10/20

SUFFRAGE

SUFFRAGE

WOMEN'S LONG BATTLE FOR THE VOTE

ELLEN CAROL DUBOIS

THORNDIKE PRESS
A part of Gale, a Cengage Company

GALE
A Cengage Company

**LIBRARY OF CONGRESS CIP DATA ON FILE.
CATALOGUING IN PUBLICATION FOR THIS BOOK
IS AVAILABLE FROM THE LIBRARY OF CONGRESS**

ISBN-13: 978-1-4328-8003-3 (hardcover alk. paper)

Published in 2020 by arrangement with Simon & Schuster, Inc.

Printed in Mexico
Print Number: 02   Print Year: 2020

To Arnie for the future,
and to my mother for the past

CONTENTS

8

INTRODUCTION

A seventy-five-year marathon through the very core of American history, the suffrage movement brought half the American people into the body politic, gave them fundamental political rights, and recognized their existence as individuals above and beyond immersion in family roles. It opened the road women would need to travel to gain genuine political power. It ushered in a pair of fundamental changes: dramatic alterations in what it meant to be an American woman, and a grand step forward toward true democracy, the largest mass enfranchisement in national history. The Nineteenth Amendment to the Constitution barring disfranchisement on account of sex was ratified in 1920, but even after that victory, the full meaning of women's enfranchisement continued to evolve.

The demand for woman suffrage meant one thing when its mid-nineteenth-century aspirants imagined full voting rights for women. It meant quite another when tens of thousands of American women mobilized for the amendment in the early twentieth century as the country entered the modern era and stepped onto the global stage. The significance of woman suffrage continues to change today, as hopes and fears for American democracy rise and fall. Its meaning alters as American women become ever more assertive in public life, and the issues that concern them, notably the right to abortion, move to the center of national politics. Its legacy grows as women's votes are solicited by political parties, even as female candidates encounter enduring misogynist taunts and sexist prejudices. Its consequences change as some women candidates for political office experience unexpected, crushing defeats, even as others win surprising victories.

This book was first conceived to coincide with the hundredth anniversary of the ratification of the Nineteenth Amendment. But it was also written and completed when American democracy was — as it has been in the past — in great upheaval, perhaps even peril. When I began this book, I was hopeful — actually certain — that it would coincide with the first female presidency. As

I wrote, that hope was dashed by a radically different presidency, one awash in misogyny, racism, and nativism. Nothing could illustrate more starkly the unpredictable path of women in American politics than the unanticipated defeat of a female presidential candidate widely expected to take the highest office, followed by unprecedented numbers of enraged women taking to the streets in the largest political demonstration in American history, and two years later by the election to Congress of a virtual flood of women candidates new to electoral politics and extremely diverse in their backgrounds and experiences.

The woman suffrage movement had incredible range. It was sustained and transformed through massive political, social, and economic changes in American life and carried forward by at least three generations of American women. The women who first raised the call for their political rights did so with limited educational and occupational opportunities, but also with memories of the American Revolution still fresh and hopes for their young nation great. They would be forgiven if they could not recognize themselves in the women who finished the struggle: "New Women," as they called themselves, with college educations and

11

aspirations for economic independence, visions of companionate marriage and sexual freedom, insisting that they be fully empowered citizens.

The suffrage movement was shaped by — and shaped — the different political eras through which it grew. First expressed in the 1840s, when abolition, temperance, and other social movements were riling politics, suffrage hopes initially peaked in Reconstruction years. Subsequent decades witnessed massive social and political reaction to the dramatic changes which the nation had undergone, and the suffrage movement was set back by the Jim Crow racism and untrammeled capitalism of those very conservative years.

Toward the end of the nineteenth century, democratic politics revived, and with it, the suffrage movement. The growing class conflict within the nation's booming economy began to be challenged and the suffrage movement advanced in its wake. Great masses of wage-earning women flooded into suffragism in its last decades. So too did a new, twentieth-century determination to use governmental resources and power to address national social and economic issues. The franchise for women might not have been won when it was had it not been for the political culture of the Progressive Era.

Some of the women who were drawn to the suffrage standard during these different phases were undeniably radical; others were conventional, even conservative. All, however, were determined that women and their concerns must be allowed to shape political debates and affect political decisions. The first important lesson of the woman suffrage movement can be found here, in the incredible determination of advocates — and their daughters and their granddaughters — who refused to stop fighting for their right to vote. To appropriate a reprimand against a defiant female fighter on the national political stage: "nevertheless she persisted." Generations of suffragists persisted, and their descendants reap the benefits of their stubborn heroism.

Because the woman suffrage movement was of such long duration, because it went through so many iterations, categorical claims about what suffragism was — and wasn't — are suspect. This book confronts two of those claims in particular. The first is that suffragism was a "single issue" movement, that as its advocates determined to win political equality for women, they ignored other claims for social justice.

This characterization may have been true

of the suffrage militancy of the final decade — the picketers and jailed hunger strikers whose heroic actions have lodged in historical memory as *the* essence of suffrage activism. But even in the 1910s, this insular suffragism was more characteristic of a few leaders than it was many of their followers, suffragists who were also dedicated peace activists, birth control advocates, and trade unionists. For the most part and in every suffrage era, as the foremothers who called the first national convention in 1850 put it, suffrage passions and beliefs were always of a piece with "the upward tending spirit of the age."[1]

Nor was it true that the woman suffrage movement was voiced exclusively by and in the name of white women and that deep-seated racism was its fatal flaw. For much of its history, the demands for woman suffrage and black suffrage were bound together, but that statement must be carefully parsed. Women's right to the vote would not have been demanded and not have entered into the political discourse in the first place if its initial leaders had not been deeply involved with the abolitionist and black suffrage movements. But in the post-Reconstruction years, this bond was broken as the mainstream woman suffrage movement excluded black women. This development was of a piece with the larger social and political reaction to Reconstruction. We have to recognize and examine that white racial exclusivity and its consequences for suffragism. The grand conclusion of the suffrage movement was tainted by the ironic fate of its coinciding with the very nadir of post-slavery racial politics.

Still it must be said that every other white-dominated popular political movement of that era similarly accommodated to insurgent white supremacy. And yet only the woman suffrage movement — not the Gilded Age labor movement or the People's Party or even Progressivism itself — has been so fiercely criticized for the fatal flaw of racism. Historical memory recognizes the cautious gains of other reform movements of that era, even as they, like woman suffrage, turned away from the rights of black people. Without minimizing the seriousness of that shift in racial politics, we must restore the historical context of the suffrage movement's decisive turn away from equal rights for African Americans in those years.

Throughout the entire seventy-five years of the woman suffrage movement, and continuing into the post-suffrage era, African American women remained stalwart defenders of women's political rights, their numbers growing over time. Some of these women were well-known national figures — Sojourner Truth, Ida B. Wells-Barnett, Mary Church Terrell — but most were not. I recognize less well known activists who were part of the larger current of suffrage history. They understood what W. E. B. Du Bois preached in the pages of *The Crisis* in 1912: "Every argument for woman suffrage is an argument for negro suffrage. Both are great movements in democracy."[2]

This history cannot stop at 1920 because it is important to examine the evolution of equality and empowerment for women in the electoral and political arenas. That full story must be the subject of another book — or several. As New York suffragist Crystal Eastman observed in 1920: While "men are saying thank goodness that everlasting women's fight is over!" women are saying "now at last we can begin."[3] Winning the vote, as Carrie Chapman Catt told her followers in 1920, had come at unbelievable cost. They must therefore prize it and use it "intelligently, conscientiously, prayerfully. . . . Progress is calling to you to make no pause. Act!"[4] Greater work even than winning the right to vote was getting men to let women into the circles of political

16

power and influence, changing the way American politics was done. That surely is a second lesson of this history: The conclusion of woman suffrage efforts, if there ever is one, depends on the continuing struggle of women.

As the triumph of woman suffrage is celebrated and remembered, as the heroism of these many devoted activists is fully incorporated into our national history, Americans should also remember the long, troubled, embattled history of woman suffrage and see it as evidence of the fragility of democracy. To this day there are forces that oppose its full realization. Today's voter suppression is the contemporary manifestation of the opposition to extending the franchise to African Americans and women. Women's right to vote was consistently resisted for three-quarters of a century, with every political tool and specious argument known to man, in state and federal constitutions, legislative debates and voter referenda. Men's active opposition lay at the root of that long history of anti-suffrage.

Throughout the history of woman suffrage, established political parties were fearful of and acted against women's enfranchisement. Starting with Reconstruction Republicans and concluding with Progressive Era Democrats, parties which were otherwise open to reform failed to support the enfranchisement of women. Sometimes politicians feared women's supposed conservatism, other times their alleged reform-mindedness, but always they feared the disruption that the doubling of the electorate would bring, especially the threat it meant to an enduring political patriarchy. Today the suspicion and harassment of women political candidates and officeholders is of a piece with that record, and knowing the history of woman suffrage can be a tool in resisting this form of voter suppression.

The woman suffrage movement can be said to have succeeded, but like the civil rights movement which has been its historic twin, it has never ended.

ONE:
THE SACRED RIGHT TO THE ELECTIVE FRANCHISE, 1848–1861

It was a hot July Sunday in 1848. Elizabeth Cady Stanton, thirty-three years old and the busy mother of three rambunctious boys, was invited to tea at the home of Jane Hunt. Cady Stanton and Hunt lived in the twin towns of Seneca Falls and Waterloo, just off the bustling Erie Canal in upstate New York. The gathering was in honor of Lucretia Coffin Mott, in town from Philadelphia to see her sister, Martha Wright. Three other local Quaker women — Mary Ann M'Clintock and her two daughters Elizabeth and Mary Ann — joined them at the round parlor table.

Lucretia Mott was a tiny, serene fifty-year-old whose modest Quaker dress and demeanor belied her standing as one of the most courageous, widely respected — and radical — female voices in the world of American social reform. Along with her Quaker convictions, her roots in the whal-

19

ing community of Nantucket had taught her about the strength and capacities of women. Her marriage to James Mott was, by all accounts, exceptionally loving and compatible. They had five children and shared strong reform commitments, beginning with a passionate hatred of slavery. James gave up his business as a cotton trader, and their household was kept absolutely free from anything produced by slave labor. Despite Mott's pacifist convictions, she was no stranger to violence. When a wild Philadelphia mob attacked an 1838 meeting of abolitionist women and burned the meeting hall to the ground, Mott calmly led the women outside to safety. Her reform convictions were broad. While visiting her sister in western New York, she took time to investigate the conditions and heard the concerns of nearby Seneca Indians and inmates at Auburn Prison.

That afternoon, the tea talk soon turned to a discussion about women's wrongs. Many such discussions no doubt took place around many such tables, but this time the outcome was different. The discussion was led by Cady Stanton, recently relocated from exciting Boston to relatively sleepy Seneca Falls, her growing family and modest middle-class resources leaving her little time or energy for anything else. Her torrent of emotions was still vivid to her a half century later when she wrote her autobiography. "I suffered with mental hunger," she wrote, "which, like an empty stomach, is very depressing. . . . Cleanliness, order, the love of the beautiful and artistic, all faded away in the struggle to accomplish what was absolutely necessary from hour to hour. Now I understood, as I never had before, how women could sit down and rest in the midst of general disorder."[1] Housewives from then until now would recognize themselves in her description.

Cady Stanton's unhappiness had reached a breaking point, and finding herself surrounded by a sympathetic group of women like herself, she "poured out, that day, the torrent of my long-accumulating discontent, with such vehemence and indignation that I stirred myself, as well as the rest of the party, to do and dare anything."[2] The small group was determined to organize a "convention," a term that had recently come into usage for public meetings to discuss and take action around compelling issues. Political parties held conventions and so did established reform movements such as temperance and antislavery. But this convention would be different; it would be the first to focus on women's wrongs and women's rights.

Time was short if they wanted to take advantage of Lucretia Mott's presence, experience, and reputation. The women placed an announcement in the local paper of a two-day public meeting for protest and discussion, to be held ten days hence at the Wesleyan Chapel, a progressive religious congregation in Seneca Falls. They would discuss "the social, civil, and religious conditions and rights of women" — note the absence of "political" in the list.[3] Then they began to consider what to do next, for they had few days to prepare. Only Lucretia Mott had ever planned such a public event, so they were a combination of bold and timid in calling this one. They did not sign their names to the announcement, and when it came time, none of them, not even Lucretia Mott, was willing to chair the proceedings. Writing with her characteristic verve, Cady Stanton looked back: "They were quite innocent of the herculean labors they proposed. . . . They felt as helpless and hopeless as if they had suddenly been asked to construct a steam engine." But the power of the Declaration they produced belies that modest memory.

They started by drawing up a statement

of principles. Instead of writing something from scratch, they decided to use as their model the Declaration of Independence, perhaps because they had just heard it a week earlier at local July 4th celebrations. We are used to hearing the Declaration of Independence cited and read often, but in the 1840s Americans had just begun to turn back to it as a powerful statement of the democratic ambitions of their still young country. What they finally produced was a bold choice, a thoroughly political statement, lacking any of the moralistic or religious flourishes expected of the "gentler" sex. And, by supplying both language and legitimacy, the Declaration of Independence also made their task easier.

They incorporated the original Preamble with a few alterations, but these were enough to make their document enduringly memorable. To the "self-evident" truth that "all men are created equal" they added the words "and women." And instead of the "repeated injuries and usurpations . . . of the present King of England," they charged the actions of "man toward woman, all having in direct object the establishment of an absolute Tyranny."

Next came the grievances. Few Americans study the eighteen grievances of the 1776

Declaration, which cite imperial taxation, standing armies, impressment, and other concerns no longer relevant to us. But many of the grievances cited in the Seneca Falls Declaration of Sentiments, the document that the women wrote, remain meaningful to this day. Marriage leaves woman man's subordinate, obliges her to obey him, and turns her into an "irresponsible being," unable or unwilling to be accountable for her own actions. Men have "monopolized nearly all the profitable employments," exclude women from "the avenues to wealth and distinction" which they most prize, and provide only "scanty remuneration" for the work left. A different moral standard punishes women severely for "moral delinquencies . . . not only tolerated but deemed of little account in man." The last two grievances, expansive in their reach, remain particularly powerful: that man usurps the right to define the "sphere of action" appropriate to woman; and that he does all he can "to destroy her confidence in her own powers, to lessen her self-respect, and to make her willing to lead a dependent and abject life." Their target was not "men" but "man" in the aggregate; they might have spoken of "patriarchy" if the word was then used that way.

Finally, the group listed thirteen powerfully worded resolutions. At the core was a grand statement of autonomy and equality: "All laws which prevent woman from occupying such a station in society as her conscience shall dictate, or which place her in a position inferior to that of man, are contrary to the great precept of nature, and therefore of no force or authority." Once the Declaration had been drafted, Cady Stanton returned home to reflect on what the group had done. It seemed to her that something was missing. The document protested woman's obligation to "submit to laws, in the formation of which she has had no voice," but wasn't this grievance the core of all the others? If so, something must be done. She resolved to call for a collective effort by women to confront women's ultimate political powerlessness, so out of place in a democratic society. She returned the next day with a proposal for a final resolution: "that it is the duty of the women of this country to secure to themselves their sacred right to the elective franchise."[4]

The right to vote eventually became the central demand of the American women's rights movement for the next three quarters of a century, changing women's lives and American politics in the process. In retrospect, this development might seem inevitable, that American democratic rights would eventually have to be extended across the gender divide to incorporate the omitted half of the nation's citizens. But at the time it was voiced by that small group of women, it had rarely been expressed anywhere. During the French Revolution, radical clubs of women had demanded the right to vote, but to no avail. In the United States, only in New Jersey between 1776 and 1807 were unmarried, property-holding women able to vote. In general, women's equal right to the franchise was a controversial and by no means obvious proposition.

An occasional advocate of women's rights or political democracy had previously contended that women should be men's political equals. But for the most part, the notion of women voting was considered ludicrous, counter to common sense, and beyond the limits of the democratic community. Political democracy, still a radical experiment in human government, required independent and rational citizens, and women were considered neither of these things. "Men bless their innocence are fond of representing themselves as beings of reason . . . ," Cady Stanton said just after the convention, "while women are mere creatures of the affections. . . . One would dislike to dispel the illusion, if it were possible to endure it."[5] It was widely assumed that women were an emotional, not a rational, sex, and wives were thoroughly — and properly so — dependent on their husbands. How could they be trusted to cast an intelligent vote? Often the possibility of women voting was discussed only to call into question other efforts to expand the franchise. Allow black men to vote? You might as well allow women! The absurdity of the notion was enough to shut down all discussion and leave voting rights in the hands of white men.

The convention was scheduled to begin on Wednesday, July 19, at 11 a.m. That morning the planners assembled early. Lucretia Mott came the fourteen miles from Auburn with her sister and husband. Elizabeth Cady Stanton walked less than a mile from her house on the outskirts of town to the Wesleyan Chapel, accompanied by her five-year-old son Henry Jr., her sister Harriet, and Harriet's son Daniel. In all the difficult work that the women had done to draft their declaration, they had forgotten a small detail, to make sure that the door of the church was opened, which it wasn't. Daniel was small enough to crawl through an open window and unlock it. Then they waited to see whether they would have an audience for their ambitious undertaking.

They did. Two-thirds of them were women, some publicly associating themselves with the convention by signing their names to its Declaration of Sentiments. Probably two or three times as many as signed actually attended. Of the hundred signers, one quarter were associated (as were the Motts) with the radical "Hicksite" wing of Quakers, and the rest were varieties of Methodists. Economically, they ranged from wealthy town-based families to farmers and their wives and daughters, who came in horse-drawn carts from villages as far as fifteen miles away. Immigration and slavery were two of the big political issues of the day, but there were no immigrants and only one second-generation young Irishwoman there. And there was one ex-slave. Ten years earlier Frederick Douglass had escaped his Maryland master. Eventually he would become one of the most famous African American men in history. In 1848, he was living and editing a weekly newspaper in nearby Rochester. He had met Elizabeth Cady Stanton seven years earlier in Boston, and each had been impressed with the other. Douglass had advertised the upcoming convention in Seneca Falls in his paper, and on the first morning he was present. Everyone else was native born, white, and Protestant.

Most of those who listened that day and the next are lost to history. But one, Charlotte Woodward Pierce, who was just eighteen at the time, lived to the age of ninety, when she was able to witness the final victory of the woman suffrage movement and to share her memories. She was one of the few working girls in the audience, though working for her meant sitting alone in her home, hand-sewing precut gloves and then returning the finished goods to the manufacturer in the aptly named village of Gloversville. "I do not believe that there was any community anywhere in which the souls of some women were not beating their wings in rebellion," she recalled. "For my own obscure self, every fiber of my being rebelled, although silently, all the hours that I sat and sewed gloves for a miserable pittance which, after it was earned, could never be mine. I wanted to work, but I wanted to choose my task and I wanted to collect my wages."[6] She brought five friends with her, and as their wagon neared Seneca Falls they joined a large flow of traffic headed for the chapel. Charlotte Woodward Pierce was an advocate of woman suffrage through the entirety of her long life.

Although the first day of the meeting had been called for women only, Charlotte and her friends found a group of men, leaders of the village, waiting to get into the church. How to involve men had put the organizers in a bind. Women meeting in public in the company of men was still considered morally questionable, in the disturbing phrase of the period, a "promiscuous assembly." Also the organizers expected that as difficult as it would be to get women to speak, the presence of men would make it that much more so. On the other hand, excluding men seemed to violate their most fundamental principles, that of sexual equality and individual rights. They decided on a compromise, to admit men but to allow only women to speak on the first day. Men would be able to speak — and they did so at considerable length — on the second day.

This last-minute small-town gathering on behalf of women's rights was not, at the time it was held, a historic event, and there are only scant records of what actually went on during those two days. Of all the women there, only a handful dared to speak. Mott, a seasoned speaker, gave a version of remarks on "the Law of Progress," which she

Lucretia and James Mott, c. 1842.

had delivered at an antislavery meeting two months before. She spoke of the thrilling cascade of developments — chief of all the progress of the antislavery movement — "of 'peace on earth, and good will to man.' "[7] Now she added her hope that women's rights would soon find a place in the pantheon of reform. For all her fierce convictions, Cady Stanton dared to make only some impromptu humorous remarks meant to soften any lasting impression that the convention was set against "the Lords of Creation."[8]

As Cady Stanton recalled, woman suffrage

was the only point on which there was any disagreement. Quakers, a large minority of the audience, found the realm of politics too corrupt, the government too sullied by its collusion with slavery, political parties too self-serving, for women to seek involvement. Others may have found it a step too far outside of woman's traditional sphere. Even Lucretia Mott, usually unwilling to give way to conservative popular opinion, thought the notion of women's equal political rights would "make us seem ridiculous. We must go slowly."[9] If they were not careful, they would undermine the entire women's rights effort they were daring to initiate.

But Cady Stanton was determined "then and there" to insist on the right to vote.[10] To her lasting gratitude, support came from Frederick Douglass, the only man there who knew what it was to be disfranchised. Forty years later, he paid tribute to Cady Stanton for seeing "more clearly than most of us that the vital point to be made prominent, and the one that included all the others, was the ballot, and she bravely said the word. . . . There are few facts in my humble history to which I look back with more satisfaction," he recalled, "than . . . that I was sufficiently enlightened at that early day, and then only a few years from slavery, to support [her] resolution for woman suffrage."[11] Between them they carried the day. At the last session, one hundred people, two-thirds of them women, publicly pledged to fulfill the final resolution and give "zealous and untiring efforts" to support all of the resolutions, including suffrage.[12]

What did women having the right to vote, so unimaginable to others, mean to Cady Stanton? As she explained in a series of articles written later, she dissented fundamentally from the widespread conviction that nineteenth-century Anglo-American society was the pinnacle of possibility for women. Women's lives in modern America were as full of "degradation and woe" as those in Turkish harems, Biblical patriarchies, and a backward Old World. In a modern society boasting political democracy, the exclusion of women from the nation's proud claim that the people were sovereign only underlined women's continuing subordination.

Cady Stanton herself was not the classic victim of women's wrongs. Most everything about her life and situation except her sex favored her, but it was this which was the source of her fierce conviction and revolt against women's subordination. Still, despite her rage against the humiliation that "drunkards, idiots, horse-racing, rum-selling rowdies, ignorant foreigners, and silly boys" had political rights while she did not, she came to a more, not less, egalitarian conclusion, insisting not on a contraction but an extension of democracy.[13]

News of a public protest meeting in favor of women's economic, civil, educational, and political rights went viral throughout New York state and into Pennsylvania and Massachusetts. Cady Stanton and her sister organizers knew that what they were doing was unprecedented, but they did not antici-pate the mean-spirited, demeaning ridicule that came down on them, drawing on every possible negative stereotype of manly women and effeminate men. The women were called "Amazons," their dignified proceedings "A Petticoat Revolution." "A woman is nobody. A wife is everything . . . ," editorialized a Philadelphia paper.[14]

Behind these insults were basic and wide-spread beliefs about women and what role they should play in a larger society. "Wom-an's sphere," as it was called, was intended by God and nature to be thoroughly domes-tic and private, self-sacrificing and modest, passive and deferential. It was a self-enclosed world in complete distinction from man's sphere, where men pursued their ambitions and took action in the public arena of money-making and politicking. Deviations from these defined roles, especially by women, were more than social gaffes; they were moral errors of the highest order. An unwomanly woman was a monster of nature and a threat to society. Sacrificing what was called her "delicacy," she might even find herself thrown off her pedestal to become the object of men's baser impulses.

This belief in mutually exclusive masculinity and femininity was more than a set of prescriptions for men's and women's behavior. Without the antidote of woman's selflessness, a nation made up only of "self-made men" would have no center, nothing binding its members together. It would fly apart, torn to shreds by the individualism and vigorous competition of which Americans in these years were so proud. Here was the root of the lurking fear that women gaining their individual rights would come at men's — and society's — expense. Rights were a zero-sum game. Were women to break through the barriers enclosing man's sphere, men must take up women's neglected role. Women at the ballot box would send men to the kitchen and nursery.

Against this barrage, advocating women's

rights would take more than conviction; it would take courage and endurance. Unwilling to be the object of such unbridled mockery, some of the people who signed the Declaration withdrew their names. But the organizers were not to be intimidated. Where others saw withering public attack, they recognized an opportunity to go even further to defend and advance their demands. "Ridicule will not have any effect on those who seriously feel themselves aggrieved," Elizabeth Cady Stanton and Elizabeth M'Clintock wrote in a letter to a local newspaper. This time they signed their names.[15]

The organizers of the Seneca Falls Convention were determined to make it the start of something bigger, to use every tool available to them to advance their goals in a steady and consistent fashion. They could refuse to pay taxes, assault their legislatures with petitions, protest publicly on election day "bearing banners, with inscriptions thereon of great sentiments handed down to us by our revolutionary fathers."[16] The word "movement" had begun to take on a new meaning in these years, designating the organized efforts of a group with a shared social or political goal. Their purpose was to give "direction to the efforts of the many women, who began to feel the degradation of their subject condition, and its baneful effects upon the human race."[17] They wanted, in other words, to start a movement.

Elizabeth Cady Stanton was not the first to recognize the centrality of disfranchisement to women's oppression and advocate full political equality. Two years before the Seneca Falls Convention, a group of six women from a rural district far away had petitioned the New York legislature for their suffrage rights. However, she was certainly the most formidable of the early advocates of suffrage.

What Cady Stanton said of her mentor Lucretia Mott was certainly true of her: she was "a woman emancipated from all faith in man-made creeds, from all fear of his denunciations."[18] A century and a half later her words still speak more clearly and compellingly to us of women's wrongs and rights than do any of her contemporaries. She could deliver a speech of several hours' length, as did many orators of the time, without it seeming excessive, antiquated, or flowery. One reason no doubt is that she had early on shed the thick Protestant ideology and language to which most social prophets of the age held. Her faith was in humanity rather than the divine. She rooted her hopes for progress in the inescapability of the here and now and the obligation of right-minded people to take action to make sure society's direction was forward and democratic.

Unlike most of her sister collaborators, Elizabeth Cady Stanton came not from the middle class, but from an upper-class family. She was born in 1815 in Johnstown, New York, to a father who had risen through the law and judiciary and by marrying a woman with money and standing. Her mother was Margaret Livingston, descended from the old Dutch-based New York landed aristocracy. It is tempting and not entirely untrue to look to this class background to credit Cady Stanton's astonishingly stubborn and resilient self-esteem, alas too rare in women, even now. When insults and male arrogance became too much to bear, which happened frequently, her self-confidence would turn to arrogance. She would default to a haughty — and infuriating — elitism, speaking in the name of the "blood of the Pilgrims," the "daughters of the Revolution," and the power of her "Saxon" heritage to explain her talents and convictions.

Margaret Cady gave birth to eleven children, seven of which lived. Elizabeth was the fifth. All the surviving children were girls except for one son, who died when Elizabeth was eleven. In Cady Stanton's telling of her life, her father's grief at this loss, her desire to fill her brother's shoes, and her inability as a girl to do so laid the foundation of her women's rights convictions. She rode horses, studied Greek and Latin, and served her father as an apprentice law clerk, but no matter what — as she recalled repeatedly — her father would say, "Oh my daughter, I wish you were a boy!"[19] Still, her father was the parent who mattered the most to her, doted on her, recognized her intelligence.

Her family's wealth provided Elizabeth Cady with as good an education as was available to girls then. At the age of fifteen, she went off to boarding school in Troy, New York, where Emma Willard had modeled the curriculum on that of men's colleges of the time. There Elizabeth studied history, mathematics, philosophy, geography, science, and literature. Her later abilities as a writer testify to the excellence of her education there. But her memories of her time at Willard's school show her already to be mischievous and high-spirited, anything but a proper young lady of means. "Our chief delight was to break the rules," she recalled.[20] Because of her family's wealth, she did not need to work, earn money for her family, or even help her mother with domestic chores after graduation.

Seventy-five miles to the west of Johnstown, just south of Syracuse, lived her cousin Gerrit Smith, and she visited there often over the next eight years. Smith was scion of one of the wealthiest families in upstate New York. His daughter, also named Elizabeth, was Elizabeth Cady's best friend. Gerrit Smith was one of the most influential reform figures of the era. He gave away an estimated eight million dollars, much of it in the form of small land grants to Mohawk Indians and African Americans. Of all the great causes of the age which he supported, antislavery was closest to his heart. It was in his home in 1858 that the first plans for John Brown's futile slave rebellion were laid.

Smith was renowned for his hospitality, and around his table an impressive array of figures ranging from descendants of "the old Dutch aristocracy" to "scholars, philosophers, philanthropists, judges, bishops, clergymen and statesmen" met and debated ideas.[21] By no means did they agree on important matters. Slave owners debated with abolitionists, ministers with free-thinking atheists. Elizabeth Cady listened to and became entranced with the intelligence and bold opinions of her cousin's many guests. "There was never such an atmosphere of love and peace, of freedom and good cheer, in any other home I visited," she recalled. "To go anywhere else, after a visit there, was like coming down from the divine heights."[22] It was here that she received her education in the ways of social change.

The Smith home was a major stop on the underground railroad, where fugitive slaves received temporary shelter, were hidden from their pursuers, and were aided in their flight to Canada. "One day, as a bevy of us girls were singing and chattering in the parlor," she recalled, "Cousin Gerrit entered and, in mysterious tones, said: 'I have a most important secret to tell you.' " He took them to the third floor of the house and introduced them to another young woman, Harriet Powell, who was escaping from her slave master. "You may never have another opportunity of seeing a slave girl face to face, so ask her all you care to know of the system of slavery," he instructed. Elizabeth Cady learned that Harriet had been sold "for her beauty in a New Orleans market," which everyone knew was notorious for advertising light-skinned black girls for sale to masters for sexual purposes. "We all wept together as she talked, and when Cousin Gerrit returned to summon us away, we needed no further education to make us abolitionists."[23]

In the Smith house, Elizabeth Cady met the second figure in her transformation from a smart and eager young woman into a dedicated social activist. This was the man who would become her husband. When she met Henry Stanton in 1839, she was twenty-four; her mother had married at age sixteen. She was a romantic at heart and had suitors aplenty, but she was in no hurry to leave behind the enjoyments and freedom of her youth for marriage. Nor had she met the man to whom marriage would bring anything like the excitement of the Smith household.

Henry Brewster Stanton was ten years older than Elizabeth, handsome and unmarried. His early family life had been tumultuous, highlighted by something that was almost unheard in that era: his mother had sought and secured a divorce from his father.[24] Henry Stanton had grown into a high-spirited and self-confident man. As Cady Stanton later remarked, they agreed as a pair "they were as nearly perfect as mortals need be."[25] He was also, like Cousin Gerrit, a devoted abolitionist, one of the best speakers in the movement, and on the verge of taking the antislavery movement out of the realm of moral appeal into party politics. Drawn to each other, the two took off on a horseback ride. "We stopped often to admire the scenery," Cady Stanton recalled, "and, perchance, each other."[26] Returning many hours later, they told their astonished friends and family that they were going to get married.

This hasty engagement was too much for Elizabeth Cady's parents. Her father could not abide her intent to tie her life to a political radical, a man who had no employment other than that as an antislavery agitator, and to make a choice that lowered her social rank. All of his other daughters were married to lawyers who had trained with him. He protested that this daughter's suitor "cannot in my judgment be overstocked with prudence — or feel much solicitude for her whom he seeks to marry."[27] Even Cousin Gerrit was brought into the family intervention, and Elizabeth Cady, subjected to intense pressure from those closest to her, agreed to break her engagement.

Cady Stanton later observed that the entire episode deeply tainted her ideas about marriage, previously "painted . . . in the most dazzling colors," but now "represented as beset with dangers and disappointments, and men, of all God's creatures as the most depraved and unreliable."[28] But despite the broken engagement, she stubbornly remained determined to marry Henry Stanton. Cady Stanton's biographer observed that this decision was one of the most fateful of her life, freeing her from "the conservative atmosphere, the aristocratic surroundings" of her Johnstown home.[29] On May 1, 1840, they were married by the Cady family minister. Despite the minister's stern sermon on the obligations of marriage, the two pledged "to love" but not "to obey" to each other.

By marrying Henry Stanton, Elizabeth Cady had also wed herself to the abolitionist movement. Women had been involved in the movement since William Lloyd Garrison founded the American Anti-Slavery Society in 1833. Albeit confined to auxiliary female societies, as Cady Stanton later reflected, "Mid violence and persecution, they learned the a, b, c of individual rights."[30] Among the most important of these early women abolitionists were Sarah and Angelina Grimké, daughters of one of the wealthiest and most powerful slaveholders in South

Carolina.

As young women, the Grimké sisters had fled their father's home, sickened by the treatment of enslaved people. Moving to Philadelphia, they became devout Quakers and abolitionists. Then, because of the incomparably intimate knowledge they had of slavery, they agreed to speak forthrightly and publicly against slavery. Testifying to the sexual abuse visited on slave women and drawing men as well as women to hear them, they found themselves in 1836 at the center of a massive retaliation from the entire Congregational Church clergy of New England. For their multiple violations of woman's sphere, they were denounced publicly from every Congregational pulpit from Maine to Pennsylvania. When a woman "assumes the place and tone of a man as a public reformer," a pastoral letter thundered, "our care and protection of her seem unnecessary . . . she yields the power which God has given her for protection, and her character becomes unnatural."[31]

Instead of shrinking from this harsh criticism, the sisters added to their original abolitionist offense a second heresy, a forthright defense of women's rights. Arguably this was the first comprehensive statement of women's equality with men in

45

American history. "Whatever it is morally right for a man to do, it is *morally* right for woman to do," Angelina Grimké declared. "I recognize no rights but *human* rights. . . . for in Christ Jesus, there is neither male nor female."[32] Soon after, she married the abolitionist Theodore Weld, one of Henry Stanton's closest and dearest colleagues. Then the couple retired along with sister Sarah to New Jersey, where they ran a progressive school to which many reformers sent their children.

In 1839, controversy broke out again, this time within the abolitionist movement. William Lloyd Garrison, who had become a full-fledged anarchist, led one side, arguing that all human institutions fettered individual conscience and action, none more so than the American government and the Constitution on which slavery rested. Accordingly, he urged his followers to have nothing to do with politics. Henry Stanton and Gerrit Smith, leaders of the other side, were labeled "political abolitionists." They were much more pragmatic and insisted that "slavery is the creature of law and can be entirely abolished only by the repeal of those laws which create and sustain it."[33] Voting for parties and candidates that could further the demise of slavery was, they argued, the duty of all true abolitionists. They were already beginning to form the Liberty Party, which, although tiny, would be the first of a series of antislavery political parties, culminating in the Republican Party, under whose banner Lincoln would become president.

In the 1839–1840 split, most abolitionist women, who after all had no votes to wield, sided with the Garrisonian wing and against the political abolitionists. In 1840, when the political abolitionists withdrew from the American Anti-Slavery Society, the Garrisonians were free to open the way for women to leave their auxiliary position and become full and equal participants. Starting with Abby Kelly Foster, many women became traveling agents, paid organizers, and abolitionist preachers throughout New England and the Midwest. Here was one of the first places in American public society where women experienced full equality with men.

Just as Elizabeth and Henry were facing down family opposition to their marriage, this split spilled out into the international abolitionist community. British abolitionists had called for a World's Anti-Slavery Convention to be held in London in June 1840. Both Garrisonians and political abolitionists arranged to go and to try to win the endorsements of British abolitionists for their side in the quarrel. Henry's plans to leave for London had no doubt hastened his marriage to Elizabeth — the lovers did not wish to be parted. What a honeymoon they would have, sailing the ocean, visiting the Old World, and watching history be made!

Before they left, Henry took his new bride to meet Sarah and Angelina Grimké. Initially, Elizabeth found the sisters a bit dowdy and Quaker-severe, but after three days — having learned the basics of the antislavery heritage, within which her own women's rights commitments would flourish — she was entranced. She began to correspond with them regularly and read everything they wrote. The sisters, for their part, immediately saw her for the promising and unusual woman that she was. "We were very much pleased with Elizabeth Stanton, who spent several days with us," Angelina wrote to Gerrit Smith. "I could not help wishing that Henry was better calculated to help mould such a mind."[34]

From the Grimké/Weld New Jersey household, the newlyweds went to New York and sailed to London. By her own recollections, the new bride had a grand time onboard ship. She was surrounded by notable abolitionists, most important the Liberty Party's presidential candidate, James Birney. She recognized that she was "a little too gay, & much too ignorant on the subject of slavery for the circumstances in which I am placed," and she listened and learned all she could.[35] But she was still the frolicsome and irreverent young woman who had entranced Henry Stanton, skittering around the decks and generally driving Birney, who was no fan of unconventional women, to distraction. He reprimanded her for calling her husband by his first name in public, which was a decidedly improper thing for a well-brought-up young lady to do.

The party arrived in Exeter and then hurried to London for the World Anti-Slavery Convention. Among the five hundred American abolitionists, there were eight women who had come as part of the Garrisonian faction. Coming to London was a courageous act for these women, who knew they were headed for a confrontation. The London organizers had to decide whether to take sides in the split of American abolitionists by granting them formal credentials. After a day's debate, the convention members decided that women delegates violated British abolitionist practice. The American women were relegated to the visitors' galleries, to watch and listen but not to participate. Although not a delegate, Cady Stanton was "humiliated and chagrined" at the exclusion of women.[36]

To commemorate this historic event, a London painter created a monumental group portrait, with individualized renderings of many of the delegates. Henry Stanton was seated in the front row, in the only surviving portrait of him as he must have looked when Elizabeth Cady met him — long noble nose, curly brown hair, thick sideburns. The painter found the Americans unpleasant and their women impious, but nonetheless he included portraits of more than a half-dozen women placed along the edge, including Lucretia Mott. In sketchy strokes and across the back of the painting, he drew the people sitting in the visitors' galleries. Though not individuated, all those portrayed are bonneted women, among whom must have been Elizabeth Cady Stanton.[37]

Because of the indomitable women abolitionists with whom she was cast, this event was a turning point in Cady Stanton's life. Prior to this, all of the people who had impressed her for their intelligence, their forthrightness, and their liberal thought were men. She had met the Grimké sisters, but they were retired from active reform. Now she met other women with whom to communicate and connect her instincts and aspirations. "These were the first women I had ever met who believed in the equality of the sexes and who did not believe in the popular orthodox religion. . . . It was intensely gratifying to hear all that, through years of doubt, I had dimly thought, so freely discussed by other women."[38]

None of these women had a more profound impact on Cady Stanton, and through her on the future of the women's rights movement, than Lucretia Mott. "I often longed to meet some woman who had sufficient confidence in herself to frame and hold an opinion in the face of opposition." Lucretia Mott was that woman. "Wherever our party went I took possession of Lucretia," she recalled, "much to Henry's vexation, as we were just then married."[39] Reminiscing many years later at Mott's memorial, she wrote that when they met, Mott was "the greatest wonder of the world — a woman who thought and had opinions of her own."[40] In the days after the World's Anti-Slavery Convention, Cady Stanton marveled at the calm, confident, and efficient way Mott disposed of the arguments by opponents of women's participation.

Mott was the third of her reform mentors, and it was under her tutelage that Elizabeth Cady Stanton grew into a great women's rights thinker. Walking the halls of the British Museum, the two vowed someday to call a public reform meeting on behalf of women's rights.

Lucretia Mott freed her young protégé from the last vestiges of the religious cloud that had hung over her since childhood. The daughter of severe Scotch Presbyterians, Elizabeth Cady had struggled against the obligation to obey the dictates of clerical authority without question. As a radical Quaker, Mott was an absolute believer in the authority of "the inner voice," and she urged her new friend to rely on her own internal sense of justice, not the pronouncements of learned theologians. "When I first heard from the lips of Lucretia Mott that I had the same right to think for myself that Luther, Calvin and John Knox had . . . I felt at once a new-born sense of dignity and freedom."[41] Breaking away from conventional religious thought was the key step for Cady Stanton. Nowhere was the power of the established Protestant churches and the men who led them greater than when acting as the gatekeepers over women's proper behavior and beliefs. Elizabeth Cady Stanton's rage at "priestcraft" only grew over the years.

The couple spent much of the next year and a half under the Cady family roof in Johnstown. To acquire a genuine profession, support his wife, and please his in-laws, Henry followed the other brothers-in-law and studied law with Daniel Cady. Under her mother's care, Elizabeth gave birth to her first child, named Daniel after her father. In 1844 and 1846 she had two more sons. She referred to these births as "productions," by which she meant not difficult labors but creative projects. In 1844, after Henry had set up his law practice in Boston, Elizabeth and the children joined him. No longer surrounded by the luxury of her parents' home, she wrote to a friend that she was absorbing "the effect of 'lessons of economy' upon my extravagant nature."[42]

Boston was an exciting city, brimming with intellectual and political stimulation, "a kind of moral museum," as she called it.[43] She attended lectures by the famous Unitarian minister Theodore Parker and socialized with William Lloyd Garrison and other important reformers. She was in Boston during the years that Margaret Fuller, the most intellectually accomplished woman in America, was regularly meeting with other women, sharing her education, knowledge, and philosophy. Perhaps Cady Stanton attended her salon. In Boston, she also met a recently escaped slave named Frederick Douglass, beginning a lifelong relationship of deep mutual appreciation. Then, in the fall of 1847, because her husband's health appeared to require it, Elizabeth began to remodel a small house given to her by her father far away in the Finger Lakes country of New York and to prepare to move her family there, to the village of Seneca Falls.

Meanwhile the promise Elizabeth Cady Stanton and Lucretia Mott had made to each other in London to initiate a women's rights movement remained unredeemed. Why then was it, eight years later, that they, along with the other women around that Waterloo tea table, suddenly and decisively moved to take action? As Cady Stanton herself observed, in considering the "preceding causes" of what happened that summer in Seneca Falls, "Fortunately, progress is not the result of prearranged plans of individuals, but is born of a fortuitous combination of circumstances that compel certain results, overcoming the natural inertia of mankind."[44] What were those multiple circumstances and how did they combine in that time and place to produce that outcome?

Far away from the village of Seneca Falls, 1848 was a historic year, as a wave of revolutions swept across Europe, driving out autocratic rulers in favor of greater political democracy. The organizers of the Seneca Falls Convention no doubt read the on-the-scene dispatches posted from Europe in the *New York Daily Tribune* by Margaret Fuller. Now, in addition to her other accomplishments, she had become America's first woman war correspondent. In June 1848, the *Tribune* published her account of revolutions across the Italian peninsula and throughout Europe. Carefully and always she described the revolutionaries in the streets as both "men and women" and proudly noted that her friend and hero the Polish patriot Adam Mickiewicz had explicitly called for "entire equality of rights" for women.[45] She wrote with the hope that the men and women of her own country, "stupid with the lust of gain, soiled by crime in its willing perpetuation of slavery," would share in the "nobler spirit" emerging across the Atlantic.[46]

As if answering Fuller's call, the Seneca Falls group recognized that its call for votes for women was of a piece with "the upward tending spirit of the age."[47] As Cady Stanton wrote at the time, women were fighting for the very rights "the maintenance of which is even now rocking to their foundations the kingdoms of the old world."[48] Newspapers covering the Seneca Falls Convention also observed the coincidence. "To whatever part of the world the attention is directed, the political and social fabric is crumbling to pieces . . ." reported the *New York Herald.* "By the intelligence, however, which we have lately received, the work of revolution is no longer confined to the Old World, nor to the masculine gender."[49]

Meanwhile, there was political upheaval in the United States. The United States had just won its war with Mexico, annexing enormous swaths of western lands into the country. Heretofore, the issue of slavery, which was established and maintained by state laws, had been the most incendiary issue of national politics. Now with the status of slavery in these new federally controlled territories in the forefront, the issue could no longer be avoided. Many northern Democrats gathered behind a congressional resolution refusing to admit states formed out of the "Mexican cession" into the union

— the first of which would be California — unless they explicitly banned slavery. Even former Democratic president Martin Van Buren, successor and advisor to pro-slavery President Andrew Jackson, joined them, insisting that states formed from the new western territories must be kept "free soil."

To Henry Stanton, it began to appear that a new party, which "fused" antislavery Whigs and Democrats, was a real possibility. A month after the Seneca Falls women's rights convention, he traveled to Buffalo to help form the Free Soil Party. The new party's political base would be broader than the Liberty Party he had formed eight years before, but its platform would be more confined: it would oppose not slavery itself but its extension into the territories, arguing that, if slavery could not expand, it would surely wither and die. Non-expansion in federal territories, the Free Soilers believed, rather than a head-on attack on slavery, was the only way for any part of the abolition platform to be brought into national politics. Van Buren was nominated as its candidate, and with a former president heading its ticket, the new party polled a very impressive 15 percent of the vote.

The increasingly political direction that abolitionist activism was taking, and her husband's leading role in it, surely underlay Cady Stanton's growing conviction in 1848 that not only should women's rights include political rights, but that suffrage must be the movement's leading demand. She was still attached to the Garrisonians for insisting on equality between the sexes within the abolitionist movement, but she shared the pragmatism of the political abolitionists. She was a kind of women's rights fusionist, combining the political focus of Henry's wing of the abolitionists with the egalitarian principles of the Garrisonians. "I am an admirer of Garrison," she wrote to a friend. But at the same time, "I am in favour of political action. . . . So long as we are to be governed by human laws, I should be unwilling to have the making & administering of those laws left entirely to the selfish & unprincipled part of the community."[50]

One other historical change in that momentous year was especially close to Cady Stanton's determination in the Seneca Falls Convention to insist that law and the power to shape it were as crucial to women's status as they were to the abolition of slavery. For over a decade, many state legislatures, including in New York, had been debating reform of the laws that governed married women's economic rights. To anyone surveying women's legal disabilities, the denial to married women of the independent right to own, purchase, sell, and contract for property was foremost. Such legal practices derived from the long-standing Anglo-American legal principle of "coverture," that the rights and interests of women, once married, were absorbed into those of their husbands. Thus, as far as the law of property was concerned, married women had no legal existence, or as Cady Stanton put it, they suffered "civil death."[51] Marriage was the condition of the overwhelming majority of adult women. The denial of property rights to wives affected not only their real and personal property but also the wages they earned, because their labor was not their own either.

When the New York legislature first confronted this issue in 1836, the only woman lobbying for reform was Ernestine Rose, a young Polish immigrant of Jewish descent. Born Esther Polotowski, she fled to England to escape her confining religious heritage. Nonetheless, her Jewish background left her relentlessly opposed to Christian influence. She came under the influence of early British socialists, who were committed to ending coverture. The socialist attack on coverture was an assault both on the tyranny of private property and the material basis of women's subordination within marriage. In 1836, Ernestine Rose moved with her husband to New York, bringing her anti-coverture campaign with her.

In 1846, when a New York constitutional convention was called to undertake comprehensive legal reform, the decade-long campaign that Rose had helped to initiate came to a head. The constitutional convention briefly considered legalizing wives' independent rights to hold property, but at the last minute, a conservative legislator quashed it when he argued that any such reform would threaten "the sacred ordinance of marriage, and the relations growing out of it."[52] Two years later, in the spring of 1848, however, the legislature passed the proposed reform. As Cady Stanton observed, "If men who make the laws were ready for some onward step, surely the women themselves should express interest in legislation."[53] The Seneca Falls women's rights convention occurred three months later.

The Seneca Falls Declaration concluded with the ambitious hope that it would "be followed by a series of Conventions embracing every part of the country."[54] Just two weeks later, many of the same participants, including Cady Stanton, Lucretia Mott, and Martha M'Clintock, traveled the fifty miles to Rochester for a quickly called second meeting. This time there was no longer any debate over the propriety of political equality for women, wage-earning women's situation was included in the consideration of women's rights, and — to Cady Stanton's initial shock — a woman chaired the proceedings. Soon women's rights meetings began to pop up, "as if by magic," in New York, Ohio, Indiana, Pennsylvania, and Massachusetts.[55]

In understanding how women were inspired by news of these women's rights conventions, consider the story of Emily Collins. Collins lived in "one of the most secluded spots" in western New York state. She was Cady Stanton's age, with much less education and wealth but similarly aware of and enraged at the laws and customs that oppressed women. A man in her neighborhood, a Methodist preacher, "esteemed a worthy citizen . . . every few weeks, gave his wife a beating with his horsewhip . . . to keep her in subjection, and because she scolded so much." When news of the Seneca Falls Convention "gave this feeling of unrest form and voice," Collins gathered together fifteen other women and formed a suffrage

61

society. They met every other week in one or the other's parlor, circulated a petition, and sent it on to the state legislature, where it was dismissed "as something absurdly ridiculous." Undeterred, Collins remained an active suffragist until she died in 1904.[56]

Although all of the previous women's rights conventions, including Seneca Falls, had been local and hastily called, so much excitement had been stirred that it seemed time for something more. In 1850, eight New England women, most of them veterans of antislavery work, announced that the first National Women's Rights Convention would be held in Worcester, Massachusetts, in October. "To consider the great question of Woman's Rights, Duties, and Relations," the organizers invited "all Men and Women of our country who feel sufficient interest in the subject, to give an earnest thought and effective effort to its rightful adjustment, to meet each other in free conference."[57] In retrospect, Cady Stanton regarded this gathering rather than the Seneca Falls meeting as the genuine start of the American woman suffrage movement.[58] It was followed by similar meetings every year (except 1857) for the rest of the decade.

The organizers agreed to divide among themselves the names of all the supporters of women's rights of whom they were aware and write to them asking for support. They appealed especially to "all the women who are accustomed to speaking in public — every stick of timber that is sound."[59] Paulina Wright Davis, a Rhode Island abolitionist who had distinguished herself by educating women about their reproductive health, was the convention's leading force, and she took it on herself to contact Cady Stanton. The Worcester meeting lasted for four days and one thousand people attended. The largest group came from Massachusetts, but sizable delegations attended from Ohio, New York, and the rest of New England. One woman came from California, another from Iowa. Great effort was made to render women's rights as a cause equally important to men as well as women, and many of the men leading the antislavery cause — including Garrison, Wendell Phillips, Stephen Foster, and Frederick Douglass — attended and spoke.

The Worcester convention did more than any other prewar women's rights convention to link African American and women's rights, and to bring attention to the sufferings of women under slavery. "The cause we have met to advocate . . . bids us remember the two millions of slave women at the

South, the most grossly wronged and foully outraged of all women," the convention resolved, "and omit no effort to raise [them] to a share in the rights we claim for ourselves."[60] This was no doubt a response to Congress's recent passage of the Fugitive Slave Law, the first major piece of federal pro-slavery legislation in many decades. By federalizing the crime and punishment of slaves' running away from their masters and obligating citizens to participate in their capture, this law sent shock waves through the abolitionist community. People who had escaped slavery could now be hunted down and re-enslaved, a fate which Frederick Douglass had dodged by fleeing to England. Even black people who had never been enslaved were being illegally dragged South, as Solomon Northrup recounted in his harrowing 1853 tale, *Twelve Years a Slave.*

Here also for the first time an African American woman appeared on the stage of a women's rights convention. Tall, dark-skinned, and in her early fifties, Sojourner Truth had been born Isabella Baumfree in New York sometime around 1797 and was enslaved there until 1826. Self-emancipated, she was a rising figure in the antislavery community. Her manner was humorous and folksy. She spoke with an accent, although

Sojourner Truth, 1863.

the "dese" and "dose" that contemporaries remembered were not that of a southern black person but rather a remnant of Dutch, her first language. "She advocated woman's rights," the newspapers reported. "She had looked on men and was sorry for them. The slaves all came on them, and now the women came on them." A self-taught itinerant preacher (thus the post-slavery name she picked as a sojourner after truth), she took on and refuted biblical excuses for women's subordination. If Eve is credited with turning "the world upside down . . . ," she suggested to the audience's great delight, "what should hinder her to turn it back again?"[61] Sojourner Truth is more widely remembered for a women's rights speech she gave the next year in Akron, Ohio, in which she challenged the notion that women were privileged and protected. She knew she had certainly not been, and asked "arn't I a woman?"[62]

Reports of this first National Women's Rights Convention circulated widely, in the United States and beyond. In England, the news caught the eye of Harriet Taylor, who published a long article describing it and laying out her own elaborate exposition of the subject in the distinguished British political journal the *Westminster and Foreign Quarterly Review*. Her readers would be especially surprised, she noted, to learn that "the agitation . . . is not a pleading by male writers and orators for women." Rather, it constitutes "a political movement, practical in its objects, carried on in a form which denotes an intention to persevere," and, of greatest importance, "it is a movement not merely for women but by them."[63] Taylor was the intimate companion and soon-to-be wife of the most famous political economist in the world, John Stuart Mill, and it was to Mill that the article was attributed for many years. Sixteen years later, after Taylor's death, Mill incorporated his wife's ideas in *The Subjection of Women,* which became the most widely circulated women's rights tract of the era, reaching an international audience and translated into numerous languages.

Elizabeth Cady Stanton was not able to attend the 1850 Worcester meeting. Her husband was often in Albany serving in the state legislature and she was now thoroughly swamped and increasingly dispirited by her household responsibilities. "Men and angels give me patience!" she wrote. "I am at the boiling point! If I do not find some day the use of my tongue on this question, I shall die of an intellectual repression, a woman's rights convulsion!"[64] She had just sent her eldest son, nine-year-old Daniel, to the boarding school that Theodore Weld and the Grimké sisters had started to help him learn to "manage" himself better. (This may have included bedwetting. A note from Angelina mentions protecting a new mattress from being ruined by Daniel's "difficulty.")[65] Elizabeth was also pregnant again, four months later giving birth to her fourth son. Her longing for a daughter was intense but not to be fulfilled until the birth of a daughter two years later. Her household struggles were lifted somewhat when Amelia Willard, a young Quaker woman, became her housekeeper. Thirty years later, Elizabeth thanked her as "one of the best gifts of the gods" without whom "much of my public work would have been quite impossible."[66] This was not a compliment she ever extended to her husband.

Now other women's rights advocates came to the forefront. Chief of these was Lucy Stone, whose name headed the call for the 1850 national convention. Born in central Massachusetts in 1817, she was the only daughter of a typical middle-class patriarch. Francis Stone was a successful farmer, a heavy drinker, abusive to his children, and overbearing to his wife. His daughter silently watched and resented her mother's unrelenting labor, numerous pregnancies, and absolute and humiliating economic dependence. From a young age Lucy Stone contributed economically, first on the farm, then hand-sewing the shoe "uppers" for a local manufacturer, and finally as a teacher no older than many of her students. Her women's rights instincts crystallized when, sitting in a gathering of her state's assembled clergy, she heard a minister read the famous pastoral letter condemning the Grimké sisters for daring to speak in public about the horrors of slavery.

The effort at clerical intimidation backfired. Lucy Stone realized that she wanted nothing more than to follow the Grimkés' path and become a public speaker on behalf of the slave. For this she needed an education, which her father refused to support. With her own money, she enrolled in nearby Mount Holyoke Academy, the predecessor of the college of that name and the best school for girls in the area. But the institution was too conservative for her, so she withdrew and waited for something better. After a decade, she found it in Oberlin Collegiate Institute, the first full-fledged college to admit women alongside men, and an institution with a solid antislavery perspective. She was twenty-seven, self-supporting, and pinching every penny she had saved for her education. In the third year of college, her father relented and helped pay.

Stone's Oberlin education was a good one but for one problem: the college refused to train her as an orator, which was her goal. So she organized a secret club of other women students to meet in the woods in the cabin of a local African American woman and teach themselves the skills of public speaking. When after five years she graduated, in the spring of 1848, Lucy Stone became the first woman in the United States with a baccalaureate degree. She immediately joined the ranks of antislavery lecturers. Her sweet voice and girlish looks in contrast to her hard-hitting antislavery lectures made her famous, and she was soon able to earn over $7,000 in three years of lecturing. Everywhere she went to advocate for the slave, she also talked about women's rights.

Stone was scheduled to be the major speaker at the 1850 National Women's Rights Convention when she was called to Illinois to nurse her brother, who had contracted cholera. After he died, she was laid low by her own severe bout of typhoid fever. As she slowly made her way back to Massachusetts, she stopped in Cincinnati to cash a paycheck she had from her antislavery employers. Henry Blackwell, an abolitionist and local hardware merchant seven years her junior, obliged her. She arrived in Worcester weak and depleted but in time to say a few words to the convention she had helped set in motion. Speaking with what a New York newspaper described as "great simplicity and eloquence," "unburdening her heart," she lamented "the inferior and slavish position of Woman," and looked to a future in which women, no longer "the appendages of Society," had become "the coequal and help-meet of Man in all the interests, and perils and enjoyments of human life."[67]

Meanwhile, Henry Blackwell had become smitten with Lucy Stone and relentlessly wooed her. He was no stranger to women's rights. His older sister, Elizabeth, was the first U.S. woman to become a fully licensed physician. For five years, Lucy Stone remained committed to her vow never to become a wife, willingly accepting the "privations" and "isolation" but also the deep satisfaction of her solitary path in life.[68] Blackwell wrote her long impassioned letters, assuring her that he would never claim authority over her and would support her heart and soul in her women's rights work. Then when he broke the law to help rescue a young woman fugitive slave, Stone was deeply moved and relented. On an early morning in the spring of 1855, dear reader, she married him. At the wedding, they read a statement that they had written together, "acknowledging our mutual affection" but repudiating any law or custom that did not "recognize the wife as an independent, rational being" or that conferred "upon the husband an injurious and unnatural superiority."[69]

To signal their determination to undertake a new kind of marriage, they agreed that Lucy Stone would not take the name Blackwell and would remain Lucy Stone even though married. Well into the twentieth century, a woman who kept her own name upon marriage was called, in her honor, a Lucy Stoner. Cady Stanton wrote that "nothing has been done in the woman's rights movement for some time that so rejoiced my heart as the announcement by you of a woman's right to her name. . . . A proper self-respect demands that every woman may have some name by which she may be known from the cradle to the grave."[70] Henry Blackwell's promises notwithstanding, however, the marriage was a difficult one, and over time, Stone found her hard-won independence, emotional as well as financial, slipping away.

The third of the women's rights pioneers in the movement's first decade was Susan B. Anthony. Unlike Stone and Cady Stanton, Susan Brownell Anthony had an extremely warm and supportive family, including a father who inspired and stood behind her in all her endeavors. Her mother was born Baptist and her father Quaker, though his independent-mindedness repeatedly ran up against the local elders' sense of propriety. Like so many other Americans in the tumultuous late 1830s, the nation's first great depression, the Anthonys suffered the dramatic economic ups and downs of the collapse. The family gained, then lost, then regained financial security. Finally, in 1845, they settled in Rochester, New York, which remained Susan's hometown for the rest of her life.

Susan and her older sister Guelma were sent to a Quaker boarding school, where a harsh schoolmistress imbued her with a lingering doubt as to her intellectual abilities. Then, when her father's fortunes again collapsed, he was forced to withdraw his daughters, and her formal education ended. Nonetheless, like so many other young women of her background, Anthony became a teacher. After fifteen years, however, she had become bored by the work and frustrated by the reality that, no matter how experienced she was, no matter how well she did her job, no matter how successful she was at taming the ill-behaved boys in her care, she was paid far less — a quarter as much! — as the men she often replaced. The experience left her with an understanding that economic independence for women

Elizabeth Cady Stanton with her second daughter, Harriot, c. 1857.

was a matter not just of equal rights to property but also of equal wages for equal work. Her lifelong commitment to self-supporting women was unequaled by Cady Stanton, Stone, or any other first-generation women's rights contemporaries.

Nor did her dedication to women's rights have its roots in festering youthful resentment and thwarted aspiration. Rather, her restless desire to do something important, to make an impact on the world, to experience directly the fast-moving society around her seems the more likely candidate. Soon after leaving her final teaching job, she wrote her mother that she would have joined the crowds going to gold-rush California "if I were but a man."[71] Instead she decided to become a public reformer, to find some "service which I can render humanity . . . to right the wrongs of society."[72] It was a path she would follow the rest of her life, though not one that ever provided her with anything like economic security or a reliable income. In her parents' home, among Rochester Quakers, she had met abolitionist leaders. But what she chose instead, perhaps because she was not ready for the disapprobation that abolition drew, was temperance. By the summer of 1851, Susan B. Anthony had risen to a leadership role in the women's wing of the western New York temperance movement.

In 1850, the abolition of slavery and temperance were the two issues most riling American society, shaking up political parties, and — of particular importance — igniting women's energies. Indeed, if at that time you were asked to pick which was the more likely to become the major reform movement of the day, you might have guessed temperance. The temperance move-

Susan B. Anthony, age twenty-eight, 1848.

ment's call for individual self-control struck a note for people living in an often chaotic society. It meant the tempering — indeed the elimination — of the widespread use and abuse of alcohol, especially by men and therefore of direct concern to women. But "temperance" meant more than that: it meant a lifestyle of moral and physical restraint in the face of any sort of uncontrolled "appetite" — be it for drink or sex

Lucy Stone with daughter, Alice, c. 1858.

or even making money. We call an uncontrolled appetite an addiction, but advocates of temperance often spoke of it as a form of enslavement.

Cady Stanton could write, Stone could speak, but Susan B. Anthony could do something the others could not do. Temperance activism unleashed her tremendous talent and enthusiasm as a reform organizer. Beginning in the early 1850s, and continuing almost without interruption until the end of the century, she traveled day after day, year after year, recruiting women and weaving them into networks in which they could act collectively and make an impact — not just on their families and neighborhoods but on the welfare of the larger society. Practical and energetic, she did the basic work in those years of turning women's rights aspirations and principles into an actual reform movement.

Anthony was five-feet-five and weighed about 140 pounds. After she gave up Quaker garb, her one personal vanity was buying occasional pieces of elegant clothing, a way perhaps of expressing and enjoying the principle of self-support to which she was so dedicated. But none of this was obvious to the public. Cady Stanton and Stone were both crowd pleasers. Anthony was not. People rarely smiled in photographs in those days, but in her pictures, her expression is more sober than most. Her seemingly severe persona fit the stereotype of the strong-minded woman. But in personal relations she was warm and generous, and in her devotion to women's rights, unparalleled. Over time this made her uniquely beloved within the nineteenth-century women's rights movement.

While Cady Stanton married in her twenties and Stone in her thirties, Anthony remained single her whole life. This inspired a great deal of curiosity as to her private love life, which she always met by indirection. She could not attach herself intimately to one man, she explained, until she was no longer a "political slave and pariah" and could meet her husband on a level field of equality and citizenship.[73] There were never-married women of the era who developed romantic, almost conjugal attachments to other women, but even this does not seem to have been the case with Anthony. What she did have were devoted and sustained friendships, none more profound and consequential than her bond with Elizabeth Cady Stanton. The Stanton/Anthony friendship was one of the most important working partnerships in American history. Cady Stanton would write thirty years later, that the two were "fastened heart to heart with hooks of steel in a friendship that . . . years of confidence and affection have steadily strengthened."[74]

By legend, the two women first met in the spring of 1851 on a Seneca Falls street. Anthony's sister Mary had attended the 1848 women's rights convention in their hometown of Rochester and told her about it. Anthony was "not yet quite convinced that these [rights] included the suffrage."[75] She was, however, seeking women of purpose and courage, and eager to meet the charismatic woman living in nearby Seneca Falls about whom they spoke. "There she stood with her good earnest face and genial smile . . . the perfection of neatness and sobriety," Cady Stanton recalled many years later. "I liked her thoroughly."[76]

The woman who introduced them was Amelia Bloomer, a Seneca Falls resident and proprietor of the *Lily,* a local temperance journal for women, to which Cady Stanton was now regularly submitting articles. Bloomer is largely forgotten to history but for one thing: her name became attached to the "reform dress" adopted in the early 1850s by bold women, including Elizabeth Cady Stanton, Lucy Stone, and Susan B. Anthony. Originally known as "the Turkish costume," it was made up of a dress raised just below the knees and worn over a pair of loose trousers that reached the ankles. It was to these "under pants" that the name "bloomer" became permanently affixed. Women who sought any entry into men's traditional sphere had long been accused of wanting to "wear the britches," and now this dire prediction had come to pass.

Amelia Bloomer in reform dress, 1851.

The "bloomer" dress was a historic women's rights development. Fashionable dress was then — as it is still — confining and bothersome. It carried the message that women are only their bodies, mere ornaments, not thinking, working, serious people. "Both our bodies and minds are now rendered weak and useless from the unhealthy and barbarous style of dress adopted," explained Amelia Bloomer.[77] Women's health was said to be impaired by the many pounds of fabric that weighed on their hips, and their organs and breath were confined by tight corsets. Shorter skirts made all of women's activities easier. Cady Stanton could climb the narrow steps of her Seneca Falls house carrying babies, laundry, and candles without struggling to hold up her long skirts; Stone could get in and out of trains and wagons and walk through the muddy streets of the towns and villages she visited without trailing mud and dust behind her. Anthony was sure that simpler, more utilitarian clothes would help women earn equal wages with men.

For a supposedly avant-garde style favored by only the most radical of women, the bloomer craze gained attention and followers far and wide. In Santa Cruz, California, Eliza Farnham and Georgiana Kirby, left alone to do their own farming because local men had all rushed to the goldfields, wore the outfit as they hoed and planted. In London, a few women of "some standing" made the news when they showed up at the famous Crystal Palace Exposition "attired according to the Bloomer fashion."[78] And from an Apalachicola, Florida, newspaper came reports of three of the "fairest daughters" of the South causing unprecedented excitement when they debuted bloomers in Pensacola.[79]

To the women for whom dress reform was not a fashion fad, however, the bloomer episode eventually became a prolonged misery. "People would stare," Cady Stanton recalled, "many men and women make rude remarks, boys followed in crowds with jeers and laughter."[80] Her whole family, including her husband, objected to the dress. Stone had the same experience. "When I go to each new city a horde of boys pursue me and destroy all comfort."[81] Especially if they were taking on new public roles, the bloomer brought them heightened and unwanted visibility and ridicule. Bloomers represented an important principle — women's freedom — but the symbol came to overshadow and interfere with the principle itself. As Cady Stanton wrote when she gave in after two years, "We put it on for greater freedom, but what is physical freedom compared with mental bondage?"[82] Anthony was the last to put on the bloomers, and the last reluctantly to give them up. Fashion is still a challenge for freedom-seeking women, but each time a woman zips up her jeans or puts on her presidential pantsuit, let us give a silent thanks to the courageous women who first put on the bloomers.

For the first two years after that meeting

in Seneca Falls, Cady Stanton and Anthony worked together in the temperance movement. Chafing under restraint from male leaders, Anthony determined to establish an independent New York State Women's Temperance Society. She convinced her new friend to serve as its president. In her inaugural speech in December 1852, Cady Stanton refracted temperance activism through her own radical women's rights ideas. She pointed out that, like abolitionism, the temperance movement was also being drawn into partisan politics. In 1851, state legislatures, beginning in Maine, began to shut down virtually all sales of alcohol. Surely women could recognize that helping to pass temperance law was so much more effective than prayer and moral supplication. "Just so soon as the women of this State say they will vote on the Temperance question," Cady Stanton argued, "the work is done."[83]

Cady Stanton went even further. Women's temperance activism must confront the inequalities that lurked within marriage itself. Temperance women already understood that men's drinking led not only to domestic violence but also to what we would call marital rape. As a solution, Cady Stanton shockingly declared, "it has been

84

left for Woman to preach the doctrine of Divorce" and called for liberalizing New York law to permit divorce on the grounds of drunkenness. Thus began Cady Stanton's lifelong exploration into the laws, custom, and practice of women's subordination in marriage. The image of women suffering poverty and abuse from, and losing custody of their children to, drunken, irresponsible husbands eventually became a staple of the argument that women needed the ability to make laws that protected them and their families. But in 1852, Stanton's audiences must have gasped.

The temperance movement could not tolerate such radicalism, and within a year Cady Stanton and Anthony had lost control of the organization they had formed. In the process, however, Anthony came to believe heart and soul in woman suffrage. She realized that for women to follow their best moral inclinations, they needed to have economic independence, and to have that, they needed legal change, and to have that they needed the right to vote. Never was a more loyal, energetic, and above all practical convert found. She determined to take "prompt and efficient action."[84] But how?

Until now, the only action that suffrage proponents advocated was to follow the

Revolutionary fathers and call for a tax protest until such time as women could represent the interests of their own property. Starting in 1852 and continuing for many years after, Harriot Hunt, a pioneering Massachusetts physician who had helped to call the Worcester convention, refused to pay her taxes. However, tax protest was an individual act, moreover, available only to the minority of women who owned property and paid taxes.

To find a more robust lever for change, one that recognized that all women were disfranchised, not just the propertied, was the question to which Anthony applied herself. There were several serious strategic obstacles. First, neither the U.S. Constitution nor federal law had anything to say about who could vote — yet. Franchise reform must be achieved state by state. Moreover, unlike wives' property rights, which could be changed by ordinary legislation, changes in suffrage had to be accomplished by state constitutional revision. Women had only one political tool to use here, the petition. Woman suffrage petitions had been submitted to constitutional conventions in 1850 in Ohio and 1853 in Massachusetts, only to be summarily rejected. Nonetheless, Anthony was determined to undertake a petition campaign for a woman suffrage amendment to the New York constitution. She was faced with a daunting procedure in pursuing a state constitutional amendment: passage through two successive state legislative sessions and then submission to a vote of the general electorate.

Such a task required a great deal of woman power, planning, and execution, all done with virtually no funds. Within months of her conversion to suffrage, Anthony was planning a campaign to petition state legislators. Cleverly she worked on two fronts: to reform the laws that disabled women economically; and to go deeper by enfranchising women to shape the laws themselves. In two months, after canvassing more than half the state's counties, she and others had collected ten thousand signed petitions, four thousand for suffrage.

Cady Stanton's role was to make the legal and political case to accompany the petitions. She had just given birth to her fifth child, her daughter, and was still breastfeeding. She tried to resist her friend's pleas, but "I find there is no use saying 'no' to you." Describing a daily routine that still speaks to women, she explained:

While I am about the house, surrounded by my children, washing dishes, baking, sewing, I can think up many points but . . . I seldom have one hour to sit down and write undisturbed. Men who can shut themselves up for days with their books and thoughts know little of what difficulties a woman must surmount.[85]

Finally, Cady Stanton relented and agreed to outline an argument, but wanted Susan to fill the speech with specific laws. Did Anthony know an "acute lawyer" nearby?

A month later, Cady Stanton had completed her address. She went up to her attic and practiced over and over again. While Anthony babysat, Cady Stanton took the train to Rochester to read the speech to a trusted mentor, William Henry Channing. Then with her two youngest children in tow, off she went to Albany. There was one last obstacle: her father was deeply concerned, though whether it was because she spoke at all or just not well is unclear. Daniel Cady was "an audience of one, and that the one of all others whose approbation I most desired, whose disapproval I most feared." He was distressed that his coddled daughter knew so much of women's sufferings, but he reluctantly gave her his approval, offered a few other legal examples, and sent her off with a kiss.[86]

Her words were addressed to an even more intimidating audience, the state's legislators. "We the daughters of the revolutionary heroes of '76," she began, "demand . . . the redress of our grievances — a revision of our state constitution — a new code of laws." In compelling detail, she examined the wide range of laws that disabled women — first "women as women" (the category that included disfranchisement), then women as wives, women as widows, finally women as mothers faced with laws that made the child "the absolute property of the father, wholly at his disposal." Women's rights were not the demand of a few, she insisted. No, we speak for the masses of women, the workingwomen, the wives of drunkards, "a very large majority [who] support themselves and their children."

Above all, it was her rage at women's humiliating subordination to which she gave voice. "Would to God you could know the burning indignation that fills woman's soul . . . how like feudal barons you freemen hold your women."[87] Bloomers had been amusing, but now newspapers reacted with fury at those who dared to bring their women's rights heresies into the legislative sanctuary. The women who "stalk into the public gaze" were unsexed; the men with them — "weak minded . . . with fingers locked across their stomachs . . . and with upturned eyes" — were hardly any better. Public sentiment would not bear this "egregious and ridiculous humbug" much longer.[88]

Cady Stanton read her address to a women's rights convention in Albany. With a loan from a male supporter, the convention made 50,000 copies of the speech, a copy of which was received by each legislator one week later when the petitions were submitted. The language of the legislators' response was more tempered than that of the newspapers, but the sentiments were the same. No law could alter the divine "mandate that man and woman shall not be equal."[89] Women could rest assured that they were faithfully represented in their families by their husbands and then in their governments by the legislators elected by their husbands' votes. Over the next many decades, innumerable legislators and congressmen would offer women endless versions of the same excuses in denying their rights.

The newspapers and legislators underestimated Anthony. Not one to give up easily, she planned for a second year's campaign, with speakers and public meetings in all the state's sixty counties, and a goal of twice as many petitions. During the frigid winter of January 1855, she traveled back and forth across the state. Many of her audiences were small. In Corning, she laid the blame for the public's "apathy" at the feet of the local clergy. In Elmira, she lost her audience to a popular Baptist itinerant preacher. To keep her expenses to a minimum she found sympathizers with whom she could stay, but in Penn Yan, her hosts turned out to be a couple quarreling over their property, and she fled to a rare hotel room.[90] After all her effort, the legislators' response was more insult and opposition. A state senator recommended that instead of the right to vote, the women petition for a law authorizing husbands to wear petticoats and wives to wear breeches.[91]

Anthony continued this New York petition work for the next half decade. Clergymen delivered sermons condemning the godless work she was doing; fearful women slammed doors in her face. As her sister activists married and had children, fewer and fewer were able to share the work. Anthony, the only unmarried childless woman in the leadership, found herself carrying more and more of the movement's burden by herself. "To leave poor brainless *me* to battle alone," she lamented, "It is a shame."[92] The loss of Stone, who Anthony thought might remain unmarried like herself, was particularly painful. After Stone's marriage to Henry Blackwell, the birth of her daughter and her husband's improvidence left her exhausted and depressed, with little time, energy, or confidence for public work.

Meanwhile, Cady Stanton could barely contain her eagerness to join with Anthony. These years of isolation for Anthony and frustration for Cady Stanton would cement their friendship. They each gained something essential from the bond. Anthony's closeness to Cady Stanton and the place she found in her home soothed her intense loneliness. "How I do long to be with you this very minute, to have one look into your very soul," she wrote from the campaign trail in 1857. "I have *very weak* moments, and long to lay my weary head somewhere . . . I sometimes fear that I *too* shall fall by the wayside and drop out."[93]

As for Cady Stanton, with Henry gone more often on political business, Anthony was her real domestic partner, almost a second mother to her children, the person who could share her burdens enough to allow her time to draft a women's rights appeal or letter to a convention she could not attend. "With the cares of a large family, I might in time, like too many women, have become wholly absorbed in a narrow family selfishness." But when Anthony entered her life, "I soon felt the power of my convert in goading me forward to ever more untiring work." At the core they shared an essential unflinching conviction about the intolerability of women's subordination. "For Miss Anthony and myself," Cady Stanton declared, "the English language had no words strong enough to express the indignation we felt in view of the prolonged injustice to women."[94]

Complicating these personal challenges in slowing down the woman suffrage work were larger developments. After long being suppressed, the issue of slavery came crashing into American politics and the women's rights movement in the form of the Kansas-Nebraska Act. Proposed by Illinois Democratic senator (and future presidential candidate) Stephen Douglas, the bill was meant to determine whether the last remaining territories of the Louisiana Purchase to petition Congress for statehood would do so with or without slavery. In February 1854, Anthony arrived in Washington, D.C., in time to witness the debate on the Kansas-Nebraska Act. It was her first venture into slavery territory, and the experience was a shock and an education. In a hotel in Mount Vernon, "I ate my dinner without once asking myself, are these human beings who minister to my wants *Slaves* . . . ," she wrote in her diary.[95]

Antislavery forces opposed the Kansas-Nebraska Act in order for Congress to retain full power to control the admission of states into the union. Pro-slavery forces approved of the bill because it authorized the people in the territory themselves to make the choice, a superficially democratic procedure that in reality threatened anarchy on the ground. When the bill passed, the real struggle over slavery began. Pro- and anti-slavery forces rushed to the territories. Each side was determined that it would control the constitution proposed by the new state, Kansas. Pro-slavery forces came from Missouri, where slavery was legal. Northern abolitionists also came in large numbers, especially from New England and New York. Among them were Anthony's two brothers, Daniel and Merritt. Were it not for the women's rights work, Anthony would have probably gone (as she did a decade later). The one women's rights activist who did join the abolitionist emigrants was Clarina Howard Nichols, a seasoned lecturer from Vermont. Just as soon as the law was passed, Nichols went to Kansas with her two older sons (her husband came later). She not only supported the antislavery forces but also recognized that, in shaping the first constitution for the new state of Kansas, she might find an opening for woman suffrage. Ultimately, she succeeded in winning a wedge, the right of women to vote for school boards. This was the first female franchise in any state constitution in the nation.

The battle in Kansas between the pro and antislavery forces, lasting until late 1856, was violent and murderous. The leader of the antislavery forces was a Connecticut tanner named John Brown, the fiery figure who in 1859 attempted and failed to ignite a slave rebellion at the federal armory in Harpers Ferry, Virginia. As a self-appointed martyr to the obliteration of slavery, Brown became an intensely polarizing figure between North and South. Merritt Anthony was suspected of harboring Brown in Kansas. Cady Stanton may have met John Brown through Frederick Douglass, but the conflict came even closer to her when her cousin Gerrit Smith was found to have helped to fund the abortive slave rebellion. Smith had a nervous breakdown. "The worse than death of my dear Cousin Gerrit, the martyrdom of the grand and glorious John Brown — all this conspires to make me regret more than ever my dwarfed womanhood," Cady Stanton wrote to Anthony just before New Year's Day, 1860.[96]

Women's rights activists became increasingly eager to participate in this historic political moment. Stone, who had followed her improvident husband to the wilds of Wisconsin, was no longer in demand nationally as a lecturer, but she still carved time out of her wifely and maternal duties to address the locals on antislavery principles. "The cause of Kansas, and of the country are still *our cause,* even tho, we *are* disfranchised," she wrote to Anthony.[97] Anthony's organizing skills caught the eye of abolitionist leaders. "The efficiency and success of our operations in New York this winter will depend more on your personal attendance and direction than upon that of any other of our workers," they wrote her. "We need your earnestness, your practical talent, your energy and perseverance."[98] She agreed to direct antislavery work for the whole of New

York state but made sure she retained the right to speak for women's rights as well.

The Kansas-Nebraska events had their most lasting impact in the creation of the Republican Party. Democratic support for the law fractured the party. Many northern Democrats came together with former Whigs who also opposed slavery in "anti-Nebraska meetings," out of which the Republican Party was born. At first abolitionists had great hopes of the new party. "I am rejoiced to say that Henry is heart and soul in the Republican movement," Cady Stanton wrote Anthony.[99] So was she, forcing her way into a Republican rally that was supposedly reserved for voters. In 1856, the Republicans ran their first presidential candidate, John Frémont of California Gold Rush fame. Frémont was married to Jessie Benton, daughter of a powerful Missouri senator, and the highest profile woman in presidential politics since Abigail Adams. Republican campaign buttons advertised Jessie as often as they did her husband. Women's rights activists had hopes that the new party would not only oppose slavery but also follow its commitment to freedom all the way to women's rights.

By the election of 1860, however, many members of the abolitionist and women's rights communities had become skeptical about the determination of the Republicans to end slavery. They did not support Abraham Lincoln as president, because his antislavery record was so vague and vacillating. The Stantons were especially disappointed that the party's nominating convention passed over their neighbor and friend New York senator William Henry Seward. In the months between Lincoln's election and inauguration, abolitionists sought to counterbalance pressure on him coming from southern threats to secede by holding public meetings designed "to rouse the people to the necessity of holding that party to its declared principles and pushing it if possible, a step or two forward." Anthony was still in charge of New York antislavery work, and now Cady Stanton, her seventh (and last) child a year and a half old, was able to join her.

It was not an auspicious moment to go on the stump for the abolition of slavery. "The whole State was aflame with the mob spirit," Cady Stanton recalled, and the meetings they held from Albany to Buffalo were interrupted and attacked.[100] Henry urged his wife and Anthony to stop speaking. "I think you risk your lives," he wrote from Washington, D.C. "I assure you, this nation is going to destruction as fast as it can. . . . Civil war is upon us." The mobs in the North, the seceding states in the South, the concerns about a Lincoln presidency, "These are mere eddies in the grand current which is sweeping Slavery to perdition. Stand out of the way & let the current run," he counseled.[101]

That current would eventually move women's rights forward, but not until the years immediately following the war. Woman suffrage would come to the fore, the movement behind it would gain new solidity, unity, and purpose, but — most consequential for the long historical record — the bond between antislavery and women's rights would be threatened.

Two:
Now Let Us Try Universal Suffrage, 1861–1869

Like most wars in which men's lives are on the line, the Civil War was not a welcoming environment for women's rights. The eleventh annual National Woman's Rights Convention was scheduled for May of 1861, the speakers set and the hall hired. Then in April, the U.S. Army's Fort Sumter in South Carolina was attacked, the war began, and the organizers decided to cancel the convention. Susan B. Anthony thought this was a mistake. Why should women sit on the sidelines while the fundamental question of the nation's commitment to unity, democracy, and freedom was at stake? History was being made, and she wanted women to help make it and do so on their own behalf. "Tried to interest myself in a sewing society . . . but sewing no longer seems my calling," she wrote in her diary. "It is so easy to feel your power for public work slipping away."[1]

Anthony was largely alone in her opinion that women's rights activity must be continued, the war notwithstanding. "It is useless to speak if nobody will listen," counseled Martha Wright, one of those to call the 1848 Seneca Falls Convention.[2] Lucy Stone's energies were still primarily absorbed in raising her daughter, Alice, and trying to save her troubled marriage. Cady Stanton's plate, as usual, was overfull. Late in 1861, with money inherited at her father's death, she moved her family to New York City, where Henry Stanton's Republican Party work had been rewarded with a lucrative patronage post. Her two eldest sons enlisted while she and her two daughters and youngest son waited at home, like so many other worried families, hoping for the best. As an old woman, daughter Harriot still had memories of "sitting in the dining room . . . cutting old linen into small squares which Susan and I then raveled into lint [small pieces used for dressing wounds]."[3]

As the months passed, the casualties increased exponentially. The war was not going well for the North. President Lincoln was deferring to his chief military officer, George McClellan, who hung back from forceful military prosecution, most believed, out of an underlying sympathy with the South. Then, over the summer and fall of 1862, Lincoln became convinced that the only way to reverse the war's course was to attack head-on what he now recognized as the core of rebel society, the system of slavery. On the first day of 1863 he issued his Emancipation Proclamation, using his presidential powers to declare all slaves in rebel territory "forever free." Black communities in the North and abolitionists rejoiced. "The millennium is on the way," women's rights supporter Theodore Tilton wrote Anthony. "Three cheers for God!"[4] The Proclamation also opened the door to African American men to "be received into the armed service of the United States," and Frederick Douglass's sons and Sojourner Truth's nephew rushed to sign up.

The long-awaited move against slavery had serious flaws. Like all executive orders, it could be undone by the next president. Moreover, the proclamation exempted slaves in the border states and freed only those under the control of the Confederate government, for whom emancipation was meaningless without the defeat of the South. "We must not lay the flattering unction to our souls that the proclamation will be of any use if we are beaten and have a dissolution of the Union," warned Henry Stanton, who was now going regularly to Washington, D.C. The Republican Party and the president needed to be pushed to make emancipation full, permanent, and secured by the force of federal law. "Here there is work for you," he directed, though not to his wife. "Susan, put on your armor and go forth!"[5]

Over the previous decade, Susan B. Anthony had matured politically and was no longer the junior member of the Stanton/Anthony partnership. She had done much speaking on her own and was more confident on the public stage. Her organizing skills had been honed by her work on the antislavery circuit just before the outbreak of the war.

Nor was the political growth hers alone. By 1861, women public figures and speakers were far more common than they had been in 1848. In general, the war was transforming northern women, sweeping them up in the mobilization of the entire society, as they joined in to resist the unprecedented threat to the American national experiment. Large numbers had stepped beyond their domestic thresholds to act on behalf of the war effort. They ran businesses and tilled fields in their husbands' absences. They formed Soldiers Aid Societies and staffed the mammoth United States Sanitary Commission, traveled to army hospitals and even to the battlefield itself to nurse the sick and wounded. A remarkable number, it was later learned, even donned men's clothes and identities so that they could take up weapons and fight as soldiers.[6] The nation's crisis was bringing northern women to the brink of national politics. Women's rights leaders would take them over the threshold.

Abolitionists were busy organizing what they called Loyal Leagues, citizens' groups that were pushing for a war policy based on total and permanent abolition of slavery. With the encouragement and support of their male allies, Anthony and Cady Stanton determined to build a nationwide women's version of these Loyal Leagues. They found that many of the veterans of the prewar women's rights movement were ready to join them. Angelina Grimké Weld came out of her long retirement to participate, and Lucy Stone agreed to undertake the work. Like the men's loyal leagues, the Women's Loyal National League would both support the northern war effort and push it to undertake a commitment to ending slavery. If maintaining the precarious balance between these two purposes was not complex enough, it would carefully attempt to educate women on their political rights and obligations in the process.

The inaugural meeting of the Women's Loyal National League was scheduled for May 14, 1863, at the Church of the Pilgrims in Brooklyn, New York. Women's war support groups in Illinois, Indiana, Vermont, Massachusetts, Wisconsin, and elsewhere promised participation. "The bells are ringing and guns firing for joy for our military victories," . . . wrote the women of the Baraboo, Wisconsin, League. "But our woman's work of educating the children into the idea and practice of true and universal justice is ever to be done."[7]

Loyal women who could not abandon their domestic obligations sent heartfelt messages of support, many of which picked up on the implicit women's rights flavor of the project. Mariam Fish, an Illinois woman, told how she had written her governor to protest her inability to exert any property rights over a mismanaged family business in which she had no rights of ownership.[8] Mary F. Thomas, a physician from Indiana who later served in Union Army hospitals, hoped that out of the conflagration of war would come not only freedom for the slave but also "the enfranchisement of women."[9] "Go forward . . . as independent human beings . . ." Anthony urged those sitting before her in the audience. "Forget conventionalisms; forget what the world will say, whether you are in your place or out of it; think your best thoughts, speak your best words, do your best works, looking to your own consciences for approval."[10]

The issue of woman suffrage made its appearance only once, when the meeting considered a resolution that "there never can be a true peace in this republic until the civil and political equality of every subject of the government shall be practically established." Unlike fifteen years before at Seneca Falls, debate was conducted openly by numerous women energetically and confidently offering a range of political views for and against asking for their own enfranchisement. Mrs. Hoyt, a member of the Madison, Wisconsin, Ladies Union League, explained that while she did not oppose women's rights, it was "an ism [that] has not been received with entire favor by the women of the country," and she thought that "nothing that has become obnoxious to a portion of the people of the country shall be dragged into this meeting."[11] "This resolution . . . merely makes the assertion that in a true democracy, a genuine republic, every citizen who lives under the government must have the right of representation," Anthony responded. "Before our Government . . . can be placed on a lasting foundation, the civil and practical rights of every citizen must be practically established."[12] Newspaper reports indicated that at first Mrs. Hoyt's position was sustained by the votes of the men in the audience, but when the men were ruled out of order and only women voted, the original resolution passed.[13]

Two months after the Women's Loyal National League meeting, the resentment of many white northerners of the proclamation, which seemed to them to mean only that they would pay the ultimate price to end slavery, about which they were concerned little, and free the slaves, about whom they cared even less, boiled over. During the infamous "draft riot" in New York City in July of 1863, more than one hundred black New Yorkers were killed and some of their community institutions destroyed. Cady Stanton experienced the riot directly from her home on 43rd Street. The Colored Orphans' Asylum, the rioters' main target, was just blocks away. She watched with horror as the children were guided two by two as "the most brutal mob I have ever witnessed" burned the building to the ground. The mob was also going after abolitionists, and she feared that it would come for her. Then, the rioters found twenty-year-old Daniel Stanton standing in front of his family's house. He had finished his two-year enlistment, but they whispered among themselves that "he was one of those three-hundred-dollar fellows," the hated men of wealth who were legally permitted to pay another to take their place and personally evade the draft. Then her son, with what his mother gratefully described as "great presence of mind . . . saved his life by deception." He diverted the mob by standing the whole lot to drinks in a nearby saloon and leading them in a three cheers salute for "Jeff Davis."[14]

Left with her two middle sons and servants, Cady Stanton feared that "the wretches" would come and break down the front door. So then, as she wrote a few days later to her cousin, "What did I do?" She sent them all to the top story, pointed the way to the roof and told them, if the house were attacked, to run over to the roof of the next house. As for herself, she determined to stand up to "the tyranny of the mob," and do what she did best: deliver a speech.

With glorious arrogance, she determined to convert the mad mob to reason and peacefulness. Luckily she did not have to test this folly. Before she could "appeal to them as Americans and citizens of a republic," Union soldiers, fresh from victory at the killing fields of Gettysburg, arrived to disperse the crowd, and the family fled to the Cady home in Johnstown to wait out the upheaval.[15]

The primary work which the Women's Loyal National League decided to undertake was to collect one million signatures to petition Congress to "pass at the earliest practicable day an act emancipating all persons of African descent held to involuntary service or labor in the United States."[16] "As women we could have no voice as to what should be the basis of reconstruction of this government," Anthony explained, "save through the one right which the nation has left to us, the right of petition."[17] By February 1864, two thousand women had collected over one hundred thousand signatures. Cady Stanton told of "one poor, infirm widow who has lost her husband and two sons in the war" and who sent in 1,800 signatures from Wisconsin. The woman carefully added the names of those who refused to sign "that they may be handed over to the future scorn they so well deserve."[18]

The Stanton children were recruited to bundle the petitions, which were arranged state by state so that congressmen would know that their own constituents were appealing to them. The League delivered the petitions — tied into a giant roll — to the Senate chamber, where they were submitted by Massachusetts senator Charles Sumner. The petitions — their numbers ultimately reaching 400,000 — still reside tightly bound in the U.S. National Archives, unwound as they were when originally submitted. Once congressional Republicans concluded that legislation would not end slavery and that a constitutional amendment was necessary, the continuing avalanche of the women's petitions was directed to that end.

In January 1865, after Abraham Lincoln had been reelected on a platform that called for the constitutional abolition of slavery, what would become the Thirteenth Amendment passed through Congress. Ratification of the amendment took place against the background of the final months of the war and the assassination of the president. By December, the Thirteenth Amendment, forever allowing "neither slavery nor involuntary servitude, except as a punishment for crime whereof the party shall have been duly convicted," became part of the U.S. Constitution.

Since the adoption of the Bill of Rights, only two other amendments, dealing with judicial and electoral matters of little general interest, had been added to the Constitution. The Thirteenth Amendment was the first addition to the Constitution since the Bill of Rights to stir popular energy, and it was women, looking forward to a full role in the nation's politics, who recognized and mobilized that energy. The Thirteenth and the subsequent two postwar amendments essentially rewrote basic elements of the U.S. Constitution, turning it into a document that could respond to challenges in national life. Eventually this change, and women's role in it, elevated the demand for woman suffrage to the forefront of the women's rights movement and to the level of the federal constitutional stage.

In the war's last year, casualties on both sides remained spectacularly high, but it was clear that the South was running out of men to fight, while the northern armies were reinforced by African American enlistees.

The end of this horrible war was only a matter of time, and talk began to turn to "reconstruction" — of the Union, of the nation, of the Constitution. In late 1864, Anthony shut down the Women's Loyal National League.

Meanwhile, Elizabeth Cady Stanton was immersed in a terrible political scandal as a result of her husband's patronage job overseeing the Port of New York. His son and clerk Daniel had taken bribes to cancel bonds meant to keep transshipments from going to the Confederacy. Son and father were caught up in a newspaper storm accusing them of corruption, and were threatened with federal charges, at one point including treason. Cady Stanton blamed rival Republican Party factions, reaching all the way up to Secretary of Treasury Salmon Chase, with waging a vicious personal vendetta. Both father and son lost their jobs. Daniel eventually rebounded, but Henry Stanton's reputation as a hero of abolition and the Republican Party was irrevocably tarnished. Cady Stanton was no longer an unbridled partisan of the Republicans, and in the aftermath of this family catastrophe, she began to develop an antipathy that subsequent events would only intensify.

As for Anthony, on her shoulders had

fallen much of the ambitious enterprise of the Women's Loyal National League, and she was ready for a new start. After her father died, she closed up the family house. Then, at the invitation of her eldest brother, a rising political figure in Kansas, she took off for the plains. His state had played a crucial role in the national crisis. Antislavery forces had won the "little civil war" of 1854–1856 there, and now Republicans, prominent among them Daniel Anthony, controlled state politics. Thousands of freed slaves and free black people, responding to the state's abolitionist reputation, flocked to Kansas to start a new life. So did Susan B. Anthony.

The train trip to Leavenworth was long and grueling, but when she arrived, the freshness of pioneer conditions and the hopefulness of Kansans invigorated her. Drawn to the state's African American communities, she taught their children, attended their churches, and met their leaders. "So far every man woman & child of them is brimful of good common sense . . . & the more I see of the race the more wonderful they are to me."[19] When a black typesetter was barred by white printers from working at her brother's newspaper office, she raged in her diary that it was "a burning, blistering shame."[20]

In mid-April 1865, the war that had seemed like it might last an eternity ended with the South's surrender. "Fort Sumter Flag raising to day — just four years since it was furled," Anthony quietly noted in her diary. Just days later came far more unexpected news: "Morning Telegram reported President Lincoln assassinated at Fords Theater in Washington."[21] Right before his death, Lincoln had laid out a plan for a postwar reconstruction that would readmit seceding states but not enfranchise African Americans. The nation's first presidential assassination was a "terrible blow," but Anthony could not help thinking it was also a divine reprimand.[22] Lincoln's plan would have been a terrible mistake, undoing the very military victory so hard won. "My soul was sad and sick at what seemed his settled purpose — to consign the ex-slaves back to the tender mercies of the disappointed, desperate, sullen, revengeful ex-lords of the lash," she said at a memorial meeting.[23]

It rapidly became clear however that Lincoln's vice president and successor, Andrew Johnson, a Tennessee Unionist, had plans for the freed people that were even more hostile than Lincoln's. Encouraged by Johnson, southern states were passing laws that reinstated slavery in all but name. "There is not an earthly chance for the loyal black man of the south," concluded Anthony.[24] Trapped in a purgatory between slavery and citizenship, African Americans were without the tools to protect themselves. In this new emergency, antislavery forces remobilized. Those in Congress most committed to black freedom and rights, now known as Radical Republicans, put forward another constitutional amendment to follow the Thirteenth, which would ensure freed people's citizenship and political rights.

With its repeated invocation of the principle of "self-government" as the only safe foundation for a true republic, the Women's Loyal National League had laid the basis for linking woman suffrage with political rights for African Americans. This perspective now reemerged as an explicit call from women's rights forces for neither black nor woman suffrage, but for "universal suffrage." The prospect of emancipation had transformed the prewar bond between women and slaves from one of their common oppression into a postwar demand for equal rights and political inclusion shared by both. "No country ever has had or ever will have peace until every citizen has a voice in the government," explained Cady

Stanton. "Now let us try universal suffrage."[25]

As reasonable as the principle of a universal, affirmative declaration of citizenship enfranchisement seemed, the politics necessary to carry it forward were very muddy. Anthony recognized that even the most radical of Republicans saw an electoral advantage in black men's votes that the enfranchisement of women would never provide. Women were as diverse as the nation, and it was even then obvious that they would vote almost as variously as their sons and husbands and fathers.

Meanwhile, Cady Stanton was learning another hard lesson: the obstacles to the idea of universal suffrage were coming not just from Republican politicians, but from former abolitionist allies. Wendell Phillips, a man whose friendship, support, and judgment were very dear to her, shocked her to the core when he publicly announced that although the principle of universal suffrage was logical, the practice was not timely. Now, he declared with finality, "was the negro's hour."[26] Cady Stanton shot back with "just one question on the apparent opposition in which you place the negro and woman. . . . Do you believe the African race is composed entirely of males?"[27]

The emerging Fourteenth Amendment, ultimately the most crucial addition to the U.S. Constitution since the Bill of Rights, had a great deal of constitutional labor to accomplish. It must undo the notorious 1857 Dred Scott Supreme Court decision, which insisted that the Founders' original intent was to exclude all African descendants — not just slaves — from enjoying the status and rights of national citizenship. To replace this interpretation of the Constitution, the amendment declared that "all persons born or naturalized in the United States and subject to the jurisdiction thereof, are citizens of the United States and of the state wherein they reside." This comprehensive and inclusive characterization of national citizenship would ultimately be the source of more litigation than any other part of the U.S. Constitution.

The Thirteenth Amendment had invalidated the clause of the Constitution counting the enslaved as three-fifths of a person for purposes of determining the basis of representation, the crucial political metric that determined a state's number of House members and of presidential electors. This "three-fifths" clause had been responsible for inflating the political clout of the slaveholding states for decades. Emancipation meant that formerly enslaved persons would now count as one whole person. Ironically, the power of the southern white vote would be enhanced unless the ex-slaves could vote.

There was as yet insufficient congressional support for an outright act of enfranchisement for the freedmen, but the Republican authors of the Fourteenth Amendment devised a back-door solution to the dual problem of black voting and the basis of representation. While the notion of federal control of the franchise was still anathema, and while the individual states could not be forced to enfranchise, they could be penalized for failing to do so by cutting the basis of representation proportionally to those whom the state disfranchised. Because the advocates of woman suffrage had been effective in putting their issue on the national political table, even this very hesitant attempt to recognize black men's voting rights raised the question of women's political place. Would failure to enfranchise women also count against a state's basis of representation?[28]

The implications of this logic thus introduced woman suffrage, with which the amendment's authors had no desire to engage, into the Fourteenth Amendment debate. To solve this conundrum, congressmen began to consider making the language of the amendment's second section more specific. Ultimately it emerged as follows:

> . . . when the right to vote at any election . . . is denied to any of the male inhabitants of such State, being twenty-one years of age, and citizens of the United States . . . the basis of representation therein shall be reduced in the proportion which the number of such male citizens shall bear to the whole number of male citizens twenty-one years of age in such State.[29]

The word "male" was repeated three times! Until this moment, the Constitution had not a word to say about the distinction between men and women. But the time had passed when "people" or "persons" could be understood to mean merely men. If only men were meant, only men must be specified. The proposed Fourteenth Amendment thus recognized women's claim to the ballot by acting to deny it. "If that word 'male' be inserted . . ." Cady Stanton wrote to her cousin Gerrit Smith, "it will take us a century at least to get it out again."[30]

Cady Stanton fought back against "that word 'male' " with all her might. "I have argued constantly with Phillips and the whole [antislavery] fraternity," she wrote to Anthony, "but I fear one and all will favor enfranchising the negro without us. Woman's cause is in deep water."[31] Anthony had already begun to make her way back to New York, stopping to meet with Lucy Stone in New Jersey.

In New York City, Anthony found a room set aside for her in Elizabeth Cady Stanton's home. The two women sat down around yet another parlor table and drew up the first petition ever submitted to the U.S. Congress on behalf of votes for women. "As you are now amending the Constitution and placing new safeguards round the individual rights of four millions of emancipated slaves," it read, "we ask that you extend the right of Suffrage to Woman — the only remaining class of disfranchised citizens. . . . We pray your Honorable Body . . . that you legislate hereafter for persons, citizens, taxpayers, and not for class or caste."[32]

Within months, ten thousand signatures were collected, but unlike the Women's Loyal National League campaign on behalf of the Thirteenth Amendment's abolition of slavery, congressional sponsors for women's political rights were much more difficult to find. Senator Sumner submitted their petitions but only under protest. As they had in Kansas, Cady Stanton and Anthony turned from reluctant Republicans and accepted help from congressional Democrats. Democrats, trailing their Negrophobia behind them, were only too eager to accept the women's petitions. "I prefer the white women of my country to the negro," explained New York Democrat James Brooks when he presented the petition of his constituent Elizabeth Cady Stanton.[33]

This first campaign for woman suffrage via federal constitutional action put forward a new and expansive political goal. As woman suffrage rose to the top of the women's rights platform and became a matter of national politics and constitutional revision, it did so under the banner of "universal suffrage." Universal suffrage meant that the right to vote should be established as a fundamental national right, tied to citizenship and nothing else. "The time for Negro or Woman specialties is passed," Anthony explained, "and we proposed to step on the broad platform of equality & fraternity."[34] Revolutionary changes were coming fast in the wake of the abolition of slavery. "Out of this struggle we must come with higher ideas of liberty, the masses quickened with thought, and a rot-

Stanton and Anthony, c. 1870.

ten aristocracy crushed forever," proclaimed
Cady Stanton.[35]

Hopeful of a grand alliance from the
forces of political reform, Cady Stanton and
Anthony proposed to the leaders of the
American Anti-Slavery Society that they
join together in a new, more inclusive
universal suffrage organization. Wendell
Phillips, now in full control of the antislavery machinery, remained adamant in his opposition. The American Anti-Slavery Society
was to meet in New York on May 8 and 9,
the day before a woman's rights conven-

tion. Undaunted, Cady Stanton attended anyway and put forth a resolution from the floor that the campaign to get the word "white" out of the suffrage provisions of the New York Constitution should be expanded to remove "male" as well. Phillips abruptly ruled her out of order. The ruling was ridiculous, an exasperated Cady Stanton noted. "It was simply a question of time, . . . demanding [suffrage] for the negro on Thursday and for woman on Friday."[36]

The next day, May 10, 1866, Cady Stanton took the chair of the eleventh National Woman's Rights Convention, the first since Fort Sumter, before which they had been held regularly. The women met at the same venue as the abolitionists, Dr. George Cheever's Church of the Puritans in Union Square. Many of the movement's leading lights, including seventy-four-year-old Lucretia Mott, were there, eager to take up the new universal suffrage campaign. On that very day, Congress passed its final version of the Fourteenth Amendment, which included "that word 'male.' " "Now in this reconstruction is the great opportunity, perhaps of the century," Cady Stanton began, "to base our government on the broad principle of equal rights for all." She did not attack the proposed amendment, and expressed the hope that all changes to the Constitution would "add glory to its foundation."[37]

Cady Stanton was followed by Henry Ward Beecher, the highly influential Brooklyn cleric who ministered to the wealthy Plymouth Congregation in Brooklyn. "Think of it for a moment! A minister advocating the rights of woman!" women's rights champion Ernestine Rose had said of him a few years before. "Even her rights at the ballot-box!"[38] These were the days of heroic oratory and Beecher went on for more than an hour, his remarks taking up a full quarter of the publication of the convention's proceedings.

Then came Wendell Phillips. Had Phillips come to make peace with the women's rights faction? If so, he did it in an odd way, insisting that women were not ready for the ballot. They were too concerned with fashion, he charged, and needed to learn to turn their heads to more important matters before the ballot could do them any good. With great restraint, Cady Stanton thanked him politely. However, Josephine Griffing, a women's rights leader from Ohio who was now in Washington, D.C., working with emancipated slaves, was appalled. "Yesterday [at the Anti-Slavery meetings] he said the ballot in the hand of the negro, was a talisman to bring him every weal and ward off every woe," she said, "while, to-day, he said it was nothing in the hands of woman."[39]

The only African American scheduled to speak was Frances Ellen Watkins Harper, a free-born poet and novelist from Maryland. This was her first time on a women's rights platform. Having lost all ownership of her property at the death of her husband, she had learned that as a woman she had few rights. She also told how she had been forcibly ejected from a Philadelphia streetcar, a discrimination that generations of black women would continue to protest. Her audience of white women gasped in disbelief. She called for black men's need of the ballot while avoiding either endorsing or rejecting that of women. Still, as she concluded, "Justice is not fulfilled so long as woman is unequal before the law. We are all bound together in one great bundle of humanity."[40]

The meeting proceeded to its main business — creating an American Equal Rights Association (AERA) with the goal of pursuing universal enfranchisement without distinction of race or sex. Lucretia Mott was made honorary president, but was too enfeebled to preside; Cady Stanton, as first vice president, took charge. "The desire of her heart," to unite these two great reforms in one overarching movement for equal rights for all, had now been realized.[41] However, to no one was the formation of an American Equal Rights Association more significant than to Susan B. Anthony. Although she was one of three corresponding secretaries, it was her organization from beginning to end, and her leadership of it was a trial by fire of her commitment to woman suffrage. Its first meeting adjourned, the conflict with black suffrage forces was effectively skirted for the time being.

Five months later, as a mark of the possibilities that the moment seemed to promise, Cady Stanton made an extraordinary move. She might not be able to vote, but she could see no legal barrier to running for office and declared her independent candidacy for the Eighth Congressional District of New York City. This was the seat held by Democrat James Brooks, who had just months before sponsored her universal suffrage petition. The planks of her platform, "free speech, free press, free men, and free trade," were traditionally Democratic elements. However, she was running as an

Frances Ellen Watkins Harper.

independent candidate in order to chasten the Republicans, as "a rebuke to the dominant party for its retrogressive legislation, in so amending the Constitution as to make invidious distinctions on the grounds of sex."[42] Over future years, in part to insulate their demand for the vote from any hint of selfish desire for office, women repeatedly disavowed any interest in the ugly business of gaining political place or power, but Cady Stanton had no such qualms. Her husband

and three eldest sons and twenty other men voted for her. She lost, but so did James Brooks.

As the Fourteenth Amendment slowly made its way through the shoals of ratification, the American Equal Rights Association continued to petition Congress. Now it was asking for a supplementary amendment (had it passed, it would have been the Sixteenth) both to assert the principle of national citizenship suffrage and explicitly to bar disfranchisement by sex. At the same time, AERA was bringing its human rights and universal suffrage vision campaign to states that were revising voting provisions in their own constitutions. Lucy Stone testified before the legislature of New Jersey to remove the phrase "white male," which had been instituted by state law in 1807, previous to which New Jersey women had actually voted. In other states, sympathetic legislators and petitioning women pressed hard for changes in their constitutions and made impressive showings in Michigan, Connecticut, and Wisconsin, but in each case they were done in by Republican determination to insulate black suffrage from woman suffrage.

AERA efforts in the historic home of the

women's rights movement, New York state, were particularly important. There a state constitutional convention was called to consider, among other changes, the removal of the $250 property qualification required of black men — and only black men — to vote. AERA was determined to have the convention expand its focus to consider woman suffrage as well. Ambitious teams of speakers, black and white, male and female, canvassed the state collecting signatures on petitions. Sojourner Truth did some touring, as did a new African American recruit, thirty-seven-year-old Louisa Jacobs. Six years before, her mother, Harriet Jacobs, had published *Incidents in the Life of a Slave Girl,* her harrowing account of the sexual abuse inflicted on her by her master's father. Louisa was one of the two children Harriet chose to have by another white man, Samuel Tredwell Sawyer, to whom she had turned for protection from her abuser.

The chair of the New York constitutional convention committee assigned to receive the suffrage petitions was *New York Tribune* founding editor and antislavery veteran Horace Greeley. Although Greeley's committee received perhaps twenty thousand petitions from women, it concluded that public sentiment did not support woman suffrage because it was an innovation "openly at war with a distribution of duties and functions between the sexes as venerable and pervading as the Government itself."[43] The antiquated rhetoric was not typical Greeley, and Cady Stanton knew something less ethereal was at work. "It is not so much the will of the people that troubles politicians as the safety of the party in power," she retaliated. "The committee denies the ballot to woman and gives it to the black man for the same reason — party success."[44] The full convention endorsed the statement of Greeley's committee. The entire constitutional convention devolved into a farce, enacting no constitutional changes whatsoever.

The most ambitious and consequential of these state-level universal suffrage campaigns was held in 1867 in Kansas, the state so dear to Anthony's heart. She and others believed that pioneer life made women likely suffrage supporters, and over the next half century, the West would prove the nation's most welcoming ground for woman suffrage. "You need not wonder . . . if after all the difficulties & dangers we have encountered," one Kansas woman told Cady Stanton ". . . that we should come to think that 'our divinely constituted heads' are on our own shoulders."[45]

Though far away from the nation's centers of power, Kansas was, as Anthony put it, "a radical State — a young State, and it is just the place to try the experiment of true Republicanism for the enfranchisement of her citizens."[46] New states like Kansas did not as yet have hidebound political establishments. Instead, they offered highly unsettled party environments, sometimes with reform opportunities and at other times cutthroat partisan struggles for power and office. Through her brother Daniel, Anthony had some knowledge of Kansas Republican intricacies. The party was not ready for universal suffrage, but it was willing to put two separate referenda, one on black suffrage and another on woman suffrage, before the state's voters in November 1867.

While Anthony stayed back in New York to raise money and cultivate political support, Lucy Stone and Henry Blackwell opened the campaign in Kansas. Their marriage, troubled by his endless business fiascoes and her emotional troubles, had survived the war years. Now they were on a slightly more stable footing. They left ten-year-old Alice, their only child, in the care of her stern Blackwell aunts, Ellen and Elizabeth. It was time for Henry Blackwell to make good on his marriage promise to Stone to share fully her reform commitments. Their political partnership, which would continue for the next thirty years, allowed Stone to come back as a public figure, while making Blackwell the most important man in the woman suffrage movement.

In April and May, the couple were "speaking every day and sometimes twice, journeying from twenty-five to forty miles daily," as Blackwell reported enthusiastically. We "address the most astonishing (and astonished) audiences in the most extraordinary places. Tonight it may be a log school house, tomorrow a stone church; next day a store with planks for seats and in one place . . . an unfinished courthouse with four stone walls but no roof whatsoever."[47] They had genuine hopes for victory for both woman and black suffrage. In the bracing atmosphere of a plains spring, Stone was regaining her old rhetorical power. "The women here are grand," she reported to Cady Stanton, "and it will be a shame past all expression if they don't get the right to vote."[48] Sam Wood, a Kansas judge and their chief Republican sponsor, reported back to AERA in New York that "with the help of God and Lucy Stone, we shall carry Kansas!"[49]

Despite this early optimism, the campaign faced serious troubles. Kansas supporters of woman suffrage had hoped for an infusion of financial support from eastern reformers, but Wendell Phillips and the Anti-Slavery Society held fast to their determination to focus the money they controlled exclusively on black suffrage. The liberal eastern press, widely read in Kansas, was also closed to AERA. "If the *Independent* would take up this question . . . as it does for the negro, that paper alone could save this State," Stone wrote Cady Stanton. She said to Anthony, "What a power to hold and not use! I could not sleep the other night, just for thinking of it."[50]

The local political situation was also worsening. While Sam Wood "has always been *true* both to the negro and the woman," other Republicans were not.[51] Stone reported that even Anthony's influential brother Daniel "don't want the Republicans to take us up."[52] In a sign of growing nasty antagonisms, one scandal-mongering Kansas Republican charged Stone and Blackwell with being unmarried "Free Lovers."[53] The skittishness of the state's Republicans led Stone and Blackwell to dally with

Kansas Democrats. Stone reported that local Democrats, "a small minority with nothing to lose, and utterly unscrupulous" were "preparing to take us up."[54]

Back in New York, Anthony was still pursuing her vision of a grand canvass of the state. If well-known eastern reformers came to Kansas, they could appeal to the New Englanders who had emigrated there ten years before to fight against slavery. Her plans included both Frederick Douglass and Frances Ellen Watkins Harper, but both had been deployed by the Republican Party to go South to enroll freedmen who were beginning to gain voting rights under friendly reconstruction governments.

The only speaker available to take up the Kansas work was Olympia Brown. A thirty-two-year-old Unitarian minister and mother of two from Massachusetts, Brown took the field after Stone and Blackwell had left. She was undaunted in her energy and determination. Speaking before one hostile crowd near the Missouri border, she turned the audience around through "unanswerable logic that if it were good under certain reasons for the negro to vote, it was ten times better for the same reasons for the women to vote."[55] Brown stayed an important figure in the suffrage movement, living long enough to cast her vote for president in 1920.

The battle within the state Republican Party, inflamed by Democratic opportunism, laid traps for the universal suffrage campaign, drawing black and woman suffrage supporters into a bitter conflict. African Americans were now 10 percent of the state's population. Their most prominent leader was Charles Langston, a hero of the prewar battle against the Fugitive Slave Act. Langston knew and respected Anthony. Although his priority was black suffrage, he was willing to support both causes as long as they were not pitted against each other. Soon, however, they were. Principled universal suffrage efforts fell victim to incendiary reports of anti-black woman suffrage supporters and African American opponents of woman suffrage, stories invented and circulated by unscrupulous politicians and newspapermen. Late in the summer, reports came in that "a condition of the question is fast approaching which we have endeavored to avert — a bitter antagonism between negro and female suffrage."[56]

In the midst of both the New York and Kansas campaigns, in May 1867 AERA met for its first anniversary meeting in New York, once again at the Church of the

Puritans. Robert Purvis, AERA's most stalwart African American supporter, held the chair. "Our simple yet imperative demand . . . ," he explained, "is equality, of rights for all, without regard to color, sex or race, and, inseparable from the citizen."[57] His daughter Harriet Jr. (Hattie) served as corresponding secretary, the lone African American woman to hold office in AERA. Anthony followed Robert Purvis with an account of the association's finances: $4,000 raised and spent, far less than its campaigns needed. (Ernestine Rose quipped that with $1,000,000 "we will have the elective franchise at the very next session of our Legislature.")[58] Then Cady Stanton delivered another one of her grand speeches.

The star of the meeting was the "venerable" Sojourner Truth, introduced by Lucretia Mott. "I own a little house in Battle Creek, Michigan," Truth told the crowd, and "I would like to go to the polls myself."[59] Since her "arn't I a woman" speech in 1851, her fame had grown, and now she addressed her prestige to black women's need for voting rights. "If colored men get their rights, and not colored women theirs," she told the audience, "you see the colored men will be masters over the women, and it will be just as bad as it was before." Votes for black men were not enough. "I am for keeping the thing going while things are stirring."[60]

Sojourner Truth's intervention could not stop the tension between black and woman suffrage from spreading from the Kansas campaign into the heart of AERA itself. Toward the end of the meeting, African American activist George Downing, a wealthy Rhode Islander, prodded Cady Stanton to choose between black and woman suffrage. When she insisted that "as a matter of principle" she claimed the vote for all classes, he was not satisfied. If he insisted to ask her, "Are you willing to have the colored man enfranchised before the woman?" she must answer, "No; I would not trust him with all my rights." Woman suffrage was necessary, she went on, so that women with "virtue, wealth and education" could use their franchises to "outweigh this incoming tide of ignorance, poverty, and vice" that universal manhood suffrage was bringing with it.[61] Anthony and others rushed to try to repair the breach, but the meeting hastily adjourned.

Four months later, Cady Stanton and Anthony arrived in Kansas. At first Cady Stanton, like Stone and Blackwell, was enchanted. "This is the country for us to move to," she wrote her husband, who had been burned in New York Republican politics. "You could be a leader here as there is not a man in the state who can make a really good speech."[62] After two months, however, she had lost that rosy view of pioneer life. She traveled by wagon over enormous distances and unmarked roads in the company of former governor Charles Robinson. Absent hotels and restaurants, they slept either in the carriage or at the home of some isolated settler, eating only the provisions they carried with them. Much later, she admitted that she was often frightened but "I was glad of the experience. It gave me added self-respect to know that I could endure such hardships."[63]

The local political situation had worsened since the spring. An "Anti-Female Suffrage" faction had taken over the state Republican Party, motivated, Olympia Brown thought, by genuine fear that "the measure would carry at the polls."[64] Its supporters spewed nasty sexualized innuendo, calling woman suffrage advocates "male women" and "poodle pups."[65] Anthony and Cady Stanton set themselves to revive the campaign. While Cady Stanton brought her considerable oratorical firepower to town after town, Anthony stayed in Leavenworth, engineer-

138

ing the entire operation. She was waiting for "some *honorable* [man]" to travel with her, when word arrived that a most unexpected ally was ready to come to Kansas and speak for woman suffrage.[66]

The man was George Francis Train, one of the most unusual, controversial, and confounding figures in the history of the woman suffrage movement. He was an intrepid world traveler, the prototype for Phileas Fogg, hero of Jules Verne's *Around the World in Eighty Days,* a major American proponent of Irish independence, financier of the Union Pacific Railroad, and later organizer of the notorious Crédit Mobilier financing scheme, and much more. He was also a wacky political performer, an egomaniac, and a dandy with delusions of becoming president. One of the few balanced historical assessments of Train was that he "occupied a space somewhere between brilliance and insanity."[67]

Train was an avid supporter of many reform causes. His most intense conviction was for temperance, which contributed to a sincere interest in woman suffrage. "How is it that men can break all social laws and remain respected," he asked his Kansas audiences, "while if woman commits the slightest fault she is damned, driven from town and ruined?" His answer: "Because man can vote and woman can't. Give her a vote and she will protect herself."[68] Despite Train's unflinching support for woman suffrage, his controversial record during the Civil War shaped his impact in Kansas. He had been a diehard unionist, but he was indifferent (at best) to the abolition of slavery. Although he was accused, with reason, of "Negrophobia," at the time he was more fiercely reviled for having been a Copperhead, one of those northerners who advocated for a negotiated armistice with the South and were even more reviled during the war than actual Confederates.

Train swept into Kansas, drawing large crowds for his two-hour performances, which included nasty swipes at Kansas Republicans, an amusing talent for casting his political observations in rhyme, half-serious self-advertisements, but always support for the woman suffrage referendum. He drew many Irish immigrants and regularly got them to pledge support for votes for women. Even hostile newspaper reporters had to admire his way with the crowds. He was respectful and kind to suffragists, especially Anthony, praising her "grand speeches . . . convincing logic and her enthusiastic manner."[69]

In an already overheated political atmosphere, the suffragists' association with Train aroused tremendous hostility. The lurking conflict between the black and woman suffrage referenda now burst into full bloom. Negro suffrage advocates joined with the Anti-Female Suffrage faction, while woman suffragists claimed that the black men's vote would turn against women. Cady Stanton revived her charge that educated white women were more trustworthy with the franchise than ignorant ex-slaves. Even Anthony, who had deep abolitionist convictions and connections with black communities, gave way to her rage at seeing her cause set aside.

Although they were condemned for it, neither Anthony nor Cady Stanton ever regretted collaborating with Train, not then nor years later. Anthony, who habitually stood in the background making the way easier for others, was for once working with someone, a man moreover, who shouldered some of the burden, especially the finances of the campaign. Train treated her like a lady, rather than as the asexual "old maid" that others saw. "For every word you have spoken — for every vote you have taken — for every dollar you have given," she thanked him three years later. "And more than all

"The Revolution and the Ladies Turn the Crank," satiric cartoon of Train's support for suffrage, 1868.

for the increase of respect for and faith in myself with which you have inspired me, my soul blesses you."[70]

When the votes were counted, both enfranchisement measures had lost, but the women's referendum came within seventeen hundred votes of black suffrage. There was enough blame to go around. Anthony believed it was "the Republican party leaders, who killed negro suffrage, and woman suffrage too."[71] Cady Stanton was enraged at long-standing male allies, none more so than Wendell Phillips who "counseled us to silence."[72] "Playing off one [proposition] against the other," she charged, they had defeated both when together they might have gone on to victory.[73] Kansas Republicans who had stayed loyal to woman suffrage blamed Train and his Democratic enablers. Former friends and allies, most painfully Lucy Stone and Henry Blackwell, blamed Cady Stanton and Anthony. The couple had left Kansas months earlier, believing the campaign to be in good shape. As they saw it, Anthony and Cady Stanton had veered away by working with Train, soiling the moral legacy of woman suffrage. After collaborating for years, Stone broke away from Cady Stanton and Anthony, conclusively and with considerable animosity. This split hobbled the suffrage movement for the next three decades.

The Kansas episode altered the future of the woman suffrage movement in even larger ways. Women's rights had come of age in association with another great reform movement against slavery and for racial justice, but now that bond was being shattered. Former antislavery allies found the association of Cady Stanton and Anthony with Train an unforgivable betrayal of the ex-slaves. "I cannot refrain from expressing my regret and astonishment that you and Mrs. Stanton should have taken such leave of good sense," William Lloyd Garrison wrote to Anthony, ". . . as to be travelling companions and associate lecturers with that crack-brained harlequin and semi-lunatic, George Francis Train! . . . The colored people and their advocates have not a more abusive assailant."[74]

Anthony and Cady Stanton saw the crisis of the moment differently, for they had learned a crucial lesson, "that woman must lead the way to her own enfranchisement . . . with a hopeful courage and determination that knows no fear or trembling."[75] Woman suffrage was becoming its own movement, and its leaders must seek out avenues to victory wherever and however they might present themselves, regardless of the counsel of others. For them, it was a coming of age.

George Francis Train's involvement with woman suffrage did not end in Kansas. Frustrated by being shut out of the male-controlled reform press, Anthony longed for a woman-run pro-suffrage publication. There had been no women's rights paper since the mid-1850s. Toward the end of the Kansas campaign, she shared her frustration with Train, who, to her utter astonishment, announced that he would give her money to launch her own weekly. "Its name is to be the *Revolution,*" he insisted, "its motto, 'Men their rights, and nothing more; women, their rights and nothing less.' "[76] Martha Wright, sister to Lucretia Mott, wrote to Cady Stanton how much she loved the title. "I am thankful it *isn't* 'a Lily, a Rosebud or a Sybil,' for its vigorous pages are what we need."[77]

Back in New York, Anthony wasted no time. She planned an initial run of 10,000, with a first issue to appear on New Year's Day, 1868. In its first few issues, *The Revolution* carried much information by and about Train, advertising his causes and his politics. Within a month, however, he had gone to Dublin, where he was imprisoned for his Irish nationalism. He joked that he was arrested for carrying a copy of *The Revolution.* His financial support evaporated, but Cady Stanton and Anthony were already set on their new path and had no intention of giving up now. They solicited subscriptions and advertisements, distributed free copies to influential politicians, and looked forward to a long and happy journalistic life. One of the rare newspaperwomen of the day found *The Revolution's* downtown offices far more welcoming than the smoke-filled workplaces of male editors. She reported meeting its two animating forces: Anthony, "the invincible — possibly destined to be Vice President or Secretary of State some day," and Cady Stanton, hard at work, joined by her sixteen-year-old daughter Margaret, "as laughing eyed as her mother."[78] Determined to succeed, Anthony began to accumulate a personal debt to keep the paper afloat, which ultimately reached $10,000 and dogged her for the next decade.

The Revolution allowed Cady Stanton to do what she had long been ready to do, write with unmatched insight about woman suffrage, but also about the whole range of women's lives, wrongs and rights. With a platform of her own, Cady Stanton was able to throw herself into controversial matters that had long concerned her: the baleful state of marriage and the unacceptable laws and customs that held women in oppressive marital bonds. She plunged into discussions of prostitution, the sexual abuse of wives by husbands (what would later be called marital rape), and women's enforced maternity. She was often enraged but rarely somber, always witty, and sometimes downright funny. Criticized for commenting on Senator Roscoe Conkling's good looks, she shot back, "Women have been looked at . . . six thousand years . . . by all men, great and small." It was time for the gaze to be reversed. "Fairy fingers shall yet write for *The Revolution* sweet sonnets to bushy whiskers, moustache, goatee, to brawny muscles, giant form, and shaggy brow."[79]

Anthony had her own concerns — the low wages and limited opportunities of workingwomen. She wanted to take her newspaper to the working girls who filled the factory towns of the Northeast to "show [them] their need of the ballot." *The Revolution* pressed men's unions to admit women and did its own bit by hiring only women compositors. It not only reported on the beginnings of a workingwoman's movement but also helped to organize all-female labor associations.[80]

The Revolution lasted only two years under the leadership of Cady Stanton and Anthony, but it was an extraordinary run. In those years, the woman suffrage movement began to expand beyond demands for legal rights to explore and advocate much more of what would later be called feminism: women's achievements, their history, their social position, and the case for their sexual, reproductive, and economic independence.

Its editors placed themselves within a long historical tradition by serializing Mary Wollstonecraft's 1792 *Vindication of the Rights of Women*. When *The Revolution* finally collapsed of its unsupportable financial weight and outsize political ambitions, Anthony was more devastated than by any of the many losses she suffered during her long advocacy career. "It was like signing my own death warrant," she wrote and "like binding out a dear child that she could not support."[81]

Congress impeached President Andrew Johnson in the spring of 1868 for opposing its will. Although the Senate failed (by one vote) to find him guilty, Johnson was left virtually powerless and radical Republicans took full control of Reconstruction policy. Republican presidential nominee Ulysses S. Grant, hero of the Civil War, won a decisive victory in November. Before his inauguration in March, his party determined to push for a third constitutional amendment, one that would go beyond the Fourteenth and directly address the obstacles faced by freedmen in securing the right to vote.

As Congress debated the new amendment, Kansas senator Samuel Pomeroy proposed the universal suffrage approach that women suffragists had previously advocated. "All national citizens, whether native or naturalized," would be equally entitled to the right to vote, leaving states with only the ability to set age and residence requirements. The editors of *The Revolution* were thrilled, but Senator Pomeroy's proposal went nowhere. Instead, the final language took the narrowest possible approach, merely establishing that "the right of citizens of the United States to vote shall not be denied or abridged by the United States or by any State on account of race, color, or previous condition of servitude." Not only was woman suffrage missing, but the universal suffrage premise that suffrage was derived from national citizenship disappeared, leaving control of the franchise where it had always been, with the states.

Emerging into the ratification process, the Fifteenth Amendment faced woman suffragists with one of the most difficult choices ever put before their movement. "When that [measure] was pending my soul travailed in anguish," recalled Cady Stanton.[82] Would they accept the Fifteenth Amendment as written, be gracious toward the enfranchisement of black men, and remain hopeful that woman suffrage would soon get its turn? Or would they recognize that the constitutional door was swinging shut, and woman suffrage would have no more opportunities for a long, long time? Would they endorse or oppose a constitutional amendment addressing only black men's disfranchisement? Blackwell and Stone (more reluctantly than her husband) accepted the Fifteenth Amendment and sought ways to advance woman suffrage without interfering with black suffrage or imperiling potential Republican support. Cady Stanton and Anthony disagreed. Despite the consequences that they knew would come from breaking with former allies, they opposed ratification, certain that the passage of the Fifteenth Amendment would firmly end Republican interest in further enfranchisement and any chances for woman suffrage.

As she took this path, Cady Stanton's approach to woman suffrage was dramatically changing in other ways as well. She no longer focused on an expanded franchise that set aside distinctions of race and sex. Now she unleashed her rhetorical power exclusively in favor of women's enfranchisement and emphasized gender difference, female superiority, and the antagonism of the sexes. "The male element is a destructive force, stern, selfish, aggrandizing, loving war, violence, conquest, acquisition, breeding in the material and moral world alike discord, disorder, disease, and death," she declared. Only "the female element," representing "power, virtue, morality, true religion," could save the nation. To raise the lowliest of men above the most elevated of women, she preached, was "a deliberate insult to the women of the nation." Her catchphrase of the season was an "aristocracy of sex," all that was left now that monarchy and slavery had been routed. "Of all kinds of aristocracy, that of sex is the most odious and unnatural," she exhorted, "invading as it does our homes, desecrating our family altars . . . exalting the son above the mother."

Though Cady Stanton now spoke exclusively in the name of "Woman," she did not really mean all women. "Woman" became reduced to white and educated, and "man" to immigrant and former slave. "Think of Patrick and Sambo and Hans and Yung Tung . . . making the laws" for women like Lucretia Mott, she frequently challenged.[83]

Disappearing in this invidious opposition was the attention that the universal suffrage framework had brought to black women, in whom race and sex disfranchisement came together. Now at the center of Cady Stanton's call for woman suffrage were "women of wealth and education, who pay taxes and obey the laws, who in morals and intellect are the peers of their proudest rulers," women who were — without her needing to say it — white.[84] At the far end of her argument, she adopted the specter being conjured by Democratic Party demagoguery, of former enslaved men, inflamed by political power, preying sexually against the pure but powerless white women who had once owned them.

There were times that Cady Stanton claimed only to be ratchetting up her rhetoric to draw attention to the danger of the moment, but over the winter and spring of 1869, as she saw constitutional chances for woman suffrage slipping away, her words carried genuine conviction. She was mobilizing her brilliant insights into the power that men held against women and using them on behalf of a fundamentally undemocratic and exclusive understanding of who was to benefit from a republic just rescued from near destruction. It was a tragic move on her part, a betrayal of the broad human rights credo she had learned from Mott and the Grimké sisters, Gerrit Smith, and William Lloyd Garrison. The taint it left on her legacy equaled and at times overshadowed her path-breaking leadership and brilliant

Frederick Douglass, c. 1870.

understanding of women's oppression.

Cady Stanton's descent into such anti-democratic, outright anti-black and anti-immigrant argument, distressing as it was and remains, deserves to be read in context. She and Anthony believed — and they were right — that a genuine opportunity for winning the vote for women by democratizing the national franchise was slipping away. To make it worse, their allies and champions of decades bore much of the responsibility. "It has been a great grief to the leading women in our cause that there should be this antagonism with men whom we respect, whose wrongs we pity, and whose hopes we would fain help them to realize," Cady Stanton admitted. Alongside her racist and nativist claims, she continued to insist, often in the very same speech, that "suffrage is a natural, inalienable right . . . of necessity belong[ing] to every citizen of the republic, black and white, male and female."[85]

In March 1869, one month after the Fifteenth Amendment went to the states for ratification, suffragist ally Congressman George Julian proposed an additional amendment, as a supplement or corrective to the Fifteenth. It was intended to do two things: it would rescue women from the ignominy of their singular disfranchisement; and, by applying the universal suffrage formula, would elevate voting rights to a fundamental right of national citizenship:

The Right of Suffrage in the United States shall be based on citizenship, and shall be regulated by Congress; and all citizens of the United States, whether native or naturalized, shall enjoy this right equally without any distinction or discrimination whatever founded on sex.[86]

154

Cady Stanton declared all honor to Congressman Julian, even as she knew the idea would go nowhere in a Congress eager to conclude the suffrage issue.

The climax in the terrible break between black suffrage and woman suffrage occurred at the third — and last — anniversary meeting of AERA held in New York City in 1869. Cady Stanton and Anthony were fresh off a triumphant spring tour around the Midwest, where they had gone in search of new energy for the woman suffrage movement. It was their first extended speaking tour on behalf of woman suffrage. In Milwaukee, Madison, Toledo, St. Louis, and elsewhere, audiences responded enthusiastically. Returning with them to New York was their prize new recruit, forty-nine-year-old Mary Ashton Livermore from Chicago. Livermore had made a national name for herself as a leader of the major northern Civil War aid society, the United States Sanitary Commission. Always "heroic and brave," Cady Stanton wrote to *The Revolution,* Livermore now was "fully awakened to the power and dignity of the ballot, and stung to the very soul with the proposed amendment for 'manhood suffrage.' "[87] "It is wonderful — this *rushing* to our lines now," Anthony wrote to Lucretia Mott. "Our Equal Rights machinery seems now all harmonious."[88] Subsequent events would prove her wrong.

On May 12, 1869, AERA convened at the capacious Steinway Hall, recently built as a public concert hall (home of the New York Philharmonic) and display space for the piano company's instruments. An enormous, eager crowd, estimated at over one thousand and predominantly women, was drawn by the prominent names scheduled to speak and the important "live questions" surely to be debated: "manhood suffrage, female enfranchisement, free love, negro emancipation, etc."[89] Cady Stanton began restating her arguments about the danger of the male element, the elevating power of the female element, and the threat to democracy and to women's rights of an electorate dominated by "iron-heeled peasants, serfs, and slaves."[90]

Then she and Anthony were ambushed by abolitionist firebrand Stephen S. Foster. Foster had been an adamant champion of AERA since its formation, but now he turned on them, challenging their right to continue to lead the organization they had founded. They had dragged AERA away from its mission by their attacks on black suffrage, the Republican Party, and the Fifteenth Amendment. He even claimed that Anthony had misused AERA funds, a ludicrous charge, as she was widely known as a penurious financial steward. Passions were high. The audience hissed, Cady Stanton in the chair tried to call him out of order, but he would not be stopped.

In the conflict that ensued, it was Frederick Douglass's remarks that have gone down in history as a stark expression of the new antagonism between the former sibling movements. "There is no name greater than that of Elizabeth Cady Stanton in the matter of woman's rights and equal rights," Douglass began. When others had shunned his "wooly head," she had always welcomed him into her heart and her home. But now, as freed people began to claim a meaningful freedom, they were facing dire circumstances. A white supremacist secret society, the Ku Klux Klan, was spreading through the South, raping, murdering, and conducting a widespread "reign of terror." Douglass was now compelled to oppose his old friend:

I must say that I do not see how anyone can pretend that there is the same urgency in giving the ballot to woman as to the negro. With us, the matter is a question of life and death, at least, in fifteen States of the Union. When women, because they are women, are hunted down . . . when they are dragged from their houses and hung upon lamp-posts; when their children are torn from their arms, and their brains dashed out upon the pavement; when they are objects of insult and outrage at every turn; when they are in danger of having their homes burnt down over their heads; when their children are not allowed to enter schools; then they will have an urgency to obtain the ballot equal to our own.

"Is that not all true about black women?" someone from the audience shouted. "Not because she is a woman," retorted Douglass, "but because she is black."[91] By way of a "little good natured criticism," he went on to call out his friend's liberal use of the terms Paddy and Sambo.[92] His great respect for Cady Stanton notwithstanding, however, he could not accept her claims that black men were more opposed than white men to women's rights.

Cady Stanton remained in the chair, while it was Anthony who rose to defend the power and meaning of the vote for women. Responding to Douglass's skepticism that the vote would not "change anything in respect to the nature of our sexes," she responded, once again speaking on behalf of wage-earning women. "It will change . . . the pecuniary condition of woman. It will place her where she can earn her own bread, so that she may go out into the world an equal competitor in the struggle for life."[93] The women had not been the ones to raise the question of political priority, she insisted; it had been foisted on them by politicians and their erstwhile allies.

Lucy Stone vainly tried to balance support for the Fifteenth Amendment and advocacy of a separate woman suffrage amendment. "We are lost if we turn away from the middle principle and argue for one class," she pleaded, but she could not halt the conflict.[94] African American champion Frances Ellen Watkins Harper also tried to mediate, but in the end confessed that "when it was a question of race, she let the lesser question of sex go."[95]

At the end of the day, the damage of AERA was irreversible and the possibility of building common cause between black and woman suffrage had been grievously set back. Mary Livermore complained that she thought that she was coming all the way from Chicago to a woman suffrage meeting and would not have done so had she known how persistently " 'the Negro question' "

Currier and Ives satirical lithograph, 1869. Note caricatures of Anthony on the right and Stanton before the ballot box.

would take over.[96] Conversely, Douglass was disappointed that the meeting had been too focused on woman suffrage. Cady Stanton finally lost her storied composure, admitting that she had taken personal insult at the charges leveled against the organization and her leadership. After a second session two days later, AERA passed into history.

The American Equal Rights Association had lasted only three years. The rancor into which it dissolved was its lasting mark on the historical record. And yet it had raised the issue of woman suffrage to the national political level and done so by attempting to assert the very basic principle of political

160

rights for all. Never again, on behalf of any disfranchised group of citizens, would Congress seriously consider taking voting rights away from the states to make them a constitutionally protected right of national citizenship. As the freedmen would soon learn to their great sorrow, the Fifteenth Amendment was insufficient because it left the right to vote fundamentally unprotected against state attempts to distort or suppress it. The battle for woman suffrage would continue, but only under these limitations and in a political context increasingly hostile to further expansion of the electorate.

THREE:
ARE WOMEN PERSONS?
1869–1875

At the May 1869 Steinway Hall meeting, Ernestine Rose had proposed that the American Equal Rights Association (AERA) rename itself the Woman's Suffrage Association, so that "we shall know what we mean."[1] Cady Stanton ruled that prior notice would be needed for such a change, but it was clear that discontent with AERA, especially among new adherents, was widespread. Two days later, on May 15 she and Anthony hosted an evening reception for delegates at the Woman's Bureau, which housed the offices of *The Revolution* and which was formally opening its meeting rooms and displays of woman-made objects for sale to the female public.

When she arrived at the elegant Manhattan town house, a Chicago visitor reported that Cady Stanton was sitting "behind an official-looking table . . . evidently doing Presidential duty."[2] The reception then became a meeting to form a new organization, to be called the National Woman Suffrage Association (NWSA). Cady Stanton was to be the president, its purpose was "to discuss woman suffrage separate and apart from the question of equal rights and manhood suffrage," and it was to concentrate its efforts on behalf of Congressman George Julian's proposed woman suffrage amendment.[3]

Cady Stanton suggested that only women be allowed to join. Her husband explained that he "had been drilled for twenty years privately and . . . was convinced women could do it better if left alone."[4] In the end, it was decided that while men would be allowed to join, leadership would remain in the hands of women. It would be some time before the National Woman Suffrage Association would be truly national and extend much beyond New York and the Midwest, but in one form or another it would lead the woman suffrage effort for the next half century.

Lucy Stone and Henry Blackwell had left New York before the Woman's Bureau reception. They then claimed that they had been deliberately kept in the dark to make sure that they would not be there when the new suffrage society was formed. Within months, they and other New England suffragists formed a rival organization, the American Woman Suffrage Association (AWSA). Men, including Republican politicians, took a prominent role. Lucy Stone chaired the executive committee, but as if in repudiation of NWSA's declaration to have only women leaders, the presidency went to Reverend Henry Ward Beecher. Besides his national reputation as America's foremost Protestant minister, Beecher was a moderate reformer, supporting abolition and temperance in the prewar years and woman suffrage after. His father had been a fire and brimstone evangelist, but the son emphasized the redemptive power of love, divine and human both. There were hopes that his national prominence could aid the cause.

In order to be loyal to the Republican Party and not criticize the Fifteenth Amendment, AWSA's pursuit of woman suffrage would initially focus solely on changes in state constitutions. In November, its first convention was held in Cleveland. Anthony attended at the urging of some of her new supporters, reluctantly offering her blessing. "Division is a healthy sign" of a growing movement, she was willing to concede. "These independent and separate movements show that we are alive."[5]

Two months later, just as Anthony was forced to give up her beloved *Revolution,* Stone and Blackwell intensified her suffering by initiating their own periodical, the *Woman's Journal.* The *Woman's Journal* lasted much longer than *The Revolution.* Stone devoted most of the rest of her life to it, and then her daughter, Alice Stone Blackwell, took over, remaining editor until and after the 1920 ratification of the Nineteenth Amendment.

Suffrage supporters outside of New York and Massachusetts had trouble choosing between the two organizations, and if it had been up to them, the rift would have been mended and the movement united. A few efforts were made to overcome what one friend of both groups called the suffragists' "civil war," but personal animosities among the principals only grew greater and they dug into their rivalry.[6] Stone and Anthony seemed unwilling or unable to forgive each other. Stone was more open to Cady Stanton. Just after she and her daughter had come to visit, Stone dared to hope that "your little girls and mine" — Alice Stone Blackwell and Margaret and Harriot Stanton — "will reap the easy harvest which it costs so much to sow."[7] Reconciliation, which Alice led and Harriot in fact supported, would take another two decades.

Contemporaries and historians alike differ about how much the split damaged the suffrage movement or whether it accelerated expansion and recruitment along two parallel lines. But either way, women never before associated with the suffrage movement were drawn by the new visibility of enfranchisement, the attraction of a broad and politically significant movement, and their own ambitions for a larger field for their capacities. The movement began to grow and to spread westward across the country.

In February 1870, one year after Congress had passed it, the Fifteenth Amendment was ratified. Once that contested issue was settled, the differences between the two suffrage organizations became less those of substance than of style. AWSA drew a more conventional crowd, NWSA a more daring group of women. AWSA spent a great deal of energy creating a thoroughly organized society, built around official delegations from the states. Men were prominent speakers at its conventions, and even opponents to women's enfranchisement, notably Catharine Beecher, were invited to the platform. Respectability, orderliness, harmony were its watchwords.

NWSA took its lead from Cady Stanton's wide-ranging radical interests and Anthony's fierce dedication to women first, last, and always. In the final chaotic years of Reconstruction, the group dipped into some of the most extreme manifestations of the feminist spirit in the nineteenth century. Then as now, the unsettled question was whether women's rights needed more moderation or more radicalism to speak to women.

By late 1870, the suffrage movement as a whole seemed to be running out of political options. AWSA was continuing to court Republican support by confining itself to state action, while NWSA pressed for a Sixteenth Amendment, with minimal congressional support. As Paulina Wright Davis, one of NWSA's leaders, plaintively wondered, "It is a fitting question to ask if there has been progress; or . . . has this work . . . failed and become a monument of buried hopes?"[8]

Cady Stanton and Anthony were exhausted by their efforts and discouraged by their defeats. Cady Stanton repeatedly told friends and family that she never wanted to go to another convention, never wanted to go where her ideas were not entertained, only wanted to speak and write about "*Womans* absolute freedom."[9] Needing money to send her last four children to college, she undertook a new career as a traveling lecturer. She crossed the country speaking on everything from woman suffrage, to women's marital woes, to the proper way to mother sons and daughters. Audiences loved her and it was a lucrative move for her.

Anthony was also desperately "tired of fighting" and eager to "lay off my armor."[10] She also went out on the national lecture circuit, determined to retire the enormous debt she had incurred in trying to keep *The Revolution* alive. She was not as smooth and pleasing a speaker as her friend, for, as a Pittsburgh paper noted, she spoke "not for the purpose of receiving applause but for the purpose of making people understand."[11] She did, however, speak on how the right to vote would improve the condition of workingwomen. These years of touring greatly helped to spread the ideas of the woman suffrage movement across the country, to a whole generation of women who pioneered it across the West.

In their absence, an enthusiastic new convert, Isabella Beecher Hooker, stepped forward to run NWSA. Hooker was the wife of John Hooker, a distinguished lawyer, legal thinker, and abolitionist, and together with him developed Nook Farm, a Hartford, Connecticut, community of artists and writers, most prominently Mark Twain. She was also the youngest child of the powerful Beecher family, sister of America's most celebrated minister, Henry Ward Beecher, as well as of two immensely popular women writers, Harriet Beecher Stowe and Catharine Beecher. Looking for her own route forward in a family overloaded with influence, she was convinced that with her connections and the respectability of her family's name, she could quickly and elegantly bring victory to woman suffrage. Cady Stanton was amused by Hooker's presumptuousness but if she "thinks she could manage the cause more discreetly, more genteelly than we do," then more power to her.[12] Suffrage leadership, it would soon turn out, took her far beyond the bounds of gentility and discretion.

Hooker took charge of the January 1871 NWSA meeting in Washington, D.C. Cady Stanton refused to attend, but Anthony was concerned about the direction of the movement and hurried to the city, D.C. She had learned that a controversial figure, Victoria Woodhull, would make a formal presentation to the important House Judiciary Committee on the same day as the suffrage convention was to convene in January 1871. Woodhull's request had been shepherded, and she had probably been assisted in writing her remarks, by committee member and Massachusetts representative Benjamin Butler. Butler had been a Union general who had made headlines in 1862 by slandering the upper-class ladies of New Orleans as "women of the town" when his troops occupied the city. Woodhull was the first woman to appear before and speak directly to members of Congress. Anthony knew that she had to be there, to hear what this unexpected advocate would have to say.

Victoria Woodhull was the most scandalous, disruptive, and transformative figure to enter the suffrage ranks in the final years of Reconstruction. Not even George Francis Train caused as much upheaval as Woodhull. Born Victoria Claflin, she came from a wildly dysfunctional family populated with carnival and con-man types. She was exploited by her parents for her talents as a faith healer, and while still young, married, divorced, and remarried. At least one of her two children was probably syphilitic as a result of her sexual activities.

Woodhull had her own instinctive women's rights sentiments, born of her sorrowful personal experiences with sexual and economic exploitation. Like more conventional women's rights advocates, she attacked the double standard that penalized women for activities that men engaged in freely, but with a difference: she wanted more sexual freedom for women, not less for men. Nonetheless, although bedeviled by her parasitical and criminal family and her own shady reputation for unconventional personal relations, Woodhull fascinated and charmed virtually everyone who met her. "No one can be with her," Martha Wright, sister of Lucretia Mott, wrote, "without believing in her goodness and her purity."[13]

Woodhull and her sister Tennessee Claflin came to prominence as the first "lady brokers" of Wall Street. They were brought there by backing from one of the Street's most powerful men, Cornelius Vanderbilt, whom Tennessee had charmed. Anthony visited the offices of Woodhull and Claflin in 1869 and was pleased to find "these two ladies (for they are ladies) are determined to use their brains, energy, and their knowledge of business to earn them a livelihood."[14] With a reported capitalization of

$35,000, in 1870 the sisters started their own bold reform weekly, *Woodhull and Claflin's Review,* which appeared almost exactly when Anthony gave up *The Revolution;* and despite advocating even more radical sexual and economic issues, lasted six years and reached a height of 50,000 copies.

By early 1871, when Woodhull made her first public appearance as a suffrage advocate, she had lifted herself to a position of wealth, influence, and public attention. She had extraordinary charisma, which the era called "magnetism." She advocated ideas held by other strong-minded women, but she was beautiful, charming, presenting the very opposite of the dreary, unattractive, unfeminine image with which suffragists were already burdened. When she wore an outfit of a jacket and loose pants, the newspapers did not attack her for her foolish bloomers, did not ridicule her for "wearing the trousers," but cooed over her fashionable appearance. Her celebrity was meteoric, publicity fueled, and ultimately doomed to collapse, but the three years during which Woodhull was associated with NWSA reminded the country just how radical the assertion of women's equality and entry into the public sphere could be.

Arriving in Washington, Anthony con-

Victoria Woodhull, 1875.

vinced Isabella Beecher Hooker to attend Woodhull's hearing before going to their own convention, and they hurried to the Capitol along with local suffrage activist Josephine Griffing. Promptly at ten a.m. on January 11, Woodhull entered into the hearing room. She was escorted by Congressman Butler, who was a close ally of President Grant. The other members of the House Judiciary Committee were assembled around a central table, and Anthony and the suffragists sat just behind them. After

173

Chairman John Bingham of Ohio opened the proceedings, Woodhull began to speak, her voice at first tremulous but gaining in confidence and power as she went on. Woodhull was there to request a new congressional approach to enfranchising women.

What Anthony and Hooker heard from Woodhull was a powerful version of an approach to women's enfranchisement that had been circulating in suffrage circles for some time. First advanced two years before by a St. Louis couple, Francis Minor, a lawyer, and his suffragist wife, Virginia, the argument rested on the Fourteenth Amendment, which had established that "all persons born or naturalized in the United States" were citizens of the nation. Inasmuch as women were assuredly persons, they must also be national citizens, protected equally with all others in a citizen's "privileges and immunities." These included, all must acknowledge, the right to vote. This argument, which came to be known as the Suffrage New Departure, was in essence a revival of the universal suffrage argument with the advantage that it did not require any new constitutional amendments. Rather, women could claim the vote based on the Fourteenth Amendment.

Woodhull concluded by requesting Congress to pass a Declaratory Act that would vindicate her interpretation and "be necessary and proper for carrying into execution the right vested by the Constitution in the citizens of the United States to vote, without regard to sex."[15]

In the atmosphere of Reconstruction, the notion that enfranchisement was an individual right that belonged to all citizens equally, rather than a government-bestowed privilege, was spreading. The Minors gave it constitutional heft. Already, some women were attempting to register and to vote. The largest group was almost two hundred women (including two African American women) from Vineland, New Jersey, a utopian community.[16] Denied access to the ballot box, they brought their own box in which they deposited their own ballots. They were accused of "playing vote," but they insisted they were dead serious and determined to make their votes count by the next presidential election. The local historical society still owns the special ballot box.[17]

Anthony and Hooker were deeply impressed by Woodhull, her ideas, and her courageous congressional presentation. This woman was in a position to bring the suffrage movement much of what it then needed: money, influential connections, a newspaper, and above all, public attention. They brought her and Tennessee back to their convention and had them read the statement. Both women wore "dark dresses, with blue neckties, short, curly brown hair and nobby Alpine hats, the very picture of the advanced ideas they were advocating."[18] Anthony rode back to New York on the train with Woodhull and found her "very charming — utterly forgetful of difference of sex in her approach to *men*."[19]

NWSA leaders immediately switched their strategy from petitioning for a sixteenth amendment to pressing this new, compelling constitutional argument. Although the Judiciary Committee issued a majority report rejecting Woodhull's proposal, Ben Butler authored a strong minority response which supported it, establishing himself as one of the suffragists' most reliable congressional allies. Members of NWSA were urged to support the New Departure in two ways: collect petitions requesting a congressional declaration of the expansive meaning of the new amendments; and test the New Departure argument by attempting to register and vote in upcoming elections. Excitement and optimism were high. "Everybody here chimes in with the new conclusion that we are free already," Anthony wrote to Woodhull three weeks later from Kansas City.[20] Women would no longer humbly have to petition men to give them the vote. The right to vote was theirs already and they must merely seize and use it. The next presidential election was looming as a major moment in the country's postwar direction, and suffragists were determined that women would have a part in that choice.

Despite all that she offered, a major danger lurked in the elevation of Woodhull as a public figure in the suffrage firmament. Her disreputable history included multiple marriages, extramarital affairs, and perhaps even bigamy. Charges that advocates of women's freedoms were guilty of unbridled sexuality were as old as women's rights itself. Frances Wright, an early and bold advocate, had been viciously attacked by the American press as a "free lover" in the 1820s.

As far back as 1860, Cady Stanton had invited similar charges merely by publicly condemning women's suffering in unloving marriages and calling for legal reform to make divorce easier and more socially acceptable. Divorce reform was still a radical idea, even to most women's rights advocates. In 1870, Cady Stanton picked up the theme again as she lectured to all-female audiences on the sexual violence women suffered within their marriages. "O! the experiences women pour into my ears!" she wrote from Kalamazoo, Michigan. Searching for a way to bring the practice out of the shadows, she called it "legalized prostitution" and controversially likened the suffering of abused wives to the widespread rape of enslaved women.[21] To newspaper charges that she was an advocate of untrammeled sexual freedom, she confidently responded, "I've lived thirty years with one man, and expect to live with him to the end, and I'll let my life speak for me."[22]

Woodhull took women's sexual rights much further than Cady Stanton, because of her open and proud advocacy of what was then called "free love." A vague but incendiary term, free love could either mean the removal of government involvement through laws in regulating the creation and dissolution of marital bonds; or a repudiation of monogamy in favor of multiple sexual partners. Instead of running from the charges that she was a free lover, Woodhull defiantly embraced both of these interpretations.

Thomas Nast cartoon in Harper's Weekly *of Victoria Woodhull as Mrs. Satan, 1872.*

A year after she joined the suffragists, Woodhull defiantly responded to an audience taunt by declaring that indeed she was not only an advocate but a practitioner of free love. "I have an *inalienable, constitutional* and *natural* right to love whom I may," she announced to a New York City audience in November 1871. She insisted that sexual choice, like the right to vote, was her inherent, individual right, and that she was free "to *love* as *long* or as *short* a period as I can; to *change* that love *every day* if I please."[23] The declaration produced the most enduring image of Woodhull, a Thomas Nast cartoon depicting her as "Mrs. Satan," complete with devilish bat wings and a call to "be saved by FREE LOVE," followed by an impoverished woman weighed down by a child in her arms and a drunken husband on her back.

Woodhull's sexual radicalism was intertwined with the ability she claimed of speaking with and through the spirits of the dead. She was a leader of Spiritualism, a quasireligion of the period which gained popularity as the massive deaths of the Civil War spread the desire of the living to communicate with those they had lost. For women like Woodhull, Spiritualism — like other trance-inducing states — allowed them to say things and speak in a manner considerably beyond the normal limits of what was allowed to their sex. The spirits gave them authority. Importantly, their claim to communicate directly with the dead allowed them to bypass the Christian clergy that did so much to shape and control women's personal lives. Ironically Isabella Beecher Hooker, daughter and sister of influential Protestant ministers, was particularly drawn to Woodhull by her spiritual talents. "How much I could do," she wrote passionately to suffragist Olympia Brown, "if *my soul could work outside my body.*"[24]

The response to Woodhull's suffrage advocacy fell along the lines already dividing the suffrage ranks. AWSA, which was centered in America's most proper city, Boston, regarded the development with horror. As a single woman, Lucy Stone had been critical of women's subordination in marriage, but now, in a troubled union to a man with his own roving eye, ironically she thought quite differently. She now believed that woman suffrage must have nothing to do with criticisms of marriage, which was the basis of a stable and healthy society and a fundamental protection for women from male depredations. "We *need* every clean soul to help us," she appealed, "now when such a flood of what is fatal to the peace, and purity of the family, is rolled on our question."[25]

By contrast, NWSA leaders were thrilled with the opening up of new opportunities for their stalled movement. "I would rather make a few blunders from a superabundance of life," Cady Stanton wrote in response to AWSA criticisms, "than to have all the proprieties of a well embalmed mummy."[26] She dismissed the gossip against Woodhull as yet another example of the sexual double standard that dogged women. If this or any woman was to be "crucified" for her moral violations, it should be left, not to women, but to "men [to] drive the spikes, and plaite the crown of thorns."[27] Although Anthony was a much more proper person than Cady Stanton, she too rejected the notion that Woodhull should be forever tainted by her "antecedents," that is her prior actions.[28] She knew too many men in power whose private lives were saturated with misdeeds.

Through 1871 and early 1872, Woodhull was largely in control of NWSA, aided by her two most stalwart followers, Paulina Wright Davis and Isabella Beecher Hooker. Cady Stanton and Anthony had gone west — perhaps fleeing the ensuing controversy — on an ambitious nationwide lecture tour. From the comfortable railroad cars that took them west, Anthony wrote, "We are just as cozy and happy as lovers." Thinking of her union with Cady Stanton in almost marital terms, she quoted a description of ideal marriage, "In all that there is real bliss, if only the two are perfect people, two loving people, neither assuming the control of the other."[29]

But going west did not protect the women from the free love taint or the suspicion of sexual radicalism. In Salt Lake City they stirred up controversy by holding a meeting only of women, who told them what polygamy meant to Mormon wives. (Cady Stanton concluded that their sufferings were not so much worse than conventional marriages.) In San Francisco, they defended a woman who had shot a lover who had deceived her, and insisted that she could not be tried fairly because no woman could sit on any jury. They also found large, enthusiastic audiences eager to receive the new gospel of women's rights and excited by the news that women might vote in the next presidential election.

Cady Stanton returned after three months, in time to get to Johnstown for the funeral of her mother, aged eighty-six. "Her death like her life was calm & serene," she wrote mournfully to cousin Gerrit Smith. "The old home is now broken up . . . & soon strangers will fill our vacant places."[30] Meanwhile Anthony stayed out west through the winter, enjoying being on her own, independent of her more popular partner, and finding new allies and suffrage energies in the Northwest. In Portland she conquered her nervousness and spoke, again to an audience of women only, against the efforts of San Francisco and St. Louis to license prostitution.[31] On her way back she stopped in Kansas, still longing to be with her brothers, then continued on to Rochester to tend to her own ailing mother. In her diary, she lamented "my fate to sacrifice love & affection."[32]

Woodhull's testimony, "Memorial to Congress," and her bid for suffrage leadership were linked to her own outsize ambition. Like George Francis Train before her, she determined that she was going to run for president of the United States. She would be carried into office by the votes of women, which Congress, responding to her constitutional argument, would declare by legislative act was their right. None of the old parties suited her, especially not the Republican Party, which was fast becoming the reliable ally of big money and booming industrialization. Groups of political radicals of all stripes — labor, socialists, "greenbackers" (advocates of paper money), free lovers, and of course radical suffragists — would combine to seize the mantle of true social change. Woodhull prepared to bring them all together in her own "Equal Rights

Party," named perhaps after the recently collapsed American Equal Rights Association. Cady Stanton was thrilled at the idea. Her own antipathy to the Republicans had only grown, and her expansive reform ambitions matched Woodhull's. Anthony was less so, suspicious that Woodhull "means to run our craft into her port and none other."[33]

After she returned from her nearly year-long tour, Anthony learned that NWSA was to hold a mass meeting in New York City in Steinway Hall on May 9, 1872, with Woodhull commanding the platform. To Anthony it was now perfectly clear that Woodhull was planning to absorb the suffrage association into a multi-reform coalition behind her presidential candidacy. Cady Stanton had not only signed Woodhull's call to form a "new political party whose principles shall . . . represent equal rights for all," but included Anthony's name without her permission.[34] "We have no element out of which to make a political party," Anthony protested. "All our time and words in that direction are simply thrown away."[35] She insisted her name be removed.

That very same day as the Steinway Hall meeting, NWSA's rival, AWSA, was bringing its case from Boston to New York City.

Henry Blackwell, now its leading spokesperson, was prepared to preach against NWSA's connection with Woodhull. He spoke for those who were "not assembled to . . . break up the social relations of men and women," only simply and without distraction advance woman suffrage by "steadily educating public opinion. . . . He was sick to death . . . of woman's suffrage associations that wanted more than woman suffrage and wanted more latitudinarian views of marriage."[36] Everyone knew who and what that meant.

Rushing from Rochester, Anthony made her way to New York City, prepared for a dramatic showdown. She was determined to wrest the Steinway Hall meeting away from Woodhull's control and to prevent any political parties, old or new, from being endorsed. The hall had been rented in her name, Anthony insisted, and she would not allow Woodhull to commandeer it for her purposes. Then she went off to see Cady Stanton to convince her that the Woodhull tie must be broken. Anthony placed a last-minute announcement in the *New York Times,* listing speakers. Woodhull's name was omitted.

Anthony's effort at taking control failed. On Thursday May 9, the NWSA meeting opened. The audience was large, filled with labor reformers, Spiritualists, and others eager to sign on to Woodhull's candidacy. Cady Stanton was there and delivered a stirring speech that barely skirted Woodhull's political plans. We will not nominate candidates, she announced, "but we now propose to descend to the political business of life. Today we are combined with . . . all classes of men who will help to roll back the constitutional doors that we may enter and enjoy the rights that belong to every free citizen of the United States." She urged women to go in numbers to the polls, try to register, "and if our votes are refused, we will contest it in the Supreme Court."[37]

Then, despite Anthony's best efforts as chair, the proceedings descended into anarchy. Woodhull "came gliding in from the side of the platform," delivered "a few vehement remarks," and instructed the audience to reconvene in Apollo Hall the next day to form the new party and nominate her for president.[38] Anthony persuaded the Steinway Hall janitor to turn off the gas lights and throw everything into darkness even "as Mrs. Woodhull persisted in talking."[39]

Abigail Scott Duniway, an Oregon suffrage leader whom Anthony had met on her

Pacific Coast tour, arrived in town too late for the Steinway Hall meeting but in time to get to Apollo Hall. Welcomed by "one or two grey-haired bohemians" at the door, Duniway witnessed Woodhull's beauty and ability to magnetize, but remained skeptical. Not present and unaware of the honor being bestowed on him, Frederick Douglass was nominated to be Woodhull's running mate. (When informed, he declined.) When Duniway was able to take Woodhull aside and ask her whether she really thought "this thing will succeed?" Woodhull responded, "Of course I do. A lot of spirits are back of it." Laura de Force Gordon from California was also in the audience, and she and Duniway compared notes. "Poor Vicky is crazy," Gordon said. "She is making a fool of herself. . . . She's done much for Woman Suffrage in the way of violent agitation" but her presidential ambitions and the crowd she had assembled around her now would doom her to irrelevance.[40]

NWSA reconvened in Steinway Hall on the second day but the audience was small — many had gone off to Apollo Hall, or were confused or just dispirited. Anthony thought "all came near being lost" and was furious at what she called the *"folly of Stanton."* It was as close to a break as the two ever came. Anthony felt that she had just barely kept the ship of suffrage from hitting the shoals but only "by a hair's breadth escape."[41]

Though they did not follow Woodhull into her quixotic presidential campaign, suffragists were still not done with her. Over the next few years she dragged many from both NWSA and AWSA into the biggest sex scandal of the nineteenth century. For some time, gossip had been swirling in reform circles of a prolonged adulterous affair between Henry Ward Beecher, nominal head of AWSA, and Elizabeth Tilton, the wife of NWSA's most important male ally, Theodore Tilton. The details of the story, and the church and civil trials that resulted, filled hundreds of newspaper pages and captivated the public nationwide until 1875.

Because many of the principals were involved in the suffrage movement, Cady Stanton and Anthony were privy to some of the details of the affair. Through them, Woodhull learned of what she regarded as a closeted case of free love, which she was determined to expose in order to protect herself from unrelenting attacks on her own propriety. By the summer of 1872, Woodhull had begun an all-out attack on the hypocrisy practiced by the most respected political and cultural leaders of postwar American society, a campaign which she was never going to win. In September, she went public with the story of what became known as the "Beecher Tilton Scandal." Boycotted by the regular press, she resumed publication of her newspaper and on October 26, with a massive print run, published the story in lurid detail.

A fanatic "purity" reformer, Anthony Comstock, who had been looking to pursue what he regarded as rampant sex radicalism, saw this as his opportunity. He was able to use an obscure postal regulation to have New York police imprison Woodhull for sending through the mails "obscene materials," that is the Beecher/Tilton reporting in her newspaper. For this questionable legal violation, Woodhull was arrested November 2, 1872, and remained in a city jail for six weeks. Comstock was subsequently able to get federal antiobscenity legislation passed, and himself appointed as its one-man enforcer. The so-called Comstock laws remained to cause trouble for all further attempts to assert women's sexual and reproductive rights and were still the major legal obstacle faced by the birth control movement well into the twentieth century.

Pictorial History of the Beecher Tilton Scandal, *1875.*

Woodhull's career, reputation, resources, and health were destroyed, as were those of many of the other parties to the scandal, with the sole exception of Henry Ward Beecher himself. In defense of his honor, the entire elite of his hometown of Brooklyn rallied. For standing up to her brother and insisting that he admit his guilt, Isabella Beecher Hooker was mercilessly attacked by her family, who publicly questioned her sanity. The Beecher Tilton

191

Scandal established the basic principle of Gilded Age morality, that the claims of the powerful were always to trump those of their victims and make the truth of such accusations irrelevant. Standing and reputation — and political and economic power — must be protected above all.

Cady Stanton and Anthony were also swept up into the scandal's ugliness, including claims that they were part of a free-love cabal surrounding Woodhull and Theodore Tilton, reform journalist and a close friend, perhaps lover to Woodhull. One trial witness alleged that she caught Anthony sitting on Tilton's lap and flirting with him, an allegation so ridiculous on its face that it was not believed even in the overheated atmosphere of public hunger for salacious details.[42]

Many, then and now, believed that the episode set the suffrage movement back several years, and perhaps it did. Nonetheless, Cady Stanton was one of those who thought that an essential truth of great moment for women had been revealed. The insatiable public interest in the scandal was "evidence, not of a depraved popular taste," she believed, "but of a vital interest in the social problems that puzzle and perplex the best of us. The true relations of man and woman, of the foundation of the family and home, are of more momentous importance than any other question of State, or Church, can possibly be." The lesson that someday must be learned from such events was that "the true social code, whatever it is, must be the same for both sexes."[43]

Even after the terrible toll that the sordid episode left on the late Reconstruction Era suffrage movement, neither Cady Stanton nor Hooker nor Paulina Wright Davis ever repudiated Victoria Woodhull. Cady Stanton, Hooker, and Davis, though not Anthony, stayed in touch with her, out of respect for what she had been, what had happened to her, and what she had tried to do. Later, Cady Stanton wrote:

Victoria Woodhull has done a work for woman that none of us could have done. She has faced and dared men to call her the names that make women shudder, while she chucked principle, like medicine, down their throats. She has risked and realized the sort of ignominy that would have paralyzed any of us who have longer been called strong-minded.

Numerous biographies of Woodhull have proved Cady Stanton right in her prediction that "she will be as famous as she had been infamous . . . in the annals of emancipation."[44]

The Beecher Tilton Scandal was in its earliest stages when the presidential election of 1872, which would determine the future of Reconstruction and the prospects for woman suffrage on the national stage, began to heat up. The first act of the election season occurred in May when a Republican faction withdrew to form the "Liberal Republican Party." Although its emphasis on individual rights might have otherwise drawn suffragists, the decision to nominate for president *New York Tribune* editor Horace Greeley, a diehard opponent of woman suffrage, made that impossible. To the regular Republicans, the Liberal Republican bolt — and other evidence of partisan discontent such as the formation of Woodhull's new party — was evidence of an impending loss of its reformist wing, and with it, perhaps the presidency. Into this moment, the energy and activism of woman suffragists and the possibility that they might be voters created a strategic opening that Anthony, looking for a direction away from the Woodhull connection, took.

Accordingly, less than a month after the

disastrous Steinway Hall fiasco, Anthony went to Philadelphia to press the Republican National Convention "to assert the duty of the National Government to protect women citizens in the exercise of their right to vote." If it were to embrace the high principles of universal enfranchisement, and human rights for all, the party might just pull itself back from the brink of historical irrelevance. The *Philadelphia Inquirer* wrote an admiring piece, describing her as "the head and front of the Woman Suffragists," whose strength and earnestness should convince Republicans of her cause.[45] Henry Blackwell had already been working the delegates but was not hopeful: "only one bitterly opposed . . . but not one thoroughly prepared to fight for it."

Somewhat to Anthony's surprise, the Republicans adopted a platform plank not quite up to her standard, but an acknowledgment nonetheless. "Mindful of its obligations to the loyal women of America," the party was willing to entertain "the honest demands of any class of citizen for equal rights . . . with respectful consideration." Because there was no specific mention of woman suffrage, Blackwell had initially dismissed this as of "no value" but eventually agreed to accept it because "anything is better than nothing."[46] Anthony agreed, and though she was not a fan of President Grant because of the disturbing indications of corruption in his administration, she felt "his wife is with us heart and soul," and his running mate, Henry Wilson of Massachusetts, was a sincere advocate of woman suffrage. A few weeks later, when the Democratic Party convention not only refused to welcome suffragists at its convention, but then signed on to the Liberal Republican platform and the presidential candidacy of Greeley, the deal was sealed. "I shall clutch [the Republican plank] as the drowning man the floating straw," Anthony wrote, "and cling to it until something stronger and surer shall present itself."[47]

Cady Stanton was less convinced. The meagerness of what the Republicans were offering, which she called a "splinter" rather than a plank, set against the collapse of her hopes for a new reform party, threw her into a deep depression.[48] Then Henry Blackwell, whose long-standing support of the Republican Party now seemed that it might be vindicated, reached out to propose a truce between their two suffrage societies. Could they not join their forces together to insure the election of Republicans? Cady Stanton wanted a reconciliation enough to agree to work with Anthony in support of the Republican Party. If women wanted to play a role in this important election, and she was certain they should, then "a proper self-respect forbids any woman to look in any direction" but the regular Republicans. The platform plank, "weak as it is . . . is a rainbow of promise to my waiting soul."[49] Common support of the Republicans, however, could not overcome the animosity, especially between Anthony and Stone, and AWSA and NWSA campaigned separately, unable or unwilling to campaign jointly.

For the past half decade, Anthony and Cady Stanton had insisted that suffragists must go their own way, not rely on the spurious promises of male supporters who would desert them in the end. Differences over whether to trust the Republican Party were once great enough to have split suffragists right down the middle. The eagerness with which Anthony and even the perennially skeptical Cady Stanton threw themselves into the reelection of President Grant is testimony to two important political realities: the upheaval in the partisan divisions that had carried the nation through the war; and the eagerness of increasing numbers of mobilized rank-and-file suffragists to play a part at this turning point of national political fate. "Now there is our opportunity," Cady Stanton observed, "to show *our capacity* to help a political party."[50] Looking back retrospectively at the disappointment that was to come, Anthony's biographer wrote that it was "most touching to observe Miss Anthony's joy over this quasi-recognition."[51]

With Matilda Joslyn Gage, an important suffrage leader from Syracuse, Anthony had issued a call on behalf of NWSA to all women who believed in their political rights to join in the campaign. No one knew better than they that politicians could not be relied on, especially when it came to voteless women. Nonetheless, what the Republican Party had dangled was a "promise of the future . . . the entering wedge which shall break woman's slavery in pieces and make in at last a nation truly free — a nation in which . . . humanity alone shall be the criterion of all human rights." Fueled by rage at the prospect of electing Greeley, "for years our most bitter scathing opponent," they urged, "Let us one and all forget our many grievances" — against politicians, against former male allies, against other suffragists — and do what is necessary to reelect Grant.[52]

The openness to suffragists in the Republican Party reached a peak in the second week of July 1872 when the Democratic Party met in national convention and fused with the Liberal Republicans, adopting their platform and seconding Horace Greeley's candidacy. There was a real fear that the old antislavery core of the Republican Party would defect, and in this atmosphere, desperate calls came to Anthony. By the time she was able to get to Washington, D.C., however, the crisis had eased. It was becoming clear that Greeley was going to run an ineffective campaign, and Anthony found that her services were no longer quite so valuable to the Republicans. She was given $1,000 to run a series of meetings for Grant and Wilson in New York. Every time she spoke, she emphasized the party's opening to woman suffrage, even as regular Republican campaigning entirely ignored the issue. What would come of the Republican "splinter"? Anthony learned the answer when she decided to join the ranks of voting women and cast her ballot.

Anthony had long wanted to join the other voting women and submit her ballot at the polls, but had never been home in Rochester for the thirty days before an election, as required by New York law of any voter, which she now believed herself to be. Now, in November 1872, for the first time in three years, she had her chance. On the Friday before election day, she and her sisters went to a nearby barbershop where official registrars were recording the names of voters. When one of them insisted that the New York constitution specifically limited the right to vote to men, Anthony gave him a little lecture, reading the Fourteenth Amendment and explaining the House Judiciary Committee's Minority Report supporting the New Departure argument. After consultation among the polling officers, the women were allowed to register their names.[53]

On Tuesday morning November 5, Anthony waited to cast her ballot at the West End News Depot near her home in Rochester. She had not expected to be able to vote, only to try to do so and be rejected. Her plan was then to sue for her rights all the way up to the U.S. Supreme Court. Her surprise at her success jumps out from the letter she wrote to Elizabeth Cady Stanton as soon as she got home: "Well I have been & gone & done it!! — positively voted the Republican ticket — strait — this A.M. at 7 Oclock. . . . Not a jeer not a word — not a look — disrespectful."[54] Anthony's voting made the news across the country. "There is a great deal of conflicting practice as to the admission and denial of the claim of women to vote," editorialized a Pennsylvania paper. Since the well-known suffragist Susan B. Anthony has been allowed to cast her vote, however, "the ladies in favor of 'suffrage' now have a first class precedent."[55]

Grant won the election easily. Over the next days, Anthony continued her normal round of meetings and correspondence, especially with other women who had also tried to vote. Then, two weeks later, she opened her front door to find a well-dressed young man, federal officer Elisha Keeney. "He sat down. He said it was pleasant weather," as she later told the story. "He hemmed and hawed and finally said [that the U.S. Commissioner for the Circuit Court of the United States for the Northern District of New York] Mr. Storrs wanted to . . . 'arrest you.' "[56] She was, to say the least, startled. "I never dreamed of the U.S. officers prosecuting *me* for voting — thought only that if I was refused — I should bring action against inspectors."[57] Anthony had her little vanities, and before the marshal took her away, she made him wait as she changed her dress. On the

THE DAILY GRAPHIC

An Illustrated Evening Newspaper.

VOL. 1—NO. 81. NEW YORK, THURSDAY, JUNE 5, 1873. FIVE CENTS.

GRAPHIC STATUES, NO. 31.—"THE WOMAN WHO DARED."

"The Woman Who Dared," published the week before Anthony's trial, 1873. Illustration by Thomas Wust.

streetcar to the federal commissioner's office, other riders noted that she complained loudly that her rights were being violated and that she insisted that she be handcuffed.

Arriving at the commissioner's office, Anthony learned she was being arrested under the 1870 Enforcement Act which specified criminal punishment for anyone voting "without having the lawful right" to do so and was intended to insure that former Confederates did not try to return to political power by voting in federal elections and undermining the rights of former slaves. In passing the law Congress had in mind recalcitrant rebels, "repeaters," and others seeking to vote fraudulently, surely not Susan B. Anthony, a respectable fifty-two-year-old woman acting out of publicly acknowledged political intention, moreover casting a vote for the Republicans!

How then to explain her arrest? Now that the election was over, the votes counted, and Grant safely reelected, the Republican Party's support for women's enfranchisement evaporated. Unlike former slaves, white American women's allegiance to Republicans could by no means be assured. The prospect of women becoming voters threatened to upend the political system and endanger the dominant party's stability. Woodhull, who had been arrested the day after Anthony had registered to vote, wrote to her, "I fear [the Grant administration] intend to crush out, in your person, the Constitutional Question of Women's right to suffrage, as they are attempting, in my person, to establish a precedent for the suppression of recalcitrant Journals."[58] Anthony did not respond.

As Anthony's case moved through endless legal maneuverings, all of the major figures arrayed against her were Republicans — the man who issued the warrant for her arrest, the judges and prosecutors involved in the various stages of her trial, and most notably Justice Ward Hunt, newly appointed to the United States Supreme Court, who would go on to make the entire trial a national cause célèbre. Each had political connections that went at least as high as Roscoe Conkling, a U.S. senator and the most powerful Republican in New York state, a man with President Grant's ear. The fourteen other women who had cast their votes along with her were also arrested, but their cases were dropped in favor of exclusive attention on Anthony. She noted in her diary that she had been made the "test case."[59]

Anthony refused to pay her bail, wanting to be jailed, but none of the prosecutors or judges had any intention of incarcerating her and making her a martyr. For the next seven months, the time it took for the entire process to play out, Anthony was placed in the custody of the same deputy federal marshal who had knocked on her door with news of the arrest. The notion that she was confined while awaiting trial was a farce, as he vainly protested against her continuing to travel around the state and country, attending suffrage meetings, telling her own story of the arrest, and raising a small defense fund from friends.

Anthony was formally indicted in January 1873, and the trial itself was scheduled for May. In March, without any public fanfare, she insisted on voting for a second time, this time in a municipal election in Rochester. During the winter and spring of 1873, while awaiting her trial, Anthony gave the most important speech of her life, "Is It a Crime for an American Citizen to Vote?" She delivered it over and over again in her home county, and then, when the presiding judge moved the trial to another venue, she canvassed in that county as well. Her goal was to take her case directly to the male citizens from whom her jury would be selected so they would know why she had done what she had done, so it would be impossible to find *twelve men* so *ignorant* on the *citizen's rights* — as to *agree* on a *verdict* of *Guilty.*"[60]

Anthony was generally not a confident speaker, but when she did speak, she was all passion. Her voice virtually shouts out across the years from her yellowing manuscript pages. In preparation, she scribbled down phrases, as if carefully crafted sentences were a distraction from the fast current of her convictions. All her speeches, like her letters, were liberally punctuated by underlinings, which convey, over a century later, exactly the meanings, understandings, and feelings she wanted those who heard her to take from her words.

This habit makes her basic points of emphasis stand out in a speech that was long and full of elaborations and arguments, judicial and otherwise. First, the people's rights were *unalienable, God-given, secure* and *sovereign,* and governments existed to *secure* and *protect* — not to *give* them. Second, "the people" meant *"we the people* — not we *white male citizens,* nor yet we *male citizens* — but we the *whole people."* Thus, the rights of all the people were both *equal and natural.* If this had not been clear in the preamble to the Constitution or the Declaration of Independence, the Fourteenth Amendment had settled the question otherwise "for *what purpose* was the grand old charter of the fathers" burdened with alterations?

Only one question was left: *"Are women persons?"* Here she was especially emphatic. Any effort to make *sex* an unbridgeable barrier to the right of franchise was to make women not *citizens* of a *republic* but "help-less, powerless — bound to obey laws made by superiors." She became bolder: women's disfranchisement made them slaves, slaves of men, for, quoting Thomas Paine, *"slavery consists in being subject to the will of another."* Here was the bridge from the Thirteenth Amendment through the Fourteenth to the Fifteenth. This time quoting Senator Theodore Frelinghuysen of New Jersey, the war's greatest lesson, "the heresy of state rights" to disfranchise or enfranchise, "has been *completely buried.*"[61]

It was good that Anthony spoke so extensively prior to her trial, because at the trial itself, every effort was made to silence her. Throughout the trial, she was refused the right to speak in her own defense. The initial presiding judge, N. K. Hall, was replaced by U.S. Supreme Court justice Ward Hunt. At that time, justices of the Supreme Court rode circuit, and upstate New York was Hunt's circuit. Putting him in charge of the trial suggests, in the words of one New York newspaper, efforts to give resolution of "the questions involved . . . an added weight of authority."[62]

Hunt supervised the two-day, June 17–18, 1873, trial with a heavy hand. He considered only two issues to be relevant: had Anthony voted in a federal election, and was she a woman, hence lacking the right to do so? All testimony as to the constitutional argument on which Anthony had based her vote was prohibited. Her lawyers were not allowed to argue that because she believed herself to have the right to vote and did so in good faith, she had not violated the law, which specified that the person "knowingly" committed a criminal act.

In her speech, Anthony had named as the most important of the "privileges and immunities" which the Fourteenth Amendment guaranteed to all national citizens to be "the *jury box* and ballot-box."[63] Now, Justice Hunt proceeded to deny her not only the latter, but also the former. He declared that her guilt was so clear and uncontested that there was nothing over which the jury need deliberate. Thus, he would take it upon himself and directed the jury to find a verdict of guilty. (Nonetheless, the jury continued to deliberate for several hours.) Reading from a written statement composed ahead of time, he declared that the states retained the exclusive right to decide who could vote. To emphasize how foolish was Anthony's case that she could not be barred from voting because of her sex, he made his point by insisting that had a state law specifying that "no person having gray hair, or who had not the use of all his limbs" could vote, it would be perfectly constitutional.[64] Hunt's action of preempting the jury's decision strongly suggests that he feared that the jury might have agreed with Anthony's interpretation of the law and found her not guilty. "The greatest outrage History ever witnessed," Anthony scribbled in her diary.[65]

After Hunt pronounced his verdict, he allowed Anthony, as an act of "outward form," to say a few words. In perhaps the most dramatic moment of the spectacle, she rose and spoke extensively and forcefully, finally making her own case despite repeated and futile efforts on Hunt's part to make her stop: "Sit down Miss Anthony, I cannot allow you to argue the question"; "the Court cannot allow the prisoner to go on"; "the prisoner must sit down — the Court cannot allow it"; "the Court must insist"; "the Court orders the prisoner to sit down. It will not allow another word."[66]

Anthony would not be stopped. What she wanted to say more than anything was that the trial had happened at the hands of men and thus was illegitimate. She had not been tried by her peers. Even if the jury had been allowed to deliberate, they were men. More than once she likened the situation to that of runaway slaves under the Fugitive Slave Law and Hunt's decision to that of Justice Taney in the Dred Scott case. "The only chance women have for justice in this country is to violate the law, as I have done, and shall *continue* to do so," she declared, striking her hand "heavily on the table in emphasis of what she said." It was as defiant a note as she ever struck.[67] In her diary she noted that as she spoke, "a sublime silence reigned."[68]

When she finally sat down, Justice Hunt ordered her to stand up again to receive his sentence: one hundred dollars plus costs. She refused to pay the fine, hoping that she would be jailed for contempt of court. Hunt would not allow any such thing, and against her expressed desires, suspended her fine. That afternoon, the three election inspectors were also tried for the crime of receiving her vote, and Anthony, now that she was in the role of witness, was allowed to speak. When asked by Justice Hunt if she had claimed her right to vote as a female, she promptly replied, "Not as a female at all, sir, I presented myself as a citizen of the United States."[69]

The highly publicized trial and sentencing drew to a halt most of the efforts of women around the country attempting to vote. When Mathilde Weil tried to vote in New York City, the registrar told her, "It cannot be done, since Miss Anthony tried it."[70] Still Anthony kept her case and her cause alive. Her lawyers requested a new trial, but Hunt was still the presiding judge and he denied the request. She filed a petition before Congress to remit her fine, but that too went nowhere. The cruelest blow was her discovery that because of Hunt's refusal to jail her, she had no basis for appeal, no reason to submit a writ of habeas corpus, and thus no grounds for taking her case all the way to the Supreme Court as she had hoped. Despite it all, she remained proud of what she had accomplished. "My friends," she said to an audience later that year, "I stand before you to-night a convicted criminal." The audience applauded.[71]

In 1874, Virginia Minor, who along with her husband had in 1869 first laid out the argument that women already had the right to vote, brought the issue before the U.S. Supreme Court. Minor was suing Reese Happersett, the St. Louis election official who had denied her the right to register and to vote. A year later, the Supreme Court pronounced on the case. It was disposed of summarily, but with grave consequences.

Along with a decision the year before denying a claim by Chicago lawyer Myra Bradwell that the privileges and immunities clause of the Fourteenth Amendment protected her admission to the Illinois bar, *Minor v. Happersett* began a century of women's rights constitutional jurisprudence.

The Court conceded that women were persons, and persons were citizens. The fundamental issue, it said, was whether voting was a citizen's right. The court's rejection rested here: "The Constitution of the United States does not confer the right of suffrage upon any one." This was not an isolated decision concerned only with women's rights: the entire fate of the Reconstruction amendments — whether they would be broadly or narrowly interpreted — hung in the balance. The very next day, the Court heard arguments in one of the first cases which would undermine the Fifteenth Amendment as a protection of freed black men's voting rights. Anthony had anticipated this. "If we once establish the false principle, that United States citizenship does not carry with it the right to vote in every state in this Union, there is no end to the petty freaks and cunning devices that will be resorted to, to exclude one and another class of citizens from the right of suffrage."[72] The court's decision in the Minor case put an end to any effort to locate women's right to vote within the general rights and protections of national citizenship.

The Minor decision did not, however, stop the suffrage movement. Now that the Supreme Court had essentially vitiated federal control over voting, states were left with almost full control over the franchise. Suffragists began to refocus on amending state constitutions to grant women suffrage rights. If and when woman suffragists could succeed in amending state constitutions, these state-by-state changes would grant women full rights to vote, including in federal elections, including for president. This would be a much more laborious and difficult path, but it was the only one open.

Four:
The Great Primitive Right from Which All Freedom Originates, 1876–1893

With prospects for a constitutional victory dimming, new potential for suffrage growth emerged in the booming post-Reconstruction phenomenon of the Woman's Christian Temperance Union (WCTU). Etched in national memory as Bible-sotted harridans wielding axes against saloons and harassing peaceful beer-drinking men, the conventional, pious midwestern women who flocked to its ranks would seem unlikely candidates to pick up the suffrage torch. But they provided the first large, popular constituency for women's enfranchisement.

Just before Christmas 1873, groups of churchgoing women in Hillsboro, Ohio, began entering saloons, dropping to their knees, and praying for an end to the liquor trade that was destroying their husbands and sons. "It was phenomenal and emotional, and sprang up suddenly, like a fire from spontaneous combustion . . ." wrote suffragist and temperance leader Mary Livermore. "It was the anguished protest of hopeless and life-sick women against the drunkenness of the time, which . . . forced women and children to hide in terror from the brutality of the men, who had sworn to be their protectors."[1]

The temperance crusade, one of the largest spontaneous women's public demonstrations in American history, quickly spread throughout the Midwest. Saloons closed, husbands took the pledge, and local governments stopped licensing the liquor trade. The next year, the praying women organized themselves into the WCTU, which went on to become the best organized women's society in the country. Within a decade the WCTU claimed forty-four state chapters and seventy thousand members.

Seasoned suffragists did not know quite what to make of the temperance crusade, but they were thrilled to see women taking public action against an acknowledged nationwide evil. Lucy Stone cautiously wished the temperance crusaders Godspeed. Although "these praying bands are not exactly to my taste," Cady Stanton observed, nonetheless she could see that "the women who are leading the war will not be easily remanded to silence."[2] "This crusade will educate the women who engage in it to use the one and only means of regulating or prohibiting the traffic in liquor," Anthony predicted, "that of the ballot."[3]

Frances Willard was the woman to fulfill Anthony's prophecy. In just a few years, she guided the WCTU into full-fledged suffrage advocacy. She was born in 1838 to parents who were abolitionists and Republicans, and her temperance speeches were frequently laced with paeans to Lincoln and emancipation. Even as a teenager, she was ambitious, and her first crusade was on behalf of her own education. Though it offered a course of study not much more demanding than the standard female academy of the day, North Western Female College transformed Willard from a shy farm girl into a confident young woman.

Willard taught and traveled for a decade and a half and then at age thirty-three, she was offered the position as dean of the Women's College of the recently established Northwestern University in Evanston, Illinois. It was a dream job for her, but her tenure was brief. She had previously turned down the marriage proposal of Charles Fowler, the reverend gentleman who had become president of the university. Determined to retaliate, he reduced her institutional independence, humiliated her in public, and charged her with failure to carry out her responsibilities. She was a woman of enormous inner strength, but finally, when he had reduced her to tears, she resigned. It was 1874, and she turned to the newly formed WCTU, which awaited a woman with her talents.

The WCTU fit perfectly with Willard's combination of organizational talents and moral and religious beliefs. Drink, she believed, was a new form of enslavement that she was called upon to fight, just as her abolitionist parents had fought chattel slavery. She knew its devastations intimately because her brother was an alcoholic and eventually died from the disease. She found the young organization the perfect place for her energies, her intelligence, and what turned out to be her broad vision for what American women could achieve, even in an increasingly conservative age. Willard loved women, both in the aggregate and as beloved friends and partners, and she sought to draw them together and move them beyond domestic life into public influence. She became the organization's first corresponding secretary, a position that allowed her to communicate far and wide with the growing membership.

Within two years, Willard had come to understand that prayer alone would not defeat the scourge of alcohol. Preparing for a lecture in 1876 in Columbus, Ohio, she dropped to her knees, searching for inspiration about how to shepherd women's desire to cleanse the nation of the sin of liquor. "What wouldst Thou have me to do?" she prayed.[4] "There was borne in upon my mind, as I believe from loftier regions," she recalled, a clear call to action, and the voice said, "You are to speak for woman's ballot as a weapon of protection to her home and tempted loved ones from the tyranny of drink."[5] Suffrage was the way.

The command was God's, but the execution was Willard's. She recognized that most WCTU women had "never even seen a 'woman's rights convention,' and had been held aloft from the 'suffragists' by fears as to their orthodoxy."[6] She must go slowly toward political engagement so as not to frighten them. In the first of her efforts to introduce — ever so delicately — the ballot as a way to dethrone the rule of liquor, conservatives who still controlled the organization stilled her.

Finally, in late fall at the national WCTU

convention, five months after receiving the divine call, Willard was ready to go public with her epiphany. A large audience of invited temperance activists listened attentively from the pews of the Central Methodist Episcopal Church in Newark, New Jersey. "Though I could but feel the strong conservatism of an audience of Christian women," Willard recalled, ". . . I felt far more strongly the undergirdings of the Spirit."[7] Her face, which she thought plain, glowed with intense inner conviction. Her first premise was familiar to the WCTU throng: "woman, who is the born conservator of the home, [is] to be the Nemesis of home's arch enemy, King Alcohol." It was her second assertion that broke new ground: the mother-spirit can "in a republic . . . through that magic lens, that powerful sunglass which we name the ballot, be made to converge upon the rum-shop in a blaze of light that . . . shall burn this cancerous excrescence from America's fair form." Willard's metaphorical excess dazzled, but the crucial word — "ballot" — stood out.

The women of her audience, she told them, must find a way to arm themselves with the vote and to become "the cavalry forces in this great spiritual war."[8] Her audience broke into applause. Despite the warning of the next speaker that they should beware of trailing their skirts "through the mire of politics," Willard knew that "the hearts of the women were with the forward movement."[9] Two years later, now in the WCTU presidency, she was able to commit the entire organization to a formal endorsement of women's enfranchisement, putting it far ahead of any other women's society in the country, with the exception of the suffrage associations themselves, years ahead of the secular women's club federations.

Anthony, who had met Willard the year before, was following her efforts and wrote to say that she "rejoic[ed] that at last you have obeyed the 'inner light,' . . . put under your feet all the timid conservative *human* counsels," and had "spoken out for suffrage as a power to help on your hearts hope & work for Temperance."[10] From that point on, despite their very different styles of leadership and advocacy, Willard and Anthony, both single self-supporting women, were friends and allies.

Willard's approach to reconciling the notoriously radical demand for woman suffrage with conservative midwestern Protestant values was nothing short of brilliant. Two months after her suffrage insight, she initiated a brilliant strategy for relaunching

Frances Willard.

woman suffrage away from its previous radical associations. She rebranded "woman suffrage" as "home protection." She appropriated the term "protection" from Republican politicians, for whom it meant raising tariffs to benefit American industry. Instead Willard attached it to the site of women's responsibilities. Women, charged with sending their children out into a dangerous world, must act to protect them and to use all the tools available to them. Foremost among these were the ability to shape legislation, elect lawmakers, and see that their government was dedicated to "the enforcement of righteous law."[11] Temperance women were already petitioning lawmakers; now was the time to move on to more direct political efforts, to the vote itself.

In 1879 Willard became WCTU national president, from which position she was eventually able to make her next move. In January 1881, Willard was ready to propose that support for suffrage become the WCTU's official policy. Anthony went to Washington, D.C., to attend the WCTU national convention, and Willard introduced her from the platform. She witnessed with glee the launching of what she called "Frances Willards Suffrage bomb-shell into the Christian W[omen's] Union Camp."[12] This was Willard's "bomb-shell" resolution: "Home Protection where Home Protection is the strongest rallying cry; Equal Franchise, where the votes of women joined to those of men can alone give stability to temperance legislation."[13] The majority voted for it and the conservative, anti-suffrage wing withdrew.

Willard was in full control and support for suffrage was now formal policy, but it took her several years to bring the bulk of the membership along with her. Over time, the WCTU became an important training ground for suffrage activists, especially from the Midwest. Undoubtedly the most important of these was Anna Howard Shaw, who eventually became one of Anthony's most beloved protégées and the nation's leading suffragist. Equally important was the deep grassroots suffragism that the WCTU put down in the nation's heartland.

Much about Willard's approach differed from classical woman suffragism. Her argument was based not on individual rights, but on the needs and welfare of the community. Women must vote, not because they had the same rights, the same capacities, and the same obligations as men — though Willard thought that they did — but because their duties and spheres were so fundamentally different. Her home-centered approach drew support for suffrage much closer to the lives of average small-town middle-class women. Few owned property and paid taxes, so "no taxation without representation" had little meaning for them. Instead, they had responsibility for their homes, and "home protection" spoke to that reality. From there Willard summoned temperance women to mother the nation itself. The brilliance of her approach vaulted these less than radical women over the alleged wall between women's private and men's public spheres, and eventually into politics itself.

Willard was particularly anxious to grow the WCTU in the South. Anthony wanted to go south with her suffrage advocacy, but her abolitionist baggage made that virtually impossible. Willard faced no such obstacles, and starting in 1879 she began touring the region. Jim Crow segregation and racial violence had not yet settled onto southern society. She spoke before African American as well as white audiences.

Over the 1880s, the WCTU, led by Willard's vision, opened up to African American women, albeit in chapters segregated from white women. The WCTU became one of the most important avenues for southern black freedwomen to begin to move into collective public activism. "[T]emperance work in small towns and communities motivated the beginning of African American women's organizational development in the post–Civil War years," writes the foremost historian of black suffragism.[14]

"The real people there . . . the great middle-class of whites and the most intelligent class of blacks," Willard was convinced, "have . . . largely abandoned politics

224

as a sectional trade."[15] Believer as she was in the common virtues that united all women and certain that hostility to alcohol was a point of womanly unity, she preached that the divisions the nation suffered — racial and regional both — could be wiped out by the common bond of temperance belief and action. Many black women, pious Protestants who subscribed to the values of respectability and morality that the WCTU advocated, identified with her charge for women to lift up their communities, to strengthen their families, to wean their men away from drink, and to make plain the true dignity of their people.

In 1881, Willard instituted a Division of Colored Work. Among its first leaders was Frances Ellen Watkins Harper, the African American antislavery and equal rights veteran of the late 1860s, who led the WCTU work in Pennsylvania. Like Willard, Harper believed that "the twin evils of slavery and intemperance . . . had foisted themselves like leeches upon the civilization of the present age" and that alcohol was "not simply an enemy to one race but an enemy to all races."[16] She quickly rose in the ranks, becoming National Superintendent of Colored Work in 1889. "The people are deeply appreciative," she reported, "and no white field is more ready to harvest than this."[17]

Sarah Early, an African American graduate of Oberlin, became one of Harper's major lieutenants. "The moral character of one people is worth as much to themselves as is the moral character of the other," Early preached. "No one should undervalue the grave responsibilities which now rest upon us."[18] She "travelled six thousand miles," bringing her recruiting work to the South, to African American churchgoers, college students, even prisoners.[19] Early urged African American women to attend to how African American men, who still had suffrage rights in some southern states in the 1880s, used their votes. "The people of African descent form no small factor in the politics of this government," Early wrote from Tennessee. "A factor whose suffrage no one can afford to turn to bad account . . . if properly informed and stirred upon this topic, [they] would be as anxious to do right as any other people."[20]

It takes a real leap of historical imagination to appreciate what Frances Willard accomplished in the WCTU. So much of her approach — her religious framework, her appeal to sentimentalism and moralism, even her flowery language — is foreign to us today. Unlike Elizabeth Cady Stanton, who believed relentlessly in individual privacy as well as rights, Willard was an advocate of social control and government policing of behavior and morality. She believed in legal prohibition, if necessary by constitutional action. That said, Frances Willard placed herself squarely in the center of the women's rights tradition, and did so in a way that spoke to women far less radical in their inclinations than the pioneers of the suffrage movement. As Willard's leadership grew stronger and more confident, her essential belief in the equality of the sexes became ever clearer. She wrote in her 1889 autobiography, *"Woman, like man, should be freely permitted to do whatever she can do well."*[21]

Willard's relentless work to build the WCTU and women's political influence through it eventually exhausted her, and she died in 1898 at the young age of fifty-nine. The WCTU survived, but without Willard at its head, its political impact lessened. Within less than a decade, a new organization, the Anti-Saloon League, had taken over the anti-liquor movement, and men, not women, were in the lead.

In 1876, just as Frances Willard received

her suffrage revelation, Susan B. Anthony was preparing to celebrate the centennial of America's revolutionary founding with a dramatic action. It was not an especially good time for such an important national celebration. The country was in the midst of a presidential election that would turn out to be one of the most contested in its history. In late June, the nation was shocked when George Custer's Seventh Army Cavalry was wiped out by thousands of Sioux warriors in the Dakota territory. Even the nation's moral compass had gone awry, as newspaper readers were fixated on the continuing reverberations of the scandal over charges of adultery against Henry Ward Beecher, the nation's most revered Christian minister.

Nonetheless, it was the country's hundredth birthday. To celebrate, Philadelphia agreed to host the nation's first world's fair. The Centennial Exposition opened in May, and on July Fourth, in the midst of an unbearable heat wave, formal proceedings were held. The distinguished men heading the official celebration sat on a podium in Independence Square, droning on and on about America's great heritage and its spectacular future. Meanwhile, that morning a small group of suffragists waited at the back of the crowds, wondering when they would get their chance to step forward and make their case.

For some time, these women had been planning to offer some sort of protest on behalf of their sex and its claims to unfinished democratic business. They were determined to insert the matter of women's rights to full national citizenship into the Exposition. What could be a more appropriate moment than the hundredth anniversary celebration of the nation's democratic heritage? The women had arranged to hold a separate meeting elsewhere in the city, but as the day approached, they decided to add something bolder: to take their protest to the very center of the day's activities at Independence Square.

The day before the group decided to stage their protest, D.C. suffragist Sara Spencer had made a personal appeal to General Joseph Hawley, Civil War veteran, Connecticut governor, and chair of the official centennial celebration. Would he please allow the women to present the document of protest they had prepared for the event and to enter it into the day's official record? The program for the Fourth was already full, he explained. "We cannot make even so slight a change as that you ask."[22] He added, "Tomorrow we propose to celebrate what we have done the past hundred years, not what we have failed to do."[23]

Elizabeth Cady Stanton and Lucretia Mott were so offended that they boycotted the entire July Fourth event. Not Susan B. Anthony. It had been a hard year for her personally. She had been in Kansas to be with her dying younger sister. She was still smarting from the U.S. Supreme Court rejection of the New Departure argument, but she was determined to make July Fourth 1876 a *"Centennial screech for freedom."*[24] The suffragists would force themselves on to the platform, Hawley's refusal notwithstanding. Cady Stanton admired her friend's bravery, her willingness "to take the risk of a public insult in order to present the woman's declaration and thus make it an historic document."[25] But she wasn't prepared to join in.

Anthony was accompanied by other protestors drawn into the movement by the direct action voting campaign of the early 1870s. With Anthony and Cady Stanton so often away on the lecture circuit, Matilda Joslyn Gage had quickly risen in the National Woman Suffrage Association's (NWSA) organization and by 1876 was effectively serving as president. Sara Spencer, the fiery Washington, D.C., suffragist who had confronted General Hawley, was determined to stand up to his dismissal. "I never yet was forbidden by a man to do a thing," she explained, "but that I resolved to do it."[26] Lillie Devereux Blake, an elegant southern woman turned New York City suffragist, and Phoebe Couzins from Missouri, one of the nation's first women lawyers, rounded out the group.

In May, they went looking for a local office from which to plan their actions. Like most states in the union, Pennsylvania did not allow married women to sign binding legal contracts. The women's rights movement had long been tackling the infuriating legal principle of coverture, which denied wives independent economic standing, but here it was, still blocking their way. Anthony was a single woman, so she signed the contract. Setting up shop a mile down Chestnut Street from Independence Hall, they decorated the walls with slogans, posters and "pictures expressive of woman's condition," filled the shelves with suffrage literature, and then opened their doors to the public.[27]

By the time July Fourth finally arrived, the group patiently waited for their chance to undertake what Phoebe Couzins called "an overt act."[28] Richard Lee, descendant of a signer — and a former Confederate officer — read the original Declaration of Independence. Next on the program was Dom Pedro II, Emperor of Brazil, the only monarch in the western hemisphere whose country still allowed slavery.

"Now is our time," Anthony announced.[29] She and the others stepped forward. Only Couzins remained at the back, "trembling with suppressed emotion" and noting the "look of intense pain, yet heroic determination" on her leader's face. Audience members stared with astonishment at this strange interruption to the carefully orchestrated ceremonial events. Some of the men recognized Anthony, but others may have wondered who was this ramrod-straight middle-aged woman, her graying hair pulled back in a bun, in a heavy velvet dress despite the heat of the day. Her act was "impertinent," she later admitted, but "otherwise the people could not have been notified of the protest of the women against the refusal to allow them to participate in the proceedings."[30]

Arriving at the front of the podium, Anthony stood before the official presiding officer, Vice President Thomas Ferry. (President Grant, badly tainted by the corruption of his administration, did not attend.) "I present to you a declaration of rights from the women citizens of the United States," she announced.[31] Ferry bowed and accepted the embossed document that the suffragists had prepared. Some said he did so politely, others that he paled and looked bewildered. Then the women turned around and walked back down the aisle. Hands reached out from the audience for copies of their manifesto. Desperate to draw this stunning interference to a halt, General Hawley signaled the band to start playing the Brazilian national anthem, and moved to welcome Dom Pedro. With their dignity intact and their bold action completed, the suffragists made their way to the back of Independence Square. Anthony, under an umbrella that Gage held to shade her from the noonday sun, read their protest to a large crowd, which applauded enthusiastically.

The 1876 Declaration of Rights of the Women of the United States had been more than a year in the making. Other dissenters had their claims against the U.S. government, but Anthony wanted to advance just one, "the demand for *our political freedom . . .* the *one & great wrong of the Nation* — that must — like *negro slavery,* be put away, before it will be possible for the Na-

Mary Ann Shadd Cary.

tion to purge itself of any, or all of its other sins."[32]

The document was drafted by Matilda Joslyn Gage and then underwent several revisions. In contrast to the first women's rights declaration, issued twenty-eight years earlier at Seneca Falls, the final product spoke not of "Sentiments" but of "Rights," the equal, natural, inalienable, and individual rights of each citizen. Instead of resolutions, this Declaration boldly appended eight detailed

"Articles of Impeachment," presumably against the government of men. Women were denied fundamental rights including: "The Right of Trial by a Jury of One's Peers," protection against "Taxation without Representation," and, of course, the indignity of exclusion by the establishment of "Universal Manhood Suffrage." The Declaration concluded with an eighteenth-century warning from Abigail Adams, mother and wife of presidents: women will not be "bound to obey laws in which we have no voice or representation."[33] Adams's prediction of feminist rebellion has been much quoted since, but the suffragists of 1876 were among the first to find a foremother in her.

The protesters then walked the six blocks to the First Unitarian Church with its elegant Doric columns, where they were welcomed by the venerable abolitionist minister William Furness. They had previously advertised that they would present their Declaration of Rights there, and the pews were filled with eager listeners. For five long, hot hours, the audience listened to Elizabeth Cady Stanton read the Declaration, Matilda Joslyn Gage explain that marriage constituted a violation of the right of habeas corpus to wives, Susan B. Anthony tell the story of her arrest four years before in Rochester, and other women speakers. Then, well satisfied with their protest and the aftermath, the weather in Philadelphia still intolerable, the suffragists left town. For weeks after, women from all over the country wrote to have their names and those of their friends and relatives added to the Declaration of Rights, preserved for the future in a beautiful leather binder. A group of women working at the Internal Revenue Bureau sent their names and a small donation. Mary Ann Shadd Cary, the pioneering African American suffragist, sent over ninety signatures, apologizing that she had not sent more.

After the Centennial, Cady Stanton, Anthony, and Gage decamped to the cool front porch of the large, elegant Stanton home in Tenafly, New Jersey, that Cady Stanton had bought in 1868. There they began their next ambitious undertaking, a history of their movement. They had thought only to compile biographies of the leaders but the project developed into a multivolume comprehensive account of the nineteenth-century woman suffrage movement. To catalogue virtually every detail of a major reform movement, even as it was progressing, was an unprecedented, indeed arrogant, task, but it is one to which later historians are deeply indebted.

Cady Stanton and Gage composed the text out of numerous contributions from suffrage activists. Cady Stanton's advice to contributors was to pay little attention to internal conflicts. "Our little dissensions are of little account in the grand onward march," she explained. "Considering the slavery of woman they have all behaved as well as could be expected."[34] Meanwhile Anthony, too impatient for the work of writing, was the project's manager. She assembled and organized documents and corresponded with innumerable local activists to send in their memories. She arranged for a professional index so that the history's enormous amount of detail was not overwhelming. At an expense of $6,000, she commissioned elegant steel-cut engravings of dozens of suffrage activists, so that history would record that these women were not ugly and unsexed, but elegant, proud, and womanly. The finished project, which turned out to take a decade, grew to three volumes and nearly two thousand pages. Eventually copies were given to hundreds of local libraries and even abroad at no expense, so that all could know this history.

Many of those copies, some signed by Anthony herself, can still be found on the shelves.

Lucy Stone, who feared (with reason) that the contribution of her wing of the suffrage movement would be underrepresented, objected to the project. "In regard to the History of the Women's Rights Movement," she wrote to Cady Stanton, "I do not think it *can be* written by any one who is alive to-day."[35] Luckily the editors did not agree with her and proceeded with their work. To answer Stone's challenge that "your 'wing' surely are not competent to write the history of 'our wing,' " Harriot Stanton convinced her mother to let her use proceedings and newspaper articles to compile a fair version of the contributions of the American Woman Suffrage Association (AWSA) in the final chapter of volume 2.

With the U.S. Constitution's doors slammed shut, new efforts to secure the right to vote were now developing within the states. Indeed, the Fifteenth Amendment had been written to leave authority over voting to the states, limited only by a constitutional ban against disfranchisement by "race, color or previous condition." Winning these victories, though they would have to be done state by state, would grant women full voting rights, including in federal elections. Anthony still did "not believe in getting suffrage by state action." She remained convinced that gaining women's voting rights through any means but the U.S. Constitution was an insult to women's claims to full citizenship and political equality. Nonetheless, Anthony was pragmatic enough to recognize that state action "is the only way the politicians will allow us to *agitate* the question — So I accept it of necessity."[36]

Two western territories had already enfranchised women, but territorial enfranchisement only meant the right to vote for a handful of territorial offices, nothing at the federal level. In 1869, in the midst of Reconstruction excitement over enlarging the franchise, the tiny legislature of the recently organized territory of Wyoming, population nine thousand, voted to enfranchise its 1,500 non-Native women residents. Perhaps the legislators wanted to attract white, family-based settlers to a territory still overwhelmingly Native in population. After vacillating a few days, the federally appointed governor signed the bill. The enfranchisement of white women became an important part of Wyoming's identity, up to and through statehood in 1890. Despite its limits, it thrilled and encouraged suffragists nationwide, who, when opponents insisted that women voting would upend the social order, often cited its beneficent effects on the territory.

The enfranchisement of women in Utah Territory in 1870 was more contentious. From the beginning it was bound up with controversies aroused by the territory's Latter-day Saints (LDS) population, which still practiced polygamy. Whether LDS elders supported enfranchising women in order to boost the LDS electorate with multiple wives or to cleanse it of any suspicion that its women were mistreated remains unclear. Non-LDS Utah residents supported women's enfranchisement because they were hopeful that when women were enfranchised, they would vote to end polygamy and regain their sacred monogamous marriage rights. In this expectation, they were disappointed. For the next seventeen years, LDS women energetically defended both their political rights and their polygamous practices. They retained their franchise.

Thus, in 1876, when Colorado Territory laid plans to become a state in time for the nation's Centennial, local supporters of woman suffrage saw the historical opportunity to come into the union as the first state with full voting rights for women. Colorado suffragists were inspired by the successes in the bordering Wyoming and Utah territories, but woman suffrage in a state was a much greater achievement than in a territory. If and when the voters of a state agreed to alter their constitution to include political rights for women, those rights reached all the way up to federal elections, including voting for president. Local suffragists petitioned the Colorado Constitutional Convention, but it resisted, fearing that Congress might block its bid for statehood if it came in bearing this radical innovation. Instead, Colorado politicians offered a compromise. Starting one year after statehood, a simplified voters' referendum, requiring only a majority, could amend the new constitution to allow women the right to vote. Suffragists accepted the offer.

Accordingly, soon after Colorado became a state in August 1876, a woman suffrage referendum was scheduled for early October 1877. The Colorado Woman Suffrage Association was promptly formed and chose Alida Avery, a cautious, handsome woman in her early forties, as its president. The first woman physician in the state, she had been one of only two women professors when

Vassar College opened its doors in 1865 and had moved from New York to Denver to serve as Colorado's first Superintendent of Hygiene. She was joined by Albina Washburn, who was active in the Colorado Grange, an important farmers' group, which gave equal voting rights to its women members.

The third of the association's leaders was Mary Shields, who served as "general agent." She traveled long distances, including to mining towns and Spanish-speaking areas, and spoke to men who knew nothing of women's voting. She was not a trained speaker, but by all reports she was very effective. She "did not lecture but 'talked' . . . to five hundred men at a time as if they were her own sons, and only needed to be shown they were conniving at injustice, in order to turn about and do the right thing."[37] One of those to whom she spoke — through an interpreter — was southern Colorado miner and legislator Agapita Vigil, who was converted and became one of the first politicians to support woman suffrage.

Enthusiasm was great, but resources were meager. Colorado suffragists requested "reinforcements: cavalry, artillery, infantry-troops by land and sea, in short, the sinews of war." From Boston, AWSA sent Lucy

Stone, Henry Blackwell, and Margaret Campbell.[38] Sneering at the organizers from New England, the *Pueblo Chieftain* ridiculed "all of the crowing hens and clucking cocks in that region of advanced ideas . . . let loose like a flock of magpies upon the people of our State."[39] Stone and Blackwell traveled from town to town, with meetings every day. Henry liked the adventure and the change, but it was hard on Lucy's health. She wrote to her daughter that her father thought he could make a better living in Colorado than Boston, but "I'd rather be hung than live here."[40]

Anthony was not eager to cooperate with AWSA, but she was a born agitator and an inveterate adventurer and the call from Colorado proved irresistible. In early September, she also arrived in Denver, ready to lecture throughout the state. She covered much of the southern tier, going up and down mountain passes, crossing the Continental Divide, traveling night and day. Although railroads were coming to the state, much of it was still difficult to reach. Anthony was unbelievably intrepid. With casual fortitude, she rode on a narrow-gauge railroad over a nine-thousand-foot peak to reach a railroad town that was barely three months old. She gave her speech in a hotel dining room, "the first nail of which was driven not over thirty days before."[41] In the morning, she took the six a.m. train to the next town.

Anthony arrived back in Denver the day before the election. Voting was still done by inserting a preprinted ticket issued by official party organizations, all of which were marked against the suffrage referendum. Suffragists tried to counter by printing up their own pro-suffrage ballots, but this device was not enough to come anywhere near winning. "The politicians . . . quietly manipulated the printing and distribution of the tickets, . . ." reported Henry Blackwell. "This fact alone was fatal." Suffrage lost badly, 6,612 to 14,053.[42] The easterners blamed the "priest-ridden," Spanish-speaking male voters of the southern mining counties despite the support of Agapita Vigil.

The deeper problems, however, extended beyond Colorado. While the WCTU helped to build mainstream support among women, it also posed new problems. Heretofore, the obstacles to woman suffrage were conservative clergy, stubborn congressmen, nasty newspaper coverage, and the many women who feared venturing beyond their homes. Now, for the first time, the movement began to face organized, well-funded opponents who recognized and feared the link between women voting and prohibition legislation. Henry Blackwell concluded that in Colorado "the strength of our opponents consists of the liquor-selling and liquor-drinking interests" and the influence he believed that they were able to wield, especially among German immigrants.[43]

Over the next decade and a half, this story was repeated in many different places. In Indiana, one of the centers of WCTU strength, "women, many of whom had never spoken before any audience save their own neighbors," became organizers for suffrage. In response, "the animosity of the liquor league was aroused, and this powerful association threw itself against submission" of a bill before the legislature for a referendum.[44]

In Nebraska, one of the few states that authorized a referendum to add women's voting rights to its constitution in the 1880s, the liquor interests made sure voters came out against it. Clara Colby, a talented journalist and rising star in the state suffrage firmament, described the situation. "Towards the close of the campaign it became evident that the saloon element was determined to defeat the amendment. The organ of the Brewers Association sent out its orders to every saloon . . . and the greatest pains [were] taken to excite the antagonism of foreigners by representing to them that woman suffrage meant prohibition."[45] "*Between ourselves* — there is no more hope to carry woman suffrage in Nebraska than of the millennium coming next year," Henry Blackwell wrote to his daughter from the campaign trail.[46] He was right. With only one third of the vote, the measure was soundly defeated.

The other major referendum in the 1880s was in Oregon. The leading suffragist there, Abigail Scott Duniway, an impoverished farm wife turned savvy political organizer, was determined to keep the temperance issue as far away from woman suffrage as possible. Personally, she was hostile to the temperance movement, but more important, she could see the danger it posed politically. She understood that too much enthusiasm among temperance women could backfire and ignite the opposition. Despite her efforts, she could not stave off the conflict. Fraud at the polls was rampant. On the morning of the election, she recalled, encouraged by liquor interests, "multitudes of legal voters who are rarely seen in daylight except at a general election, many of whom were refugees from Washington territory, crowded forth from their hiding-places to strike the manacled women down."[47] The measure was defeated, again two to one.

Where suffrage campaigns to amend state constitutions were defeated by voters, suffragists regularly concentrated their resentments on immigrants, "foreigners." The universal suffrage promise had faded. The entire political class was losing faith in democracy. Immigration rates were rising, and Catholics and Jews were beginning to arrive in greater numbers, threatening the heretofore uncontested Protestant character of American society. As the country became more nativist in response, so too did the suffragist movement.

Germans and Italians particularly had reputations as heavy drinkers, and so suffragists were sure that the liquor industry was encouraging them to vote against suffrage whenever it came up on the ballot. Facing opposition from immigrant men who had gained the right to vote without any struggle, when no woman could do so no matter how hard she pressed, suffragist resentment intensified. In the wake of the Colorado defeat, Anthony wrote to her friend and reliable congressional ally Ben Butler, to question why he had drawn on immigrant support throughout his political career. She angrily protested against "Bohemians, Swedes, Norwegians" and what it felt like to be "begging *them* to vote to *let you vote.*" She added, "*You'd feel* the insult quite as keenly as I do."[48]

By the end of the 1880s, the backlash against woman suffrage was erasing most of the movement's gains, modest as they were. In 1883, Washington Territory had followed Utah and Wyoming to give women a limited territorial franchise. Although they could not vote in federal elections, women there could sit on juries, which put them in a position to take action against the saloons, brothels, and gambling houses that thrived in Seattle and Tacoma.

Anti-suffrage forces mobilized to undo this small victory. Politicians and vice purveyors arranged for a case to be brought before territorial courts. The plaintiff was the wife of a saloon owner and a dance hall girl who had the fantastical name of Nevada Bloomer. Her claim to have been denied the right to vote was a pretext to get the courts to rule against the legality of women's enfranchisement. In 1886, two territorial supreme court justices ruled that the legislature had exceeded its authority by enfranchising women, and the law was undone.

"The liquor forces, having thus illegally disposed of the woman vote, conducted a successful campaign to elect a [constitutional] convention that would represent their wishes," concluded later historians of suffrage.[49] Washington Territory became a state in 1887 without its women voters.

Woman suffrage in Utah Territory also came under attack, the opposition in this case coming from Congress. In seeking to punish the territory for the LDS practice of polygamy, congressional Republicans targeted the practice of women suffrage there. Both to defend their own enfranchisement but also to work for suffrage nationwide, some LDS women became strong advocates of woman suffrage.

Emmeline Wells, the seventh wife of a prominent LDS elder, was an early and important Utah suffrage advocate. As editor of the Salt Lake City–based *Women's Exponent,* Wells circulated a petition to Congress calling for passage of a sixteenth amendment enfranchising women. She collected an astonishing seventeen thousand signatures from Utah women. The next year she was invited by suffrage leaders to attend NWSA's Washington, D.C., convention. They brought Wells with them to meet President Hayes, and she took the opportunity to appeal to the president and his wife, emphasizing the terrible damage anti-polygamy legislation would wreak on plural wives and their children. She signed a personal plea to Lucy Hayes, "Please accept this token of the esteem of a Mormon wife." The first lady received her politely, which Wells mistook for support. If anything, reports of the meeting inflamed popular anti-polygamy sentiment and strengthened the president's anti-polygamy position.[50]

Although support for LDS suffragism was a manifestation of NWSA's baseline commitment to maintaining an open and broad suffrage platform, hostility to polygamy was growing, including in suffrage circles. The WCTU objected strongly to plural marriage under its "home protection" rubric. AWSA followed suit. In the 1880s Anthony herself began to pull back. In 1887, Congress intensified its attack on woman suffrage in Utah with a bill disfranchising all of the territory's women regardless of their beliefs about or past practices of plural marriage. The *Women's Exponent* published "burning articles, letters and editorials upon this uncalled-for and unwarranted interference with the affairs of the women of this territory," and NWSA strenuously objected that the disfranchising legislation constituted "a disregard of individual rights which is dangerous to the liberties of all."[51]

Nonetheless, the anti-suffrage legislation passed handily, and after seventeen years of voting, Utah women lost their political rights by action from a Congress that was willing to disfranchise but not to enfranchise. Wells and others continued to press for the reinstatement of woman suffrage until, in 1896, when Utah (which had by then agreed to outlaw polygamy) became a state, women's comprehensive voting rights were reinstated in its inaugural state constitution.

Over these difficult years, only the women of Wyoming Territory were able to maintain their franchise rights without interruption, joining with men voters when statehood was secured in 1890. At last and at least, somewhere in the United States, women had full and equal voting rights. In Wyoming they could cast their votes for Congress and for president.

Despite her concession to campaigns to amend state constitutions, Susan B. Anthony refused to give up on an amendment to the U.S. Constitution. On January 25, 1887, she and several dozen other suffragists settled into the visitors' gallery of the

U.S. Senate to hear, for the very first time, a congressional debate on an amendment to the U.S. Constitution to enfranchise women. Gone was the universal suffrage approach which had been advanced by NWSA for almost two decades. Instead the Senate debated a different sort of amendment, one patterned exactly on the Fifteenth Amendment, except that it replaced "race, color or previous condition of servitude" with "sex" as a prohibited disfranchisement. Like its precedent, this proposed amendment otherwise left control over voting rights to the states, which were already finding ways to erode national protections for the suffrage of black men.

The bill had first been brought forward ten years earlier by California senator Aaron Sargent. Now the sponsor was Henry Blair of New Hampshire, advocate of many franchise reforms including congressional restoration of suffrage rights to the residents of the District of Columbia. Anthony had been working closely with him for at least a year, urging him to find ways to overcome the opposition of his Senate colleagues and bring the amendment bill up for a general vote on the Senate floor. She was, of course, relentless. "I thought . . . you would come fussing round before I got your amendment reported to the Senate," he wrote her. He was in control of things, he assured her. She should not "meddle," and he suggested that she "go off and get married!"[52] Anthony took it as a joke.

The basic arguments in this first senatorial debate would be repeated endlessly for decades to come. In support of the bill, Blair spoke about the importance of political rights being available to all. "The right to vote is the great primitive right in which all freedom originates and culminates. . . . It is impossible to conceive of the suffrage as a right dependent at all upon such an irrelevant condition as sex. It is an individual, a personal right, and if withheld by reason of sex it is a moral robbery." He was followed by Senator Joseph Dolph of Oregon, who emphasized that women were already voting in the Utah, Wyoming, and Washington territories, with none of the catastrophic results opponents had predicted. "Nature had continued in her wonted course. . . . Marriages have been quite as frequent and divorces have not been more so."[53] Leaders of the WCTU, backed by their 200,000 members, submitted a petition supporting the amendment.

Then came the opposition. Senators Joseph Brown of Georgia and Francis Cockrell of Missouri waxed poetic about woman's sacred place within the family. God also ordained men's exclusive responsibility not only to vote, but to wield the sword in war, and "of constructing and operating our railroads."[54] From Great Britain, where she had gone to be with her daughter and care for her granddaughter, Cady Stanton read of their arguments. The "one pleasant feature . . . is the harmony of the view of these gentlemen and their Creator" though "they cannot tell us when, where and how they interviewed Jehovah."[55]

Sixteen senators voted for Blair's bill, which was, to the surprise of no one including its suffragist advocates, defeated. For their championing of women's right to vote, the *Chicago Daily Tribune* called Blair and Dolph "the two old ladies of the Senate." It also ridiculed Anthony for being just as "emotional and impulsive" as the rest of her sex, because she had expressed her determination to campaign for the defeat of prominent opponents.[56] In fact, Anthony was quoted as having no regrets at all. "A defeat!" she exclaimed. "Why no. It was a triumph for us. You see we have on our side one-third of the United States Senate."[57]

Nonetheless it would be a long time before greater gains were realized at the federal level. A woman suffrage amendment to the U.S. Constitution was not debated again in Congress for almost twenty years, by which time Anthony had passed away and woman suffrage had lost its place in line to three other constitutional amendments.

The creation of a unified woman suffrage movement was of a piece with an enthusiasm for organizational federation throughout turn-of-the-century women's activism. The General Federation of Women's Clubs, the National Association of Colored Women, and the National Association of Jewish Women were all formed in the 1890s. In February 1888, NWSA had initiated an International Council of Women, which resulted in a National (U.S.) Council of Women. All of these federative groups reached across a wide range of interests, in some cases going so far as to include anti-suffragists. Even in the National Council of Women, which had been formed by suffragists, the issue of woman suffrage was deliberately sidelined in favor of a broader, less controversial mission of encouraging women's public activism, whatever the object.

In late 1887, two decades after their separate and acrimonious formations,

AWSA and NWSA began negotiations to come together in a single, united national suffrage organization. Now that both worked simultaneously on campaigns to amend state constitutions and supported a federal constitutional change patterned after the Fifteenth Amendment, there were few substantive differences. Although Lucy Stone and Susan B. Anthony still disliked and distrusted each other, Stone took the initiative and Anthony responded positively. At the first meeting Stone and her daughter, Alice Stone Blackwell, met with Anthony and Rachel Foster, a wealthy young woman from Philadelphia, and Anthony's chosen "suffrage daughter." From there, discussion moved out to the larger leadership circles of each organization. "These two organizations are like parties," NWSA leader Isabella Beecher Hooker said, unconvinced that union was the right path. "You have got attached to them. You work harder than you would if you were one party."[58] The process of unification was difficult and fraught. Disagreements ranged from the name of the new organization to how the two groups of suffragists would combine so as not to favor the larger NWSA. But after two contentious years, unity was effected. The new name combined that of its two preceding associations and was to be the National American Woman Suffrage Association (NAWSA).

As NWSA and AWSA proceeded to unite, Cady Stanton was not universally welcomed into the united organization. Stone and AWSA had tried to make it a condition of unification that she (along with the other two founding pioneers) not take a leadership position. Anthony and other NWSA stalwarts, who considered Cady Stanton the essential philosopher of the suffrage movement, "who had borne the burdens of our cause for forty years," would not hear of it. "To cut her head off," as Isabella Beecher Hooker put it, "fills me with disgust."[59] Even though Cady Stanton was increasingly focusing not on suffrage but on the role of Christianity in creating and prolonging women's oppression, Anthony and Hooker would not go forward without her. Eventually NWSA's objections prevailed and when the two organizations met as one for the first time on February 18, 1890, Cady Stanton became president of NAWSA. Even then, several other pioneers, who believed that the radical tendencies of NWSA had been lost in unification with AWSA, went their own separate ways, forming break-off societies, none of which survived very long.

Cady Stanton held the presidency for just

two years. In January 1892, she delivered one of the most powerful suffrage speeches in American history in a hearing before Congress. "The Solitude of Self" was essentially her suffrage swan song and is the most eloquent and enduring expression of what equal political, economic, and personal rights for women meant to her. The case she made was neither political nor sociological nor economic but profoundly philosophical. "The point I wish plainly to bring before you on this occasion is the individuality of every human soul, . . ." she began. "The strongest reason why we ask for woman a voice in the government under which she lives; in the religion she is asked to believe; equality in social life, where she is a chief factor; a place in the trade and professions, where she may earn her bread, is because of her birthright to self-sovereignty." No one, not even a loving husband or kind father, could ultimately protect a woman from the exigencies of life. The unavoidable responsibility one had over oneself, the inescapable fact that no one else can know each soul's true needs, were to her the ultimate reason that each individual deserved, indeed required the right to participate in public governance.[60]

"The Solitude of Self" painted a bleak

and beautiful portrait of existential isolation, the thoughts of a woman soon to enter her ninth decade. "We come into the world alone, unlike all who have gone before us; we leave it alone under circumstances peculiar to ourselves." In an era in which politics were increasingly emphasizing class and other group positions, when some of the best thinkers of the age were trying to understand the social dimensions of human life, Cady Stanton was insisting on a profoundly individualist basis for women's rights. It was a perspective that looked backward to the origins of the movement and forward to a modern era, to a feminism not yet in existence; above all, it was a perspective unique to this one woman. Anthony thought that it was *"her crowning speech,"* and she reported that some of the most obdurate congressmen who heard it wiped tears from their eyes.[61] The next day, Cady Stanton announced she would no longer serve as NAWSA president.

FIVE:
NEW WOMEN, 1893–1906

Eighteen ninety-three was the year after the four hundredth anniversary of Christopher Columbus's arrival to ("discovery of") the New World, and the United States was ready for a much more ambitious, a much more truly "world's fair" than the 1876 Centennial. Chicago, the booming center of America's new industrial might and aspiring global power, was the chosen site. While the rest of the country fought a collapsing economy, in Chicago visionary architects and an army of workers created a six-hundred-acre city within the city. Fourteen new gleaming white buildings advertised the expanse of American achievement and the great changes that the future would bring. An atmosphere of great national celebration pervaded all. Twenty-seven million visitors eventually came from all over the country and abroad.

The suffrage movement was also growing

in new directions. While there were still no opportunities for a federal amendment, new political forces, especially in the West, were reigniting campaigns for enfranchising women in state constitutions. African American women were coming together in their own clubs and federations and including demands for votes to offset the disfranchisement of men of their race. Finally, some of the leaders of the female wage-labor force, which was providing many of the workers in the new industrial economy, were beginning to see the relation of political power to securing better economic conditions.

Overall, American womanhood was more confident and well positioned for this exposition. Their clubs and societies were now organized into large national organizations, and they were invited to play a major part in the fair's design and leadership. Seeking to stand at their head was forty-four-year-old Bertha Palmer — though she preferred to be called Mrs. Potter Palmer so as to invoke her husband's great wealth and social standing. Palmer was active in Chicago's vibrant women's public culture, concerned with the condition of wage-earning women, mildly progressive in her political opinions, and extraordinarily well connected to the highest circles of wealth and political power.

She was not, however, a suffragist, and pressing too hard for women's political equality was not part of her vision for women's presence at the fair.

Meanwhile, Susan B. Anthony was also working to ensure women's full involvement at the exposition. She had moderated her approach, and unlike the 1876 fair, when she burst into the proceedings, this time she worked behind the scenes from the nation's capital, seeking the help of "ladies of influence," meaning "wives and daughters of the judges of the Supreme Court, the Cabinet, senators, representatives, army officials."[1] She worked to get Congress to include special funds for women in its fair authorization, and succeeded partially. She had urged that women be members of the official national commission in charge of the fair. Instead, the congressional authorization left the main commission entirely to men and specified a separate "Board of Lady Managers." Leadership of this group went to Bertha Palmer.

A great deal was at stake in this high-profile, government-funded world's fair. How was the place of American women in the great national enterprise to be represented and by whom? Palmer, who had unparalleled faith in herself and her high social standing, believed that only by personally keeping firm control would women's contribution to the Columbian Exposition be a success. Her plan was to emphasize "women's place in the charitable and reformatory work of the world." "Lady" was not an insignificant designation for her framework: upper-class female philanthropists were to oversee everything. This put her into a series of conflicts with career women, suffragists, African Americans, and finally white working-class women, all of whom had their own ideas about how they and their achievements should appear at the fair.

The site of women's organized activity was the elegant Woman's Building, funded by Congress and situated on the edge of the main grounds. To design it, Palmer chose twenty-one-year-old Sophia Hayden, the first woman architecture graduate from MIT. Hayden had never before undertaken a major project (and never would after). Palmer also selected women painters, sculptors, and designers to ornament the building, which was to be filled with exhibits of women's artistic, intellectual, mechanical, and scientific achievements. "Far more important than the discovery of Columbus . . ." Palmer declared at the building's dedication, "is the fact that the general government has discovered women."[2]

Closed out of Palmer's inner circle and most of these major decisions, suffragists secured control over one project at the fair, an elaborate, weeklong "World's Congress of Representative Women." There, questions of equality, rights, and suffrage would get proper attention. Palmer had been warned to be careful that the radical tendencies of these few "powerful women, exerting tremendous influence over the whole country," not be allowed to dominate. Those women she feared were Anthony, Frances Willard, and May Wright Sewall, an Indiana suffragist and a leading figure in the National Council of Women. Sewell was to be the director of the World's Congress of Representative Women.[3]

Palmer was wrong in thinking that suffragism would damage the women's standing at the fair. The World's Congress of Representative Women drew a bigger attendance that any other meeting in Chicago except for the World's Congress of Religions. It was so crowded with events and attendees that it had to be held at a building offsite, which eventually became the home of the Chicago Art Institute.

Lucy Stone attended, in what turned out to be the last major speech of her life, for she died five months later. Elizabeth Cady Stanton was too obese and immobile to travel and remained at home in New York, but her speech was read for her. Elsewhere in her speeches from these years, Cady Stanton partook of the era's suspicion of political democracy by calling for an educational qualification for suffrage, but not in Chicago. One of those stirring declarations that she had been grinding out for almost a half century, "The Ethics of Suffrage" insisted without hesitation or qualification on the basic, universal, individual right to self-government and on women's right to be fully included.[4]

However, it was Susan B. Anthony who was the undoubted star of the World's Congress of Representative Women. Most of her adult life she had been the object of public derision and ridicule. Now, for the first time, she found herself widely acknowledged as a champion of women's advancement. She was a celebrity! Visitors seized the chance to see this woman about whom they had heard so much. "The way she walked along the corridors in her flight from meeting to meeting, the untiring energy with which she made opening addresses . . . was nothing short of miraculous," crowed the *Chicago Tribune*. "And wherever she went the cause of woman suffrage screamed. Indeed all other subjects sank into insignificance against this burning one."[5]

Twenty-eight-year-old Ellis Meredith of Denver traveled to Chicago to attend the National American Woman Suffrage Association (NAWSA) meeting that was part of the World's Congress. She had a specific goal: to request Anthony's support for a second try at enfranchisement in her home state of Colorado. Meredith was not prepared for the revered woman's initial response. Anthony had not forgotten the 1877 defeat in Colorado, nor forgiven the state's Spanish-speaking citizens whom she had blamed for the loss. Still believing deeply in a federal amendment, Anthony regarded state campaigns, even though they could grant women full suffrage including for federal office, as a waste of time. But Ellis Meredith represented a new generation coming into the suffrage movement, bringing with it new sources of enthusiasm and support, prepared to take over from Anthony and her aging cohort.

Ellis Meredith was a second-generation suffragist, daughter of Denver suffragist Emily R. Meredith. She was both a married woman and a professional journalist, a combination difficult to imagine just a few years before. Her mother and her mother's generation called her Mrs. Howard Stansbury, but she preferred to be called Ellis Meredith, a gender-neutral first name of her own invention and the last name she was born with. In 1893, she was already a journalist for the *Rocky Mountain News*. A contemporary observed that "her pen," and "the magnetic influence of her contact with the people wielded a large influence."[6]

Ellis Meredith represented the emergence of the "New Woman," the popular name for an 1890s female style radically different from the conservative ladies of her mother's generation. These "New Women" no longer thought of themselves primarily in domestic terms, but were educated, independent minded, and career oriented. They were proudly athletic, playing tennis, riding bicycles, and dressing in simpler, less confining clothes. Illustrator Charles Dana Gibson popularized them as "Gibson girls." Artist Mary Cassatt, a suffragist herself and a rising star in the French impressionist circle, honored them in a grand three-part mural in the Woman's Building, depicting young women gleefully pursuing knowledge, science, fame, and the arts.

Despite Anthony's skepticism, Meredith

explained why Colorado suffragists were ready for another try after the defeat of 1877. Much had changed. The state had adopted the secret ("Australian") ballot system. No longer would voters use a ballot prepared and pre-marked by the parties. They would mark their own officially printed nonpartisan ballots in the privacy of a voting booth.

Even more important, the political environment was shifting dramatically in favor of reform. A new political party, the People's Party (or Populists, as they were nicknamed), had been founded in 1891. Populists were drawn from rural discontents in the Farmers' Alliance, labor activists in the Knights of Labor, and temperance women in the nation's heartland. Unlike the established parties, Populists were determined to address the unregulated power of large economic interests and the massive disparities of wealth that led Mark Twain to disparage the age as "Gilded." Unlike the Republicans and Democrats, they were unafraid of the massive influx of new voters that women's enfranchisement would bring; indeed, they welcomed their new, not yet affiliated political energy. In the spring of 1893, the Populists controlled the Colorado state legislature and passed a bill authorizing a referendum for the fall election to add women voters to the state constitution. This was the opportunity that Meredith and her sister suffragists were determined to seize.

Meanwhile the nation's economic crisis, a depression that would not be equaled in severity until the 1930s, deepened. Colorado suffragists were desperately short of money, but the political shifts offered them other resources. They positioned themselves as champions of a threatened democracy and allied themselves with critics of the nation's growing inequality, confident that they could find allies among men who were "their natural partners in all things else save political prestige and political power."[7]

Instead of temperance, Colorado suffragists were linking women's right to vote to issues that male voters cared about, and from whom they could possibly win support. " 'Equal rights' is a life-long principle with the Knights of Labor and the Populists," wrote Ellis Meredith.[8] In recognition of this ideological repositioning, Colorado suffragists no longer spoke of woman suffrage but of "equal suffrage" because, as Meredith argued, "in the word 'equal' there is an appeal to justice which does not seem to exist in the word 'woman.' "[9]

"These are some of the straws that make

us believe the wind is coming our way," Meredith concluded what she said to Anthony. "I was born a suffragist," she wrote in an introductory letter, "so you can understand that a word of encouragement from you would go a long way."[10] Anthony could see that here was a new generation of suffragists, looking forward, not backward. She agreed to put national suffrage resources into the campaign. She would send a rising young star of the movement to Colorado. Her name was Carrie Chapman Catt.

Carrie Chapman Catt was also a New Woman. Born Carrie Lane in 1859 to a middle-class farming family, she had overcome her father's reluctance and was able to attend Iowa Agricultural College (later Iowa State University) in Ames, where she was the only woman in her graduating class. She had thought to study law, but needing to earn money, she switched to teaching and quickly rose to the position of school superintendent of Mason City. A striking-looking woman with dark, deep-set, slightly sad eyes, she then married a crusading local newspaperman, Leo Chapman, and because she was now a wife, the school board required her to give up her job. Within just a year, her husband contracted typhoid and died. Again in need of a way to support herself and finding that she had a taste and talent for public speaking, she became a successful lecturer. Drawing on the evolutionary sociology she had absorbed in college, she railed against the danger that immigrants were posing to American democracy.

As a young girl, she had already shown interest in woman suffrage, and by 1885 she was collecting petitions to the state legislature in favor of municipal suffrage. For a while she worked through the WCTU, but by 1889 she was active in the Iowa State Woman Suffrage Association. In October of that year, she heard a speech by Lucy Stone, who wrote admiringly in the *Woman's Journal* of the young eager suffragist she met in Iowa. The next year, she traveled to Washington, D.C., to attend the first convention of the newly united NAWSA. There she met Susan B. Anthony, who may have already heard enough about this young woman to recognize that she had the same sort of superb talent for grassroots organizing that Anthony had brought to the movement three decades before. She had married again, and was now known as Carrie Chapman Catt. Would she like to be one of

NAWSA's organizers in the 1890 South Dakota campaign? Carrie Chapman Catt agreed to go.

The South Dakota referendum, the first that the newly unified suffrage organization undertook, was a gruesome trial by fire. The state was impoverished, travel across distances was difficult, and former political supporters had dropped the woman suffrage amendment to the state constitution. South Dakota women had been educated about woman suffrage by the WCTU, but more than a quarter of the population were immigrants, whose strong anti-temperance prejudices set them against woman suffrage. "It is the most difficult sort of a campaign," Anthony, who spent four months in the state, wrote from the field. "The strongest argument to win the Prohibition men . . . is the very strongest to drive from us the high license [pro-liquor] men."[11] "Ours is a cold lonesome little movement," Carrie Chapman Catt, who had joined her, wrote of the situation, "which will make our hearts ache about November 5."[12] Two-thirds of the state's voters rejected the suffrage referendum.

Three years later, however, Carrie Chapman Catt was ready for another campaign. When she arrived in Denver on Labor Day,

1893, she found a considerably different situation. The 1877 Colorado campaign had trained a small cohort of skilled state suffragists who had bided their time for another opportunity. Now they had identified a diverse coalition of supporters. Upper-class Denver women were on board. Elizabeth "Baby Doe" Tabor, the scandalous second wife of a wealthy mining magnate (whose amazing life became the basis of the opera *The Ballad of Baby Doe*), made Denver's stunning Opera House available to the campaign. To encourage working-class women to the cause and bring working-class men to vote yes on the state constitutional referendum for women's full voting rights, Leonora Barry Lake, the leading female organizer for the Knights of Labor, came to the state. Caribbean-born Elizabeth Piper Ensley organized the small African American community. Carrie Chapman Catt toured much of the state, leaving local leagues behind to do the work. Her two months in Colorado established her organizing skills and instincts and reputation as the movement's sharpest strategist. She was increasingly regarded as Anthony's likely successor to head the national suffrage movement.

Colorado suffragists used what funds they

had to distribute massive amounts of pro-suffrage literature across the state. "Are you not interested in politics," one of their leaflets read, "when in spite of the strictest economy want creeps into the household, when the mother is forced to pinch and save and deny her children; when the self-supporting woman sees her wages reduced, and when on every side arises a long, low undertone of sorrow, the cry of the suffering poor? No matter how hardly economic conditions press upon men, except in the cases of a few favored ones they press harder on women. . . . Drop all other things from now till November 7 to work for suffrage," they urged. "Nothing else is so important."[13]

In the midst of the campaign, news came from Boston that Lucy Stone had died of a prolonged bout with stomach cancer. Even in her last months, she had weighed in on the Colorado campaign, introducing Catt to activists she knew from her 1877 trip there. Anthony seems not to have honored Stone's death — their antagonism surviving the unification of their two groups three years earlier — but Stone's passing was a signal that the pioneering generation, which had held on so long, would not be able to direct the movement much longer. Meredith wrote that in the midst of their hard work, Colorado suffragists felt "regret and sorrow" that Stone would not be there to see what they hoped would be their victory.[14]

Indeed, equal suffrage, women's enfranchisement, won in Colorado and won strongly. Suffragists' political sophistication was growing. They put poll watchers to guard against election fraud in Denver, Colorado Springs, and other cities. Labor unions did a great deal of door-to-door canvassing in the mining districts. (A hostile Colorado Springs newspaper suggested that miners had voted for woman suffrage because they wanted to attract women from the East to marry them.[15]) Opponents, especially the liquor dealers who were lulled into overconfidence by suffragists' decade of inactivity, did not mobilize until it was too late. The measure won 60 percent of the vote. Next door, Wyoming women were already voting in all elections, including federal, because the new state legislature had acted to protect the rights women had enjoyed as territorial citizens. Colorado, however, was a first because a majority of male voters had supported a state constitutional amendment for woman suffrage. "I can't yet believe it is true — it is too good

Colorado women voting, 1907.

to be true!" Anthony wrote to Ellis Meredith. "How glad I am that at least we have knocked down our first State by the popular vote!! — it fills us with hope that we may knock down No. 2 & No. 3."[16]

The next November, when the polls opened, the lines were long, and half of those waiting were women. They filed into the polling places early in the morning to make sure their votes were recorded. Elizabeth Piper Ensley described the African American women, who "stepped forth . . . with enthusiasm unbounded, to exercise for the first time the crowning act of citizenship." Most of them energetically voted for "the ticket strait" of the Republican Party.[17] Nor were they alone. Republicans organized energetically among women, and when the Populists lost control of the state, women reaped much of the blame for their defeat.

Ensley went on to be the foremost organizer of Colorado's African American women, helping them to form a Republican Women's Association and a state Colored Women's Federation. She died in 1919, aged sixty-two, having voted, presumably always for the Republican candidates for president and Congress, for a quarter of a century.

The 1893 suffrage campaign also set Ellis Meredith on a lifelong political path. For years, she testified about the beneficial aspects of enfranchisement for both Colorado women and the state itself. At the 1904 national suffrage meetings, she caught the attention of her audience when she disavowed the idea that woman suffrage was a "divine, far off event toward which the whole creation moves." Rather, she made a more pragmatic case. "To my mind, [the ballot] is simply one of our many modern labor-saving devices. . . . In the ten years that women have been voting in Colorado, I believe they have done at least five times as much as all the rest of the non-voting women in the United States together."[18] By the time the suffrage movement drew to a close in 1920, she was working from within the Democratic Party to win support for a federal constitutional amendment.

■ ■ ■ ■

Through the 1880s, the numbers of women involved in the suffrage movement had expanded significantly. The WCTU had spread suffrage sentiment among women, but at the cost of generating a determined opposition built on men's anxiety that women would vote against their right to drink alcohol. In the 1890s, the new challenge facing suffragists was to cultivate men's support. "All goes well — so far as the *women go*!!" Anthony observed in 1894, "but how are we to get at the *men*?"[19] The liquor industry was proving itself increasingly successful at convincing men that woman suffrage meant the prohibition of alcohol, especially, many suffragists believed, immigrant men.

In the three years after the Colorado victory, state constitutional suffrage referenda went before the voters of three states, winning only in lightly populated Idaho. More important campaigns were held in Kansas and California, which, despite enormous effort, were lost. The 1894 campaign in Kansas was personal for Anthony, who regarded the state as a second home. That election was largely a battle between Republican regulars and Populist insurgents. At first, when Republicans dismissed woman suffrage, Populist suffragists got their party to endorse a woman suffrage amendment to the state constitution. Anthony broke her lifelong commitment to the Republican Party and promised to stump for the Populists. "I have been like a drowning man for a long time," Anthony exulted. "And have been waiting for someone to throw a plank to me."[20]

However, when Republicans won the election by promising to "redeem" Kansas from Populist radicalism, the suffrage amendment went down to defeat. In Carrie Chapman Catt's angry analysis, strong pro-suffrage sentiment had been done in by political leaders' "jealousy and suspicion." Years later she still regarded the Kansas defeat as "the bitterest in the whole history of the movement, for they were sold out by their friends for a wholly imaginary political advantage."[21]

Next and last came the 1896 California campaign, a promising, challenging, and ultimately crushing loss. In the winter of 1895, two veteran suffragist lawyers, Laura de Force Gordon and Clara Foltz, succeeded in getting the state legislature to authorize a referendum to add woman suffrage to the state constitution for the next year. The state was already a political prize: its economy was strong, the population was booming, and the women of the state were well organized in a large network of women's clubs. In 1895 and 1896 clubwoman Sarah Cooper organized two grand "Women's Congresses" patterned on the 1893 Chicago World's Congress of Representative Women.

The WCTU was strong in the more rural parts of the state. It was planning a national convention in California in 1896, but after a direct appeal from Anthony, who was fearful of a backlash against suffrage, Frances Willard graciously agreed to relocate, leaving the California suffrage field untrammeled by an overt connection to prohibition. Suffrage loyalists were also active in the more radical end of the political spectrum, not only among the Populists but socialists as well. As in Colorado, a dedicated organizer worked among African American voters.

Against the advice of her friends and family, Anthony journeyed twice to California for the campaign. Now age seventy-five, she took a rare personal break to explore the Yosemite Valley. Returning to the campaign, she spent most of her time living in the San

Francisco home of Ellen Sargent, widow of California's first senator. With a touch of the old abolitionist faith, Anthony spoke at San Francisco's American Methodist Episcopal Zion Church: "The black man has proved his ability to make a right use of the elective privilege. Can we believe that woman, black or white, is inferior to the negro, only recently let loose from slavery?"[22] Five weeks before the election, she traveled across San Francisco Bay to Sausalito, "where I spoke in a pool-room." She was truly ready to meet men wherever they were. "The gamblers . . . printed [an announcement of our talk] in red and white chalk on a great blackboard on which they keep the tally of the games."[23]

Forty-nine-year-old Anna Howard Shaw was now Anthony's constant companion. Shaw, like her mentor a lifelong unmarried and self-supporting woman, had come from a more impoverished background than virtually any other major suffrage leader. At age four, she immigrated from England with her family to the factory town of Lawrence, Massachusetts. After eight years, her father, an improvident man prone to thoughtless decisions that usually imperiled his family, bought fallow land in the wilds of Michigan and sent his wife and young children there while he stayed back east to earn wages. His family barely survived the first year.

Through these experiences, Shaw grew up to be a self-sufficient, resolute young woman, determined to gain an education, no matter what it took, which was a great deal. She gave up her early habits of wearing pants and short hair to assume a more modest style that drew less undue attention. After years of defying her family, working in any job she could find, she received church support to attend Albion College, a small Methodist institution in Ohio. Shaw went on to a series of dazzling professional achievements, securing two advanced degrees, first as a Methodist minister and then as a physician.

Shaw's commitment to female autonomy, her determination, and her affection and attachment to women made her a natural suffragist. She became one of the movement's great orators and was eventually able to earn $4,000 per year. She was said to be able to convert an entire legislature with a single speech. "When I plan a speech I decide how many points I wish to make and what those points will be," she explained of her method. "I always make my points on my fingers and have my fingers named for points."[24] She began her suffrage tutelage under Frances Willard in the WCTU, then moved on to work with Lucy Stone and Henry Blackwell in AWSA. Finally, in 1887, she met Anthony, to whom she became devoted, remaining so for the final twenty years of Anthony's life. Shaw was comfortably situated to rise in the ranks when the two suffrage associations united in 1890.

Anthony assigned Shaw to be NAWSA's point woman for the 1896 California constitutional amendment campaign, the first time she had been given such a leadership role. She traveled back and forth across the state, using a railroad pass from Jane Stanford, widow of the president of the Southern Pacific Railroad, to give a lecture at least every day. Initially the political situation looked very good. State Republican and Populist parties passed pro-suffrage planks with virtually no opposition.

The only holdout was the Democratic Party. The small suffrage contingent sat for "two long hot days" through the party's June convention, only to become "very, very wrathy" as they watched their issue about to be dismissed with no discussion. Then, Anthony rose and rebuked the convention. Shaw followed her. "The little fighter was at the boiling point but with that sarcasm of which she is a complete master," reported

Ida Husted Harper, the movement's historian. She brought the convention to its feet to demand a reconsideration.[25] Although the suffrage plank was defeated, suffragists were proud of forcing the Democrats at least to reconsider. Later, although the majority of Democrats voted against the referendum, a larger than expected Democratic pro-suffrage vote was tallied, and the suffragists felt that their bold challenge had reaped unanticipated rewards.

The year of the California referendum, 1896, was not only a presidential election year but one with exceptionally high stakes, which reminded the parties that enfranchising women would bring them into federal elections. Would the Populist Party continue its impressive rise to bring down the Grand Old Party, as the Republicans had done to the Whigs forty years before? The national Republican Party defensively passed a plank that welcomed women's "cooperation" but only inasmuch as it would help to rescue "the country from Democratic mismanagement and Populist misrule." "Women want the suffrage as a sword to smite down Democratic and Populist misrule!" Anthony raged. "Infamous!"[26] Suffragists had been promised they could speak at California Republican rallies, but when the time came, they were told that they would bring "too many bonnets at their meetings" and not enough voters, and they were kept off the platform.[27]

Then the bottom dropped out of the political situation. In a final desperate move to counter the Republicans' no-holds-barred, well-funded campaign, Populists fused with the Democrats, a move that effectively nullified the new party's pro-suffrage position. Woman suffrage as an issue was jettisoned. "We were sold out," raged one temperance suffragist. "That is the truth of the matter."[28] Alerted by the Colorado victory to the growing strength of the suffrage ranks, the liquor-based opposition had fully mobilized. It issued a letter to San Francisco saloon operators ten days before the election urging them to get their patrons out to vote against the referendum.

The California constitutional amendment was defeated by a margin of 55 to 45 percent. Despite the unrelenting opposition of the conservative *Los Angeles Times,* Los Angeles voters supported suffrage, but it was not enough to offset the vote in Northern California. Almost the entire 27,000-vote margin against the referendum could be credited to San Francisco and Alameda counties. Still it seemed like the wealthier neighborhoods, standing behind the Republican anti-Populist crusade, returned more votes against the suffrage referendum than the immigrant Democratic districts, which suffragists had expected would be responsible for their defeat.

The night of the election, in the company of Ellen Sargent and in the darkness of night, Anthony "went down the street, peering into the windows of the rough little booths where the judges and clerks of the election were counting votes." "The rooms were black with tobacco smoke and in one they saw a man fall off his chair too drunk to finish the count," Anthony's official biographer wrote. "They listened to the oaths and jeers as the votes were announced against the suffrage amendment, to which they had given almost their lives. Then in the darkness they crept silently home, mournfully realizing that women must wait for another and better generation of men to give them the longed-for freedom."[29]

A month after the election defeat, Anna Howard Shaw, back in Boston, learned that her friend Harriet Cooper, daughter of San Francisco clubwoman and suffragist Sarah Cooper, had been found dead by asphyxiation alongside her mother. The police ruled it a murder/suicide. Harriet had long suf-

Ida B. Wells, 1893.

fered from serious depression, and her father had killed himself. Sarah's death was an especially grievous loss to the California movement. The California press covered the deaths, but only one suffrage newspaper connected the deaths to the referendum. Those dealing with the "taint of insanity," it noted, should probably avoid the intense pressure and overwork of a suffrage campaign.[30]

After California and for the next fourteen

years, there were only three state constitutional suffrage referenda, all in Oregon, all defeated handily.

Several months after Ellis Meredith met with Susan B. Anthony, Ida B. Wells also came to the Columbian Exposition. Wells was a New Woman, African American style. She had been born to slave parents in Mississippi just six months before the Emancipation Proclamation. When her parents died in the yellow fever epidemic of 1878, she became the guardian for her five younger siblings. To support her family, she taught in segregated schools until, like Susan B. Anthony, she could no longer stand the conservative standards imposed on women teachers. She moved to Memphis, where she became a journalist and developed a powerful, direct style well suited to her bold political opinions. Eventually she became part owner of a small black newspaper, the *Memphis Free Speech and Headlight.* She was a petite, handsome woman and had an active social life, searching the Memphis African American community for a husband who appreciated her ambitions and shared her activist commitments.

Wells had come to Chicago to protest the absence of her people from any formal recognition at the Columbian Exposition. Local groups of African American women had been fighting since 1891 for representation on the all-white board of lady managers, but to no success. Several African American women, led by Chicago clubwoman Fannie Barrier Williams, had been included in the World's Congress of Representative Women, but elsewhere they were largely absent.

The freedpeople's tremendous achievements in less than three decades since emancipation should have been highlighted as testimony to the power of American democracy and the progress of the century, but instead they were ignored. Together with seventy-five-year-old Frederick Douglass, who had become her mentor, Wells — who always took her people's protest to the next step — published a scathing ninety-six-page pamphlet entitled *The Reason Why the Colored American Is Not in the World's Columbian Exposition.*

Though slavery is gone, "its asserted spirit remains," wrote Douglass. Now "a new determination is born to keep [the former slave] down."[31] Never fully safe or free, African American lives, especially in the South, were under new and drastic threats. Southern white Democrats were determined to recapture state governments from "Black Republicans," meaning both the party and the race. Through the 1890s, state after southern state enacted laws effectively shutting out black male voters. These state governments proceeded to legalize segregation in every facet of social life through the infamous "Jim Crow" laws. Once again, as in antebellum times, the substantial power of the South in national politics was in the hands of committed white supremacists.

Douglass and Wells especially focused on the illegal, violent side of this attack on black rights, the murderous assaults on African Americans that went completely unpunished. "In the time of slavery if a Negro was killed, the owner sustained a loss of property," Douglass, who knew of what he wrote, explained. "Now he is not restrained by any fear of such loss."[32] It was Wells's job to document "Lynch Law," the epidemic of extrajudicial punishment against African Americans for alleged crimes. "Over a thousand black men, women and children have been thus sacrificed the past ten years," she wrote. "Masks have long since been thrown aside and the lynchings of the present day take place in broad daylight."[33] She described bodies hanged, burned, and mutilated. These crimes are memorialized more than a century later in the widely circulated photographs of smiling white mobs in front of black victims' bodies. Civilized America did not want to face these details, and certainly not from the pen of an African American woman from the South.

Wells's anti-lynching campaign had begun the year before when three black friends were murdered by a white Memphis mob for daring to build a successful grocery business. She investigated this and other lynchings, especially disproving the scurrilous, spurious claim — of black men's sexual attacks on white women — by which these assaults were justified. She countered with a daring assertion that went over the ultimate line of racial division. Black men and white women, she boldly suggested, were engaged in voluntary sexual relations, which the society refused to admit and so recast as rape. She published her findings, emphasizing that lynchings were the result not of black crimes, but of white resentment and jealousy at black political and economic achievements. In retaliation, Wells's press was burned to the ground and she was forced to flee Memphis.

In 1893, when Wells went to the Columbian Exposition, she had just finished a successful tour of England. There she got the audience and support for her anti-lynching crusade that she could not find from white America. Returning a second time to England, Wells came into political conflict with Frances Willard, who was also living in England with her new partner, Lady Henry Somerset. The American racial atmosphere had worsened precipitously since Willard had cautiously opened the WCTU to southern freedwomen. Now Willard's mild condemnation of the violence of lynching was undermined when she publicly accepted the claim that the liquor-filled sexual rapacity of black men was its cause. "Great dark faced mobs whose rallying cry is better whisky and more of it," she insisted, were guilty of the crimes with which lynch mobs charged them.[34] Wells determined not to let these slanders stand. "The fact is, Miss Willard is no better or worse than the great bulk of white Americans on the Negro question," Wells daringly wrote. "They are all afraid to speak out."[35] Wells's British supporters sided with her, but back in the United States, the fight with Willard lost Wells sympathy, even among some African American leaders.

Wells's bold antilynching campaign was a crucial factor in laying the basis for an independent African American women's rights movement. Black women in Brooklyn organized a major speaking and fundraising event for Wells in 1892, which they followed up by organizing the Women's Loyal League. Supporters in Boston similarly formed the New Era Club to support Wells's antilynching work. Wells herself formed a group in Chicago, the eponymous Ida B. Wells Club, later to be renamed the Alpha Suffrage Club. This coming together for collective action represented a major advance beyond what Mary Ann Shadd Cary and Frances Ellen Watkins Harper had tried to do decades before, when as lone individuals they had challenged American sexism and racism, unshielded by a larger movement from accusations that they were violating sexual norms and defying racial deference.

In 1896, these and many other clubs came together as the National Association of Colored Women (NACW). This first national organization of African American women and the hundreds of clubs that made it up provided a fertile ground for breaking through the racist barriers confining suffrage support to white women. The gradual spread of African American women's suffragism over the next two decades, sheltered within these all-black organizations, was all the more remarkable given that it took place during the worst years of Jim Crow racism. African American women's collective public activism arrived just as the final stage of southern black men's disfranchisement was being effectuated. Anna Julia Cooper, the eloquent Washington, D.C., suffragist, put their determination to take up the political cudgel and defend, not just their sex but also their race, this way: "Only the BLACK WOMAN can say, 'when and where I enter, in the quiet undisputed dignity of my womanhood, without violence and without suing or special patronage, then and there *the whole Negro race enters with me.*' "[36]

Mary Church Terrell became the first president of the NACW. Like Wells, she grew up a child of slave parents in Memphis, but there the similarity ended. Terrell's father, who made his money in real estate, became African America's first millionaire, and his daughter enjoyed the best possible schooling available to young women, race notwithstanding. Her culture, her education (she spoke three languages fluently), and — it must be acknowledged — her light skin made her one of the handful of women of her race to be accepted by white suffragists.

Nonetheless, Terrell always used her position to draw attention to the condition — and the capacities — of African American women. Addressing NAWSA in 1898, she made it clear that "not only because they are women, but because they are colored women, are discouragement and disappointment meeting them at every turn" and yet "the progress made by colored women . . . has never been surpassed by that of any people in the history of the world."[37] Where Wells provoked, Terrell conciliated, but the two were equally devoted to political rights for their sex and equality for their race. Together they made an incalculable contribution to the political possibilities of organized African American women at the turn of the century.

In 1895, Ida B. Wells moved to Chicago as part of the growing stream of blacks fleeing north to escape southern violence. Now in her mid-thirties, she finally found the partner she had been searching for when she married widower Ferdinand Barnett, one of the leaders of the city's black community, a journalist and lawyer with strong Republican ties. Among the first prominent women in the country known to have hyphenated her name, she continued her political work as Ida B. Wells-Barnett. She continued her travels and speaking while still nursing her first-born child, but she could not keep this up after the second (of an eventual four). She confessed her decision to retire temporarily to Susan B. Anthony, who disapproved of talented women sacrificing their careers to motherhood. "I could not tell Miss Anthony that it was because I had been unable, like herself, to get the support which was necessary to carry on my work," she recalled with shame, "that I had become discouraged in the effort to carry on alone."[38] Unlike Elizabeth Cady Stanton, Wells-Barnett had no Susan B. Anthony to help her through her years of motherhood.

Nor was the political situation for outspoken African American women improving. After Frederick Douglass's death in 1895, southern educator Booker T. Washington assumed the position of the race's leading spokesman. Had it not been for her gender, Wells-Barnett might have taken Douglass's place and been able to mount a worthy challenge to Washington's conservative leadership. Washington advocated gradual educational and industrial advancement and advised against any direct challenge to the mounting forces of white supremacy. He counseled accepting the disfranchisement of southern men and thus was no friend of expanding black suffrage to women. Wells-Barnett would have none of it. "Mr. Washington's theory [is] that we ought not to spend our time agitating for our rights; that we had better give attention to trying to be first-class people in a jim crow car than insisting that the jim crow car should be abolished. . . . Of course, fighting for political rights [has] no place whatsoever in his plans."[39] Opposition to Washington, who controlled whatever Republican patronage came his people's way, cost Wells-Barnett and her husband dearly.

Still, from the beginning of her life in Chicago, Wells-Barnett was an advocate of political power and influence for African American women. Unlike the South, where black disfranchisement was a settled fact, Chicago was one of the northern cities where the Republican Party was strong and somewhat willing to extend protection to its black partisans. Like a few other states, Illinois had attempted to appease women's demands for full voting rights by granting them partial suffrages, the most common of which was "school suffrage," the right to vote for elected education officers. In 1894, Illinois women attempted to use their "school suffrage" to elect a woman to the board of trustees of the state university.

Lucy Flower, a white Republican candidate for trustee, reached out to African American women voters, with a promise to secure them college scholarships if they helped her. Wells-Barnett, who like most African Americans was a solid Republican, became one of the leaders of this campaign. She was invited to join the Illinois Women's Republican Educational Committee. Flower won her seat, and Wells-Barnett went on to campaign among African American men in Chicago on behalf of William McKinley for president in 1896. She also worked — selectively — with white Chicago women reformers who met her standards for racial ethics.

Wells-Barnett's suffragism can be obscured by her antilynching work, but the two were intimately connected. African American leaders had never given up on protecting enfranchisement for men and expanding it to women at the national constitutional level. Southern state opposition did not allow them that option. Moreover, while the "lynch law" Wells-Barnett fought was not really law, an episode during her time in Illinois showed how it could become a matter for electoral politics and an argument for the female franchise. In

298

1908, in the aftermath of a deadly race riot in the state capital of Springfield, an African American state legislator was able to get an "anti-mob" bill passed, which made local law enforcement responsible for mob violence.

The next year, in the southern part of the state, an African American homeless man was brutally tortured and murdered for the death of a white woman, with which he was not involved. After he was hung from an electric pole, Wells-Barnett wrote, "five hundred bullets were fired" into the dead man's body, and the mob, including "women pushing baby carriages, . . . burned it to a crisp."[40] As the relentless detail of her description indicates, Wells-Barnett's standard tactics were to use her words to generate moral outrage. However, this time she also had Illinois law on her side. She organized the local black population to petition the governor, a Republican who understood that black votes were important to his party, to apply the anti-mob law and dismiss the sheriff. "That was in 1909, and from that day until the present there has been no lynching in the state," she proudly concluded in a 1910 article.[41]

In that article, entitled "How Enfranchisement Stops Lynchings," Wells-Barnett described this episode and the power of law duly enforced. "Having successfully swept aside the constitutional safeguards to the ballot," she observed, "it is the smallest of small matters for the South to sweep aside its own safeguards to human life." The vote in African American hands could do a great deal to ensure decent schools, equal law enforcement, and ultimately black lives themselves. But it was not just the utility of the ballot that moved her. It was its transcendent meaning. "The enfranchisement of all manhood" along with the abolition of slavery represented, for her, "the flower of the nineteenth century civilization for the American people."[42] Black men's right to vote must be defended, and it must be extended to black women. Over the next decade, Wells-Barnett continued her work in Chicago and waited for the right moment to bring these convictions and black women's aspirations for political rights onto the national stage.

The growth in African American suffragism at the turn of the century coincided with and may have been the reason for NAWSA's decision to undertake an explicitly racist policy. An occasional exceptional woman like Terrell might be accommodated, but not entire African American clubs and federations. After Reconstruction, the mainstream suffrage movement had veered away from its historic connection to black rights. As the nation's racial politics descended, so did those of leading white suffragists. Recognizing that constitutional suffrage could never be won without the support of the white politicians who controlled the South, they embarked on a campaign to cultivate an exclusively white suffrage movement there. This meant absorbing into the national movement the region's increasingly openly white supremacist politics.

Laura Clay of Kentucky first advanced these ideas in the 1890s. She was the daughter of Kentucky Unionist Cassius Clay and a distant cousin of Henry Clay, author of the Compromise of 1850. Her attitude toward black people is extremely distasteful to the modern ear, but in the late nineteenth-century southern context, she was a racial moderate. Southern states disfranchising black men was to Clay an opportunity for woman suffrage. Her argument was that coupling woman suffrage with a literacy qualification like hers would favor white women and depress black women's enfranchisement. Clay argued that her approach was a far more civilized way to undo constitutional protections of black men's right to vote than lynching, and it would be legally more defensible than fraudulent voting rules directed against black voters.

Clay's "southern strategy" was not solely a regional product. Indeed, it had its roots in an argument put forward by Lucy Stone's husband, Henry Blackwell, as far back as 1867, when the suffrage movement was still committed to universal suffrage. Blackwell was as much an abolitionist as any other suffragist of his generation. However, his relentless political pragmatism led him to urge southern states still fighting Reconstruction to recognize that "four millions of Southern white women will counterbalance your four millions of negro men and women, and thus the political supremacy of your white race will remain unchanged."[43]

Now, three decades later, Laura Clay's strategy coincided with the recent "educated suffrage" arguments of Elizabeth Cady Stanton. After the 1894 defeat of a campaign to get woman suffrage into the New York State constitution, Cady Stanton's elitist tendencies once again took over, and she denounced immigrant voters, whom she blamed for the loss. In one of her last forays into suffrage policy, she championed literacy qualifications for woman suffrage. Such limitations would not only meet the needs of white southerners but of nativist northerners too. "With the ignorant and impecunious from the Old World landing on our shores by hundreds every day, we must have some restrictions of the suffrage for our own safety and for their education."[44] Her own daughter, Harriot Stanton Blatch, now a socialist, publicly disagreed. "Every workingman needs the suffrage more than I do," she responded, "but there is another who needs it more . . . and that is the working woman."[45]

The "southern strategy" was a more difficult move for Susan B. Anthony. Her longstanding sympathies with African Americans held her back, as did her abolitionist reputation across the South. "I have longed to go South for *thirty years*," she wrote to Clay, "— and never could go — because I knew of no one to welcome me."[46] Now a new generation of national leaders who shared none of her convictions or compunctions responded enthusiastically to the idea of a campaign to recruit southern white women and bind North and South together in suffrage reconciliation. They absorbed the narrative that the Fifteenth Amendment had betrayed woman suffrage, but without knowledge of the prior history of abolitionist/women's rights collaboration. Carrie Chapman Catt was one of them, and in 1895, Anthony toured the South with her.

The organizing tour ended in Atlanta, where NAWSA was to hold its first convention outside of Washington, D.C. The night before, Anthony spoke at Bethel African Methodist Episcopal Church, before an audience of a thousand African Americans, "some *whiter* than me."[47] The next day, at the NAWSA convention, Catt struck a far less inclusive note. "There is a race problem everywhere. In the North and the West, it is the problem of the illiterate immigrant; in the South it is the problem of the illiterate negro," she explained. "The solution of the race problem is the same everywhere, the enfranchisement of women with an educational qualification."[48]

Returning home to Rochester from the Atlanta convention, Anthony met several times with Ida B. Wells-Barnett, from whom she seemed to need some sort of absolution. She confessed that she had earlier asked her old friend Frederick Douglass not to attend lest his presence offend southern whites. The 1869 conflict over the Fifteenth Amendment notwithstanding, Douglass had been a steadfast supporter of woman suffrage. In an impassioned speech delivered in 1888 at a Washington, D.C., gathering of international suffragists, he declared that when "a great truth" like women's equality "once gets abroad in the world, no power on earth can imprison it or prescribe its limits or suppress it."[49]

Just weeks after the Atlanta conference, Douglass had died, no doubt intensifying Anthony's guilt. "I did not want to subject him to humiliation," she explained, "and I did not want anything to get in the way of bringing the southern white women into our suffrage association." Was she wrong to do that? she asked. Yes, she was, Wells-Barnett answered, for "although she may have made gains for suffrage, she also confirmed white women in their attitude of segregation."[50]

The second author of suffragists' turn-of-the-century "southern strategy" was Kate Gordon, a fierce suffragist from New Orleans. Unlike Kentucky, Louisiana had a majority black population, and Gordon was a much more uncompromising white supremacist than Clay. "The question of white supremacy," Gordon declared, "is one that will only be decided by giving the right of the ballot to the educated intelligent white women of the South."[51] She guided the Louisiana legislature to enact a partial suf-

NAWSA officers in 1900: Shaw, Anthony, and Catt standing in front.

frage for women on issues involving taxes, one of the few breaches in the solid southern wall of hostility to women's votes. Gordon's day in the sun was the 1903 NAWSA convention, held in New Orleans. This time, African American women were explicitly prohibited from attending, though Alabaman Adella Hunt Logan, light-skinned enough to pass, infiltrated the meeting.[52]

The New Orleans convention formally agreed to a "states' rights" policy, by which each state affiliate was allowed to set its own terms for membership and its own legislative strategies, no matter how racially exclusive. This time, support was voiced by

306

Anna Howard Shaw, now NAWSA vice president. Bringing her best oratorical power to bear, Shaw endorsed the attack on black men's enfranchisement. "Never before in the history of the world," she insisted, "have men made former slaves the political masters of their former mistresses."[53] A letter published in the New Orleans press and signed by Shaw and Anthony clarified that the national suffrage association allows "each auxiliary State association [to arrange] its own affairs in accordance with its own ideas and in harmony with the customs of its own section."[54]

Eventually, enthusiasm for the "southern strategy" at the national suffrage level began to wane. The calculation that it would provide new hope for national suffrage was not only morally bankrupt; it was strategically ineffective. Other than Louisiana's female taxpayer franchise, southern states provided no openings for woman suffrage. Southern white male political leaders, their sexism almost as obdurate as their racism, remained unmoved by the argument that white women could save them from black power. Soon it became clear they had no need for white women's votes. In its 1896 *Plessy v. Ferguson* decision, the U.S. Supreme Court put the cap on its readiness to roll back black people's rights and accede to the Jim Crow regime of segregation and disfranchisement. As other strategic avenues for suffragism began to surface, the "southern strategy" went latent. It would reemerge a decade later, when national suffrage politics began to open up once again to a constitutional amendment and southern politicians' fear of black women's enfranchisement.

White working-class women had been almost as invisible in the formal structures of the 1893 Columbian Exposition as African American women. Among the very few exceptions was an evening panel on "Trade Unions and Women" at the World's Congress of Representative Women. The three speakers were Susan B. Anthony and two women named Mary Kenney and Florence Kelley. Superficially an unlikely pair, Kelley and Kenney would go on to play major roles in the next decade in opening the door to the suffrage movement to white wage-earning women.

When Mary Kenney stepped forward and began to speak about "Organization of Working Women," her leisure-class audience probably imagined she was talking about working girls' social clubs. Kenney made it clear she meant trade unions, and that these were the key to workingwomen's betterment. Like the handful of other women labor organizers before her, Kenney understood the enormous challenge of the enterprise. "To say that it is difficult to organize women is not saying the half," she explained. The deepest problem was not exploitation by employers or hostility from male workers. It was that women in the labor force saw themselves as only temporary visitors in the world of work, waiting to be saved by marriage and the dream of a kind husband to support them. "The only protection they expect is protection given them by men," she insisted, "not realizing that it is their duty to protect themselves."[55]

Mary Kenney was a twenty-nine-year-old Irish American bookbinder who had moved to Chicago from Iowa. "Tall, erect, broad-shouldered, with ruddy face and shining eyes," as Florence Kelley described her, "she carried hope and confidence whithersoever she went."[56] Kenney was already an important figure among Chicago trade unionists for her brilliant work organizing wage-earning women. After succeeding in unionizing the women of her own trade, the bookbinders, she formed unions among women cloak-makers and retail clerks and even male cabdrivers. She came to the attention of Samuel Gompers, president of the American Federation of Labor, in 1890, when she submitted a resolution putting organized labor on record in favor of woman suffrage. In 1892, Gompers appointed her a special organizer of workingwomen, the first such appointment in the history of the labor federation. After six months, however, the appointment was not renewed. At the 1893 Chicago Fair she came before a group of leisure-class women in search of alternative support for organizing women workers.

Florence Kelley, five years older than Kenney, could not have been more different in her origins, though not, as it turned out, in her passions. She was the daughter of William Kelley, a champion of black rights during Reconstruction and a congressman from Philadelphia for three decades. After graduating from Cornell, Florence Kelley went to Switzerland to get the postgraduate education unavailable to women in her own country. There she became an avid socialist, married a Russian comrade, and translated several of the major works of Karl Marx and Friedrich Engels into English. In 1886, she returned to the United States determined to find a way to pursue what she now knew was her life's work, to fight on behalf of wage-earning women.

Kelley's links to Anthony and to the woman suffrage movement went far back. Her great-aunt Sarah Pugh was an intimate friend of Lucretia Mott and Elizabeth Cady Stanton. "I wish profoundly for the franchise for every woman in America," twenty-five-year-old Kelley wrote in 1884 to Anthony, but "I am far from able to write eloquently . . . about it." Rather, she explained, "I shall give myself to work for the best interests of the working women of America."[57] Though her life's work would not be woman suffrage, neither was it unrelated. Kelley believed that industrial reform was going to be dependent on "the slowly growing power of women as citizens." "Little did we foresee," she later reflected, "that women in the United States would not everywhere have suffrage" for years to come.[58]

Kelley and Kenney were already working together by the time of the Columbian Exposition. They had met about a year and a half before at Hull House, the pioneering settlement house that was the center of women's reform activities in Chicago. Jane Addams, another daughter of a first-generation Republican congressman, had established Hull House in 1889. Deter-

311

mined to find a way to live and work as an unmarried leisure-class woman, she moved into a once-fine mansion in a dense immigrant neighborhood in order to connect with poor families who were her neighbors. Others joined her, and Hull House became a center for New Women with ambitions to help deal with Chicago's multitude of social and economic troubles.

Jane Addams realized that while the nation's booming economic growth may have made for greater wealth, it had put America's democratic heritage at great peril. The threat to democracy that she felt most strongly was not so much political or even economic, but social and ethical. She wanted to remedy the lack of meaningful connection across the great gulf of economic inequality and the ignorance among well-to-do women like herself of the lives lived by the masses. Under her direction, Hull House veered away from leisured women's traditions of charity work to become a genuine bridge between rich and poor. Its goal, Addams wrote, was "to make social intercourse express the growing sense of the economic unity of society and to add the social function to democracy."[59] Efforts like this were under way in other big cities — New York, Philadelphia, Boston — but

Chicago's standing as the first city of America's industrial age made Hull House uniquely influential.

Mary Kenney came to Hull House sometime in early 1892. Addams later wrote of their meeting, "She came in rather a recalcitrant mood, expecting to be patronized."[60] "I had never heard of Miss Addams or Hull-House," Kenney recalled. She was already "class conscious" and told her mother, "No club people for me!" Then Addams, who knew about Kenney's organizing work, threw her off guard by asking her, "Is there anything I can do to help your organization?" "I couldn't believe I had heard right," recalled Kenney. She told Addams that she had looked with longing at the comfortable public rooms of Hull House. Her union women had been "meeting over a saloon on Clark Street and it is a dirty and noisy place, but we can't afford anything better." Addams offered her Hull House rooms to which she could bring groups of workers to organize. "When I saw there was someone who cared enough to help us and to help us in our way," she wrote, "it was like having a new world opened up."[61]

Addams invited Kenney and her mother to move into Hull House, but Kenney was uncomfortable among the leisure-class residents there. Instead, she proposed the establishment of separate apartments for wage-earning women. Addams agreed, and the "Jane Club," named in her honor, was established. Kenney used her skills and principles as an organizer in setting up the club. The residents ran everything, unlike "working girls' homes," where outside matrons conducted strict oversight. Even the housekeeper and cook were included in the cooperative meetings that managed club affairs. Within a year, thirty-five working-women were living there. A long newspaper article described the Jane Club in glowing terms. "Love of the club and regard for the public sentiment of its members have proved strong enough to keep all in harmony."[62]

Although Florence Kelley was of the same class and education and family background as Addams, her arrival at Hull House was considerably more freighted than Mary Kenney's. She arrived in the winter of 1891 late at night, a fugitive from an abusive marriage, with her three children in tow. Her Russian husband, who had moved with her to New York, had turned violent, beating her frequently. Servants and friends remembered seeing the bruises on her face each time he hit her. Fearful for herself and her children, Kelley moved into Hull House and found a place in a Chicago suburb to hide the children from their father. Four months later, she was in a Chicago court, fighting for and winning custody of her children, as newspapers around the country reported the sordid details of her marriage.

Addams not only gave Kelley safety; she provided her with an environment where she could do the work for which she had been preparing herself. Addams's empathy with the poor was profound, but there was a naiveté to it, as if no woman before her had ever recognized or sought to address class inequality. Kelley's pragmatic socialism and her unwavering focus on working-women changed that. She soon linked up Hull House with labor leaders and labor allies in an ambitious program to develop robust state protective laws to remedy the worst abuses workingwomen and children suffered. Labor reform brought woman suffrage involvement in its wake.

Kelley began working with Kenney to tackle Chicago's massive "sweatshop" sector, where one-third of the city's women workers cut and sewed clothes. The term "sweated work" meant labor that drove workers to the point of ill health and exhaustion. Working with the Chicago City Labor

Federation and others, the two women designed a model law to regulate sweatshops and then went to the state capital to lobby for it. Peter Altgeld, the state's reform governor, signed the Illinois Factory Act in 1893. When asked why she thought the legislature had passed such an ambitious labor law, Kelley responded that employers expected it would be "put on the books" and nothing would happen.[63] She was determined that this would not be the case, and when the governor asked her to serve as the state's chief factory inspector, she agreed. This was a position of major executive authority previously unmatched by any other woman in the state government. Kelley appointed Kenney one of her twelve deputy inspectors.

Just after the law was passed, in the late summer of 1893, the Columbian Exposition closed. "Alas for its ephemeral effect upon the community which produced it!" Kelley wrote. "When it vanished, Chicago was outwardly as though the Fair had never been."[64] The economic depression suffered by the rest of the nation now descended with full force on Chicago. The next summer, the workers at the Pullman Railroad Car factory on the outskirts of the city walked out in response to a drastic cut in their salaries, drawing most of the nation's railroad network to a halt. In Chicago, the cross-class bridge that Hull House had built all but collapsed. "The fact that [Hull House] maintained avenues for intercourse with both sides," wrote Addams, "seemed to give it opportunity for nothing but a realization of the bitterness and division along class lines."[65]

Political and judicial tolerance for industrial reform vanished. In 1895, the Illinois Supreme Court struck down the portion of the states Factory Inspection Law establishing a limit of eight hours a day labor for women. The court contended that among the Fourteenth Amendment's guarantees was an individual's right to contract, which was violated by any attempt by a labor union to establish limits for a group of workers on a day's work. As the daughter of one of the men who had crafted the Fourteenth Amendment, which she knew had been intended to increase the freedoms of former slaves, not the power of bosses, Kelley was enraged at this distortion of William Kelley's legacy to diminish the conditions of poor women workers. Then in 1897, Florence Kelley was fired as factory inspector.

The collapse of the laws overseeing sweatshop workers' hours showed female reformers and women workers that without their own political power they would never be able to force legislators, judges, and politicians to meet their demands and to hold them to their obligations. A decade later, Kelley reflected on the painful lesson she had learned in Chicago. For all the effort that she and others had put into "obtaining or promoting legislation on behalf of workingwomen, girls and children," little permanent improvement had been gained. "It has become [my] settled conviction . . . that, until women are universally admitted to the franchise, direct measures involve almost certain illusion and disappointment."[66] She was now committed to suffrage activism.

Mary Kenney and Florence Kelley both left Chicago. Kenney moved to Boston to marry trade unionist John O'Sullivan. Her first child was born in 1895, followed by two more. As she had told the young women she organized, marriage and motherhood did not solve workingwomen's problems. She continued organizing, connecting workingwomen with middle-class reformers and pressing women's demands at the American Federation of Labor.

After her bad marriage, Florence Kelley never remarried. In 1899, she left Chicago and moved to New York to take a well-paying job as executive secretary of the National Consumers' League. The league organized women consumers to use their buying power to improve working conditions for women workers in both manufacture and retail. It was not quite the direct working-class action that Kelley had once advocated, but it was effective. The National Consumers' League became a major force in redirecting middle-class women's reform energies toward support of wage-earning women.

From their different political and geographic locations, Kelley and Kenney together opened up the woman suffrage movement to the energy, perspectives, and needs of the enormous numbers of wage-earning women pouring into the U.S. labor force in the new century. Kelley could see that NAWSA had fallen into a deep torpor. "The whole movement suffers from belatedness," she wrote to her son. "The women of my generation had shirked their duty and left it in the hands of older pioneers, whose faces are turned to the past."[67] In 1898, she gave the first woman suffrage argument focused on workingwomen ever delivered in Congress. "No one needs all the powers of the fullest citizenship more urgently than the wage-earning woman," she argued. She needed the vote not only to raise her wages but also to assert "her wider needs as a human being and a member of the community."[68]

In 1903, NAWSA created a Committee on Industrial Work. Florence Kelley took it over and infused it with energy and urgency, bringing together her labor and suffrage work. Three years later she agreed to serve as NAWSA's vice president. Her task was nothing short of turning around the association's approach to the working class. Suffragists had long been talking about working-class men as foreign, ignorant, and manipulated by liquor interests to become suffrage's major electoral enemy. This was a profoundly losing political approach. Kelley argued that taking on the issues that motivated labor — she particularly pointed to passing laws to ban child labor — could win support from working-class male voters.[69] "I've enlisted for the war!" she again confided in her son.[70]

In Kelley's second year in the office, NAWSA held its annual convention in Chicago, and repeatedly emphasized the importance of drawing in "the industrial woman" and highlighting her political needs. In 1908, NAWSA met in Buffalo, another booming industrial city, at which the Sunday-afternoon meeting traditionally devoted to suffrage and religion was switched to an "industrial meeting." Kelley finally left her NAWSA office in 1911, at which point she felt her goal had been met.

Meanwhile, Mary Kenney O'Sullivan was laying the basis for working-class women to come forward from the other end of the bridge they were building between labor and suffrage. In 1903, she cofounded the all-important Women's Trade Union League (WTUL). O'Sullivan's lifelong goal was organizing working-class women to act on their own behalf on the bases both of their class consciousness and of their gender identity. The WTUL had the potential to combine the energies of the labor and women's movements, neither of which was sufficient alone, behind workingwomen's efforts to organize. By the end of its first decade, it had become the major recruiter for working-class women into the suffrage movement.

The WTUL was founded on a November evening at a Boston restaurant. The year before, O'Sullivan's husband had been killed in a streetcar accident. Despite the pressures of being a widow and single mother, she responded immediately when presented with the opportunity to form this

First national meeting of the Women's Trade Union League, 1907. Mary Kenney O'Sullivan is fourth from left.

new national organization. The proposal came from William English Walling, a wealthy young resident of the University Settlement House. The project would rely on wage-earning women recruits, male trade union leaders, and sympathetic leisure-class women drawn from the settlement house community. These women would be known as "allies," to designate that they intended to support the working-women's efforts, not supplant them.

Walling had learned about a similar organization formed thirty years earlier in Britain and decided to borrow its name, the

322

Women's Trade Union League. A wealthy and politically well-connected Boston reformer, Mary Kehew, was designated president, but O'Sullivan, as vice president, did the day-to-day organizing. Branches were formed in Chicago, Boston, and New York. O'Sullivan, Walling, and a handful of others sought to enroll wage-earning women interested in trade unionism who were willing to put energy into this visionary organization. The work proceeded slowly.

At its first national convention, the WTUL added full citizenship for women to its mission statement, and the next year formed a Suffrage Department. O'Sullivan herself began to appear at suffrage meetings and rallies in Massachusetts and New York. However, the continuing search for genuine labor federation support and for enough wage-earning members inclined to support suffrage put the issue on the back burner at WTUL. As an organizing leaflet prepared by the Chicago chapter put it, the ballot in the hands of the workingwoman will be "one of the most decisive devices by which she can command a hearing," although trade union organization was still the most immediate opportunity before her.[71]

Kelley's efforts inside NAWSA and O'Sullivan's in the WTUL began to come together at the 1906 NAWSA convention in Baltimore. The convention turned out to be Susan B. Anthony's last. Four years earlier Elizabeth Cady Stanton had died. "It seems impossible — that the voice is hushed that I have longed to hear for fifty years, . . ." Anthony wrote when she heard. "What a world it is — it goes right on & on — no matter who lives or dies!! . . . I can think of nothing."[72]

By 1906, Anthony, now eighty-six, was herself quite ill but insisted on attending the NAWSA convention. She was made comfortable in the elegant home of Mary Elizabeth Garrett, wealthy daughter of the president of the Baltimore and Ohio Railroad, and her life partner, M. Carey Thomas, founder and dean of Bryn Mawr College. Both were new to the movement, and among the very earliest wealthy women drawn to suffrage.

In Anthony's honor, Garrett and Thomas pledged the extraordinary amount of $60,000 to the suffrage cause. This was by far the largest donation yet made to the movement. "To you, Miss Anthony, belongs by right, as to no other woman in the world's history, the love and gratitude of all women in every country of the globe," Thomas declared. "We, your daughters in the spirit, rise up today and call you blessed."[73]

There was a kind of historical confluence here. Just as Anthony's decline meant the final passing of the founding generation, a new vision for the suffrage movement was coming into its own. Suspicion of Catholic and Jewish immigrants was beginning to give way to engagement. A Baltimore rabbi, Adolf Guttmacher, opened the proceedings. Throughout the 1906 convention, Florence Kelley repeatedly invoked "industrial issues," especially child labor, a horror which she insisted women's votes could do a great deal to end.[74] O'Sullivan also spoke, her topic being "The Duty of Women of Opportunity," urging Congress and the dominant political parties to support a woman suffrage constitutional amendment.[75]

The theme of industrial age suffragism was picked up by Gertrude Barnum, middle-class ally and official organizer for the WTUL. This wasn't a representative audience, she began, seeking to shake her listeners out of their habits of self-congratulation. They all knew they needed workingwomen to come out for suffrage, but where were they? Her answer: "We have been preaching to them, teaching them, 'rescuing' them, doing almost everything for them except knowing them and working with them for the good of our common country." To an audience who thought of workers as unlettered and narrow-minded, she described trade unions as schools for politics, preparation for suffrage itself. "These women of trade unions, who have already learned how to think and vote in them, would be a great addition, a great strength to this movement."[76]

After the convention ended, Kelley and O'Sullivan traveled the thirty miles to Washington, D.C., to testify before Congress. This was another first for O'Sullivan. Disfranchisement, she told the legislators, was one of the reasons the three million women for whom she spoke were underpaid and treated dismissively by their employers. Organized labor had done its part by endorsing woman suffrage. "I am asking you, in the name of the women I represent," she demanded of the congressmen, "at least to do for us what our working brothers are trying to do — give us our rights." Florence Kelley followed her. She reminded these men that her father, William Kelley, was a powerful congressman and a supporter of woman suffrage for decades. She would continue his campaign, follow his persistence. She and her comrades would persist as long as they must. "I assure you," she challenged them, "that I and the rest of the women throughout the country will come from generation to generation, just so long as necessary."[77]

The next day was Anthony's eighty-sixth birthday. "Ill from a severe cold," she was accompanied from Baltimore to Washington, D.C., by a nurse provided by Mary Garrett so that she could attend the celebrations planned in her honor. "She took very little part . . . except to smile and nod as things were said that pleased her," newspapers reported.[78] As one of her biographers wrote, she "was dying on her feet, dying as she lived, a stoic."[79]

Brought back to Rochester, she was no longer able to get out of bed. Her niece, Lucy Anthony, wrote to friends that — predictably — "it is the progress of the Cause that touches her most deeply every time."[80] Lucy's life partner, Anna Howard Shaw, who had taken over the NAWSA presidency two years before, solemnly agreed to the dying woman's request that she stay in the post "as long as [she was] well enough to do the work." Toward the end, Shaw recalled, Anthony roused herself just long enough "to utter the names of the women who had worked with her, as if in a roll-call."[81] Finally, on March 13, 1906, Anthony passed away. She had been in "a comatose state for two nights & a day," her nurse reported. "Dear old soul rather hated to die. She wanted to live to gain just one more victory."[82]

Six:
A POLITICAL CAUSE TO BE CARRIED POLITICALLY, 1907–1915

Even as Susan B. Anthony was on her deathbed in Rochester, a new era in suffrage politics was beginning four thousand miles away, in Great Britain. Emmeline Pankhurst and her daughters, Sylvia, Christabel, and Adela, formed the Women's Social and Political Union (WSPU). The WSPU was not polite, but obstreperous. It did not request, but "clamored." A reporter from the *Daily Mail* coined a new term to describe these impatient radicals: "suffragette."[1] The term spread amazingly quickly and widely — went viral, as we would say. "If you are not familiar with 'suffragette,' " a small-town Vermont newspaper predicted, "you will be sooner or later."[2] Something new and exciting was happening in Great Britain, and American suffragists were paying attention.

Anna Howard Shaw was determined to witness the suffrage upsurge in Great Britain. She was going to Europe for a meeting in Amsterdam of the International Woman Suffrage Alliance (IWSA). Formed and led by Carrie Chapman Catt, the IWSA reflected the vigorous growth of suffrage activism internationally. Full voting rights had already been won in New Zealand (1893), Australia (1902), Finland (1904), and Norway (1908), but worldwide attention was drawn to what was happening in Great Britain.

In London, Shaw arrived in June 1908 in time for a mass public demonstration for suffrage, estimated at fifteen thousand persons. Public demonstrations were just beginning in the United States, but they were tiny, at most a hundred, nothing compared to what was occurring in London. The marchers finished by crowding into Albert Hall; they were determined, by their numbers and their energy, to put to rest the claim that women did not want the vote. Shaw was invited to speak. "They tell us if we want to vote we must show them we do," she declared. "We are here to make the exhibit."[3]

Nebraskan Clara Bewick Colby, also in Europe for the IWSA meetings, participated in a second London demonstration one week later, which dwarfed the first. An estimated 50,000 suffragists, drawn from all over the country, and a crowd of perhaps 500,000, coming from seven different directions, overflowed Hyde Park, where twenty platforms and speakers delivered the case for national enfranchisement. The WSPU had organized this "monster demonstration" and designed it to "call upon the Government to give the vote to women without delay."[4] Soon British suffragettes had moved beyond mass parades to breaking store windows and other forms of civil disobedience, for which they were arrested and imprisoned. When the suffragettes went on hunger strikes in prison, the British government responded with a gruesome policy of forced feeding.

American suffragists, even those who were inspired by news of the British militants, were confident they would not need to go that far. One reason for their optimism was that just at the moment British suffragettes encountered obdurate parliamentary opposition, American politics were undergoing a promising new political development bubbling up from numerous states. Newspapers labeled it as "Progressivism." Progressivism was a big-tent politics ranging from moderate Republicans to socialists, from champions to opponents of racial equality. Its proponents shared a determination to upend legislative paralysis and government corruption wherever they found them, regardless of party loyalty. Rejecting the late-nineteenth-century "laissez faire" principle of legislative minimalism, Progressive reformers pursued a wide range of new state laws, designed both to ameliorate economic inequalities and to advance political democracy. Of these, the most relevant to women activists were limits to the working hours of wage-earning women, banning child labor, and — of course — enfranchising women. Without the Progressive Era revival of reform political possibilities, a constitutional amendment to enfranchise women would have remained much longer in the wasteland in which it had so long languished.

The first sign of the new possibilities that Progressivism brought to American suffragism was in the state of Washington. While still a territory, Washington had enfranchised its women, only to have this undone by territorial courts in 1888. Therefore, when Washington became a state in 1889, it had an exclusively male electorate. Twenty-two years later, a revived suffrage movement succeeded in restoring the right to vote to Washington State's women. In the midst of the campaign, a Seattle newspaper published a banner headline declaring "The Great World Sweep of the Woman Suffrage Movement."[5] The victory there was due to several things: support from "suffrage states" Idaho and Colorado; reforms to the election process pressed by Progressives; and involvement by organized labor. Mary Kenney O'Sullivan sent a message directly addressed to the state's working-class men. "When women organize and vote," she predicted, not only would women "get equal pay for equal work," but that they would no longer compete unfairly with men by undercutting their wages.[6]

The decade-and-a-half suffrage drought since securing full voting rights for women in Colorado and Idaho was over.

In 1910, fourteen years after their previous referendum defeat, California suffragists began to mobilize for a new campaign inspired by the Washington victory. In the first direct primary ever held in a California state election, voters elected reformers who took over the state Republican Party. The insurgents included the submission to voters of a woman suffrage amendment to the state constitution in their election platform. A referendum was scheduled for October

1911. "Suddenly, almost unexpectedly, . . . we found ourselves at the beginning of the shortest campaign any State has ever had to face," California activists realized. "Only eight months . . . to do propaganda work which many States had failed to do in two years!"[7]

The 1896 California defeat had made it clear that suffrage needed a vigorous initiative among workers in order to win enough voters to succeed. The woman who tackled this problem was Maud Younger, a wealthy San Franciscan. Like so many other New Women of her generation and her class, she was restless and in search of a more purposeful life. She moved to New York, worked in a settlement house, joined the Women's Trade Union League, and became a waitress. She got "to know the wage-earning woman and her problems far better than I had ever known anything else."[8] When she returned to San Francisco, she was both a determined suffragist and a devoted labor unionist. Her sobriquet was "the millionaire waitress." In 1908, she organized a Wage Earners Suffrage League, one of the earliest suffrage groups in the United States led by wage-earning women.

At first, the members of the California Wage Earners Suffrage League were uneasy about their relation with other suffrage groups. "You want to use [your votes] for someone else," Minna O'Donnell, a former printer and a labor journalist, told middle-class suffragists. We want the ballot "for self-protection." Our men "are with us heart and soul," she bragged; "your men simply smile."[9] By the spring of 1911, when the state suffrage referendum campaign began in earnest, the Wage Earners Suffrage League was ready to collaborate and was clear about its own goals, foremost among which was securing the votes of working-men. Labor federations officially supported suffrage, thanks in large part to the earlier work of Mary Kenney O'Sullivan, but motivating the rank and file of the unions to vote for woman suffrage remained a challenge.

Through the summer and fall of 1911, wage-earning suffragists visited unions in San Francisco, Oakland, Richmond, Stockton, and San Jose. Younger was proudest when wage-earning women succeeded in winning over the Brewery Workers Union. Her standing with the Waitress Union, whose members served beer and liquor in saloons and bars, made her a different sort of suffragist, untainted by temperance. She proudly reported that the Brewers "listened attentively" when the wage-earning women spoke and then "expressed themselves as favorable to the amendment."[10]

By 1911, other specialized suffrage groups joined the referendum work. The decentralization of the California movement gave it a unique flexibility and ability to draw on the energy, styles, and capacities of a wide range of women. African Americans were only 1 percent of the state's population but they were extremely loyal Republican voters. Black women organized primarily through their own suffrage clubs — the Colored Equal Suffrage League of Oakland, the largest — but also pushed for interracial suffrage work. Fifty-one-year-old Sarah Massey Overton, wife of an ex-slave, did this work in San Jose and became vice president of the racially mixed Political Equality League there.[11]

Spanish-speaking citizens were an even larger population, but were only beginning to draw reformers' attention. Maria de Lopez seems to have been the lone Hispanic organizer. She was born into a family that had lived in the San Gabriel area before statehood. Her father was a blacksmith, her mother a seamstress, and both were determined to secure education for their children, including their daughters. When Maria de

Lopez joined the suffrage movement in 1910, she had already made her mark, graduating from the University of Southern California with two degrees. Eventually she would work as a lecturer in Spanish at the recently established Southern Branch of the University of California (later UCLA) and would translate and publish several important early-nineteenth-century texts. Newspapers reported her speaking in Oxnard and Ventura, and at an election eve rally in the Plaza in downtown Los Angeles.[12]

The most active and innovative group of California suffragists was the College Equal Suffrage League (CESL). The first College Equal Suffrage League was formed in 1900 by two Radcliffe College graduates, Inez Haynes Irwin and Maud Wood Park. In 1906, it was reorganized into a national organization, with Bryn Mawr College president M. Carey Thomas at its head. When the women of the California CESL branch determined to "go out into public life and make a personal canvass for the cause we had advocated," wrote Louise Herrick Wall, who chronicled their suffrage work, "we caught a great breath and looked each upon the other. . . ."[13] By the time the campaign was in full swing, the CESL had organized dozens of large meetings and scores of smaller ones, "with programs especially adapted to local conditions." "Our chief need was to place the subject before the people, again and again, in a way that must hold their attention."[14]

These New Women did all they could to distinguish themselves from the lingering memory of suffragism's past and of the 1896 campaign. While their mothers' generation had insisted on accepting the rules of female respectability, they reveled in breaking them. They liked making their case in public, enjoyed the splashy news coverage they got (even the attacks), and loved drawing public attention. Suffragists had been appealing to the public's reason with very limited results. This new generation went for the emotions: excitement, attraction, desire. They treated their audiences as consumers, and their job was to sell their product. "The proposition that women should vote," one California suffragist asserted, "will at first be established . . . much as the virtues of breakfast food are established — by affirmation."[15]

The CESL used every opportunity and every new method and technology available to deliver simple, effective, attractive, and compelling messages. They drove their automobiles to the far reaches of the state,

California suffrage poster by Bertha Boye, 1911.

rode right into the town center, and stood on the seats of their cars to deliver their short, punchy speeches. They developed a slide show, illustrating the need for women's votes to protect children and families, showing the many faces of workingwomen, and making the case for votes for women as basic patriotism. Promising that it would bring in paying audiences, they convinced

339

proprietors of movie theaters to show it.

To develop a signature image for the campaign, they ran a well-publicized contest among local artists. Bertha Boye, who had once sued her art school for not paying her for use of her work, won with a stunning graphic featuring a beautiful woman dressed in Native American style, holding a scroll that read "Votes for Women."[16] Yellow was already the color associated with the suffrage movement, but Boye tweaked it in a California direction, by framing the woman with the halo of a golden sun and setting her against the Pacific Ocean Golden Gate. The poster was reproduced in leaflets and cards as the campaign's major advertisement. It remains one of the most enduringly beautiful pieces of American suffrage art.

None of the activities of the college suffragists was more controversial than street speaking. Older suffragists advised them that they would appear undignified and unwomanly if they went out into public to address strangers, but the method was too effective, too simple — and too exciting — to resist. Once "we felt that the time had come for us to reach the man on the street . . ." wrote San Franciscan Ernestine Black, "we went forth. That first night we caught the wind of success and thereafter it sang in our banners."[17] The campaign was so creative, so relentless, so upbeat, that success seemed assured. "Oh, yes, it will come," suffragists were told. They knew better. Woman suffrage was not "some blind force in nature that operated upon a passive society," wrote Louise Herrick Wall. "Reforms come at the cost of infinite labor."[18]

On election day, October 11, 1911, suffragist watchers were in place at as many polling stations as possible. The Colored Equal Suffrage League monitored two African American districts.[19] When there were not enough women volunteers available, the campaign hired Pinkerton detectives. Elections like these, where reform elements were trying to rout established party power, were especially at risk of fraud. Wall described the scenes with much irony: "To stand a hundred feet from one of these unholy, and peculiarly masculine places . . . to enter, as official watchers, the polling places themselves and in tallying the count to sit there until midnight with creatures of the same dire sex as our husbands and fathers — this surely was a feat for a few brave spirits!"[20] Everyone was brave.

The first returns the next morning were bad. Suffragists remembered it as "Black

Wednesday." Newspaper headlines around the country announced that the suffrage measure had been defeated in California. "To many who had never faced the thought of loss, who had believed that the powers of good were with them, the news came as a fearful, grinding shock," Wall wrote. "Strange faces at midnight, pallid, flushed and blotched faces, gazed across the Election Day headquarters at each other."[21] Then, slowly, returns from more distant districts came in, and the numbers began to shift. It took two days before the full vote was tallied, and it showed that suffrage had won by the narrowest of margins, 3,500 votes out of almost 250,000 cast. Los Angeles and rural districts were the strongest supporters, but the "no" vote in working-class districts in San Francisco and Oakland was smaller than it had been in 1896 and smaller than the "no" vote in the silk-stocking districts. The suffragists' goal had been to eat away at working-class opposition, and they had succeeded. "Maud Younger's work in the unions . . . saved us," a local suffragist reported.[22] Women would now have full voting rights in California.

Because of California's economic and demographic diversity, and the sheer extent of the campaign, its significance was unprecedented. "The agony is over," a suffrage paper in faraway Iowa reported. "The victory is ours in California. . . . It is the grandest success yet achieved in the United States."[23] From Massachusetts, eighty-six-year-old Antoinette Brown Blackwell wrote to her California friend, ninety-one-year-old Caroline Severance, who was "almost my only very elderly friend of long ago . . . to congratulate you that you are an actual voter."[24]

Nevada and Arizona joined the column of states in which women had full voting rights after California. Oregon went through five grueling defeats before the state's voters passed a suffrage amendment in 1912. In 1914, it was Montana's turn. Thirty-four-year-old Jeannette Rankin, who had apprenticed in the Washington State campaign, led that victory. In 1917, three years before the federal suffrage amendment was adopted, the women of Montana did their part to elect Jeannette Rankin to be the first woman to sit in the U.S. Congress.

California was the sixth state to give full voting rights to its women — after Wyoming, Colorado, Idaho, Utah, and Washington. The "precocity" of western suffragism was due, according to its foremost historian, to "the unsettled state of regional politics, the complex nature of western race relations, broad alliances between suffragists and . . . progressive reformers, and sophisticated activism by western women."[25] Could the suffrage revival cross the Mississippi? Everyone was asking this question. New York State was the big prize in the East, with 5 percent of the nation's population and one-tenth of the delegates to the House of Representatives. State politics there were in turmoil as both the Republican and Democratic parties were being shaken up by the Progressive insurgency. A new generation of young Democratic Party politicians, including Franklin Roosevelt, Robert Wagner, and Al Smith, were rising fast and poised to lead the drive for legislative reform.

The problem was that Democrats, even these young Progressives, regarded woman suffrage as a wealthy woman's hobby. This began to change when, over the winter of 1909–1910, New York City experienced one of the most consequential events in Progressive Era women's and labor history. Spreading out from three large factories, women shirtwaist makers struck their employers, demanding better wages. ("Shirtwaists" were the inexpensive factory-made blouses that were all the rage, especially among young workingwomen themselves.) Here was the opportunity that the Women's Trade Union League (WTUL) had been waiting for. The members of its New York branch rushed forward to offer time, money, and any other support they could. Working-class picketers were being roughed up by police and thugs, arrested, and thrown in jail in large numbers. When Mary Dreier, WTUL ally and New York chapter president, joined the picket line and the police arrested her, the charges were dismissed once the judge realized the consequences of mistreating the strikers' wealthy supporter. At that point the newspapers finally took notice.

The Monday before Thanksgiving, the WTUL, in collaboration with the small, male-dominated Ladies Garment Workers Union (LGWU), called a mass meeting of these young strikers in lower Manhattan. Thousands of young women listened impatiently as speakers debated whether to declare an industry-wide ("general") strike of all shirtwaist shops in the city. Women workers had never attempted anything this ambitious, and union leaders doubted that young women had the stamina for it. Then a twenty-one-year-old Jewish woman rose from the floor to speak. "I am one who feels and suffers from the things pictured," she said. "I move that we go on a general strike."[26] The speaker, Ukrainian immigrant and socialist Clara Lemlich, was no anonymous worker: she was the lone woman officer of the LGWU and "the most famous striker on the East Side."[27]

The audience rose as one and approved her motion. Within two days, twenty thousand young women workers were out on New York's streets. Their numbers eventually growing to forty thousand, they stayed out into the new year. Finally, in January 1910, garment shop owners conceded some of their demands and the strike ended. Strikers secured better wages and conditions but not union recognition. It was only a partial victory.

The story of the Shirtwaist Strike has been told many times and in many ways. Not often told is the suffrage side to this story. The height of the strike coincided exactly with a highly publicized visit to the United States of Emmeline Pankhurst, the pioneering British suffragette. British suffragettes were just at that moment gaining international attention for their dramatic acts of civil disobedience and their government's hostile response. An immense audience crowded into Carnegie Hall only to find that the fearsome Pankhurst was "a slight woman with curly graying hair." Nonetheless she was defiant. "It is by going to prison, rather than by arguments . . . that we have won the support of the English working man."[28] Direct action had returned to the U.S. suffrage movement.

The images of these very different women protesters — wage earners in New York streets and militant suffragettes standing up to the British government — being brutally treated by police, arrested, and thrown into jails, flowed into one another. Both groups were made up of determined, aggressive women, fighting to win their economic and political rights. "There was no doubt that many of the women in the union were in favor of woman suffrage," the *New York Times,* which supported neither woman suffrage nor trade unions, reluctantly conceded.[29] Clara Lemlich observed that the abrupt dismissal of the strikers' appeal for better treatment by the police and in the city courts would simply not have happened if the mayor had known that "we girls have a vote."[30]

Into this overheated environment came Harriot Stanton Blatch, sixth child and second daughter of Elizabeth Cady Stanton. Blatch, now fifty, made the enfranchisement of New York women her personal crusade. She knew the state in all its varieties. Her mother had been born near Albany; Harriot and her siblings had grown up along the Erie Canal; she had lived her teenage years in New York City, and had gone to Vassar College in Poughkeepsie. Her family ties gave her access to some of the state's major political figures. Prepared by her mother for suffrage leadership, she embodied the link between the radicalism of the pioneering generation and the vitality of the new suffragism. Since the 1880s, Blatch had been living abroad with her British husband and daughter, Nora (named after the Ibsen heroine). In England, she was exposed to the democratic socialism of the Fabian Society. She also became friends with the Pankhurst family.

Blatch visited the United States frequently during her mother's final years but waited until Anthony's death in 1906 to return for good to assume her suffrage legacy. She regarded the New York branch of NAWSA, the descendant of the organization that her mother and Anthony had formed forty years before, as "completely in a rut." "It bored its adherents," she recalled, "and repelled its opponents." To offer an alternative, she formed the Equality League of Self-

Supporting Women (ELSSW). Among its initial members were politically active working-class women and young college graduates, some of whom would go on to lead the birth control and women's peace movements. The ELSSW's goals captured all the elements of the new suffragism: "that suffrage propaganda must be made dramatic, that suffrage workers must be politically minded . . . the need of drawing industrial women into the suffrage campaign and that these women needed to be brought into contact, not with women of leisure, but with business and professional women. . . ."[31]

At first, small donations supported the ELSSW, but Blatch's idea for a winning campaign required money, lots of it. She had no intention of following NAWSA's self-defeating habit of trimming its operations to fit its financial constraints. She believed that you decided what you needed to do to win and then you found the money to do it. So just as she was building a suffrage constituency from workingwomen, she began to cultivate wealthy women who could fund her ambitious plans. The suffrage movement had long been proudly middle class. The accelerating class divide of these years, of great wealth at one end and enormous numbers of workers at the other end, ushered in a different approach.

The first wealthy woman of importance in New York was the multimillionaire Alva Belmont. She had accumulated her wealth by marrying William Vanderbilt, then divorcing him for his flagrant philandering and marrying the transit magnate Oliver Belmont. She had been to England and met Emmeline Pankhurst and her daughters. Back at home she accumulated her suffrage credentials by funding the December 5, 1909, public support meeting during the Shirtwaist Strike. Within a few years, Belmont would shift from state to federal suffrage work. A great deal of what occurred among the radical adherents of the U.S. suffrage movement in its last decade would not have happened without her money.

Belmont was not the only "society queen" who came into suffrage in these years. There were others, and Blatch recruited many of them. Katherine Mackay's husband was the founder of the International Telegraph and Telephone Company and an enthusiastic supporter of her activism. She began her suffrage career in 1905 by making use of New York women's school suffrage and winning a seat on her local school board. Helen Rogers Reid was married to the publisher of the *New York Tribune* (and later took over this role herself). Louisine Havemeyer was the widow of the "sugar trust king" and with her husband was a wealthy art collector. Their collection was a major contribution to the holdings of the Metropolitan Museum of Art. The first money she raised for suffrage came from an exhibition of paintings by Mary Cassatt, a personal friend who, it was reported, had introduced her to suffrage activism.[32] These women accomplished the unimaginable: they put suffrage on a solid financial footing and made it fashionable. Their money allowed Blatch to increase the budget of her suffrage operation sevenfold, to almost thirteen thousand dollars. These funds meant that women who needed to earn their living could now be paid as suffrage organizers, publicists, lobbyists, and office managers.

Blatch brought a profoundly political sensibility to the revival of New York suffragism. Through her mother, woman suffrage was in her bones, but through her father, politics was in her blood. "Our chief problem was to rouse the Legislature out of its indifference to woman suffrage," Blatch insisted.[33] The suffrage bill had not seen the light of legislative day in New York since her mother's failure to get it into the state constitutional convention in 1894. Traditional suffrage methods assumed that getting laws passed was a matter of gradually educating legislators to the justice and necessity of enfranchising women.

Blatch believed that education and justice were beside the point. She insisted on the fundamental "connection between the advancement of woman suffrage and politics as they existed in our native state."[34] In 1910, she renamed the ELSSW the Women's Political Union (WPU). "We adopted political work because we were convinced that ours was a political cause to be passed politically," she insisted.[35] This meant taking advantage of the partisan upheaval in the state, engaging and confronting the major political parties, and using the same tools that male party leaders used to get and hold power.

The California suffragists had not had to battle to get the state legislature to submit the referendum bill, only to win voters' support. By contrast in New York, just the campaign to get the state legislature to authorize a voter referendum on woman suffrage took three years of intense work. With money from her wealthy supporters, Blatch built a full-fledged suffrage lobbying enterprise. She set up offices in Albany, hired office staff and a professional lobbyist, and compiled information on every legislator whom she would need to press for support. The Republican Speaker of the Assembly did not support suffrage, but Blatch's feats of derring-do convinced him to take her on as a kind of political protégée. He taught her how to get the Judiciary Committee to release its hold on the bill and send it to the floor of the legislature. She expected they would probably lose their first floor vote, but she had been "taught by two such veteran campaigners as my mother and Miss Anthony . . . [to] be willing to accept temporary defeat."[36] There was no other route to victory.

As a new generation of Democratic legislators rose to power in New York, it became clear that working-class suffragists were key to winning their allegiance. One of Blatch's first legislative forays was bringing working-class women to testify before a state legislative committee. "Gentlemen, we need every help in the battle of life," Clara Silver, a British-born garment worker, spoke, her voice low but insistent. "[T]o be left out by the State just sets up a prejudice against us. Bosses think and women come to think themselves that they don't count for so much as men."[37]

Blatch relied heavily on Leonora O'Reilly, an Irish American garment worker, veteran reformer, and ultimately the most important working-class suffragist in New York. Progressive Democrats were trying to pass a bill limiting women's working hours, which was supported by labor unions but opposed by manufacturers who depended on underpaid and overworked female workers. O'Reilly linked the maximum hours bill to woman suffrage. She spoke to the Senate and Assembly Judiciary Committees on behalf of the "50,000 women in this State and the 800,000 in the country [who are] mauled in the mill, fagged in the factory, and worn out behind the counter. We can only strangle the organizations that want to make our hours longer at the ballot box."[38]

The struggle to win Democratic support for the state woman suffrage referendum was making little headway until, in April 1911, the political calculus shifted dramatically. Just before closing on a Saturday night, the Triangle Shirtwaist Factory, the very center of the 1909–1910 Shirtwaist Strike, burst into flames. The factory was located on the upper floors of the Asch Building, which although brand new, had inadequate fire escapes and no sprinklers. However, the real scandal was that the factory owners had locked the doors to keep out union organizers. One hundred forty-six workers, nearly one-third of those working at the time, almost all of whom were young Italian and Jewish immigrant women, died horrible deaths, burning or jumping from upper-story windows. The fire was one of the great tragedies of New York City labor history. The state legislature formed a special Factory Inspection Commission, which eventually enacted a comprehensive set of industrial laws, including a nine-hour daily limit and a prohibition on night work for women workers.

The Triangle Fire stretched the links between working-class women and their upper-class supporters to the breaking point. Rose Schneiderman, another founding member of the WTUL, finally had had enough of wealthy women's support. She was less than five feet tall and not yet thirty years old, but she was a powerhouse. By this time, she had joined the Socialist Party and the fire finally exhausted her patience for "good fellowship." Workingwomen were still without the protection of either unions or labor laws. "The life of men and women is so cheap," she thundered at a memorial rally for the dead, "and property is so sacred."[39] The women workers were gone, but the building stood — and still stands — more than a century later. Within a month, some New York City working-class women followed the California example and formed their own Wage Earners Suffrage League. Democratic Party leaders began to listen. The cultivation of workingwomen's suffragism was now fully in motion. "Every class that ever lived on another always told the slaves that it was good for them to be slaves," Schneiderman addressed the New York State Senate. "We are here Senators. We are 800,000 strong in New York State alone."[40]

Despite outrage over the Triangle Fire, yet another year of sustained work was required before the state legislature passed enabling legislation for a suffrage referendum. Judiciary Committee chair and leading Democrat Robert Wagner was keeping the measure from a floor vote. Blatch brought a train full of suffragists to Albany to chase him down — literally. "Some fifty or sixty of us crowded into the committee room, the rest gathered in the corridor outside . . ." she wrote in her memoirs. "At what point the Senator took in his predicament, I do not know. . . . There was not an anti-suffragist to rescue him, not an orthodox suffragist to show some human sympathy.

There were only all about him, the convinced, the ruthless members of the Women's Political Union."[41] Wagner had no choice but to give in and allow the Senate to vote on the measure.

Still two votes short of passage, Blatch now turned to popular pressure. She had been following the lead of British suffragettes and organizing suffrage parades in the city since 1909, but the May 3, 1912 New York City parade greatly exceeded all that had come before. "To impress the legislators," Blatch told Leonora O'Reilly, "the parade must not be for this class of women or only for that, it must draw out the largest number of women of all sorts."[42] All the women marchers of whatever class wore white and marched in disciplined rank. For the first time significant numbers of men, harassed by the crowds as "mollycoddles," participated.[43] The march began on Saturday at 5 p.m., late enough to allow many working girls to come and early enough to get good coverage from the Sunday papers. College women marched under the banners of their schools, wage earners under the signs of their trades, and African American women proudly had their own division. Estimates ranged from ten to seventeen thousand marchers. Crowds

Harriot Stanton Blatch, exhorting Wall Street crowds, 1910s.

along the sidewalks were massive, good humored, and impressed.

In the summer of 1912, the shift in national politics finally broke through the New York legislative logjam. Progressives came together on the national level behind the third-party presidential candidacy of former Republican president Theodore Roosevelt. Nationally, his candidacy split the Republican Party — ultimately enough to elect Democrat Woodrow Wilson to the presidency, making him only the second Democratic president since the Civil War. In New

York, Republicans took control of the Assembly and Democrats held the Senate. Blatch was able to play competing parties against each other and to gain support from all sides. Two months before Wilson's inauguration, the New York bill authorizing a suffrage referendum for amending the state constitution passed both houses, and the issue was on its way to the voters.

As magnificent as this victory was in one of the most intricate political environments in the country, now suffragists had an even more difficult task: to win the majority of New York's voters. The referendum was scheduled for November 1915, two years hence. It did not escape Blatch's notice that a victory then would celebrate the hundredth anniversary of Elizabeth Cady Stanton's birth.

The new excitement and energy flowing into New York suffragism in the 1910s crossed the river into Brooklyn and breached the race barrier to African American women. The dean of New York black suffragism was Sarah J. Garnet. Born in 1831, she came from a mixed African American and Native American background, and her family had lived for many generations on Long Island. The first black public school principal in New York City, she married a local minister, and after his death, she married again, to Henry Highland Garnet, one of history's great abolitionists. By 1882, she was twice widowed. Soon after, she organized the Women's Loyal League, the courageous organization that, in the 1890s, had defended Ida B. Wells through the storm that her bold anti-lynching activism had set off.

In 1902, Garnet, now seventy-one, along with her younger sister, physician Susan Smith-McKinney, founded the Brooklyn Equal Suffrage League (ESL), the first black women's organization devoted exclusively to woman suffrage in New York. It met monthly at the all-black YMCA branch in the Fort Greene neighborhood, where many middle-class black people lived. In 1907, the group scored a great coup by inviting Anne Cobden-Sanderson, the first British suffragette leader to visit the United States, to speak to them. Three years later, perhaps inspired by meeting Cobden-Sanderson, Garnet traveled to London and brought back news of the full flowering of radical suffragette activism there. Garnet died, age eighty, in 1911.

In the North, in those states where black men still voted and where their numbers were rising, the hostility of white suffragists to African Americans began to alter about 1910. The first white suffragist to reach out to black women in New York was Alva Belmont. In early 1910, she approached Sarah Garnet and another leading black suffragist, Irene Moorman, with a proposal. If they could recruit at least one hundred women into an all-black division of Belmont's own independent suffrage organization, she would provide them with their own meeting room in Harlem. Garnet and Moorman accepted, two hundred women attended the meeting, and Belmont fulfilled her promise.

Belmont's deeper motivation for reaching out to African American women has never been fully explained. She was a powerful woman with big ambitions for achieving high visibility leadership in the suffrage movement. As her divorce indicated, she was also a woman not afraid — indeed quite drawn to — giving offense to conservative social norms. Eventually, her ambition outran her convictions and she lost interest in cultivating black suffragists. She did, however, open the interracial door in New York. In 1911, the Brooklyn wing of NAWSA followed her lead and invited black women to join their organization. That same year Alice Chipman Dewey, wife of philosopher John Dewey, tried to host an integrated suffrage meeting in her home near Columbia University, but when her neighbors threatened to sue her for violating a restrictive housing covenant, she canceled.

In April 1911, W.E.B. Du Bois came to speak to the Brooklyn black suffragists. He had left his position as professor of sociology at Atlanta University and moved to New York to serve as executive director of the recently formed National Association for the Advancement of Colored People (NAACP) and the editor of its ambitious monthly magazine, *The Crisis.* Mary Church Terrell was a founding member of the NAACP, though not Ida Wells-Barnett, who was regarded as too divisive even for that organization. Several progressive white suffragists — Jane Addams, Florence Kelley, Leonora O'Reilly, and Harriot Stanton Blatch — were also early members, but Du Bois would not yet commit himself to woman suffrage. Instead, he concentrated on calling out white suffrage racism. *The Crisis* reported that Anna Howard Shaw, NAWSA president, had recently resurrected the old Reconstruction Era canard that "white women have no enemy in the world who does more to defeat our amendments . . . than colored men."[44] Du Bois called it a "barefaced falsehood."[45]

Yet within a little more than a year, Du Bois was writing regularly in favor of woman suffrage. "The same arguments and facts that are slowly but surely opening the ballot box to women . . . must open it to black men," he wrote in a featured editorial in the May 1912 issue of *The Crisis*. "It only remains for us to help the movement and spread the argument wherever we may."[46] He introduced his readers to the women of Sarah Garnet's ESL and to black suffragists in other cities. In the September 1912 issue, suffragist Mary Church Terrell was featured in the regular "Man of the Month" (sic) feature. Terrell wrote that "for an intelligent colored man to oppose woman suffrage is the most preposterous and ridiculous thing in the world."[47] As part of a "symposium on woman suffrage," Adella Hunt Logan of Tuskegee University promised that the African American woman would use her voting rights with more care than her "colored brother, who . . . has become too indifferent to his duties of citizenship."[48]

Despite these breakthroughs in places like New York, nationally, white suffrage racism would never disappear, and in the later part of the decade, would return to be a major complicating factor in the final push for woman suffrage.

The third major state to modernize suffrage activism in the early 1910s was Illinois. Chicago, the nation's second largest city, was home to a particularly vital group of women political activists, including both white wage earners and black women. The 1912 presidential election had a major impact in the state, making for a three-way split of the legislature among Democrats, regular Republicans, and Progressives. This created a very promising situation for suffragists. The biggest problem was that the state constitution permitted only a single amendment at a time, and woman suffrage was not the governor-elect's top priority.

There was, however, a daring backdoor approach that might allow Illinois women to vote for president without having to secure — and then win — a state constitutional amendment via a voters' referendum. Ever since the late nineteenth century Henry Blackwell, Lucy Stone's husband, had been arguing for what he labeled "presidential suffrage."[49] He argued that there was a way through simple statute that women in a state could weigh in on presidential elections. The U.S. Constitution explicitly left the method of selecting presidential electors to each state legislature, and Blackwell sought to exploit this fact on women's behalf. He contended that instead of laborious voter referenda, state legislatures could simply pass legislation to authorize women to vote for members of the electoral college, which was the functional equivalent of voting for president, as opposed to granting women full voting rights, which required constitutional change. "Presidential suffrage" was thus a partial suffrage, like school suffrage or the temperance vote, but with infinitely greater political significance.

Blackwell died in 1909. Four years later, Illinois suffragists took up his idea, pressing for state legislation that would enact presidential elector suffrage for women in combination with securing their rights to municipal suffrage. A team of three led by Grace Wilbur Trout went to Springfield to run the campaign. Naive and politically inexperienced, Trout at first was "indignant at the way the suffrage committee was treated" by politicians.[50] Soon, however, she was taking instruction from legislative adversaries about which committees should vet suffragists' bills, how to deal with opponents, and how to get the bills onto the full legislature floor for a vote.

The state senate voted for the presidential suffrage law, but there was opposition in the house. To counter the charge by the Speaker of the House that there was little enthusiasm for voting among women, suffrage leaders organized a "telephone brigade, by means of which he was called up every fifteen minutes by men as well as women . . . from early Saturday morning until late Monday night," then followed that up with a "deluge" of letters and telegrams. When the floor vote was taken, suffragist minders were assigned to each legislator so that "if any of these men were missing [from the vote], . . . a cab was sent for them" to get them onto the floor. After a ferocious five-hour floor fight, the House followed the state Senate and voted for the presidential suffrage law. The governor signed it despite tremendous pressure not to do so. Politicians declared it a miracle "but it was a miracle made possible by six months of unceasing toil, during which the suffrage lobby worked from early in the morning until late at night."[51] Chicago attorney Catherine Waugh McCulloch, who had helped to design the strategy, characterized the passage of the bill as "the biggest thing to happen east of the Mississippi since the Civil War."[52]

After the governor signed the bill, Illinois suffragists celebrated their victory with an automobile cavalcade down Michigan Avenue. Nineteen suffrage organizations and at least 150 automobiles participated. The parade was led by a brass band, and banners and balloons in suffrage yellow festooned the automobiles. The *Chicago Tribune* gave the parade major coverage, including a three-column-wide photograph of autos crowded with women (and driven by male chauffeurs). "The paraders looked quite dainty in their summer gowns," it reported, adding that the women nonetheless appeared "decidedly intelligent enough to vote."[53]

Five of the automobiles carried African American suffragists.[54] They were members of the Alpha Suffrage Club, which had just been formed by Ida B. Wells-Barnett. The Alpha Suffrage Club went on to play a major role in transforming the right to vote into genuine political power for African American women in Chicago. Five months later, when state suffragists announced a massive drive to register women in time for the November elections for municipal aldermen, Wells-Barnett and the Alphas plunged into their own registration effort. Within three years, the Alphas had become the determining factor in the election of Chicago's first black alderman in the city's second ward.

As these state enfranchisements mounted, it became clear to all serious suffrage strategists that the possibilities of winning a federal constitutional amendment, which had lain fallow for three decades, had drastically improved. In 1914, the Illinois Supreme Court found the state legislature's enactment of presidential suffrage legislation constitutional. Other states followed the Illinois precedent until four million women in fifteen states representing ninety-one votes in the electoral college could vote in presidential elections. It was no longer men and men only who had the political power to put pressure on Congress and determine the outcome of the fight for a U.S. constitutional amendment. Women were no longer a "voteless constituency."[55]

While numerous suffrage organizations, constituencies, and approaches were proliferating in California, New York, and Illinois, pursuing full voting rights for women in their states, winning women's voting rights in this way was both immeasurably laborious and sure to fail in southern states. There needed to be a return to the campaign of the post–Civil War years for a U.S. constitutional amendment. NAWSA, however, was unable to translate energy from the states into a comprehensive strategy. In 1904, Anna Howard Shaw had become the national president. Though popular with rank-and-file suffragists, she found it difficult to manage conflicts among other officers or to corral state chapters to work together for suffrage at the federal level. The campaign for a constitutional amendment stagnated. The organization had no permanent presence in Washington, D.C., and NAWSA's congressional committee, which was responsible for pressuring Congress for a constitutional amendment, was unfunded and had virtually disappeared. Every January a handful of suffragists had dutifully gone to Washington to testify on behalf of a woman suffrage constitutional amendment before a tiny group of legislators. The entire process had become a meaningless ritual.

Finally, in 1912, the excitement, youth, and optimism of twentieth-century suffragism came to the national movement in the person of Alice Paul. Born in 1885 to a wealthy New Jersey Quaker family, she was exceptionally well educated, first at Swarthmore College, and later earning a

PhD in political science from the University of Pennsylvania. In 1907, she went to London, where she served an apprenticeship to Emmeline Pankhurst and learned the ways of the suffragettes.

Paul had experienced all of this — including arrests, a brutal imprisonment, and a gruesome month-long hunger strike — by the time she returned to the United States in early 1910. She was celebrated by journalists as America's first genuine suffragette. She was just twenty-six years old. Two years later, with the help of Jane Addams and Harriot Stanton Blatch, Paul's proposal to revive NAWSA's campaign for a federal amendment was accepted by the group's executive board. Anna Howard Shaw agreed to let the young ambitious woman take over the association's nearly defunct congressional committee. Paul assembled a small group to join with her to reinvigorate the constitutional amendment campaign. She was closest to Lucy Burns, daughter of Irish immigrants, who had gone abroad to continue her studies, was drawn into the Pankhursts' orbit, and there met Alice Paul. In addition, Mary Beard, who was just beginning to write with her husband, Charles, their path-breaking history *American Civilization,* joined, as did Crystal

Eastman, a New York–based writer and legal expert. Dora Lewis, fifty-two-year-old suffrage veteran from Philadelphia, was the senior member of the group.

Paul had learned from the British suffragettes to deploy public demonstrations for maximum popular attention and to hold the political party that was in power responsible for inaction on women's enfranchisement. To do both, she determined to begin her constitutional amendment campaign with an unforgettable demonstration in the nation's capital that would be directed at the incoming Democratic administration. Just as Blatch had timed the November 1912 New York parade to coincide with state elections, Paul scheduled her event for March 3, 1913, the day before the inauguration of newly elected president Woodrow Wilson. Wilson's coattails had carried a Democratic majority into Congress, and this made him exceptionally powerful. The parade was designed to demonstrate the suffragists' numbers, organization, and determination. When Wilson stepped off the train from his home in New Jersey for his inaugural ceremonies, he asked why there were no crowds to meet him. They were all on Pennsylvania Avenue he was told, watching the suffrage parade. Or so the legend goes.

Paul had a way about her, a unique kind of charisma that had already convinced veteran leaders to trust her with major responsibility. She did not advance herself personally at all. She was neither particularly warm nor intimate. Her considerable authority came from her absolute clarity about her intentions and her faith that other women could do whatever was necessary, even when they themselves had no such conviction. Working with her made them into more than they ever thought they could be.

It was as if a whole generation of young women were waiting for someone like her to call them into service. Matilda Gardner, wife of a Washington, D.C., journalist, recalled Paul telling her to find replacement trappings for the horses that the suffragists would ride in the March 1913 parade. Gardner "had no more idea how to order a trapping than a suspension bridge, but — magic-ed as always by Alice Paul's personality," she agreed and eventually found a neighborhood tailor who solved the problem for her. "She does not argue with you when you say no — but you rarely say no, . . ." Inez Haynes Gilmore wrote. "Perhaps it is the intensity of devotion which blazes back of the gentleness of her personality and the inflexibility of purpose which gives that greatness power."[56]

When Paul began her work, she and Lucy Burns rented a three-room basement office in Washington, D.C., below a realtor's office and began to raise funds. Ultimately they generated over $27,000 for the parade, much of it from restless women of wealth. Within three months, they had organized an unparalleled suffrage spectacle. Virtually every suffragist in the area and many who were new to the movement, including wives and daughters of congressmen and senators, were involved.

The parade was meticulously planned. There were seven sections. The first, led by Carrie Chapman Catt, would show the worldwide reach of the suffrage movement; the second, its long historic arc from 1848 to the present day. The five others depicted how women worked together with men to build the country; women in businesses, occupations, and trades (including one thousand college women); clubwomen; state and local suffrage associations; and finally, the only participants allowed to ride along the route, the movement "pioneers," too old to walk. The marchers in each section and subsection would wear distinctive capes, costing two dollars each, designed by a suffrage supporter in New York to provide warmth and protection against possible rain.

Vans were on hand to provide coffee and sandwiches to marchers. Trumpet-wielding heralds along the mile-long route would announce the arrival of the parade. Street corner suffrage speakers posted at the edge of the crowd would address onlookers who could not get a good view of the parade. The parade would conclude at the front steps of the U.S. Treasury Building, where there would be an elaborate pageant depicting an allegory of Columbia, to whom homage was paid by Charity, Hope, Justice, and Peace.

In 1913, the new term "feminism" began to appear in connection with the suffrage resurgence. The French had been using *feminisme* since the 1890s, and the word began to show up in histories of women's long resistance to subordination. Occasionally U.S. newspapers reported on this interesting, new, but decidedly exotic French phenomenon. Then as now the term was evocative but defied precise definition. In the wake of the new bold spirit of the Washington, D.C., parade, suffragism became connected to "feminism" by adherents and opponents in equal measure.

The one hitch in plans for the parade was the question of African American women's participation. Washington, D.C., once the vibrant national center of African American activism, had fallen victim to the invidious spirit of Jim Crow, and African American women were now marginalized in the suffrage movement there. Moreover, the newly installed Democratic Congress was controlled by its all-white southern wing.

Southern Democrats were opposed to any federal suffrage involvement, and some were even calling for repealing the Fifteenth Amendment, the single constitutional restraint on state voter policy. Southern states had succeeded in disfranchising black men, among other ways by claiming that they had misused their political rights and also sexually harassed and assaulted white women. Black women had no history of such inflammatory charges against them and southern white political leaders realized it would be much more challenging to defraud them of their rights. For their part, suffragists realized that to bring the white South into their movement would require great delicacy. The race problem faced by Paul in

1913 pointed to a political situation that would only become more challenging for suffragists. Suffragists' "southern strategy" came back to life.

Meanwhile African American suffragism was growing in strength and determination. The reaction among white suffragists to this new enthusiasm was divided: while some white suffragists sought to make sure that black women participated, others were opposed, sure that the presence of black women would inflame racial prejudices. In setting parade policy, Alice Paul was caught between her abolitionist/Quaker origins and her belief that any substantial black participation would distract from her goal of advancing the woman suffrage constitutional amendment.

In the end, Paul followed NAWSA "states' rights" policy by allowing local groups to set their own racial standards, hoping that the few black parade participants she expected would not be particularly noticeable if they were dispersed among white marchers. However, one substantial group — several dozen Howard University students — was determined to march together, proudly displaying their banner, in the college division of the parade. In this case, Paul decided on a segregation policy — to sepa-

JUST LIKE THE MEN!

Votes for WHITE women.

Cartoon by suffrage supporter *Boardman Robinson*, New York Tribune, *March 1, 1913, before the Washington, D.C., suffrage parade.*

rate the Howard group out from the larger college procession and surround them by friendly white men, presumably to shield them from hostile crowds.[57]

Mary Church Terrell and Ida B. Wells-Barnett differed on how to deal with this policy. Terrell marched with the separate contingent of Howard University students, but Wells-Barnett was determined to challenge Paul. Wells-Barnett had come to Washington, D.C., along with sixty-five white Illinois suffragists, then in the midst of their own state battle. Perhaps because Illinois had its own southern white contingent, Grace Trout, head of the state delegation, announced that Wells-Barnett would not be included. Other Illinois marchers did not agree. "It is autocratic," insisted a white suffragist who had worked with Wells-Barnett. "We have come down here to march for equal rights. . . . If the women of other states lack moral courage, we . . . should stand by our principles. If not the parade will be a farce."

Then Wells-Barnett spoke up. "The southern women have tried to evade the [race] question time and again," she said, "her voice trembling with emotion," it was reported. "If the Illinois women do not take a stand now in this great democratic parade, then the colored women are lost. I shall not march at all unless I can march under the Illinois banner," Wells-Barnett declared. "I am not taking this stand, because I personally wish for recognition. I am doing it for the future benefit of my whole race." The *Chicago Daily Tribune* reported that her "face [was] set in lines of grim determination."[58]

Just after 3 p.m. on March 3 the parade began. It had taken a month and a half and endless meetings with city and federal officials to secure a permit for the mile-long route. The women would begin under the shadow of the Capitol and move along Pennsylvania Avenue, turning right just before the White House to end at the Treasury Building. The day before had been quite cold, but by the time the parade began, the temperature had risen to 55 degrees. Inez Milholland, the young and beautiful equestrian queen of the New York parades, led off the demonstration, astride her beautiful gray horse. She was followed by NAWSA officers and a horse-drawn flower-festooned cart featuring in large letters the parade's demand for an "Amendment to the Constitution of the United States Enfranchising the Women of the Country." The *Washington Post* page one article was headlined "Women's Beauty, Grace and Art Bewilder the Capital."[59]

When the Illinois delegation folded into the line of march, Wells-Barnett was not there at first. Had she conceded to her state's determination to bar her? Hardly. Midway along the route, "suddenly from the crowd on the sidewalk," the *Chicago Tribune* reported, "Mrs. Barnett walked calmly out to the [Illinois] delegation and assumed her place." She was flanked by two white allies.[60] "All praise to Mrs. Barnett for her firm stand against the bitter prejudice of the women of the South," the African American *Chicago Defender* wrote.[61]

In the end, the black presence in the parade caused none of the predicted disruption. *The Crisis* reported favorably on the outcome. Twenty-five Howard students marched in caps and gowns, and perhaps a dozen other African American suffragists participated throughout the parade. "The attempt to draw the color line in the woman's suffrage movement has received, let us hope, a final setback . . . ," *Crisis* editor W. E. B. Du Bois reported. "There was, to be sure, a struggle . . . and the forces of caste are not demoralized; they are however beaten at present and a great and good cause can go forward," he concluded, "with unbedraggled skirts."[62]

Parade organizers turned out to have far more serious problems than black and white women marching together. They had worried that rowdy crowds, drawn to the city for the inauguration, would be difficult to control, but Chief of Police William Sylvester dismissed their concerns. Their worries turned out to be more than justified. As the parade began, enormous crowds, perhaps twenty persons deep on either side of the street, lined the sidewalks. Only a few mounted police were there to keep control, along with a small army of Boy Scouts whom the police had recruited to help.[63] Faced with police intransigence, Elizabeth Rogers, one of Paul's inner circle, had convinced her brother-in-law, Henry Stimson, who was just about to leave his tenure as secretary of war, to move an Army regiment to the edge of the city in case they were needed.

Suffragists' concerns proved well founded. Halfway along the route, crowds broke through the police lines and closed the open space, trapping the marchers. "It was like marching into a funnel," one demonstrator explained.[64] Rowdies in the crowd grabbed at the women, pulled at their signs and clothes. Marchers were harassed "with all manner of smutty conversation."[65] The police stood by so passively that some thought they were intentionally enabling the rioters. Finally, the Army regiment arrived and pushed back the crowd to allow the procession to proceed. Hours late, the parade got to the Treasury Building, where

Crowd breaking up the March 1913 parade in Washington, D.C.

the pageant performers, shivering in their flimsy costumes, had been waiting. "The woman's procession at the National Capital was broken up and the participants insulted," Blatch, who was there, challenged, "because the State taught lack of respect for the opinion of women . . . and the unthinking element, the rough element in great crowds, reflected the State's opinion of its women's citizens."[66] The next day, the presidential inauguration went on without a hitch.

Paul had learned well from the British suffragettes. She was able to use the mob's behavior and the failure of the D.C. police to protect the marchers to enhance the political impact of the parade. Two days later, the U.S. Senate resolved to hold an investigation into police misconduct during the parade. Senator Wesley Jones from the suffrage state of Washington headed the investigation, which ran a full month. The proceedings were eventually published as a 600-page government document. Forty women who had participated in the march, many onlookers, and police themselves testified. The committee concluded that while some police had "acted with apparent indifference and in this way encouraged the crowd to press in upon the parade," there was no evidence to "single out any particular individual for reproof or condemnation."[67] Clearly this acquittal was directed at Chief Sylvester. He was allowed to continue in his post for another two years, but his law enforcement career was permanently soiled by the episode.

The parade, its coverage, and the Senate hearings produced exactly the kind of sordid publicity that traditional suffragists abhorred, but Paul welcomed. As she hoped, the episode jump-started the constitutional amendment campaign. The Senate Special Committee on Woman Suffrage, which had been inactive for many years, was reinstated, now composed mostly of senators from suffrage states. The committee voted to submit

Julia Lathrop, Jane Addams, and Mary McDowell in Washington, 1913, on a suffrage mission on Capitol Hill.

a resolution calling for the constitutional enfranchisement of women to the entire Senate for a vote, the first time this had happened in two decades. While no one expected the bill to get the necessary two-thirds vote, it was no longer trapped in congressional purgatory.

The entire episode illustrated the vast difference of attitude and approach between the suffrage establishment, still concerned to demonstrate its ladylike probity by avoiding conflict and unpleasant publicity, and this new generation. Paul's goal was to show determination, not dignity, and to gain attention for suffragists' demands, however it came, and she had done this. The parade and its aftermath had resulted in significant forward legislative motion. A new generation had come to town, determined to complete suffragism's long road to the ballot box.

In December 1913 after the great parade conducted in its name in Washington, D.C., NAWSA met in its annual convention. Anna Howard Shaw was holding on to the presidency despite growing discontent with her leadership. Jane Addams, one of the nation's most revered female public figures, who agreed to serve as vice president, was one of the many trying to revive the organization. Addams argued that the political environment of the country was changing dramatically and suffragists must change with it. Forward-thinking legislators were looking beyond diplomacy and economics to tackle problems in the way people lived their lives, and "men and women will solve them

Alice Paul, 1915.

together with ballots in the hands of both."[68] Arguments and approaches for suffrage had to change to meet the new conditions of a modernizing country. Would the spirit unleashed at the March parade be allowed to spread further into the national suffrage environment?

Alice Paul and the rest of her congressional committee were the most organized suffragist group in Washington, D.C., and they had put together NAWSA's December 1913 convention. In addition to the great March 3 demonstration, her group had organized two other parades, collected two hundred thousand petitions, maintained a heavy schedule of indoor and outdoor meetings in Washington, and raised almost $28,000. They had brought three deputations to President Wilson and launched a new periodical, the *Suffragist,* dedicated to the federal amendment. Within Congress, they were planning for the upcoming Senate debate on woman suffrage, the first in over a quarter century. They wanted to pressure the House to establish its own standing woman suffrage committee.

To provide financial support for all this work, Paul had organized a partially independent organization, the Congressional Union for Woman Suffrage (CU). It claimed one thousand members from all over the country and considered itself auxiliary to NAWSA, as did other specialized suffrage organizations such as the College Equal Suffrage League. Paul had done a great deal to move the federal amendment forward.

Then, in what one reporter called a "bomb," executive committee member Carrie Chapman Catt rose to criticize Paul's report. Catt had always insisted on a tight and hierarchical organization, and charged Paul with creating a rogue group of suffragists. She said that the CU had simply grown too big, too ambitious, and too independent. "I am more or less razzle dazzled by the relationship between the Congressional Union, the Congressional Committee and the NAWSA," Catt insisted. "Are we to have two national organizations? I am for one cause and an army under one flag."[69] NAWSA's executive committee then told Paul that she must dissociate herself from the CU. She refused and was summarily removed from her position as head of NAWSA's congressional committee, effectively removing her from NAWSA.

Ruth Hanna McCormick, a politically powerful Illinois woman fresh off the victory of presidential suffrage in her home state, took over the congressional committee from Paul. McCormick's father, Mark Hanna, was the legendary advisor to President William McKinley, and her husband, Medill McCormick, was the publisher of the *Chicago Tribune* and one of Theodore Roosevelt's closest advisors.

The California, New York, and Illinois state campaigns had flourished with multiple centers of suffrage activism. Why then did organizational diversity and decentralization cause such acrimony at the national level? One reason was that NAWSA leaders did not approve of Paul's association with the Pankhurst wing of the British suffrage movement, which was becoming more lawbreaking by the day. While Paul had not advocated breaking the law nor courted arrest in the United States (not yet), still, to many in established leadership, the spirit of open challenge to political authority that she unleashed was untenable. Demanding rather than requesting change was objectionable and smacked of suffragette militancy. Suspicions were confirmed when Paul's group began to use the green and purple of Pankhurst's WSPU, instead of the American suffragists' traditional yellow.

A second reason for NAWSA's suspicion of Paul was, as it so often is, money. NAWSA was chronically short of funds and had just instituted a controversial new organizational structure which taxed all state branches and other affiliated societies in proportion to their size and wealth. Paul had initially been authorized to raise her own funds, but now NAWSA's top officers insisted that she channel her money through NAWSA's treasury. This she would not do.

Finally, the two factions confronted the national political challenges faced by the suffrage movement in different ways. The fundamental problem was the obdurate refusal of the president and the Democratic

Party to support a federal amendment. Suffrage, including woman suffrage, was an issue of states' rights, national Democrats insisted. The president agreed and insisted that the states alone should have control over granting women the franchise, with which the federal government had no business interfering. The lack of forward motion in the House of Representatives was due to southern Democrats who controlled the Judiciary Committee and refused to recommend the woman suffrage bill for a floor vote.

NAWSA's response to Democrats' states' rights concern was problematic, to say the least. Relying solely on advice from her friends in Congress, Ruth McCormick decided it was time to devise an entirely new constitutional approach to suffrage. Unlike the classic suffrage amendment, which had been before Congress steadily since 1878, McCormick's proposed amendment would operate state by state. It would require that 8 percent of each state's voters must formally petition for woman suffrage, which would then put into motion a state referendum, which would then have to be accepted by a majority of that state's voters for women to be enfranchised in that state. This cumbersome procedure would have to be repeated state by state. Senator John Shafroth of Colorado and Representative A. Mitchell Palmer of Pennsylvania (later Wilson's notorious attorney general) agreed to sponsor the constitutional alternative.

McCormick was naively betting that southern states would be more amenable to woman suffrage in this form than by straightforward federal action, but predictably they were not. From the southern perspective, instead of creating a middle ground between federal and state action, the proposal violated the essence of states' rights by asserting federal control over the structure of constitutional action at the state level. Nor was any congressional opponent convinced by the change. Under the leadership of Laura Clay and Kate Gordon, southern suffragists had recently organized their own Southern Suffrage Association to head off federal suffrage and black women's enfranchisement, and rejected McCormick's initiative entirely.

The Shafroth-Palmer proposal was surely one of the worst policies ever undertaken in the long history of American suffragism. Opposition in NAWSA's ranks was fierce. Harriot Stanton Blatch characterized the move as a device designed to give "women some political crocheting to occupy their hands and relieve Congress of their disconcerting attentions."[70] Jane Addams resigned her NAWSA office in protest. The now completely independent CU, under Paul's unfettered leadership, took advantage of the disarray by laying its claim to the classic constitutional proposal, which it renamed "the Susan B. Anthony Amendment" as its own. The name stuck.

Instead of trying to conciliate Democrats, the CU decided on an all-out attack. "Today the Democrats . . . control the executive office, the Senate, and the House, . . ." its newspaper, the *Suffragist,* editorialized. "Assuming that the Democrats yield nothing in the present session, we can . . . concentrate our forces on those points where the Party is weakest. . . . To defeat even a few Democratic Senators in November, 1914 [in the midterm election], would make a serious breach in the Party organization."[71]

By targeting Democrats, the CU's strategy defied American suffragism's rock-solid devotion to maintaining neutrality with respect to partisan warfare, a policy instituted by Susan B. Anthony herself. In going after the national Democratic Party, the CU was using the model that the British suffragettes had employed against the British Liberal Party. But the U.S. federal system, which splits sovereignty between state and federal governments, made American politics quite different. Attacking the Democrats as a party, despite their national power, led to serious conflicts with important ongoing state campaigns, including, most important, in New York. There Democrats were the key to victory. Harriot Blatch, who was otherwise in sympathy with the CU, tried to convince Paul to keep her forces out of the state. "If we win the Empire State," she wrote to Paul, "all the states will come down like a pack of cards."[72] Notwithstanding the strategic centrality of a New York victory, the money and resources available in the state were too attractive to ignore, so Paul refused to keep out of the state.

In one crucial way, however, the strategies of NAWSA and the Congressional Union converged. Neither wanted to challenge the Democratic Party's white supremacy convictions. Both continued suffragism's "southern strategy," first instituted in the 1890s. Both groups accepted the deteriorating racial climate in Congress as the situation within which they must work. Paul, despite her Quaker family legacy of abolitionism, had only one concern, a single-minded focus on enacting a federal suffrage amendment. Ironically, and despite the

CU's tactical radicalism, NAWSA's decentralized structure left greater room for affiliates in northern states such as New York and Illinois to take more racially liberal positions and reach out to black women.

Alva Belmont, who had been a fan of suffragette militancy since her visit to London in 1909, now switched her largesse from NAWSA to the CU. In August 1914, she brought the CU leadership to her magnificent Marble House mansion in Newport, Rhode Island. Mary Beard wrote to Paul that she could not in good conscience attend what she called "the Newport stunt," but she was alone in her objections.[73]

In the gold ballroom, decorated by masses of yellow lilies, Alice Paul spoke to what she called "the war council," laying out plans to go after the Democratic Party in the midterm elections. The CU's weapon would be the votes of enfranchised women in the suffrage states and its target would be all Democratic officeholders in those states, regardless of their position on suffrage. "All of these years we have worked primarily in the States," Paul explained. "Now the time has come . . . when we can really go into national politics and use the nearly four million [women's] votes that we have to win the vote for the rest of us."[74] The president would then see that unless he fought for woman suffrage, his party would pay a serious political price.

The CU's 1914 anti-Democratic election campaign was small but well organized. It sent fifteen organizers to cover nine western suffrage states. Lola Trax traveled on a freight train to Osborne, Kansas, where she found a large group ready to meet her near the station. "The temptation to hold a meeting overcame fatigue," she reported. "I jumped into an automobile nearby and had a most interested crowd." In Portland, Oregon, Jessie Stubbs urged the women of the garment and waitress unions to vote against Democrats and "stand by the working women of the East." In Wyoming, where more than two generations of women had been voters, a large audience braved a severe snowstorm to hear Gertrude Hunter. She reported that they were thrilled, having "never heard a Suffrage speech in their lives."[75]

Democrats lost half of their western seats, but it was difficult to assess the precise impact of the CU campaign. The Progressive insurgency was winding down, inflating the regular Republican vote. Nonetheless, the suffragists were pleased with the outcome. "There is every reason to believe," observed one activist, "that the Party leaders have met and studied the Democratic returns from the Campaign states."[76] Her assessment was vindicated when, soon after, the Democrats controlling the House Rules Committee allowed the suffrage amendment bill, which it had held back for two decades, out to a general floor vote.

Thus, in January 1915, the House of Representatives conducted its first ever full debate on woman suffrage, lasting six hours. Both wings of suffragists were there in numbers, and so were members of the National Association Opposed to Woman Suffrage (NAOWS). They too could now see that the federal arena was key and the fight must be waged in Congress. Congressmen trotted out all the old canards against women in politics. One member announced he was going to vote against the amendment "to protect womankind against itself."[77] Another wanted to protect men from women — at least this kind: A woman might be able to cut a side of beef better or patrol the city streets better than a man, he explained, but "who wanted to court the butcher . . . or marry a policeman?"[78]

The final House vote was 174 in favor to 204 against the bill to enable the amendment process. Misogyny notwithstanding, the defeat was driven by the Democratic Party's firm states' rights opposition to any further federal enfranchisement. "The result was what we expected," declared the NAOWS leader Josephine Dodge (or, as she preferred to be called, Mrs. Arthur Dodge). "It means the suffrage movement festered by hysterical women is on the wane."[79] Nonetheless, for the first time in history a full House vote had finally been held. Gains could not be made by avoiding defeats. The CU had put the president on notice for the 1916 presidential election.

Even as more and more attention was turning to the federal amendment and therefore to national politics, action was still ongoing in the states. In an effort to move across the Mississippi to the eastern states, referenda on state constitutional amendments were scheduled for 1915 in New Jersey, Pennsylvania, Massachusetts, and most important, New York. Carrie Chapman Catt was now working full-time on the campaign there. Since 1903, she had devoted most of her attention to the International Woman Suffrage Association, which she had created. In 1913, she turned her attention back to the United States and to the New York state campaign.

Catt was as powerful a leader as Alice Paul. She had a cool confidence that inspired trust. Her "crowning achievement," wrote one follower, was "to sway an audience to emotion by the symmetry and force of her appeal to its mind."[80] "She made those who had supposed themselves the most ardent feel that their zeal hitherto had been a pale ineffectual flame," wrote Alice Stone Blackwell, Lucy Stone's daughter.[81] "When she looks at me," one of her lieutenants recalled, "my heart comes up in my throat. I see in her face all she has lived through and I can refuse her nothing she might ask."[82]

It is difficult to overstate how absolutely Catt subscribed to the Progressive Era faith in "organization." The gospel of organization for her meant putting all suffrage work within a unified framework, working under a common strategy and being responsible to a single leader. She understood herself to be building a suffrage machine, based on and targeted at the great political party machines men had built.

Therefore, when Catt established the New York City Woman Suffrage Party (NYCWSP), and a companion organization to cover the rest of the state, the Empire State Coordinating Committee (ESCC), she insisted that Blatch subordinate her efforts to them. Blatch refused, no more willing to dissolve her independence in New York than Alice Paul had been in the national work. Catt and Blatch, New York's two "suffrage bosses," coexisted, albeit uneasily. Blatch, with her excellent connections in Albany, continued to watch over the state legislature. She made sure to meet the requirement of the state constitution to secure a second legislative vote to authorize the referendum. She also succeeded in reinstating a crucial law establishing women's right to be poll watchers.

Meanwhile Catt's city and state groups tackled the enormous task of convincing the male voters of New York to vote to enfranchise the state's women. They raised a campaign war chest of $150,000 and established "suffrage schools" to train women as political organizers. The state was divided into twelve legislative districts, which were further subdivided all the way down to the election district level. Years after, Catt recalled the totality of the structure she had built with immense pleasure. "Plans for simultaneous action . . . were formulated and executed with such precision," she recalled, "that every woman engaged in suffrage stint or stunt, knew that she was companioned by hundreds of other women who . . . were doing the same thing at the same time."[83]

Catt put the bulk of her effort into New York City, home to half the state's population. She was suspicious of the immense immigrant population of the city, fearing its ignorance and susceptibility to the dictates of Tammany, the city's powerful Democratic machine. Nonetheless, she set her organization the goal of canvassing the entire voting population of the city. "Hundreds of women spent long hours toiling up and down tenement stairs, going from shop to shop, visiting innumerable factories, calling at hundreds of city and suburban homes, covering the rural districts, the big department stores and the immense office buildings with their thousands of occupants." She estimated that they reached 60 percent of male voters.[84]

Arguably the New York referendum campaign of 1915 was one of the most expansive popular campaigns for woman suffrage ever held. Thus, its defeat on November 2 was also historic. The referendum lost 42.5 percent to 57.5 percent, defeated by 200,000 votes. Only six of the state's sixty-one counties voted in favor. Every New York City borough voted against. Speaking to her followers, "Mrs. Catt, pale and worn with the strain of the last days, read the bulletins as they came in in a cool and steady voice."[85]

Like the many suffrage losses over all those years, the failure of the 1915 New York State woman suffrage referendum could not be attributed to any single factor. The suffrage vote was complicated by the fact that at the same time the ballot contained an unpopular proposal for a state constitutional convention. Blatch had fought hard to prevent voting on both issues but lost the battle. The voters were not in a particularly welcoming mood and voted down the constitutional convention even more emphatically than they did woman suffrage. Neither political party had endorsed the referendum, most crucially not Tammany, which held sway over so many of the immigrant districts.

And then there was the war raging in Europe. The relationship between the franchise and military service, which had been used to justify men's exclusive claim to the right to vote, had not been invoked since the Civil War, but it now came back to life. The venerable idea that war was a matter that concerned only men called into question women's claims to an equal right to the franchise. Suffragists disagreed, linking

401

the momentous decision to go to war with women's political empowerment. "When war murders the husbands and sons of women, destroys their homes, destroys their countries, and makes them refugees and paupers," declared Catt, "it becomes the undeniable business of women."[86]

The well-organized New York anti-suffragists worked hard to defeat the referendum. The days when anti-suffragists emphasized women's domestic obligations and kept out of the public sphere were long gone. Now, with little awareness of the irony involved, they mimicked the very movement that they disparaged. They aggressively sought recruits, testified before legislative committees, and left their parlor meetings behind to hold public rallies. Even their arguments against suffrage mirrored those of the suffragists: women should certainly have a role in ameliorating social problems and shaping public policy, but they could do this better without the vote than by entering into the muck of partisan politics. Whether or not the "antis" deserved any credit for the outcome, they took it. Their official statement declared that the defeat "is conclusive evidence that its advocates have mistaken woman suffrage for true progress."[87]

New York suffragists would have none of it. To them, the 500,000 votes cast in favor of amending the state constitution to give the women of New York full voting rights were a down payment on eventual victory. The *New York World* called the 1915 referendum "a revelation of the astonishing growth of the movement." Vera Whitehouse, who had initially been brought into suffrage work by Blatch, drove about the city, reporting the returns and announcing a mass meeting two days later to initiate a new campaign. As suffragists filled the seats in Cooper Union, the audience cheered repeatedly as Catt's first lieutenant, Mary Garrett Hay, proclaimed, "Suffrage was not defeated, only postponed!"[88] The meeting aimed to raise $100,000 for a second referendum and quickly exceeded that goal. The state legislature that had not expected so strong a showing in the first referendum now resisted a second, but eventually passed enabling legislation in March 1916. The second New York referendum was scheduled for November 1917.

Even as the New York campaign for a state constitutional amendment revved up for a second try, national suffrage mobilization for a U.S. constitutional amendment grew in strength and conviction. Carrie Chapman Catt expected to stay focused on New York until national obligations might call her. Then Anna Howard Shaw announced that she would no longer serve as president of NAWSA. Faced by the heartbreaking defeats of the four major eastern state referenda in which victory would have immensely strengthened the national movement, she could see that someone else must take over. Carrie Chapman Catt was obviously that woman.

More than a decade earlier Catt had turned away from suffrage work in the United States to focus on building an international suffrage movement. She had recognized that "the cause would never be won, unless its campaigns were equipped, guided and conducted by women fully aware of the nature of opposition tactics and prepared to meet every maneuver of the enemy by an equally telling counteraction," but that the national suffrage movement was not yet ready for that sort of focus.[1] Now in 1915 Catt believed that she could take the National American Woman Suffrage Association (NAWSA) along a disciplined and coordinated political path. Even so, her face grew "deadly pale" when she was faced with the call to take over the NAWSA presidency.[2] Reorganizing the thousands of members of NAWSA into an orderly suffrage army would not be easy. Nor would keeping state chapters from flying off on their own or keeping national officers from quarreling with each other.

By the time she walked onto the stage at NAWSA's annual convention on December 15, 1915, Catt had thoroughly composed herself and was ready to assume its leadership. Addressing the five hundred suffragists assembled from all around the country, she spoke with great authority, like in "the days of the matriarchate" one admirer noted.[3] "Let organization be the watchword," she told them. "It has been my hobby for the last hundred years."[4] In no uncertain terms, she explained that major changes would be necessary. All of NAWSA's resources would be concentrated on winning a federal constitutional amendment. The Shafroth-Palmer amendment, the disastrous attempt to compromise with states' rights objections, would be abandoned in favor of the original Susan B. Anthony amendment to the U.S. Constitution, the simple federal prohibition of state disfranchisement by sex. Long-serving board members would be replaced with women who had been tested and tried in their own state campaigns.

Competing with Catt's commitment to winning a federal constitutional amendment was her deep involvement with the international suffrage and women's peace movements. War had been raging abroad for a year and a half. She watched with great distress as devastation descended on Europe. Her peace activism was deeply feminist: women's connection to peace rooted in motherhood and new life must be empowered to head off masculinist warmongering. Now as Catt began her tenure, she understood that too much connection between the issues would hurt both. Suffrage radicals would tarnish the women's peace effort; peace activism while war was raging would split the suffrage movement.

Yet her own deep convictions made it difficult to restrain her commitment to peace.

The very day Catt took over the NAWSA presidency, the assembled suffragists were challenged by presidential advisor Dudley Field Malone to endorse Woodrow Wilson's preparedness program, to arm and mobilize in the event of American entry into the European war. The appearance of women being "peace-at-any-price," he admonished, was costing the movement public support. Deeply offended, Catt could not allow this man, twenty-five years her junior, to lecture her on her political obligations or options. Nor would she be bullied into joining war fervor. "Behind preparedness," she insisted, "is a bigger thing — the right to maintain peace." She gave Malone a lecture of her own: this looming war was precisely why women needed full political rights. "We would find a way to settle disputes without killing fathers, husbands and sons."[5]

Speaking before a hostile House Judiciary Committee just the day before, Catt had faced a similar provocation. When congressional Democrats tried to tarnish the entire suffrage movement with the strategy being followed by the Congressional Union (CU) of attacking the Democratic Party, Catt could not restrain herself. What were the aggressive acts of a few overwrought suffragists compared to the much greater violence engulfing the entire world? she challenged. What was the threat of so-called suffrage militancy faced with the threat to entire peoples and countries by actual militarism? She declared, "10,000,000 men have been killed, wounded or missing through militant action, but all of that is held as naught." Instead the U.S. Congress was preoccupied with a few acts of suffrage defiance and aggression.[6]

Meanwhile, the CU was also undergoing an infusion of energies. Harriot Stanton Blatch had helped introduce Alice Paul onto the national stage in 1913. Now, deeply discouraged by the New York loss, she was ready to join Paul's CU, serving as a senior advisor, urging her closest followers to do the same. "Never again will I speak from the street corner," she declared in the aftermath of the defeat. "Never again will I make an appeal to an individual voter." She believed in democracy, she celebrated the fact that young men new to the country could vote, but as if drawing on the elite strain inherited from her mother, she called it "tyranny and license for them to have the power to pass on me and the native born women of America."[7] Many of her most devoted followers followed her lead.

Hopeful that Catt's presidency might be a new start, a CU delegation brought a white flag to the 1915 NAWSA convention. "All suffragists have a common cause at heart," pleaded Zona Gale, a Wisconsin-based CU member (and later the first woman to win a Pulitzer Prize for Drama). "Difference of methods is inevitable," she urged, but need not be an insuperable obstacle to working together.[8] But the obstacles to unity could not be overcome; the recent attacks by Democratic congressmen were making clear how great the gap between the two groups really was. This was not merely a difference of method but of basic orientation to political realities, conciliation versus confrontation. Negotiations failed and, as the *Washington Post* reported, "the dove of peace . . . returned last night badly battered."[9] This was the last attempt at healing the breach between suffrage factions.

Instead of agreeing to abandon its partisan attacks, the CU now proceeded to double down on its campaign against the Democratic Party by appealing to the voting women of the western states. In April 1916, Blatch led two dozen younger organizers on a five-week railroad tour, entitled the Suf-

"The Awakening," Puck Magazine, *1915, portraying states where women could vote, in white, reaching out to disfranchised women.*

frage Special, to establish CU chapters in suffrage states. Blatch was the star of the tour. "Her youthful face and winning smile," one reporter wrote, "makes one forget the streaks of silver hair that told of her years of battling for suffrage."[10] Blatch was retracing the steps taken four decades before by her mother when she was also in her sixties and toured the West under much less modern conditions. "I wanted to shake hands with you," one woman in Seattle told her, "and tell you that you are not nearly as good looking as your mother."[11]

The indefatigable CU organizers reached out to states and to women to which

NAWSA had paid little attention. Mabel Norman and Doris Stevens went to New Mexico, which had only recently become a state. Its Hispanic population was thought to be inherently conservative. Among those they recruited was Adelina (Nina) Otero-Warren, member of a powerful Hispanic political family. She rose to become the leader of New Mexico suffragists — ultimately a crucial factor in bringing state politicians to support a federal constitutional amendment — and ultimately a political power in her own right.

In early June 1916 the CU organizers completed their tour in Chicago, where five thousand excited suffragists were gathered in the Blackstone Theater. Returning with a good report on their response from western women, they were there to undertake a new strategy proposed by Blatch, a more ambitious version of the 1914 electoral campaign run by the CU. She proposed that the many women who already had full voting rights in the suffrage states were now ready to be brought together into an actual political party, made up only of women and featuring one and only one plank on its platform: securing a constitutional amendment to enfranchise all American women. Their party would be called the National Woman's

Party (NWP), and its partisans would pledge to vote against all Democrats, up to and including the president. Like the Progressive Party in 1912, the NWP would threaten to be a spoiler, potentially throwing the presidency back to the Republicans, unless the Democrats came to terms. "Why should not the women of the East find champions among the politically powerful women of the West?" Blatch wrote in a letter to the *New York Times*.[12]

Maud Younger from California, five years a voter, chaired the Chicago Blackstone Theater meeting. "A new force marches on to the political field . . . ," she announced. "Four years ago, women voted in six States — today in twelve. . . . [They] constitute nearly one-fourth of the electoral college, and [cast] more than one-third of the votes necessary to elect a President." She finished with a ringing call: "The women's votes may determine the Presidency of the United States."[13] Thirty-six-year-old Helen Keller, already a national celebrity, made headlines in newspapers across the country by praising the new plan because it "embodies the aspirations of millions of intelligent women . . . it focused our struggle for independence."[14] Blatch pledged to organize a half-million women's votes, and Alva

412

Belmont, who had transferred her largesse from NAWSA to Alice Paul, promised half a million dollars for the new NWP.

Just one week after the CU formed the NWP in Chicago, Catt was bringing the NAWSA forces to the city. The Republican Party was holding its national convention there. No major political party had ever fully endorsed a federal constitutional amendment, and she was determined finally to make that happen. The closest that suffragists had come was far back in 1872 when the Republicans offered suffragists the platform "splinter" of ambiguous support. The Republican Party was the partisan preference of many suffrage leaders, and so the most likely source for a full-fledged platform plank. This is where Catt began.

Catt prepared for the Republican National Convention by securing public endorsements from powerful party politicians and by having NAWSA activists lobby as many convention delegates as possible. The capstone was to be a grand spectacle on the opening day of the convention. An enormous crowd of suffragists drawn from all over the country would march through the city and directly into the convention arena. Catt even arranged with the city zoo to borrow a baby elephant to carry a wooden board symbolizing the "suffrage plank" that she was determined to gain from the Republican Party.[15] The spirit of spectacle initiated by Alice Paul in the March 1913 Washington, D.C., march had now spread to NAWSA.

When the day of the demonstration arrived, however, a rainstorm of biblical proportions hit the city and deluged the NAWSA paraders. Instead of the hoped-for crowd of 25,000, slightly over 5,000 hearty souls showed up, and as "the wind tore at their clothes and rain drenched their faces . . ." reported the *Chicago Herald,* "they marched in unbroken formation, keeping perfect step." The resulting demonstration was "neither colorful nor picturesque," but "no fair weather parade," Catt recalled, could have had more impact. The marchers entered the hall just as the anti-suffragists finished their remarks before the resolutions committee, insisting that women did not actually want the vote. "Through the doors of the hall came the drenched and bedraggled marchers for suffrage," undeterred from their demonstration of determination. No one on the committee could ignore the "incongruity."[16]

Newspapers had been reporting that the

Republicans were prepared to put a plank endorsing a national suffrage amendment into their platform, but now that this might actually happen, opposition emerged from the party's conservative right wing, led by Senators James Wadsworth of New York and Henry Cabot Lodge of Massachusetts. Wadsworth's wife was head of the National Association Opposed to Woman Suffrage (NAOWS). These two men would be suffragists' most determined Republican adversaries.

Thousands of suffragists in the galleries, still dripping wet from the gale, started to cheer when they heard a plank being read using the language they had wanted — "The Republican Party . . . favor the extension of the suffrage to women." Then they grew quiet as Senator Lodge finished the resolution. Support for suffrage notwithstanding, the party must *recognize the right of each state to settle this question for itself.*[17] So determined were Republican anti-suffrage forces, the women now saw, that they were willing to revert to states' rights, the signature position of Democrats. Catt swallowed her disappointment and announced herself pleased that, for the first time since 1872, a major party had put a pro-suffrage plank on its platform.

Frustrated and angered by the Republicans, NAWSA went on to the Democratic National Convention in St. Louis. This was to be a smooth affair, united behind the renomination of Woodrow Wilson. Careful not to step too far over the boundaries of femininity, local suffragists, aware that they were in a border state where suffrage had made no gains, did not march. Instead they organized a dignified gauntlet, a "walkless, talkless parade."[18] "Six thousand women, each under a yellow parasol and encircled by a yellow sash, lined both sides of the street. . . . All day long delegates trudged back and forth through the 'golden lane' reading its banners and reminded of its appeal."[19] Even an African American delegation, more likely Republican than Democratic, took part. One young participant, new to suffrage activism, watched as the men walked by and "wondered what they thought about us — whether we impressed them favorably or not." Then some delegates riding by in a carriage, "very handsome," she noted, "smiled and looked at us in a very flattering way . . . and I could not help but feel encouraged."[20]

Catt had negotiated a plank with national Democratic leaders, reportedly accepted by the president, representing the best she thought she could get. The plank would endorse woman suffrage without mention of the state versus federal method. Even this, it turned out, was too much for southern Democrats. Suffrage eavesdroppers listened throughout the night as an argument raged behind the closed doors of the party resolution committee as to whether to support suffrage at all. The compromise plank that emerged endorsed suffrage but specified state action. Catt's lieutenants wanted to protest, but again their chief counseled restraint. "We have got them to give us a plank, even if it is rotten."[21]

Still, the anti-suffragists were not done. On the convention floor, there was more opposition. Governor James Ferguson of Texas wanted to remove the suffrage plank completely. Ferguson was a prohibition opponent and notoriously corrupt. He was sure that women voters would close down the liquor industry and clean up state politics. (Irony of ironies, when Ferguson was driven out of office a decade later, his wife, Miriam "Ma" Ferguson, replaced him as governor.) Then Senator Key Pittman, from the suffrage state of Nevada, rose with a challenge. An admiring suffrage lobbyist described his "blazing dark eyes and quiet manner . . . the most dramatic figure" in the Senate.[22] "Are you *men* that cheer every denunciation of women?" he challenged the Texas delegation. Once again the weather heightened the political drama. As "a blinding flash of lightning and heavy explosion of thunder" startled the auditorium, Ferguson's motion was roundly defeated and the Democrats' modest suffrage plank, not much worse than the Republicans', stood.[23]

Two pro-suffrage planks on national platforms going into a presidential election were an achievement of sorts, but still neither party had proved itself willing to endorse a federal constitutional amendment. Faced with mounting evidence that powerful opponents in both parties were poised to stop the amendment's progress through Congress, Catt announced that NAWSA would hold an emergency convention to reconsider its strategy once the presidential campaigns were fully under way.

Thus, the first week of September, when crowds of suffragists came together in Atlantic City, Catt addressed them with a new sense of urgency. NAWSA could not go on as before, uncoordinated, unfocused, undetermined. "The crisis is here," she warned, "but . . . if our women think it means the vote without a struggle . . . the hour may pass and our political liberty will not be won." They should not count on "other women" — thinking no doubt of the militants of the National Woman's Party — to "pay the price of their emancipation" for them.[24] She had arrived at the same conclusion as Blatch and Paul: suffragists must take an active role in the fall elections. Catt audaciously invited both presidential candidates to the meeting. Republican presidential nominee Charles Evans Hughes, a moderately progressive though unexciting candidate, had already issued a terse endorsement of the suffrage amendment. He did not think it necessary to go any further and declined to attend. President Wilson surprisingly accepted.

On the afternoon of the suffrage meeting's fifth day, a thousand women crowded into the New Nixon Theater on the Atlantic City boardwalk, while many more waited outside to learn what the president of the United States had to say to them. Wilson delivered a brief speech, honoring women, believing in the eventual victory of their cause, but promising nothing. "I have not come to ask you to be patient, because you have been," he concluded, "but I have come to congratulate you that there has been a force behind you that will beyond any peradventure be triumphant and for which you can a little

419

while afford to wait."[25] The audience seemed stunned until Anna Howard Shaw raised her powerful voice. "We have waited so long, Mr. President, for the vote — we had hoped it might come in your administration."[26] The suffragists stood up as one, as Wilson, with his new and decidedly anti-suffrage wife, Edith, on his arm, promptly left the auditorium. Nonetheless, in Catt's judgment, his move toward the federal amendment had begun.

Catt then called together her new hand-picked executive board. The past five days of meetings had been long, the seashore weather hot. One member recalled vividly "the tired faces of most of the women there, the huge map hung on one of the walls; and, most vividly of all, Mrs. Catt herself."[27] In contrast to her stubbornly optimistic public stance, in this private meeting Catt let out all her anger and impatience. She was enraged at the "stupid inability of newly formed untrained committees" from chapters who had run state campaigns that were destined to fail.[28] (Such a campaign in her home state of Iowa was her particular target.) From now on, state work must be subordinated to the federal campaign. Only states with a good chance of winning full voting rights or efforts to get state legislatures to follow Illinois's lead to allow women to vote for presidential electors would receive NAWSA's support. Fundraising was to be substantially increased, new larger offices were to be acquired, and the suffrage congressional lobby, which had been working for two years, would intensify its efforts.

Meanwhile, through the summer and fall of election season, Alice Paul and the newly formed NWP campaigned hard to inflict as much damage as they could on the president and his party. Wilson was going to the voters on the basis of his liberal domestic record while trying to keep the divisive war issue to the background. His supporters nonetheless promoted him by insisting that "He Kept Us Out of War," to which the NWP retorted, "He Kept Us Out of Suffrage."[29] The NWP was pursuing its own kind of neutrality. It would not advocate for the nation staying out of or preparing to go into the war, but would keep an eye solely on the amendment. In defense of this position, Paul cited the experience of Susan B. Anthony, who had deeply regretted setting aside the issue of woman suffrage during the Civil War. Now, as the country confronted entering the first full-fledged war effort in a half century, she was determined not to repeat the error.

While Paul was genuinely agnostic toward the war, that was not so for many of her followers. The young, radically inclined feminists on whom the NWP counted for its dynamism tended strongly to pacifism, to a world without war. Inez Milholland Boissevain, the equestrian star of the 1913 Washington, D.C., parade, was one of these determined young pacifists. As a pioneering female war correspondent, she had gone to Italy to write passionately against the war mobilization of young men there. In December she had traveled on Henry Ford's "Peace Ship" as part of its feckless journey to convince the belligerent nations of Europe to negotiate an end to the war. However, her growing celebrity — and her father's money — had overcome Paul's concerns about her appropriateness and stamina, and she became the beautiful face of the NWP. Of the several dozen intensely committed organizers who fanned out across the West, she received the most press attention and the most enthusiastic audiences.

To maximize Milholland Boissevain's impact, Paul designated her a "special flying envoy." So rapid and extensive was her campaigning — in one month she was scheduled to hit all twelve states where women already had federal voting rights — that she might as well have been traveling in the air as on the rails. (Indeed, Montana suffragist Hazel Hunkins did fly in a single-engine airplane to drop suffrage leaflets near San Francisco.) Milholland Boissevain, the supreme New Woman, was renowned for her determination and fearlessness; and Paul was an unrelenting taskmaster when it came to suffrage work. So both sought to press Milholland Boissevain despite her failing health. She had been diagnosed with tonsillitis but put off any operation until after the tour. The more she spoke, the more her throat ached and the infection poured into her body. Doctors at every stop gave her painkillers at her request.

Milholland Boissevain's fundamental message was a passionate appeal to the enfranchised women of the West from the voteless women of the East. "Now, for the first time in our history, women have the power to enforce their demands, and the weapon with which to fight for women's liberation," she declared. "You, women of the West, who possess that power, will you use it on behalf of women? We have waited so long and so patiently and so hopelessly for help." The approach skillfully combined the plea of the weak with the power of the strong. Women, not men, could save women, if only they were willing to put "the interests of women above all other political considerations." Her speeches were dotted with indirect references to America's possible involvement in the war. "Other considerations press upon you," she conceded, "but surely this great question of women's liberty comes first. How can our nation be free with half of its citizens politically enslaved? How can the questions that come before the government for decision, be decided aright, while half the people whom these decisions affect are mute?"[30]

In Los Angeles, in the third week of her tour, Milholland Boissevain was in the midst of a rousing appeal to a large audience when she collapsed. Legend has it that she was just at that moment saying "Mr. President, how long must women go on fighting for liberty?"[31] She was carried off, but fifteen minutes later dragged herself back to the stage to finish, then was taken off to the hospital, where she was diagnosed with severe aplastic anemia. That explained the ashen pallor that many had noticed of her. Despite operations, blood transfusions, and other drastic measures, Inez Milholland

Boissevain died November 25, 1916. She had just turned thirty.

By that time, President Wilson had been reelected. The NWP campaign to unite western women to vote against and defeat him had failed. Anxiety about the United States entering the war had helped Wilson secure a modest popular vote margin of 600,000 (and an even narrower electoral college victory). Wilson's reelection was hard enough for suffragists to bear, but harder still was the evidence that it had been California, with its rich lode of women's votes, which had put him just barely over the top.

Milholland Boissevain's parents considered her death a private family matter, but her sister Vida believed that she would have wanted something different. She authorized the NWP to use Inez's sacrifice to further the cause. "It sounds cold-blooded," Vida wrote, "but you understand the situation."[32] Paul understood only too well. Deprived of Wilson's defeat, the NWP needed a weapon to continue to pressure him, and Inez Milholland Boissevain as martyr was that.

Early in December, the NWP brought a deputation to the newly reelected president. Sara Bard Field was selected to address President Wilson. She and two other

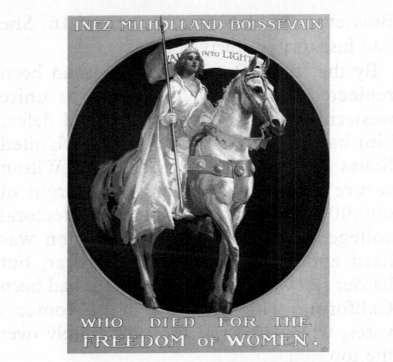

Poster commemorating Inez Milholland Boissevain's death, 1924.

women, her chauffeur and machinist, had spent almost three months driving five thousand miles across the country to deliver a mammoth petition — four miles long and 500,000 signatures — of western women who were asking for a constitutional suffrage amendment. "In the name of all women who had fought and died for this cause, and . . . with our hearts bowed in sorrow, in the name of this gallant girl who died with the word 'Liberty' on her lips," she implored, would Wilson help them in

426

their cause? The president at first seemed "very human, sympathetic" and "listened cordially." Then, when someone mentioned Charles Evans Hughes, his recent opponent, "a cold wave passed over him. . . . The look in his eyes became so cold" that all hope drained from the suffragist deputation. He admonished them to "court public opinion" and then abruptly left the room.[33]

Still the NWP's apotheosis of Milholland Boissevain continued. Speaker of the House "Champ" Clark of Missouri, a suffrage supporter, arranged for an elaborate memorial service to be held for her on Christmas Day in the Statuary Hall of the Capitol Building — perhaps because it was the only day the Hall was not open to the public. No woman had ever been honored there before. Carl Sandburg, who may have known Milholland Boissevain, memorialized the event in a poem: "They are crying salt tears / Over the beautiful beloved body / of Inez Milholland."[34] A thousand people on the floor and more in the balcony listened as Maud Younger delivered a passionate eulogy and call to arms. "As in life she had been the symbol of woman's cause, so in death she is the symbol of . . . the toll of the prolonged women's struggle. . . . We are here to-day to pay tribute to Inez Milholland Boissevain, who was our comrade. . . . Let it be . . . that we finish the task she could not finish."[35]

Now that President Wilson had made it clear that he would do nothing for the federal amendment, the NWP began a new approach. Again, the idea came from Harriot Stanton Blatch. In the lead-up to the first New York State referendum, suffragists had conducted a "Silent Sentinel," standing mute outside the Albany state capitol day after day. Their purpose was to draw publicity and shame the legislators for their inaction. Paul took this tactic, brought it to the national stage, and raised it to a new, more dramatic level.

On January 10, 1917, NWP members began a silent picket of the White House. They had rented a residence just across from the White House lawn. Every day protesters walked out the front door, crossed the street, and stood wordlessly outside the gates. The slogans on their elegant silk banners spoke for them — "MR. PRESIDENT WHAT WILL YOU DO FOR WOMAN SUFFRAGE?" and "HOW LONG MUST WOMEN WAIT FOR LIBERTY."[36] Picketing the White House has since become almost a cliché of national activism, but as was true with the 1913 Washington, D.C., parade, suffragists were among the first protesters to use the tactic. The picketers continued over the winter and even when the weather was not cooperative, the cold and the rain only emphasized their determination and drew greater publicity.

For the first few months of 1917, onlookers were either amused by or curious about the suffrage picketers. Helena Hill, a Vassar graduate, described the generally sympathetic response passersby gave her. Her only complaint was the flirtatious men who bothered her, causing her, in the words of a *Washington Post* reporter, to "stamp her little foot in apparent vexation."[37] Occasionally the president and his wife drove out of the main White House gate past the picketers, smiled, and waved. Wilson was not irritated — yet — but neither was he moved to action.

On March 4, the day of Wilson's second inauguration, one thousand suffrage demonstrators marched completely around the White House chanting their slogans. Paul warned reporters that their protest might bring down the walls, just as Joshua had in Jericho. The march was led by Vida Milholland, Inez's sister. This time, when the president drove by the pickets, he did not wave genially but stared straight ahead.

For twenty-nine-year-old Doris Stevens, this was the turning point in her life. Born in Nebraska, she had begun her suffrage work with NAWSA after graduation from Oberlin and then had switched her allegiance to the CU, then to the NWP to become one of its organizers. This day, however, fully ignited her passion and she carried the fire within her for the rest of her life. She began to grow deeply resentful of the president, a conviction which deepened to implacable rage over the next three years. Standing in the rain and cold as the president ignored them, Stevens, who became the great chronicler of the picketing campaign, wrote that this one day "probably did more than any other to make women sacrifice themselves."[38]

This dramatic ramping up of national suffrage work was made possible by tremendous new attention to and success in fundraising. Money was necessary for spectacular demonstrations, traveling organizers, congressional lobbyists, and sophisticated publicity efforts. Throughout the nineteenth century, suffrage work had been done on a shoestring, drawing on the uncompensated devotion of its adherents. But now that was changing. As more and more young women entered the labor force, many expected to be paid for their labor. At the same time, great new fortunes were being accumulated, to which some women had some access. The two came together in a new financial environment for suffrage.

It will be remembered, that, in the last months of her life, Anthony had convinced Mary Elizabeth Garrett, daughter of the wealthiest family in Maryland, to give a donation of what was then an immense sum, $60,000. Three years later, Alva Belmont had begun contributing even greater sums. First her money went to Anna Howard Shaw and NAWSA to establish modern headquarters in New York City. (Prior to that, NAWSA worked out of the treasurer's home in Warren, Ohio.) After 1913, she shifted her immense largesse to the CU. Catt sought out other wealthy donors to replace Belmont, to fund the New York 1915 referendum campaign.

Even as she did, Catt had learned of much greater financial rescue to use as she best saw fit for the entire suffrage movement, funds that completely dwarfed everything that had previously come into the movement. The donor was a woman named Mrs. Frank Leslie. Born in New Orleans as Miriam Follin, she had risen from obscure origins to lead a colorful and scandal-ridden life. Frank Leslie was her third husband and the head of a publishing company, which she was able to lift from near failure to great success. (She eventually took his first name.) After her husband died in 1880, she became one of the wealthiest and most controversial figures in New York high society. She had previously given small amounts to suffrage work, and clearly had strong opinions about women's rights, but just a week after her death in 1914, a lawyer informed Catt that Leslie had left most of her fortune to Catt for the sole purpose of woman suffrage work. The amount was just shy of two million dollars. Over the next three years, descendants' challenges and lawyers' fees ate up half of that amount, but even so what was left amounted to the largest gift by far ever given to the suffrage movement.

Now that Catt was president of NAWSA, the residual of the legacy finally became hers. The first installment arrived in the form of jewels, which were brought directly by lawyers to Catt herself. Her lieutenants ran their fingers through the gold and pearls, and one of the women "perched a diamond tiara on Mrs. Catt's crisp white hair."[39] Then the jewels went off to be sold. Checks began to arrive in May 1917. One of the first dispensations of the Leslie money was $25,000 given to the second New York suffrage campaign.

The bulk went to establishing a comprehensive press and propaganda office in New York, giving NAWSA an effective and far-reaching publicity arm. Perhaps in deference to a lingering sense that inviting publicity was unwomanly, the operation was called the "Bureau of Suffrage Education," but the effort, employing a staff of twenty-five in six different departments, was anything but modest. The impact could be seen in newspapers across the country. Previously unable or unwilling to develop their own coverage of the accelerating suffrage war, newspapers from Montana to Texas now reprinted the bureau's press releases word for word. The entire reading public of the nation was able to follow what was happening in Washington, D.C., the dramatic suffrage tactics, the relentless political opposition, and the shifting positions of the president of the United States.

Aided by the Leslie money, Carrie Chapman Catt was also able to upgrade NAWSA's congressional lobbying. In January 1917, she asked thirty-five-year-old Maud Wood Park to join NAWSA's congressional lobbying effort. Within two months,

Park was leading it. Lobbying was already a dirty word, regarded as special interests seeking to use antidemocratic means to influence legislation. Women's votes were going to clean up politics. Their lobby would be different. Park called it the "Front Door Lobby."

Park had graduated from Radcliffe College in 1898. She was one of only two members of her class to admit supporting woman suffrage. The other was Inez Haynes, her closest friend, whose own path to suffrage activism eventually took her to NAWSA's rival, the CU. "We were feminists," she recalled, "but in those days no one in America used the word feminist."[40]

Maud Wood Park has left behind a unique archive of self-examination that provides unprecedented insight into the highly personal path that led at least one woman into a life shaped by suffrage activism. After graduation she married an improvident man, keeping their union secret because she believed it would interfere with her political work. Desperately searching for meaningful work and self-expression — suffering terribly from "the snare of preparation," which Jane Addams once called the chief dilemma faced by first-generation college women — she became deeply depressed, at times

434

suicidal. She wrote in despair about what she called "the sex problem." To "a woman of brains," limited opportunities and the humiliations of sexuality would "eat into her soul." All the while she kept up suffrage work, paid a small salary by a philanthropic suffragist.[41]

When Catt tapped her for the lobbying job, she demurred that she was "too much a reformer and too little an opportunist to be of use in Washington." Nonetheless, she "felt like Moses . . . after the Promised Land had been shown to him. . . . For the first time I saw our goal as possible of attainment in the near future."[42] She accepted Catt's charge and found that she could not only do the task, but also do it well. The purpose and accomplishment of suffrage work lifted her out of her slough of despair. She remained completely dedicated to Catt for the rest of her life.

Park's guide through the intricacies of congressional lobbying was Helen Hamilton Gardener. Park's "first recollection of a woman of genius who was to teach me almost everything of value that I came to know during those years in Washington" was of a "small woman with gray hair" who said little.[43] Gardener had taken her own eccentric path to become what one admirer called "the chief diplomat" of the suffrage movement. She was a generation older than most twentieth-century suffrage activists, born in western, pro-Union Virginia in 1853, before college education became available to women. She started her women's rights career as a full-fledged radical in the 1890s.

Because of her bold criticism of organized religion, advocacy of divorce reform, and outspoken condemnation of men's predatory sexual activities, she became Elizabeth Cady Stanton's most important late-life protégée. In these years, Gardener's most remarkable campaign was a crusade to prove that women's brains were in no way inferior to men's. She convinced intelligent, accomplished women to will their brains to science. Among them was Cady Stanton, though after her death, her children overrode her wishes and her brain was buried with her.

In the twentieth century, Gardener dramatically shifted styles from provocation to pragmatism. Moving to Washington, D.C., she cultivated close relationships with powerful Democratic politicians, including Speaker of the House Champ Clark, the president's private secretary Joseph Tumulty, and ultimately Woodrow Wilson himself. Toward the end of his presidency, Wilson appointed her to the Civil Service Commission, making Gardener the highest placed woman in the federal government. When she died, her brain went to Cornell Medical College.

Gardener's diplomatic gifts rested on her uncanny ability to cajole and convince powerful men to grant her political requests. Where others saw male power and hostility, she saw insecurity and weakness, and knew how to get around it. She taught Maud Wood Park to see politicians neither as heroes or villains but, as Park put it, merely "representative of the run of men."[44] She opened a backdoor channel to the president and was eventually able to arrange a meeting with him whenever Carrie Chapman Catt requested one. Tiny, attractive, and exceedingly clever, she was, one biographer observed, possessed of "unfailing tact, [and] sensitivity to human nature."[45] "Her work can rarely be reported because of its confidential nature," Maud Wood Park explained. Nonetheless, "whenever a miracle has appeared to happen in our behalf, the facts . . . would nearly always have proved that Mrs. Gardener was the worker of wonders."[46]

Gardener taught Park the delicacies of effective lobbying, which Park boiled down to a few basic guidelines: don't nag, boast, lose your temper, overstay your welcome, allow yourself to be overheard, permit a congressman to declare his opposition, and most important, "don't do anything to close the door to the next advocate of suffrage."[47] There were special rules for lady lobbyists: make friends of the secretaries, knock before entering (but then walk in promptly) so as not to catch the congressman in an embarrassing situation, make sure the door to the congressman's office stayed open so no one would suspect anything untoward, and retreat to the congressional ladies' rooms to write notes immediately after every interview.

When Park consulted with Democratic congressmen, they told her that the NWP picketing had so irritated them that they were in no mood to help the NAWSA lobbyists. Park's opinion was that "the fuss made over the banner and the picketing is all out of proportion to the actions themselves." She did not think it changed the convictions of either supporters or opponents in Congress ("who had the picketing to talk about"), but it made unresolved "waverers" more timid.[48]

For some time, Carrie Chapman Catt had

been preparing a response if and when the country went to war. In late February 1917, in response to renewed submarine attacks on American shipping vessels and news of secret German attempts to turn the Mexican government against the United States, the president broke off relations with Germany. After two days of difficult discussion, NAWSA's executive committee voted to support the government.

They were specific about the work they would do. NAWSA would recruit and guide women into whatever positions the nation needed to free men for combat; organize homemakers to help the government to conserve crucial resources; and send support funds abroad, especially to women and children who were displaced by war. Suffragists would also assist in the cultivation of loyalty among recent immigrants whose patriotism the president doubted and whom he disdainfully called "hyphenates." However, winning a constitutional amendment would remain the first objective of the association. The organization's stance was sent to the president. The president wrote back his "great and sincere admiration of the action taken."[49] The tentative bond of collaboration and mutual trust between Wilson and Catt was growing.

Objections to Catt's leadership and NAWSA's carefully crafted pro-war policy were considerable. Members resigned, some to concentrate exclusively on war preparations, others to shift to the NWP. Catt's style was to reconcile conflicts, but dissent in the face of war was beyond even her control. Former colleagues declared that she had betrayed the cause of pacifism. Catt was ousted from the New York branch of the Woman's Peace Party and she resigned from the national organization, which she had helped to found with Jane Addams two years before.

A week after NAWSA committed itself to judicious support of the government's war policy, the NWP set its own war policy. If and when the nation went to war, it would continue as before, with daily pickets, appeals to the president, and unrelenting pursuit of a constitutional amendment. It would take no stance on war. Members who wished would be allowed to do war work, just not via the NWP. For this refusal to champion the war, newspapers began for the first time to refer to these suffragists disdainfully as "militants."

When the 65th Session of Congress opened in March 1917, suffragists' suspense over

Representative Jeannette Rankin, 1917.

the looming prospect of war was momentarily set aside in celebration of their new political star, thirty-seven-year-old Jeannette Rankin. Rankin was a suffrage activist who had apprenticed in the 1910 Washington State referendum, served as a NAWSA organizer in California in 1911, and led the successful campaign for votes for women in her home state of Montana in 1914. The first vote Rankin cast in Montana was for herself when she ran in November 1916 as the Republican candidate for one of her state's two congressional seats.

On April 2, Rankin entered the House of Representatives as the country's first woman member of Congress, put there by the votes of women as well as men. She embodied the crucial fact that growing victories in the West provided the lever for ultimate triumph in the national arena. She was average height, attractive but not stunning, dressed in a "modish" blue suit and sporting a short bob haircut. She was, in other words, much like other modern women of her generation who were drawn into suffrage work. She was distinguished by this one thing, her presence in a body that had not included a member of her sex for its entire 128-year history. The entire House stood, not just her fellow Republicans but also Democrats, supporters of suffrage and opponents alike, all acknowledging the historic transformation that her presence signified. Not only were political men united in recognition of Rankin's accomplishment, so were suffragists. Both suffrage wings, NAWSA and the NWP, claimed her as their own. She had worked with and supported both and, like the good politician she was, avoided taking sides.

That very evening, the president came

before a joint session of Congress. The time had come to call for a declaration of war. As Rankin sat with her fellow congressmen, Maud Wood Park scored a seat in the back of the House gallery and listened. The tension was profound. Wilson was taking the country into its first major war effort in a half century. Industrial production, food and fuel preparation, and a massive and rapid increase in military strength were going to transform the society, national politics, women's lives, and the president himself. These were the days when Congress still held to its constitutional obligations to declare war. The Senate quickly did the president's bidding, but the debate in the House went on for two days. To avoid calling a vote on the third day, which was Good Friday, the session went on late into the night and the roll was finally called at two a.m.

Many suffragists expected that, as a thoroughgoing pacifist, Rankin would oppose the resolution, but, as Park recognized, "if she voted 'no' her political future would be in jeopardy." "What do you think Jeannette Rankin will do?" Park asked a companion.[50] Rankin did not answer when her name was called on the first roll call. On the second round, she rose to say that she could not in

443

good conscience vote to send other women's sons to war, she herself being childless. The House officer instructed her that she must simply vote yes or no without explanation, and so she said no, joining forty-nine other members of Congress who voted against going to war. Newspapers reported that she wept as she cast her vote, but Park and others saw that she did not cry, even though several male Congress members did. There is some evidence that Alice Paul had urged her to vote no and Carrie Chapman Catt had pushed for yes, but publicly they took the same stance: Jeannette Rankin had voted her conscience and that was the honorable thing.

The president and both parties agreed that all other legislative business would be suspended during a special war Congress session. A pending suffrage resolution, previously scheduled to be the first order of business when Congress convened, could not be introduced. How long it would remain in limbo was not clear.

Wilson's April declaration of war did not immediately put the country on a full war footing. Troops needed to be assembled and trained before they were sent abroad. Even so, the atmosphere surrounding the picketing became openly hostile. Newspapers wrote that the picketers were "flaunt[ing] their banners in President Wilson's face."[51] Under the pressure of war, the rift between the two suffrage wings deepened. NAWSA's enhanced press operation responded to more than 250 newspaper editorials to clarify that, representing the great majority of suffragists, it was distinct from the NWP and did not support picketing the president. Catt issued a formal statement urging Alice Paul to halt the pickets because they were hurting the suffrage cause in Congress and constituting an "unwarranted discourtesy to the President."[52]

Finally, on June 21 the picketers were physically attacked by onlookers, who tore their banners, cursed, and spit on them. The suffragists were carrying an extra-large banner directed at a visiting delegation from Russia. The provisional Russian government of Alexander Kerensky, which had helped to depose the czar, had announced that it would enfranchise its women. Suffragists wanted to underline the irony of the president's resistance to women's enfranchisement. "President Wilson and Envoy [Elihu] Root are Deceiving Russia . . ." their banner read. "We, the women of America, tell you, America is not a Democracy."[53] A line had been crossed. Peaceful picketing now began to look like treason.

That first day that the picketers carried "the Russian banner," the only person who was arrested was a female anti-suffrage federal worker who had led the attack on the picketers. She was released without charges. The next day, however, the Capitol police began arresting picketers. Congress had just passed the Espionage Act, outlawing any "attempt to cause insubordination, disloyalty" or "willfully obstruct the recruiting" of troops for the war.[54] The picketers were guilty of none of this, so they were charged with milder, patently spurious charges, like obstructing traffic and disturbing the peace. The court dismissed the arrests. Both the *New York Times* and the *Washington Post* insisted that the picketers were after "as much publicity out of the incident as possible" and obligingly gave it to them.[55]

Four weeks later, sixteen picketers were arrested, again on charges of obstructing traffic. Among them was Doris Stevens. In her detailed book-length account of the picketers' experience, Stevens described the courtroom officers as incompetent, nervous, and "pathetic," and the arrested suffragists as interested, observant, and unrepentant.

Message to the Russian envoys outside the White House, June 1917.

They watched as the normal "Saturday night's disorderlies — both black and white" were treated dismissively and summarily sentenced because they couldn't afford lawyers. The picketers could, but chose to do without representation. "We shall speak in our own behalf," said their chosen spokeswomen. "As long as the . . . representatives of the government prefer to send women to jail on petty and technical charges," they would go to jail rather than pay fines.[56] This time the sentence was carried out.

The suffrage picketers were remanded to serve their sentences, not at the local jail in Washington, but at Occoquan prison farm, administered by the District of Columbia twenty miles over the Virginia state line. There the suffragists would be isolated far from the city, the press, and their supporters. Stevens called it "our temporary summer residence," where they were immediately "struck by a little terror." Meant to be an emblem of modern prison reform, the Occoquan Workhouse was in fact a hellish place, under the control of a sadistic warden, W. H. Whittaker. Upon arrival the protesters were stripped, put in rough prison clothes and ill-fitting shoes, denied soap, toilet paper, and drinking glasses, and given unpalatable food. "We try so hard to eat . . . for we are tired and hungry," she wrote, "but no one is able to get it down. We leave the table hungry and slightly nauseated."[57] They slept on unwashed bedding and were housed with prisoners with communicable diseases.

Warden W. H. Whittaker made sure to house the white suffrage picketers within the regular, largely black prison population and to assign black prisoners, including men, to guard and restrain them. Whittaker was no racial liberal, and Stevens accused the prison administration of deliberately encouraging "race hatred" by housing the suffrage prisoners with black women prisoners.[58] But this gave her a chance to witness the very worst of the conditions under which black District residents suffered. Her account was both sympathetic and condescendingly stereotypical. She learned of regular beatings conducted by the warden himself. " 'Yous all right' . . . a young negress prostitute" told the suffrage prisoners, Stevens recorded in exaggerated dialect. " 'What chance has we niggahs got, I ask ye. I hopes you all gits a vote an' fixes up SOM'TINGS for women!' "[59] At nighttime, the black prisoners sang songs and the picketers joined them.

Three days later, Stevens and the others learned that the president had pardoned them. The details of their imprisonment had been presented to the president by his close counselor, Dudley Field Malone, who had been gradually won over to the suffragists' side. He had listened to their stories and their arguments and, of no little importance, had begun to fall in love with Doris Stevens, whom he would eventually marry. "It was sad to leave the other prisoners behind. . . ." Stevens wrote. "It was hard to resist digressing into some effort at prison reform. That way lay our instincts. Our reason told us that we must first change the status of women."[60] Upon learning that she had been pardoned, Allison Hopkins, whose husband had served on the Democratic National Committee, returned to picket the day after she was released. Her banner read "We Ask Not Pardon for Ourselves but Justice for All American Women."[61]

In August 1917, still frustrated by congressional inaction, the picketers sought a way to go further. By now, draftees had begun to sail to Europe. This time their banners addressed the President as "Kaiser Wilson" and read "Have You Forgotten Your Sympathy with the Poor Germans Because They Were Not Self-Governing? . . . Take the Beam out of Your Own Eye." Perhaps instigated by the police, the crowd became a raging mob, chased the picketers to their headquarters, scaled the building, and tried to pull women off the balcony, and one man fired a gun into a second-story window.

"Our fight was becoming increasingly difficult — I might almost say desperate," wrote Stevens. "Here we were, a band of women fighting with banners, in the midst of a world armed to the teeth. And so it was not very difficult to understand how high spirited women grew more resentful."[62] Arrests were resumed, but picketing continued.

In her account of the picketing, Stevens

bragged that the earliest arrested picketers included daughters of ambassadors and descendants of the signers of the Declaration of Independence. Later, the appeal of the campaign, the chance to make history, and the bold outlaw thrill of civil disobedience drew a much wider range of women. Overall, the spirit was one of gender solidarity reaching beyond class difference. Among the more than one thousand women who eventually became picketers were business and professional women, teachers, and librarians.

In the fall, no doubt in response to events in Russia, where Bolsheviks were moving to seize the provisional government, much more radical women, including Eastern European Jewish immigrants and veterans of trade union and socialist activism, joined the picketing. Anna Gventer, a shirtwaist worker and a member of the Socialist Party, came from Baltimore to protest and was arrested and jailed. She smuggled out a letter to socialist congressman Meyer London. "I am more revolutionary than the Woman's Party," she told him, but she was moved to help American women win the rights that those in her homeland of Russia had already secured. "Conditions here are so bad that I feel I must stay. . . . We are enslaved here."

451

The food was unpalatable, and as a vegetarian, she could not eat the bits of meat provided. (This detail gained Gventer a place in the history of vegetarianism.) Stevens included her letter in her account. Gventer served her entire thirty-day sentence and when she came out, already a tiny woman, she had lost thirty pounds.[63]

While it would not be an exaggeration to say that the NWP picketers constituted the most thoroughly cross-class body of women's rights activists in American history, racially the party's campaign was anything but diverse. Black women suffragists were active in northern states including New York and Illinois, but national suffrage politics were almost entirely closed to them. There were white members of the NWP for whom racial equality was an important political principle, but not Alice Paul. As committed as she was to challenging the norms of congressional politics, she had long before made it clear that she would accept without question the Democratic Party's allergy to black people voting.

Although the NWP did not publicize the fact, at least one African American woman, the indomitable Mary Church Terrell, did join the White House pickets. A D.C. resident, she was frequently summoned to join the pickets, and she sometimes brought her daughter Phylliss with her "to swell the number."[64] Picketer Hazel Hunkins recalled that Paul considered Terrell a personal friend, an exception to her generally low opinion of African Americans. Terrell was a light-skinned woman, and the crowds who were already angry at white women protesting their president would no doubt have been enraged if they had realized that an African American woman had the audacity to do the same thing. As circumstances would have it, Terrell did not picket on the July day that the suffragists were first sent to Occoquan. It is chilling to imagine what might have happened to her.

In October, Paul, who had captained the pickets from headquarters, decided it was time for her to join the others — to get arrested and go to jail. The police seized her even before she could reach the picket line. The judge sentenced her to six months, then suspended her sentence. Two weeks later Paul picketed again, and this time the judge reinstated her sentence, adding one extra month for good measure. "Were they beginning actually to perceive the real strength of the movement and the protest that would be aroused if she were imprisoned?" Doris Stevens asked.[65]

Suffrage picketers in prison uniforms, Doris Stevens on the left.

Even in jail, Paul was ever the organizer. Within two days of her imprisonment she conducted an act of civil disobedience, breaking a window to allow in fresh air for the other prisoners. For this, she was transferred from Occoquan to the D.C. City Jail and put in solitary confinement. After two weeks, she ended up in the prison hospital, weak from confinement and bad food. There she concocted a new tactic, along with another picketer lying in a bed next to her. Rose Winslow was a Polish-born trade unionist who had been working with the NWP since 1916. Together they decided to undertake a hunger strike, announcement of which made the newspapers from New

York to Chicago to San Francisco.

A decade before, British suffrage militants had used the practice and gained international coverage for it. Irish Sein Fein radicals had also refused food to gain treatment as political prisoners, as did immigrant conscientious objectors in Arizona. Just that January, birth control advocate Margaret Sanger's imprisoned sister Ethel Byrne had not eaten for over a month and was finally force-fed. Paul would be the first suffrage activist in the United States subjected to forced feeding. Newspapers had been eagerly awaiting the moment when American women would follow the British suffragettes' precedent and starve themselves, and they had been disappointed that the first sentences of three days early in the picketing did not produce such a spectacle. Hunger striking was a "coveted goal of the American militant," the *Baltimore Sun* and other newspapers confidently reported.[66]

Forced feeding was an intentionally gruesome procedure. Speaking of the prison physician sent to feed her by tying her down, forcing a tube down her nose, and pouring a foul, thick liquid into it, the famously stoic Paul recalled, "I believe I have never in my life before feared anything or any human being" until "the hour of [the doctor's] visit."[67] Rose Winslow was also force-fed and kept notes, reprimanding herself. "I always weep and sob, to my great disgust, quite against my will. I will try to be less feeble-minded."[68] An African American cleaning woman at the prison hospital passed notes back and forth between Paul and NWP leaders on the outside.

Unable to get Paul to eat, discomfited by the negative publicity they were receiving, the jail authorities tried a new tactic — to convince her, or at least the public at large, that she was insane. This was another first: the first documented use of psychiatric diagnosis and confinement as a deliberate form of political repression in the United States, perhaps worldwide.

Psychiatrists came to the city jail from St. Elizabeth's, the federal mental hospital, and repeatedly interviewed Paul. She suspected nothing and willingly gave her interviewers a long explanation of what she was doing and why. "I must say it was one of the best speeches I ever made," she recalled.[69] Searching for some mental pathology to pin on her, the doctors settled on what they considered an irrational obsession with her mistreatment at the hands of the president of the United States.

Meanwhile, still at Occoquan and encouraged by the socialists among them, the other suffrage prisoners collectively composed a letter demanding to be treated as political prisoners — to be allowed visitors, counsel, letters, books, decent food, and not to be required to do forced labor — and smuggled it out to supporters and lawyers. They also demanded to be housed and fed separately from the Negro prisoners. The African American daily, the *New York Age,* called out the suffragists for this demand but accepted the suffragists' explanation that they had asked to be separated only from prisoners who were sick, not those who were black. Their demand to be treated as political prisoners became the picketers' new cause. "We have taken this stand as a matter of principle after careful consideration, and from it we shall not recede."[70] Instead of easing up, the prison administration cracked down.

On November 10, forty picketers were arrested in a demonstration meant to draw attention to the imprisonment and mistreatment of Paul and the unmet demand for political prisoner status. Fifteen of the forty took up the hunger strike and were forcefed. Any resistance, Warden Whittaker repeatedly threatened, would be met with "the brace and bit in our mouths and the straightjacket on our bodies."[71] The NWP called it "the Night of Terror." With Paul isolated in the D.C. City Jail, Lucy Burns led the Occoquan resistance. As the leader, she was subjected to particularly violent treatment. Her hands were cuffed and fastened over her head all night to the cell door. In front of male guards, she was stripped of her clothes, and her lawyer found her the next day curled up on the floor, wrapped only in a blanket. Held down by "two doctors, matron, [and] four colored prisoners," she was force-fed. She kept her lips clenched and so the feeding tube was pushed up her nose. "Nose bleeds freely," her smuggled notes reported. "Tube drawn out covered with blood."[72]

Twenty-year-old Dorothy Day participated in the hunger strike. After many days of not eating, "I lost all consciousness of any cause," she later wrote in her autobiography. "I had no sense of being a radical, making protest against a government, carrying on a nonviolent revolution. I could only feel the darkness and desolation around me."[73] Day's experience made her into a lifelong advocate of nonviolent resistance and led her to found the Catholic Workers Movement in the 1930s. The violence and mistreatment went on for days and the warden began to realize that a prisoner — one of them, Mary Nolan, was in her seventies and very roughly treated — might die on his watch.

Lawyers for the suffrage prisoners were eventually able to serve the Occoquan warden with a writ of habeas corpus and get the women transferred back to the D.C. City Jail. Even if not under better conditions, they were closer to supporters and observers. The lawyers convinced the court that the district's use of the Virginia workhouse was illegal. Then on November 27 the doors of the city jail were suddenly opened, and all suffrage prisoners were released, Paul among them. She had served five weeks of her seven-month sentence and had refused to eat for three.

Women prisoners who were not suffragists benefited from the court's decision. "Hundreds of persons . . . had been without money or influence enough to contest this doubtful procedure in the courts," Doris Stevens wrote of the practice of sending D.C. prisoners outside the city to Occoquan.[74] The workhouse there was closed. (It is now an arts district and tourist destination.) Since June, over two hundred suffragists had been arrested, nearly half of whom had served prison sentences. The

NWP celebrated its victory and Paul's release by raising almost $80,000 to refill its coffers. Five months later, a higher court threw out all of the suffrage prisoners' sentences.

In September, the House Rules Committee, which had functioned, as one suffragist put it, as "a willing morgue" to the suffrage bill, narrowly voted to form a standing Woman Suffrage Committee to take over management of the bill.[75] In December, the House formed the new committee, populated by congressmen from suffrage states. This dramatically increased the chances that the entire body would eventually vote on the amendment. The Senate, which already had a standing suffrage committee, reported the bill out favorably, only awaiting for it to be placed on the calendar for a full vote.

The NWP took much of the credit for these achievements. "The creation of the suffrage committee in the House proved that the pressure of women's agitation had forced the Democratic leader to turn from his obstinate stance against national suffrage," its newspaper, the *Suffragist,* boasted.[76] But other developments were at least as important. Chief of these was the all-important electoral victory in November

1917 in the second New York State suffrage referendum. The suffrage victory in the Empire State dramatically changed the political calculus, particularly in the House, where the state's forty-three representatives were the largest congressional delegation. Once suffrage passed in that state, most of them could be counted to vote on the federal suffrage bill before Congress.

For two years since the November 1915 referendum defeat, the women of the Woman Suffrage Party (WSP), now enlarged to cover the state as well as the city, had been busy reorganizing themselves around the two pillars of steady organizing and fundraising. The campaign was led by a quartet of women who had worked in the 1915 campaign. Vera Whitehouse exploited her access to Wall Street to build the suffrage war chest. Helen Rogers Reid was given the huge job of managing the money. Gertrude Foster Brown had been an accomplished concert pianist in her youth. Her husband was an advertising executive, and she became the leading spokesperson for the campaign. Mary Garrett Hay led the New York City work. The "Big Boss," as she was called, had become Carrie Chapman Catt's companion, sharing her home and taking responsibility for making sure that "the Chief" did not drive herself to exhaustion. She was also one of the most important women in the Republican Party.

Hay, Brown, Reid, and Whitehouse followed the approach that Catt had set in the 1915 referendum and carefully organized the state and city suffrage organizations to mirror the structures of regular party machines. Each voting precinct elected its own leaders, and a similar structure was instituted all the way to the top of the organization. The point was both to familiarize suffragists with the methods of political parties and to facilitate reaching out to the largest possible numbers of voters before the referendum.

In contrast to the previous campaign, "that of 1917 was of the byways, of quiet, intensive work reaching every group of citizens."[77] A statewide petition was circulated which ultimately boasted a million signatures. No longer would the opposition be able to claim that women did not want the vote. To reach women in rural areas, suffrage headquarters prepared mail-order training programs to teach about politics and how to canvass. These "suffrage schools" were a brilliant innovation, drawing in women far away from the cosmopolitan centers of easy access to suffrage activism.[78] For an enlistment sum of twenty-five cents every week for two months, subscribers received lectures covering everything from the history of the movement to the structures of government. They received arguments, statistics, endorsements, to counter the flimsy arguments of opponents to the referendum. A separate course of suffrage preparation was made available to wage-earning women and through them to gain their men's support.

The work of the second New York referendum to organize voters was thorough and relentless. Nearly one million women were listed as members of the WSP, boasted Vera Whitehouse, "a larger membership than either the Republican or Democratic Party of New York State."[79] Five hundred thousand dollars — five times the 1915 referendum budget — was raised. The money was used, among other things, to pay hundreds of organizers modest monthly salaries. Doors were knocked on, postcards were sent out, and when New York City subway companies refused to allow suffragists to advertise (although the antis had been permitted), women walked into and through the subway stations wearing boards urging voters to support suffrage in the November 6 election.

The Wage Earners Suffrage League was folded into the WSP, securing it greater resources but less political autonomy. Statewide, the leader of the newly designated "Industrial Section" of the WSP was a Women's Trade Union League ally and former president Mary Dreier. In New York City, veteran trade unionist Leonora O'Reilly was in charge, followed by socialist Rose Schneiderman. Schneiderman, tired of fighting male trade union leaders, eagerly took up the post. On the eve of the election, Schneiderman led a group of organizers to reach out to workers leaving after a day's hard work.[80]

In stark contrast to the near total absence of African American women from the national politics of woman suffrage, the 1917 New York campaign was distinguished by its efforts to involve them. The New York City Colored Woman Suffrage Club was also absorbed into the WSP. It kept its offices in an upscale neighborhood in Harlem and was assured that in heavily black precincts its own leaders would be placed within the organization's hierarchy. Anne K. Lewis, a thirty-four-year-old married woman from Georgia, was the leading figure in this group. She was a determined interracialist, and when a group of African

American women associated with black nationalist Marcus Garvey objected to the decision to fold their all-black club into the larger suffrage machinery, Lewis fought back the challenge. Even Ida B. Wells-Barnett, who had concentrated on work other than suffrage for years, came to New York to speak in favor of woman suffrage.

The emphasis was on getting African American men, Republican Party loyalists, to vote for the referendum. Helen Holman, younger than Lewis and an avowed socialist, took the campaign for African American men's votes to the streets. "A forcible and eloquent speaker," she gave noon stump speeches, including one at a Hudson River pier where she spoke to black longshoremen, carrying the message that "colored women want their own men to vote in favor of woman suffrage."[81]

W. E. B. Du Bois was already on record in *The Crisis* as a strong supporter of woman suffrage. As the election neared, Reverend Adam Clayton Powell Sr., pastor of the enormous Abyssinian Baptist Church, added his endorsement and perhaps his congregation to the campaign. In the last weeks of the campaign, the *New York Age,* a leading African American paper in the city, carried regular advertisements for the referendum. The WSP donated ten thousand dollars to an African American army regiment, not so much out of charity but because New York State allowed residents serving in the military to vote. No possibility would be overlooked.

African American women joined other New York suffragists in the crowning effort of the campaign, a parade of twenty thousand suffragists. "Viewed as a spectacle merely," the New York Sun conceded, "it was less beautiful than the great suffrage march of 1915." The only note of brightness were the "relentless American flags."[82] The march was studded with groups of women war workers. Indeed, it was almost as much a display of patriotic womanhood as of suffrage. "Women had taken on a value which nothing but war seems to confer on human beings in the eyes of men," wrote Mary Grey Peck.[83] Care was taken to distinguish the New York campaign from the militant actions in Washington, D.C. Signs read: WE ARE OPPOSED TO THE PICKETING OF THE WHITE HOUSE. WE STAND BY OUR COUNTRY AND OUR PRESIDENT.[84] Nonetheless, NWP newsies stood on the sidewalks of the WSP's giant parade, selling copies of their paper, the Suffragist.

The suffrage referendum won by a

hundred-thousand-vote majority, most of it in New York City. Just ten days before the election, the New York City Democratic Party had made a critical announcement. While Tammany did not endorse suffrage, it indicated that it would not take any official position on the referendum, and thus voters were free to vote their consciences. By this time, suffrage activism had expanded to include wives and daughters of Tammany operatives. Tammany's strategic neutrality is generally credited with the strong vote in New York City, more than enough to offset a small loss upstate.

Tammany may have been following the president's lead. In response to Helen Gardener's careful cultivation and Carrie Chapman Catt's promise that her suffragists would not protest or picket him, in August he had announced his hope that "the voters of the State of New York will rally to the support of woman suffrage by a handsome majority."[85]

Catt called the New York victory the "Gettysburg of the woman suffrage movement."[86] But as after Gettysburg, there were still battles to fight, still casualties to suffer, before the suffrage war could finally be won.

Eight:
Enemies Died Hard,
1918–1920

As 1918 began, the picketing had been suspended, and New York State — where resistance to votes for women had finally fallen to the relentless suffrage onslaught — had joined the list of states where women had full voting rights. This victory brought in two million new women voters and forty-three seats in Congress indebted to them. The president was gradually moving toward support of a federal suffrage amendment. Female relatives of Washington politicians, all the way up to Wilson's own daughter (and wife of the secretary of the treasury) Eleanor Wilson McAdoo, were now actively aiding the suffrage cause. Maud Wood Park recalled that she "saw the change as soon as the members of Congress began to come back" and "the mercury in our thermometer of electoral votes had jumped from 172 to 215."[1]

American military involvement was increasing in intensity in 1918. A million American men were fighting in Europe, and the nation was focused on trench warfare and German offensives. At home, war was making a distinct impact on American women. Women were needed to replace men gone off to fight and to meet the production of war matériel. They took jobs in industries in which women had never before worked, and performed well. The notion of equal pay for equal work for women began to be raised seriously for the first time. African American women especially took new steps forward. They began to be employed in factories, and though usually in menial jobs, they were no longer confined to domestic work in white women's houses.

The last time the country had been fully mobilized for war, Cady Stanton, Anthony, and Stone had found ways for a small number of women to participate and contribute. Now, a half century later, many more women were accustomed to organizations and used to steady involvement in politics and policy. They were eager to leave their homes to play a major part in the nation's mobilization. They were on the verge of being voting citizens, and ready to answer the nation's call to unity and action with wholehearted patriotism. Much has been written, in retrospect, of what the Great War did to promote the U.S. suffrage movement and contribute to its ultimate victory, but it can justly be argued that suffragism affected women's involvement in the war as much or more so than the war affected suffragism.

The decisions and experiences of four suffragists demonstrate how they responded to the war's pull. Anna Howard Shaw, retired from the presidency of the National American Woman Suffrage Association (NAWSA), was selected by President Wilson to chair the Woman's Committee of the Council of National Defense. She structured the committee along the intricate federative lines that women's organizations had been perfecting for decades, and attempted to draw together the resources of nearly a hundred national women's organizations. Most of these groups were apolitical, some of them even anti-suffrage, but Wilson's appointment of Shaw indicated his growing willingness to associate himself with the demand for a federal amendment. Although the committee was only advisory, it represented, as Missouri suffragist Emily Newell Blair wrote, "mobilizing women officially for the country's service."[2] Shaw worked to transform the limited role initially granted to the committee into something substantial. She worked closely with federal food administrator Herbert Hoover to get housewives to conserve food, and through the Labor Department, to protect standards of employment for women workers, especially safety in munitions production. She died eight months after the armistice was declared, at age seventy-two.

Harriot Stanton Blatch also began as an enthusiast for the war. In 1915, just before the first New York referendum vote, she had been called to England to settle the estate of her deceased husband. Britain was already at war, and she was thrilled to see British women undertaking work that was needed, often dangerous jobs, performing it with great patriotism. The lesson she brought back was that "the effective use of woman-power would win the war."[3] "When men go awarring," she wrote in her 1918 pro-war book, *Mobilizing Woman Power,* "women go to work. . . . That is one of its merits."[4] Blatch served as director of the Woman's Land Army of America, patterned after a British organization and ultimately involving twenty thousand "farmerettes."[5] Going back abroad again two years later she saw hunger, poverty, and devastation and radically changed her position, authoring a second book, *A Woman's Point of View: Some Roads to Peace.*

Rheta Childe Dorr, the first editor of the National Woman's Party (NWP) newspaper, the *Suffragist,* became determined to go to Europe to witness, write about, and get as close to the war as possible, even before the U.S. entry. She had no compunctions about leaving behind her work with women. The suffrage movement "was past history," she wrote. "We had gone to the mat with a whole anti-suffrage administration . . . and had beaten them to a frazzle."[6] Now she was ready for a real war. The bravado and fearlessness of her suffrage activism made her hungry to experience the thrill of real combat and immerse herself in solidarity with American men fighting the enemy. Although she served as a journalist, she got herself to the center of the action, from the Russian Revolution to the trenches of France. "I want you to know," she told her nineteen-year-old son, who had enlisted, "that I too have had the time of my life in this war."[7] After she returned to the United States, she was run down by a motorcycle on a New York City street. In her delusions in the days after, she believed she had been captured and tortured by Germans. She recovered and lived a long life, dying in

1948 at the age of eighty-one.

Addie Hunton, a forty-nine-year-old African American suffragist, widow, and mother of two young children, also followed the troops abroad. She did so through the YMCA as one of only three African American women assigned to provide support services for 150,000 black troops segregated and serving in France. "We were crusaders for democracy on a quest for Democracy!" she wrote with deliberate double meaning. "How and where would that precious thing be found?"[8]

Like Blatch and Dorr, Hunton too wrote about her experiences, especially to praise the nobility and bravery of the black troops and to call out the discrimination she and they faced from the army and the YMCA. Hunton had been to Europe before, gaining fluency in both German and French, but this experience was different, and gave her "the greatest opportunity for service that we have ever known."[9] Coming from an educated middle-class family, she gained new respect for the masses of black men who served, and like them, developed "a racial consciousness and racial strength that could not have been gained in a half century of normal living in America."[10] "Sobered by her encounter with the war," she returned much more radical in her outlook than when she had left. She switched her activism to the NAACP and became a dedicated peace activist and internationalist.[11] The war had changed her, as it had others.

The picketing, arrests, and forced feeding that had absorbed public attention through most of 1917 have been written into history as one of the great examples of feminist heroism. But the difficult, painstaking effort to navigate the political shoals necessary to bring the constitutional amendment to fruition had its own kind of quiet heroism.

In the first week of January 1918, the new House Woman Suffrage Committee scheduled a four-day hearing on a "joint resolution proposing an amendment to the constitution of the United States extending the right of suffrage to women." Anna Howard Shaw spoke primarily about women's war work. She rejected charges that women's continued suffrage work and their prior pacifism disproved their patriotism. Instead, she insisted, those who opposed women's enfranchisement were themselves guilty of "treason to the fundamental cause for which we, as a nation, have entered the war," greater democracy.[12]

Carrie Chapman Catt followed with a powerful speech that lasted much of an afternoon, emphasizing the fact that America's war partners — Great Britain, Soviet Russia, and Canada — had already granted franchise rights to their women. Did the United States really intend to be such a laggard in this worldwide democratic upsurge? Catt also confronted the charge that woman suffrage would dangerously inflate the black vote. Southern white men, she noted, regularly suggested that "the colored women are more intelligent, ambitious and energetic than the men," thus even more dangerous to enfranchise; meanwhile they simultaneously claimed that their own women "are too weak minded to have an opinion of their own." Male pride was always a rich target for Catt. "Do these men realize that they are saying . . . that the colored woman is superior to the colored man but that the white woman is the inferior of the white man?" Rather, she concluded, "the men of the South are afraid of both the white and the black women."[13]

Finally, Catt took on the claim that passage of a federal amendment violated the sacred principle of states' rights, a cover for fears of inflating the black vote. She pointed out that many of the southerners who made this argument had just voted for a federal constitutional amendment banning the sale of alcohol. For virtually its entire history, the cause of woman suffrage had been mixed up, for better or worse, with that of temperance. In December 1917 the anti-alcohol movement had been able to get a federal constitutional prohibition amendment through Congress, in striking contrast to the long stall faced by federal woman suffrage. A constitutional amendment that did nothing to alter the electorate was apparently an easier sell — if a less enduring one — than expanding political democracy by doubling the number of voters. Although the rapidity with which the prohibition amendment moved forward may have privately angered suffragists, its swift ratification in March 1919 decisively removed a complication that had long dogged woman suffrage, the threat that women would vote for prohibition.

In their testimony before the new House Woman Suffrage Committee, opponents of the amendment also reacted to the growing likelihood of winning suffrage. The November 1917 victory of the second New York referendum had been a serious blow to them, and anti-suffragists began charging suffragists with socialism, pacifism, and most terrifying, feminism. Anti-suffrage leader Alice Wadsworth, the wife of James Wadsworth, the powerful New York senator and leader of the congressional opposition, moved the National Association Opposed to Woman Suffrage (NAOWS), which she headed, to Washington, D.C., where the battle was now centered. Speaking to the Woman Suffrage Committee, she tactlessly blamed legislators whom she thought too weak on suffrage. They were "spineless opportunists who for political expediency or because they are too lazy to fight are proposing to surrender their principles for the sake of a dishonorable and we believe, temporary peace."[14]

In the midst of the debate before the House Woman Suffrage Committee, on January 8, 1918, the president delivered his historic "Fourteen Points" speech to Congress, outlining what he hoped would be the terms for a just and lasting world peace. The next day he summoned a group of House Democrats to the White House finally to ask them to vote for a federal constitutional woman suffrage amendment. He was willing at last to say that he believed this "an act of right and justice."[15] And he needed women's support for his peace plan.

Suffragists were waiting outside "in the

snow," when Representative John Raker, chair of the House Woman Suffrage Committee, came out to report the good news. Although the president was not yet ready to go public, he "has declared for the Susan B. Anthony Amendment." The next morning the chief executive would not play his regular game of golf but instead stay at home "to see any Congressman who wishes to consult with him."[16] The Woman Suffrage Committee promptly scheduled a full House vote two days later. Popular evangelist Billy Sunday, in town for a crusade, publicly urged a vote for woman suffrage.

To lead the debate, congressional Democrats appointed Republican congresswoman Jeannette Rankin. Despite her vote against the war declaration, Rankin touted women's contributions to the war effort as a reason for their enfranchisement. "I think no woman among us . . . failed to rejoice that at last a woman's voice could be raised in the Congress on behalf of her own sex," Maud Wood Park recalled.[17]

Despite the president's support, everyone knew that the vote would be close. "Beset by nauseating fear," Park took her seat in the gallery. Four reliable supporters heroically struggled to make it back to the House in time. One man arrived despite a railroad wreck, which held him up outside of Chicago, another came from his hospital bed, and a third held back from having a broken shoulder set so that he would not be too groggy to vote. Most dramatically, Representative Frederick Hicks of New York, whose wife had died overnight, came to Washington to cast his vote "because she had been ardently in favor of woman suffrage."[18] Efforts to amend the resolution to limit ratification to seven years failed.

In the end, the measure passed, 274 to 136, without a vote to spare. "One more negative vote," suffrage supporter Speaker Champ Clark "chuckled," and "the amendment resolution would have been lost in which event I would have directed the clerk to call my name." But he didn't have to break the tie.[19] The two-thirds vote was there. Women in the galleries cheered. From outside the hall, it was reported, a woman began to sing praises to God, and the galleries took up "the song of gratitude."[20]

The House had done its part, and because support for the suffrage amendment in the Senate had long been greater than in the House, a quick victory was anticipated. Carrie Chapman Catt even bought a new dress to be ready for the ratification drive. She was far too optimistic. Despite the recent ratification of the Seventeenth Amendment, which required that senators be popularly elected, the upper house was still "farther from the people . . . much harder to move."[21] Senate rules gave individual senators many ways to stall action. Tactics of public pressure that proved effective in the House were counterproductive in the Senate, and senators complained about what they called women's "nagging."[22] The core of Senate opposition came from a combination of obdurate southern Democrats, with outsize influence in their party, and a few conservative northeastern Republicans, who were determined to delay what now appeared to be an inevitable suffrage victory.

To win the Senate, both wings of the movement mobilized their lobbies. While Maud Wood Park ran NAWSA's work, Maud Younger, heroine of the California campaign, was in charge of NWP efforts. The "two Mauds," as they were called, developed a highly nuanced sense of the character of each senator, his vulnerabilities, and the best way to influence him. As lobbyists they were thoroughly professional, amazingly effective, all the more so since male politicians they sought to influence expected none of those things from women.

NAWSA had more resources than NWP, but was supporting several state referenda and presidential suffrage bills, as well as providing direct support for the war effort. Its greatest advantage was strong backup groups in almost all of the states, women who could be called on to pressure their senators from back home. The NWP was a smaller but tighter organization. A cadre of young, talented, and very courageous organizers did the bulk of the work. For these "women of spirit," it was difficult to "be quiet; deferential; to listen to long intervals of complaint and abuse, to seem not to notice rebuffs."[23] Behind the young NWP organizers stood a corps of wealthy party members, many of whom had come into the organization at the bidding of Alva Belmont and out of a desire to curry her favor. Usually each congressional visit paired a veteran organizer with one of these wealthy supporters, chosen because she "had political, social or economic influence in her home state or city."[24]

Senate resistance proved surprisingly strong and continued throughout the winter and spring. Lobbyists narrowed their efforts to a few senators, among them Republican senator William Borah of Idaho. Women in his state had been voting for president since

1896 and Borah was otherwise a progressive who had been a strong supporter of the federal suffrage amendment as recently as 1910. Then he reversed his position, it seems, because of sympathy for southern fears of doubling the black vote, compounded by anxieties about Asian voters in his own region. As time went on, Senate prospects got worse. Ten sitting senators died in office, during the 65th Congress, seven of whom were suffrage supporters. With gallows humor, Anna Howard Shaw quipped that "if she were the wife of a suffrage senator and wanted to preserve his life, she would try to have him change over to the opposition."[25]

Once in May and once in late June, the Democratic chair of the Senate Woman Suffrage Committee, Andrieus Jones of New Mexico, scheduled a full floor vote, only to conclude that he didn't have the votes and pulled the bill. Arizona senator Marcus Smith, who claimed he had left his wife's sickbed at suffragists' bidding for the May vote, was so angry when it was canceled that he declared that he would not return if and when the vote was rescheduled. Later Park learned "that he had gone down for the Kentucky Derby and that his indignation was really due to his fear of having to miss the race for the first time in many years."[26]

After the first cancellation in May, Carrie Chapman Catt burst into Senator Jones's office, enraged at the "fiasco." Maud Wood Park went back the next day to soothe the senator's feathers. Having made every effort "to conceal my feelings . . . before I knew it my emotional struggle registered itself in a violent outburst of sobbing, and I put my head down on the table and cried like a baby." Crying was what all women lobbyists feared. The senator's response? He "patted my shoulder in a fatherly way" and said to her, by way of consolation, "Why now, it just shows that you're nothing but a woman after all." Park was learning a hard lesson about the strength of weakness in women's appeals: "from that time on the Senator was staunchly and consistently our friend."[27]

When Congress reconvened in the fall, leading Democrats, suffragist lobbyists, and crucially the president himself recognized that unless Senate Democrats could vote the bill authorizing the suffrage amendment through and initiate the ratification process, Republicans would use that failure to good effect in the November midterm elections. For some time, Helen Gardener had been writing to the president (at one point from a hospital bed) to suggest that "the time has come for you to say to the Senate and the country some of the splendid things you have said to individuals" in support of federal enfranchisement.[28] Now Wilson was ready to yield.

On September 26, 1918, Senate Democratic leaders finally agreed to schedule a floor vote. Over the preceding several days of debate, much of the time was spent with Democrats and Republicans accusing each other of the unforgivable sin of being weak in the face of aggressive women lobbyists and picketers. Democrats said Republicans were collaborating with demonstrators to hurt the president, while Republicans charged that Wilson had allowed women to bully him into supporting the amendment. On the last day of September, the afternoon before the full Senate was to vote on the bill, with only a half hour notice, President Wilson arrived in the Senate chambers, accompanied by his entire cabinet. It was most unusual for a president to intervene while senators were actively debating a bill. The atmosphere was solemn. Waging war tried and tired a president as nothing else could. "He had aged noticeably during recent months . . ." wrote one suffragist, "and his gaunt figure bore witness to the mental and physical strain under which he was living."[29]

Passage of the woman suffrage amendment, the president told the senators, was "vitally essential to the successful prosecution of the great war of humanity in which we are engaged." The United States had entered the war to "lead the world to democracy," and that could not happen unless "democracy means that women shall play their part in affairs alongside men and upon an equal footing with them." Women had been partners in the prosecution of the war. "Shall we admit them only to a partnership of sacrifice and suffering and toil and not to a partnership of privilege and right?"[30] The president's eloquence deeply stirred Maud Wood Park. "Those words were the most impassioned that I had ever heard the President utter, and it seemed impossible that they could be spoken in vain."[31]

But the president had waited too long. He no longer had the power that he once had. The war had eroded that. Opponents to the suffrage amendment were not moved. Votes were not changed. The president had spent too many years preaching against a federal constitutional amendment. His new conviction seemed sudden, unmotivated, even self-serving. "The President's belief in the power of words" was insufficient, Doris Stevens wrote. His speech, "eloquent as it was, [could not] break down the opposition in the Senate which he had so long protected and condoned."[32] "He had lost command over his own party," a NAWSA officer observed.[33]

As soon as the president left the chamber, an anti-suffrage member of his own party jumped up to lambaste those, including Wilson himself, who had been pushed around by "petticoat brigades." The amendment was lost in the Senate by two votes. The women in the galleries "began slowly to put on their hats, to gather up their wraps," recalled Maud Younger, "and to file out of the galleries, some with a dull sense of injustice, some with burning resentment."[34] Catt, "more disappointed and upset than I ever knew her to be about anything else," told Park that she would never again enter Congress to await a suffrage vote, and she remained true to her vow.[35]

Widespread sentiment in the press was that nothing more could be done for the remaining half year of the 65th Congress. "The general public believed and the politicians hoped," wrote a popular syndicated columnist, "that the troublesome issue had been put to sleep for a long time."[36] But neither suffrage nor suffragists would disappear. Despite the now raging flu epidemic and a national health directive against public meetings, both suffrage organizations mobilized for the upcoming midterm elections to take the issue to the voters and to get the enabling legislation passed by defeating crucial suffrage opponents in the Senate.

The NWP had built its reputation by an unrelenting electoral assault against Democrats. It again announced it would work against western Democrats who were up for reelection into the Senate. Now, however, it also went after two Republicans running for open seats in the Senate, in New Jersey and New Hampshire. But 1918 was a bad time to change horses and champion Democrats. The Democratic pro-suffrage candidates in New Hampshire and New Jersey were not able to unseat the anti-suffrage incumbents, and fell victim to the powerful headwinds in favor of the Republicans. Another casualty of the Republican surge was Democrat John Shafroth of Colorado, who despite the disastrous federal suffrage amendment that bore his name, had remained a staunch defender of the Anthony amendment. The NWP boasted of bringing him down, despite the fact that he was one of the most long-running, dedicated suffrage supporters in the Senate. Democratic resentment at Shafroth's defeat dogged suffragists for the next two years. At least Shafroth was replaced by another pro-suffrage senator, Lawrence Phipps.

Unlike the NWP, electoral work was a first for NAWSA, which had never before been active in appealing directly to voters. "The fight idea was scary," wrote Rose Young, editor of NAWSA's periodical, the *Woman's Journal.* "It nearly broke the backs of the women who had had the campaigns directly in hand, but it was worth it."[37] Like the NWP, NAWSA selected anti-suffragists, two Democrats and two Republicans, for defeat. They succeeded in two of these campaigns.

Suffragists' success at defeating John Weeks, a powerful Massachusetts senator whom most thought invulnerable, was particularly satisfying. Weeks had a long and varied antiprogressive record, and campaigners emphasized his many conservative positions, not just his opposition to suffrage. The campaign was led by Blanche Ames. An artist and botanist, she came from a multigenerational Republican family, but she dared to go after a powerful member of the party. Emphasizing Weeks's vote against the nomination of Louis Brandeis to become the first Jewish member of the Supreme Court, Ames got financial support from Mary Fels, a wealthy Massachusetts Zionist, and used the money to lobby "every Jewish organization in the state."[38] Weeks was also an opponent of labor, and "women of the industrial section inaugurated three auto tours" and held outdoor rallies at mill gates.[39]

The other victim of NAWSA campaigning was Democrat Willard Saulsbury Jr. of Delaware, a member of the powerful du Pont family and another reliable conservative. Mabel Willard, a close friend of Maud Wood Park, came from Massachusetts to run the campaign against him. The Allies were at the height of their push in Europe, Delaware was a big munitions-producing state, and Willard organized meetings of women munitions workers to rally against Saulsbury. Hannah Black, an immigrant from Scotland and, a local paper reported, the only woman tool maker in the country, conducted large open-air suffrage rallies outside factory gates. Like Weeks, Saulsbury lost his seat to a candidate, L. Heisler Ball, who pledged to vote for suffrage. These were the long-sought-after two seats, and a Republican majority would be a reality in the new congress.

Jeannette Rankin did not run again for the House. The problem was not only her antiwar vote. The seat she held was redistricted out from under her. Undaunted, instead of running again for the House, she ran instead for Montana senator in November 1918. Despite a hard-fought race in which she lost the Republican Party primary by less than two thousand votes, she ran in the general election as an Independent. The man who won, Democrat Thomas Walsh, was a supporter of suffrage, and his campaign featured a letter of endorsement from Catt. In her departing speech on the closing day of the 65th Congress, Rankin thanked her colleagues for their genuine welcome, spoke of her unhappiness at leaving before the woman suffrage amendment had been voted forward by Congress, and solemnly charged those who remained "with the great trust of enfranchising the women of this country."[40] She would return to Congress two decades later, in time to cast the only vote against the Second World War, again losing her seat as a result.

The outcome of the November 1918 election, in which Democrats lost control of both houses, had surely been affected by the costs of the war. Wilson's Fourteen Points, his hope for a generous and nonvindictive settlement, did not appeal to the electorate. Just two days after the election, Americans learned that Germany had petitioned for peace. The war was over. The magnitude of the casualties on both sides was unfathomable: 10 million soldiers worldwide had died, 20 million had been wounded, and perhaps 50 million civilians had perished; as well 4.7 million American men had served; 53,000 had died in combat. The global influenza pandemic settled on the country in the war's final months, costing the lives of 600,000 civilians and 60,000 members of the military.

While the country rejoiced over the end of the war, suffragists, who were determined to build on their electoral victories, took no time off their work. Park rushed back to Washington, determined to convince Democrats that it would be "idiotic" to let one or two votes allow Republicans to gain credit for passing suffrage.[41] Although they had won their two crucial seats in the next congress, suffragists very much wanted to see the bill enabling the amendment passed before the 66th Congress convened.

By the time the 66th Congress convened, even should the Republicans in control vote the woman suffrage amendment out for ratification promptly, the majority of state legislatures would have adjourned for the year. Suffragists would face the very difficult process of convincing governors to call (and pay for) special sessions to ratify the amendment. If, on the contrary, it was necessary to wait for regular legislative sessions, women would not be voting for president until 1924. Catt was determined that this would not happen. The job must be done in time for women to vote in the 1920 presidential election.

After the November 1918 election and before the new congress, one new vote was gained in South Carolina, when anti-suffrage senator Ben Tillman died and the man selected by the governor to replace him declared himself a suffrage supporter. In a surprising announcement, the Senate Woman Suffrage Committee then announced that a full vote on the amendment enabling bill would be held in the remaining days of the 65th Congress, on February 9, 1919. Republicans, who had no incentive to give the Democrats a chance to pass the suffrage bill in the waning days of their congressional power, were rumored to be letting the vote go forward, confident that it would be lost and would further embarrass their opponents.

"It seemed to me that everyone in the

United States knew that we were just one vote short," wrote Maud Wood Park. "But no one except ourselves appeared to realize how hard it was to get that one."[42] It was in fact impossible. Democratic Senate leadership sought everywhere for it. Crucial and dangerous alterations to the suffrage bill were devised to get just one opponent to change his vote and save the party from itself. Since October, New Jersey senator Joseph Frelinghuysen had been proposing a modification of the bill to prohibit immigrant women who could gain citizenship by marriage from federal voting privileges. This modification failed.

A more serious threat came from Senator Edward Gay of Louisiana. He proposed rewriting the enforcement clause of the bill so as to locate protection for women's right to vote in the separate states rather than in the federal government. An obvious sop to states' rights objections, this effort showed the hand of renegade Louisiana suffragist Kate Gordon. Always a pronounced Negrophobe and a believer in enfranchisement state by state, Gordon had switched from her earlier, albeit reluctant, support for the federal amendment to determined opposition. She now called it "a form of kaiserism."[43] She had in essence become an anti-suffragist. Gordon charged that northern suffragists had become agents of Negro suffrage and southern humiliation. A federal woman suffrage amendment, she now argued, would reinforce "the frauds of the 14th and 15th Amendments" and subject the South "to the ideas of an inferior race."[44]

By February, Senator Gay had the support of Andrieus Jones, chair of the Senate Woman Suffrage Committee, for his states' rights revision. Had this version of the amendment passed the Senate and gone on to ratification, the historical meaning and the political impact of the Nineteenth Amendment would have been fatally tainted by replacing federal oversight with that of the states. But now Republican opponents, for their own highly partisan reasons, would not let any version of the bill with a chance of passage go through so long as Democrats still controlled the Congress. Up to the very last day of the 65th Congress, Wadsworth of New York and Weeks of Massachusetts kept the Senate from voting on it.

Even though it was the Republicans who were responsible for this obstruction, the NWP still held the president responsible. "His own early hostility, his later indifference and negligence, his actual protection given to Democratic opponents of the measure, his own reversal of policy practically at the point of a pistol, the half-hearted efforts made by him on its behalf," Doris Stevens insisted, her rage unabated, "were all coming to fruition at the moment when his continued prestige was at stake."[45]

Wilson had been in Paris, struggling with previously warring nations to create a fair peace and establish a League of Nations to obtain it. He returned to the United States to develop public support for his work abroad, only to be met by NWP pickets. Outside the New York Metropolitan Opera House, two dozen picketers prepared to steal the headlines from the president, but before they could get to him, they were mobbed by an angry crowd. As participant Rebecca Hourwich recalled, "All Hell seemed to break loose."[46] Hourwich, who was pregnant at the time, stumbled home and three months later barely survived the difficult birth of her daughter. Still, Doris Stevens boasted, "What a magnificent thing for those women to rebel."[47] The 65th Congress ended without taking final action on the woman suffrage constitutional amendment.

In May, seven months before the regular session of the 66th Congress, the president agreed to call a special session so that the suffrage bill could be passed promptly. Because this was a new congress, the House was required to revote on the amendment. The new Republican head of the House Woman Suffrage Committee, James Mann, scheduled the vote before all members had yet been sworn in. A large majority of Republicans as well as more than half of the Democrats voted aye, and after a mere two hours of debate, the bill passed 304 to 90. A moving picture company recorded Maud Wood Park energetically pumping the hand of Representative Mann in appreciation.

The two new votes in the Senate assured victory there, but Park could not shake the fear that something would go wrong at the last moment. Intraparty Republican wrangling over committee appointments and chairmanships delayed the vote a week and a half. Once the debate started, it went on for two days. Despite all that their party would gain politically from passing the amendment bill, Republican senator James Wadsworth condemned women's enfranchisement as an attack on American individualism and Senator Lee Overman of North Carolina railed against woman suffrage as a "postscript" to the Fifteenth Amendment.[48] Once again revisions of the bill were submit-

Vice President Marshall signing Senate suffrage bill, June 1919. Maud Wood Park to the left, Helen Gardner to the right.

ted — this time one explicitly limiting the amendment to white women — all of them rejected.

Supporters of the bill did not speak, not wishing to add to the delay. After wearying repetition of ancient objections, on June 9, 1919, a full vote was taken, and two-thirds plus two voted aye. Catt was true to her vow and was not there to witness the passage, but NAWSA treasurer Harriet Taylor Upton was present and gave way to a single sob of joy. When the final vote was announced, however, instead of erupting in cheers, suffragists in the galleries rushed home to start the campaign for ratification. The vote in the Senate had been much longer and more troubled than anyone had imagined. The prospects for ratification were, if anything, even more challenging. There was still much work to be done, and little time for celebration.

"A whole year had passed in the winning of two more votes," observed Maud Younger. Walking back to NWP headquarters, she and the others were silent. "This was the day to which women had been struggling for more than half a century! We were in the dawn of woman's political power in America."[49]

Maud Wood Park was also in a reflective mood. Her congressional work was done: ratification would fall to other workers. "Nearly a century of struggle seems an excessive price for the simple justice of votes for women," she wrote in her memoirs. What then had finally won the congressional battle? Not the Great War, as may have been the case in Great Britain. Not even the president's support, which had come so late. The ultimate responsibility for this precious victory, she wrote in the final pages of her account of the congressional lobbying she had led, was "the campaign carried on by two generations of suffrage workers."[50]

Congressional passage of the suffrage bill, as Carrie Chapman Catt described it, was "like the electric touch that sets a vast and complicated machinery in motion. Already wheels are turning, sparks are flying, wirings are humming."[51] NAWSA, with its elaborate state chapter structure, and the NWP, with its cadre of devoted, undaunted organizers, were ready. Both knew that Congress had been a difficult battle but that ratification might be even harder. To win ratification in the necessary number of states, they would have to face thirty-six separate legislatures with their political complexities and party conflicts. The nation was facing other major challenges — a series of major strikes, deadly race riots, and a vicious national campaign to imprison and deport left-wing radicals. It would not be easy to focus political attention on women's enfranchisement.

When first advanced by Cady Stanton and Anthony in the 1870s, federal protection for women's rights to vote would have entered into the U.S. Constitution as its Sixteenth Amendment. Now, four decades and three amendments later, following a federal income tax, constitutional prohibition, and popular election of U.S. senators, woman suffrage was poised to be the Nineteenth Amendment, and that is how the newspapers began to refer to it.

Ada James and her father, David, were determined that their state, Wisconsin, would be the first to ratify. As a child Ada had attended suffrage meetings with her mother, Louisa Briggs James, who had helped to form the Wisconsin State Suffrage Association in 1882. In 1911, David James was elected to the legislature and, working with his daughter, authorized a suffrage referendum, but it had failed. Ada James was increasingly drawn to more aggressive tactics, forming her own adventuresome group in 1912, and finally in 1917 joining the NWP. "I have believed for years," she explained to the head of the Wisconsin branch of NAWSA when she left it, "that it is as deadly to suffrage to have one organization as it would be to politics to have but one political party."[52]

Ada James had worked for years to cultivate support in the legislature. On June 10, 1919, the day after the U.S. Senate vote, her work was rewarded as the Wisconsin legislature voted to ratify the new amendment, taking less than two hours, with only a small number of nays in the Assembly and one in the Senate. In honor of his history of championing suffrage, David James was chosen to carry the formal notice of ratification to the U.S. Secretary of State. The only obstacle which the Jameses faced in winning the ratification race was from Illinois, which also aimed to be first. The Illinois resolution actually reached Washington, D.C., just before David James did, but the legislative clerk in Springfield had miscopied the ratifying resolution and the state legislature had to redo its vote. Illinois came in second, followed the same day by Michigan, and five more states by the end of the month.

The excitement of these first ratifications notwithstanding, suffrage leaders knew they faced considerable obstacles. The most obvious were in the South. Texas in 1918 awarded women the right to vote in primary elections, the equivalent of full voting rights in that one-party state, and became the ninth state to ratify. Border state Missouri soon followed, as did Arkansas and then, in early 1920, Kentucky, where the powerful suffragist Madeline Breckenridge had great influence. But this still left eleven southern states. Assuming all would refuse ratification, suffragists had only the narrowest path to victory. Two more non-ratifications, and the amendment would fail.

Southern antis were devoted to states' rights, fearful of black women's voting, and more than anything opposed to any further federal interference in the franchise. A new generation of anti-suffrage women ready to take a more public role was bolstered by state legislators, who were themselves backed by textile manufacturers and other industrial interests. Southern anti-suffrage diatribes always emphasized the dangers of black electoral power, but child labor, which these employers depended on and expected to be the target of women's votes, was an important underlying issue. Regional anti-suffrage forces were determined to keep a solid phalanx against the amendment, and thus hoped to doom federal woman suffrage.

NAWSA had largely given up on making suffrage gains in the South, but NWP had developed several southern specialists. Twenty-five-year-old Anita Pollitzer was a dark-eyed beauty with considerable southern charm, and she drew a great deal of newspaper coverage as the youngest officer of the NWP. She was a third-generation Jewish South Carolinian, her grandparents having arrived in the United States in 1848. Her maternal grandfather was a rabbi. Her paternal grandfather had become wealthy as a cotton merchant. The family belonged to the oldest Reform Jewish synagogue in the United States, and Anita and her sisters were progressive southerners, impatient with constraining southern ideals of femininity.

Pollitzer was a New Woman southern-style, eager for education and opportunities unavailable at home. She received a BA degree from Columbia University in 1916 and frequented New York City's avant-garde cultural scene. Herself a painter, she met and befriended another young artist, Georgia O'Keeffe, who in turn was reputed to have introduced her to the city's exciting suffrage movement. In 1915, Pollitzer joined the Congressional Union (CU), picketed, and was arrested. She rose quickly through the ranks as the CU transformed itself into the NWP, and was appointed legislative chairperson, charged with lobbying members of congress on behalf of ratification in their home states.

In the summer of 1919, Pollitzer left Washington to go to Virginia, where the legislature was already scheduled to hold a special session. Local suffragists warned that trying to raise the woman suffrage issue would only inflame anti-suffrage sentiments there, but the NWP was not daunted. Going up against determined opponents was the party's specialty, faith in the fortitude of its activists its greatest weapon. From Richmond, Pollitzer wrote to O'Keeffe, "We are here — making the Va. Legislature — a lot of old men with such sad souls — ratify."[53] In the NWP weekly, the *Suffragist,* she described traveling from one side of the state to the other, in pursuit of state legislators. "After a few times you become used to the perhaps veiled surprise with which you yourself are greeted because you may not happen to measure up in size and . . . impressiveness to the notion the man had of a would-be-woman voter." Pollitzer was a beautiful young woman, and southern gentlemen were quite willing to be in her presence, to listen politely, only to tell her that they would nonetheless oppose ratification. She was left feeling "about the most useless and ineffectual person in the world."[54]

No political fight in Virginia could occur without reference to the state's revolutionary history. Anti-suffragists called on the sacred memory of Thomas Jefferson, the great defender of states' rights against tyrannical federal power. The suffragists summoned up their own founding father, George Mason. His direct descendant, Lucy Randolph Mason, was a full-fledged progressive and suffragist, and she charged antis with distrusting women and allying themselves with politicians "afraid of democracy."[55]

When the state legislature convened, Pollitzer found herself up against a ruthless opponent, Senator (or "Colonel") Robert Leedy. In what was described as "one of the hottest parliamentary fights in the history of the Virginia Senate," Leedy offered a substitute resolution to reject ratification, using language which suffragists described as "obnoxious" and "offensive."[56] Leedy's bill was defeated, but so was ratification. Pollitzer angrily reported that "sixty-one Virginia men had ruthlessly clapped their hands over the mouths of millions of American women."[57] State suffrage leader Adele Clark tried to sound hopeful. "In a sector in the southeastern battlefront, the full quota of men failed to go over the top," she declared. However, the war would continue, she insisted. "The South-western, Western and North-western lines would continue on."[58]

In contrast to what they knew would happen in the South, suffrage leaders had counted on quick and easy ratification in the West, assuming that the states where women already enjoyed the right to vote would be among the first to ratify. They were wrong. Some suffrage organizations had entirely disbanded and governors where women already voted felt under no pressure to pass an amendment that would enfranchise women elsewhere. A nationwide miners' strike in the fall of 1919 hit the West hard, absorbing all the political attention and further complicating the political situation.

In Colorado, where women had been voting for a quarter of a century, Republican governor Oliver Henry Shoup, considered to be a long-standing friend of suffrage, was one of those who refused to call a special legislative session to ratify. Like governors in several other states, he insisted that it would cost too much money and that legislators would use the opportunity to introduce other bills which he opposed. If suffragists insisted, the governor said they would have to pay all expenses — variously reported at somewhere between $2,500 and $250,000 — before he would call the session. Suffragists' counteroffer was to serve as "stenographers, pages and clerical help" without pay.[59] In mid-June, Shoup accepted and announced he would call a special session. Still he delayed setting a date.

National leaders mobilized. The NWP sent its champion organizer Doris Stevens to Denver, and as part of her "Wake Up America" tour across the West, Carrie Chapman Catt spent three days in the fall there. "It doubtless is impossible for you, who had lived all your life in a State where women had had equal suffrage with men . . ." she chastised voters, "to realize the feeling of hundreds of thousands of American women who have borne the brunt of the struggle in this country for their own enfranchisement. Women have lived long lives and have died in advanced years and yet have given their very all during their lifetime to this struggle."[60] Perhaps she was thinking of Anna Howard Shaw, who had just died. Western governors "politely tell me they will call their special session when they are ready and not before, . . ." she wrote to her friend Mary Grey Peck. "I have been down to the bottom of the dumps today."[61]

In October President Wilson had a major stroke. His health had been failing throughout the time that he was in France. Fighting the other heads of state over the terms of the peace treaty had weakened him terribly and he had come home only to find that the Republican Party, which now controlled Congress, was determined to fight him on everything, most especially his beloved idea for a League of Nations. The severity of his disability was kept out of the news, and although he made no public appearances, statements continued to issue from his office pressing states to act on ratification. The constitutional amendment providing for a transfer of power in the case of a thoroughly disabled president would not be passed for another half century. Instead, in a great irony as suffragists were fighting their ultimate battle, Wilson's second wife, Ethel, was effectively running the presidency. Neither wing of the suffrage movement acknowledged — or perhaps knew of — the situation.

Back in Colorado, Governor Shoup gave in and called a special session for the second week of December. He was less moved by the pleas of suffragists than by the need "to deal with the present industrial crisis" as rumors were circulating that Denver would be "shut down . . . unless there is a change in the local coal situation."[62] When the session opened, the three women sitting in the legislature were given the honor of putting forward the suffrage ratification bill. On December 12, both houses of the Colorado legislature passed the ratification bill. There was no opposition.

Into the winter, Wyoming remained a holdout and a particularly infuriating one. The state was just then celebrating the fiftieth anniversary of Wyoming women's enfranchisement, dating back to its territorial days. The problem was not with state legislators, who were eager to vote, but with the governor, Robert Carey. Carey's father, Joseph, had also been governor and was often quoted in support of woman suffrage. However, the son refused to act even after many other western governors had given in to suffragists' demands and agreed to call their legislatures into session. His reason? "Wyoming women enjoy the rights of suffrage."[63] Anti-suffragists were beginning to charge that Wyoming was refusing to ratify because suffrage there had been a terrible failure. So, in late January, the governor admitted that it was necessary for his state to defend its history and honor and called the special session. It took the legislators slightly over a half hour to complete the act of ratification, seven months into the process.

Wyoming became the twenty-seventh state

to ratify the federal woman suffrage amendment. In addition to the eleven southern and border states, there were still five western states — Nevada, Arizona, New Mexico, Oklahoma, and Washington — outstanding, as well as Delaware, Connecticut, New Jersey, and Vermont.

In February 1920, in the depths of a Chicago winter, and despite the fact that ratification had not yet been accomplished, NAWSA held its "victory convention." Among its hundreds of attendees were five African American women, including Eva Bowles, head of "Negro work" for the YWCA during the war. As luck — or deliberate planning — would have it, February 1920 was the hundredth anniversary of Susan B. Anthony's birth. It was also the association's last convention. Carrie Chapman Catt had begun the process of transforming NAWSA into a new, post-suffrage organization, the National League of Women Voters (NLWV). "The only way to get things in this country," she told her audience, "is from the inside of political parties."[64] Yet, like its predecessor, the new organization would be nonpartisan, because women were already joining both parties. It was a conundrum that would soon face post-suffragism.

Even as a premature celebration, NAWSA's "victory convention" was a strange mixture of joyous anticipation and grief at the conclusion of an effort that had given identity, purpose, and unity to the lives of so many women. "Women looked into each other's eyes and saw old, endearing memories of long, hard work together leap into life," Catt recalled of that day. "They were facing new things, new affiliations, separate ways, but the recognition of what the old things, the old supreme affiliation, the old way together, had done for them, singly and collectively, rested on them with a poignant inner compulsion."[65] The suffrage movement was in the process of turning into history. Helen Gardener announced that she had arranged with the Smithsonian Institution to archive its artifacts, including the table around which Elizabeth Cady Stanton and her colleagues had written the Seneca Falls Declaration seventy-two years before.

In February and early March 1920, seven more states ratified. Each was a struggle, each was a victory, but two dramas stand out. In Oklahoma, the ratification campaign found its first martyr, thirty-four-year-old Aloysius Larch-Miller. Although ill with the flu, she had gone to her county Democratic

511

Party convention to testify on behalf of ratification. The legislature voted to ratify, but she died the next day of pneumonia. In West Virginia, pro-suffrage state senator Jesse Bloch was summoned back from the West Coast to break a tie in the legislature. Over the five days that it took him to cross the country, the other pro-suffrage legislators remained in Charleston. "Telegraphic despatches constantly arrived," reported NWP activist Mary Dubrow, "saying Senator Bloch was in New Mexico or Omaha or some other remote place." Suffragists chased down one particularly restless West Virginia legislator who had escaped and had gotten "as far as his comfortable seat on the train."[66] After five days, Senator Bloch arrived, and his one vote made West Virginia the thirty-fourth state to ratify.

On March 22, Washington State, which had given women full voting rights in 1911, provided the thirty-fifth ratification. Legislators were eager to ratify, but Governor Louis Hart, a cautious progressive, did not want to call a special session for fear of other bills which might be brought forward. His state was being rocked with labor radicalism. It was the home of the "Wobblies," the Industrial Workers of the World, which Attorney General A. Mitchell Palmer was seeking to drive into the ground or out of the country. In this tense atmosphere suffragists struggled to draw attention to the crisis that they faced. "We were a pioneer state, the fifth to be enfranchised," the newly formed state branch of the NLWV telegraphed the governor. "Therefore we resent the disgraceful humiliation put upon us by the stubborn refusal of our Governor to listen to our united demand for a special session to ratify the Suffrage Amendment."[67] Hart relented and convened the state legislature in March to consider the suffrage bill.

The session, despite being so long delayed, was an oddly courteous affair. Washington suffragists, some in their eighties, were escorted into the chamber. One of the few women legislators, Frances M. Haskell, was given the honor of sponsoring the ratification bill. Haskell was serving her first term. (She lost her seat in the next election to an opponent whose victory was subsequently ruled invalid; but no matter — she had been defeated.) The vote was unanimous, at a mere twelve minutes breaking a record for state ratifications. "The mother of suffrage" in Washington, seventy-two-year-old Emma Smith DeVoe (she had been born a month after the Seneca Falls Convention), was then invited to address the chamber. "I am proud of the Legislature of Washington because of this patriotic act," she told legislators. "I thank you in the name of our forefathers who proclaimed that 'taxation without representation is tyranny.' "[68]

This left the challenge of winning the thirty-sixth state. It would turn out to be the most difficult battle of the ratification war, among the most demanding in the whole seventy-five-year campaign for the federal suffrage amendment. Victory had to be won from one of the remaining fourteen anti-suffrage states. As the presidential election loomed, leaders of both parties worried about how women would vote. Democrats were burdened with an unpopular president and a fractured party. Republicans were eager to return the country to "normalcy" and protect it from radical elements at home and abroad. Would women's votes affect the outcome? Could they determine it?

Suffrage leaders thought they might gain ratification in one of three eastern states: Vermont, Connecticut, or Delaware. Although Vermont and Connecticut were solidly Republican and both state legislatures were prepared to ratify, neither governor was willing to call a special session.

514

In Vermont, the governor, enraged at the passage of the three previous constitutional amendments (federal income tax, popular election of senators, prohibition), believed that one more — woman suffrage — would be the death blow to "free popular government."[69] Four hundred women came to the state capital from all over the state "overcoming the obstacles of long distances, almost impassable roads and poor train service." So many suffragists answered the call that two separate audiences before the governor were scheduled. Women presented a barrage of reasons for Governor Percival Clemens to act, to which his response was succinct and dismissive: he "did not care to make a decision at once."[70]

In Connecticut in May 1920, Governor Marcus Holcomb hid his opposition to the amendment by insisting that he was prohibited by the state constitution from calling a special session except in cases of "emergency." Suffragists took up the challenge to prove to him that there was indeed an emergency. From all forty-eight states, "doctors, lawyers, scientists, business and professional women, professors, and public officials, a group of women which in size, prominence and ability had never been equaled in the United States" came to Hartford.[71] Divided into four groups, the visiting suffragists covered the state, collecting resolutions insisting that the need for ratification constituted an emergency, not just for Connecticut, but for the nation. The governor, backed by the influence of obdurate anti-suffrage Connecticut senator Frank Brandegee, would not give in.

Delaware had a mildly pro-suffrage Democratic governor, but the problem again was the Republicans, who controlled the legislature but were deeply split. Now that Delaware was beginning to look like ratification's last chance, suffragists and antis alike flooded into the state as little Delaware became the center of national attention. Catt spoke to the state legislature. Her message was that federal enfranchisement of women was coming. Delaware had the historic opportunity to deliver the decisive victory. Alice Paul also arrived.

The anti-suffragists were equally determined to turn the state their way. Charlotte Rowe, field secretary of NAOWS, arrived to work with Mary Wilson Thompson, wife of a wealthy Delaware textile manufacturer and fierce anti-suffragist. Thompson opposed woman suffrage, she told reporters, not because "I feel women cannot vote or are not the mental equal of our men folks," but because to do so would deprive them of their distinct, special form of social and community influence to merely mimic that of their men.[72] Women such as Thompson and Rowe showed how far anti-suffragists had come from the early days of reluctant public involvement. They now undertook a level of political engagement rivaling that of the suffragists themselves.

The congressional battle for the Nineteenth Amendment, occurring as it did during a period of high Jim Crow repression and under the waning days of a segregationist Democratic administration, had not made it possible for black women to participate on the national stage. However, once the struggle moved to the states for ratification, the situation was different. Especially in states where the size of the black population was significant, the Republican Party still existed, and African American men could vote, black women might play a role. Delaware was such a state. An estimated nine thousand black Delaware women, including an extraordinary group of active suffragists, met all these requirements. Many were college graduates and educators and belonged to the Equal Suffrage Study Group, organized in 1914. Its president was renowned poet Alice Dunbar-Nelson.[73]

"When the colored women become impressed with the responsibility that rests on them as a part of the electorate," she wrote in 1920, "they will appreciate their obligations to the State, and will realize, as all good Americans realize, that the highest privilege of a citizen is to cast a free and untrammelled (sic) ballot."[74]

In mid-April, while legislators were struggling over whether to bring up the ratification bill, suffragists came together in a mass rally on Dover's historic city green. "The crowning feature of the day was a parade of suffrage children," a response to the opposition's argument that votes will cause women to neglect their families. "A long line of boys and girls waving suffrage banners and mounted on ponies and bicycles" led the parade, while "wee tots whose kiddie carts were guided by their mothers" brought up the rear.[75]

Timed to coincide with the state Republican convention, the demonstration succeeded in getting the party to adopt a prosuffrage plank in its platform. Two weeks later, the Delaware Senate passed the ratification bill. All parties knew that the Delaware House was going to be a much more difficult hurdle, and the legislative devices flew fast and furious as each side sought the advantage. For the next month, suffragists and their supporters did everything possible to secure the needed votes but to no avail. Finally, on June 2, the final day of the special session, the House bill was not even granted the dignity of a straightforward vote up or down. Instead the anti legislators simply adjourned the session without considering it. Anti leader Mary Thompson was elated. Given "the splendid character and steadfastness" of Delaware legislators, she effused, "any mother might be proud to raise her sons in a state where such men can be found."[76] State suffrage president Mary Ridgely had to be more restrained. "Failure to ratify is a fearful disappointment but it really is only a brief delay. The women will win inevitably and soon."[77]

Despite the failure of Republicans in many states to act, the national Republican Party was already claiming credit for the amendment's victory and beginning to solicit women's votes and money. Why then wouldn't its leaders put more pressure on these recalcitrant states? Suffrage leaders began to sense that there were what they called "sinister forces" at work. Perhaps the Republican Party feared that its opposition to Wilson's League of Nations proposal would drive peace-oriented and internationalist women into the hands of Democrats. "The political machine that could make a President certainly could easily whip a determined Governor into line," Catt insisted, but it did not.[78]

The NWP responded to the situation by directing the energy and ire with which it had once targeted the Democrats at the new party in power, the Republicans, blaming them for these losses. Five days after the Delaware defeat, Republicans met in national convention in the Chicago Coliseum to select their presidential candidate. Alice Paul issued a call for thousands to come to protest this inaction. Republican leaders, she charged, were "seeking to prevent rather than enable women to vote in the presidential elections next fall."[79] Pickets circled the convention headquarters and a few got inside, unfurling a banner that read "We Do Not Want Planks. We Want the 36th State."[80] If the situation didn't change, and quickly, the majority of American women would not be able to vote in the presidential election.

NAWSA also sent its people to the convention. Well-connected Republicans, they were able to work from the inside. Harriet Taylor Upton, the association's treasurer, was a neighbor and friend of the man who would soon gain the nomination, Warren G.

Harding. Catt's companion, Mary Garrett Hay, had risen to prominence in the New York Republican Party. At the convention, Hay stood in for Catt, who was out of the country, called to an important meeting of the International Woman Suffrage Association. Hay submitted a platform plank to the resolution committee, which urged the Republican governors of Vermont and Connecticut to get their legislatures to ratify, but even that was too strong. When the plank went into the platform, the language was softened from "urged" to "earnestly hope."[81]

After forty ballots, Senator Harding received the presidential nomination. He was a compromise candidate, and few were enthusiastic about him. He was a wavering supporter of suffrage, although his wife, Florence, was a genuine suffragist (and, it was later discovered, a betrayed spouse). Harding delayed any public statement on suffrage, saying it was unseemly until he received the party's formal nomination in July. Alice Paul announced that the NWP would take its pickets to the candidate's doorstep in Marion, Ohio. By the time the picketers got there, however, Harding had pledged his support and sent a telegram urging Republican delegates in Tennessee to do their best to put ratification over the top. To that state, all eyes now turned.

Tennessee had been off the ratification map not just because it was a southern state, but because the state constitution required legislators to go before the voters in an election and make their stand on ratification of a federal constitutional amendment explicit before they could take such action. The provision dated back to the Reconstruction Era, when it had been directed at keeping a Republican-dominated legislature from ratifying the hated Fifteenth Amendment (which Tennessee did not do until 1997). On June 2, 1920, the U.S. Supreme Court issued a ruling which many constitutional experts thought called into question the Tennessee prohibition, and all other state attempts to circumvent the federal constitution's bestowal of responsibility on state legislatures for ratification of federal amendments.

The case on which the court ruled, *Hawke v. Smith,* did not deal directly with the woman suffrage amendment, but with its direct predecessor, the Eighteenth Amendment. In Ohio, anti-prohibition ("wet") forces sought to undo the legislature's ratification by securing a state referendum

that would supersede it. Voters obligingly —
and narrowly — passed the referendum to
reject the legislature's prohibition ratification. The case indirectly involved woman
suffrage because Ohio, Massachusetts,
Texas, and New Jersey were attempting the
same device of securing voter referenda on
the suffrage amendment to undo their
states' legislative ratification. Catt and other
suffrage leaders believed that the point of
the strategy was less to defeat ratification
via these referenda than to throw such
doubt and confusion within state legislatures that the entire ratification process
would fail. By March 1920, when state
ratifications had drawn to a halt on the
verge of the necessary thirty-six, it seemed
like the strategy might have worked.

The referendum strategy was challenged
in the courts by George W. Hawke, a lawyer
and prohibitionist from Cincinnati. The
Supreme Court ruled that the Constitution's procedures for the ratification of
amendments could not be altered by state
law. Did this ruling go beyond the prohibition case to apply to the woman suffrage
amendment and protect state ratifications
of the Nineteenth Amendment from attempted referenda? NAWSA's counsel,
former presidential candidate (and Wilson's

523

1916 opponent) Charles Evans Hughes, believed it did. Three weeks later, in answer to Catt's request to President Wilson, his acting attorney general also agreed: "the power of the [state] Legislature to ratify an amendment of the Federal Constitution is derived solely . . . through the Federal Constitution. . . . [It] cannot be taken away, limited or restrained in any way by the Constitution of a State."[82] The battle for final ratification could now focus on the Tennessee state legislature.

In these battles for ratification, every state had its complexities, and perhaps some were equal to those in Tennessee, but because of how much was at stake there, the legislative intricacies, intraparty conflicts, and oppositional dirty tricks there have received unparalleled attention. Newspapers across the country covered it day by day. Books have been written about how the fate of the woman suffrage amendment teetered on the balance in Nashville during that steamy August of 1920. The root of the Tennessee drama lay in efforts to depose Governor Albert Roberts by enemies in his own party, the Democrats. Roberts was pro-suffrage but he was unwilling to move on ratification before an early August Democratic gubernatorial primary, at which his fate would be determined. Support for ratification from the residual state Republican Party, located in East Tennessee, was shaky but would be crucial.

Tennessee suffragists made their case at the Democratic National Convention in San Francisco in late June. Despite Republican boasting, suffragists pointed out, there still might be time for the Democrats to win this last and critical battle for ratification, take credit for women's enfranchisement, and convince a critical mass of the many millions of new women voters to keep the presidency in the hands of their party. Tennessee was the key to this possibility. After the Democrats nominated the other Ohio senator, John Cox, for president, the party passed a much stronger resolution in favor of the federal amendment than had Republicans, and the delegates united in urging Governor Roberts to call a special session. Soon after, the governor did so, "whereupon a long-drawn breath of relief swept over the nation."[83] He set the date for August 9, three days after the Democratic primary, which he hoped would secure his nomination and thus the governorship.

Knowing that this would be their most difficult challenge yet, both suffrage factions put all their resources into Tennessee. The

NWP had a head start. One of their most intrepid organizers, thirty-three-year-old Sue Shelton White, was a Tennessee native who had considerable inside knowledge of her state's politics. So valuable was she to suffrage prospects that when she had defected from NAWSA to the NWP in 1918, Carrie Chapman Catt lost her usual composure and reprimanded her harshly for her disloyalty. By late June, White was already in Nashville gearing up for the ratification battle, aided by the NWP's other veteran southern-born organizer, Anita Pollitzer.

To organize NAWSA's work in Tennessee, Catt sent Marjorie Shuler of Buffalo, who had accompanied or stood in for her in major ratification efforts across the West and Northeast over the last year. Shuler, now in her mid-thirties, was a certified suffrage daughter. Her mother, Nettie Rogers Shuler, was a suffrage leader in western New York. (Her knowledge of the entire national suffrage movement was so comprehensive that in 1923 Catt asked her to coauthor a history of American suffragism.) In 1918, Marjorie Shuler wrote *A Guide to Women Voters,* the first in a series of handbooks issued by NAWSA, anticipating the work of the National League of Women Voters (NLWV) to educate women about how best to use their franchise. By the last grueling months of the ratification battles, she had become a skilled and professional publicist and journalist.

In Nashville, Marjorie Shuler was able to rely on several experienced and well-placed local activists. One of the most important was Anne Dallas Dudley, who had replaced the renegade Louisiana suffragist Kate Gordon as the most influential southerner in NAWSA. Dudley's father had come to Tennessee just after the Civil War as a "scalawag" and had risen to be an important cotton manufacturer. Brought up as a "belle of the New South," Anne had developed into a leader of southern women's Progressivism. An exceptionally beautiful woman, she crisscrossed the state, often with her two handsome children, drawing on local women's clubs and Woman's Christian Temperance Union (WCTU) chapters to lay down a solid statewide suffrage network. Her southern charm was a resource except when it wasn't, as when, during the height of the ratification struggle, she flirtatiously straightened the string tie of an opposing legislator while urging him to vote for ratification. "Without a word, Senator Mc-Farland had whipped out his pen-knife, cut himself free, and walked away, leaving Mrs.

Dudley standing, tie in hand, in the Capitol corridor."[84]

In January 1918, when Dudley had appeared before the Woman Suffrage Committee of the U.S. House of Representatives as the spokesperson for southern suffragists, she addressed the "negro problem." Seeking to lay to rest "once and for all this old, old ghost that stalks through the halls of Congress," she called it a "phantom."[85] Dudley gave the standard pragmatic refutation: in most states many more white women than black would be enfranchised; and where that was not the case, educational qualifications would keep down the black vote. This was as much as a southern white woman could say in public without damaging suffrage prospects.

Actually the racial situation on the ground in Tennessee was much more promising. In 1919, presidential and municipal suffrage were secured in Tennessee, after which white and black women in Nashville developed a successful working and voting alliance, perhaps unique in the South. The city, home to two major black educational institutions, Fisk University and Meharry Medical College, had a substantial population of educated, civically engaged African American women. Among its leaders were Frankie

Seay Pierce and Dr. Mattie Coleman. Coleman, a teacher before she became a physician, initiated an alliance with white suffragists. She proposed that black women voters join white women in using their new voting rights on behalf of the Democrats' municipal reform slate. In exchange for this, she wanted white women to support improved social services for the black community. This was a daring move, for it meant asking African American voters to abandon the Republican Party, but both groups agreed to the plan.

Frankie Pierce was the daughter of a free father and slave mother, and was a church and civic activist. In May 1920, while ratification was pending, Pierce was invited to address the city's white suffragists on "What Will the Negro Woman Do with the Vote?" "Yes, we will stand by the white women," she promised. "We are going to make you proud of us," boldly adding "because we are going to help you to help us and yourselves."[86] "I don't believe the 'nigger question' will be raised here," a leading white suffragist told Catt, "since Negro women have voted now in the five largest cities of the state, and in every instance made good."[87]

This racial compromise did not prevent

anti-suffragists from harping endlessly on the "race peril" that woman suffrage would bring to the South. Suffragists might assure a worried public that there were more white women voters than black, but anti-suffragists were there to tell the legislators that this was wrong. Black women, antis warned, would rush to vote, while respectable southern white women would "disdain to mingle at the polls with both sexes and races." "White domination," a term which antis did not hesitate to defend, ". . . as every intelligent person knows is essential to civilization," and it would be brought crashing down if and when woman suffrage doubled the black vote.[88]

The leading Tennessee anti-suffragist was Josephine Pearson. She was an educator and had been active in women's organizations including the WCTU and the 1893 Woman's Centennial Committee at the Columbian Exposition. Pearson was a fierce opponent, as indefatigable in her faith that woman suffrage would fatally harm white southern women as Catt and Paul were that it would benefit them. The amendment was named after Susan B. Anthony, she reminded her audiences, a known "propagator of *Abolition*," closely associated with the much-hated Frederick Douglass.[89] Pearson was joined by Alabaman Nina Pinckard. Pinckard had impeccable credentials for the job, for she was a descendant of the South's greatest advocate of state's rights, John C. Calhoun. Louisianan Kate Gordon and Kentuckian Laura Clay, who had left behind their suffragist past to serve as aggressive anti-suffragists, were also coming to Nashville, prepared, as Catt wrote, to "appeal to Negro phobia and every other cave man's prejudice."[90] Also Mary Gilbreth, the third president of the NAOWS in as many years, arrived in Nashville.

These women were the public face and passion of anti-suffragism, but just behind them stood men who provided the money and backroom political pressure that was necessary to turn the Tennessee legislature against ratification. The American Constitutional League, formed by Everett Wheeler in the wake of the successful 1917 New York referendum, led the men's wing of the anti-suffrage movement. Stocked with right-wing politicians and lawyers, it attacked woman suffrage as a front for everything progressive, culminating in the charge of lurking Bolshevism. The special contribution of these men was in mounting successive legal challenges, the final one not rejected by the Supreme Court until 1922.

In mid-July, Carrie Chapman Catt arrived in Nashville. She had expected to stay only a few days, but the situation she found was so dire that she remained for the next month to see the battle through to the end. Suffrage organizers across the state were reporting that, despite judicial rulings and legal opinions to the contrary, legislators still insisted that they would be violating their oath of office by acting on ratification before going before the voters. Publicly Catt was very positive, telling reporters that ratification had sufficient votes in both houses of the state legislature. Confidentially, she did "not believe that there is a ghost of a chance for ratification in Tennessee."[91] A month later, she was even more explicit. "Never in the history of politics has there been such a force for evil. . . . I have been called more names, been more maligned, more lied about than in the thirty previous years I worked for suffrage."[92]

The special session called by Governor Roberts finally opened on Monday, August 9, two days after the primary that secured his renomination. "The eyes of all America are upon us," Roberts grandly told the assembled legislators. "Millions of women are looking to the Tennessee legislature to give them a voice and share in shaping the destiny of the republic."[93] The weather in Nashville was very hot, and combatants fought and sweltered through the corridors of the statehouse and the rooms of the city's major hotel, the Hermitage.

Legislative rituals and oppositional devices delayed action in both chambers until the end of the week. On Thursday evening, at the insistence of the anti-suffragists, a joint hearing was held, attended by "one of the largest crowds ever assembled in the Capitol."[94] Suffragists had taken care to have only Tennessee women present their case so as not to arouse resentment at "outsiders," but opponents made the mistake of featuring a woman from New York. Charlotte Rowe complained that suffragists were Bolsheviks in disguise and that Tennessee women were following them down a dishonorable path. This tactical error, especially Rowe's unwise insults to southern womanhood, cost antis one crucial vote. A legislator who was personally against woman suffrage was so offended by the northern woman's insult that he would vote for ratification so that the South could have the pleasure of blaming the franchise on the women of the North.

Just after the hearing, the state senate committee in charge met and reported in favor of ratification. The next day was ominously Friday the thirteenth, but the full Senate, with greater support for ratification than either side had anticipated, voted twenty-five in favor, four against and two abstaining. One of the nays was Herschel Candler, a Republican whom Anita Pollitzer had chased up and down the hills of eastern Tennessee, trying and failing to win his support. Candler could undoubtedly see that his side had lost the senate battle, which may account for his extremely insulting remarks. The suffragists swarming over his state, he angrily charged, were "low-neck, high-skirt suffragists who know not what it is to go down in the shade of the valley and bring forth children."[95]

Both sides knew that the Tennessee House would be a much more difficult struggle. Antis succeeded in having the vote delayed over the weekend as they sought to woo, threaten, and bribe legislators over to their side.[96] Suffragists, staying in rooms in the same hotel, got much closer and more disturbing access than they had ever had before to electoral politics at its sordid worst. They were particularly appalled at the strategic plying of liquor to legislators in the Jack Daniel's Hospitality Suite at the Hermitage Hotel. "Legislators, both suffrage and anti-suffrage men, were reeling through the hall in a state of advanced intoxication — a sight no suffragist had before witnessed in the sixty years of suffrage struggle," Catt and Shuler wrote. Blatantly ignoring the prohibition amendment, for which Tennessee legislators had enthusiastically voted, was the way of state politics, the women were told. "Whiskey and legislation go hand in hand."[97]

Liquor was not the only, not even the worst, enemy. On Monday evening, suffragists learned that Seth Walker, powerful speaker of the house (and close friend of the governor), had gone from support for ratification to leading the opposition. In his sudden switch, they saw the shadowy power of railroad money. Alice Paul went to the newspapers to make the charge. The Tennessee legislature was in the pocket of the Louisville and Nashville Railroad, part of a national conglomerate seeking to protect its powerful U.S. Senate backers, who they feared would lose their seats to the votes of progressively minded women. The plot, Paul charged, reached all the way to Connecticut, where anti-suffrage forces had already blocked ratification in order to protect that state's crucial railroad man, U.S. Senator Frank Brandegee.[98] Here, it seemed, were the "sinister forces" at work that Catt had also suspected. "We are terribly worried and so is the other side . . . ," Catt wrote to her close friend Mary Gray Peck. "It is hot, muggy, nasty and this last battle is desperate. We are low in our minds. Even if we win we who have been here will never remember it with anything but a shudder."[99]

Having the powerful Walker as their enemy was partially offset by a new legislative champion. Young (and as the newspapers observed, unmarried) Joe Hanover took over the floor leadership of the pro-suffrage forces in the House. He was a tireless and effective champion. Hanover was a Polish-born Jewish immigrant, later crediting his commitment to woman suffrage to "the way I was born." Legislators on the other side were reported to have called out "Bolshevist" as he walked by. The threats were sufficient to get the governor to assign him a personal bodyguard.[100]

Finally, Wednesday, August 18, five days after Senate passage, Speaker Walker allowed the ratification bill to come up. Suffragists and antis jammed into the galleries and the overflow gathered in the back of the chamber. Newspaper reporters from around the nation were there to cover the event.

Confident that the ratification bill would not be passed, Walker declared, "The hour has come. The battle has been fought and won."[101] Catt stayed in her hotel room to await news. Legislators on both sides spoke through the lunch hour. When the House convened, Walker left his role as chair so that he could make a motion to table the bill. This had happened in other southern legislatures. It could well be the mortal blow, the postponement that would keep ratification from ever coming to a vote. There was considerable suspense. Two legislators nearly fought it out. Disagreement about the count forced the clerk to call the roll again. The turning point occurred when Democrat Banks Turner resisted Walker's attempts to coerce him and voted against the motion to table.[102] To suffragists' relief, the vote on Walker's motion split evenly, forty-eight to forty-eight, and so it did not pass.

Despite this narrow victory, there was still considerable reason to worry. One of the legislators whom suffragists had thought they might count on, twenty-four-year-old Harry Burn, had disappointed them by voting to table. Burn, a handsome young lawyer, was the youngest member of the House (Joe Hanover was the second youn-

Banks R. Turner, far left, Harry Burn, center, and Sue Sheldon White, far right.

gest). He was a Republican, from the party's stronghold in the hills of the eastern part of the state. He lived in the small town of Niota with his widowed mother. Anita Pollitzer had spent a great deal of her time trying to chase (and pin) him down, but had never succeeded. He had, however, told her that he "would do nothing to hurt you."[103] This might be true, but Burn was a protégé of Herschel Candler. Recently elected and with little legislative knowledge of his own, Burn would probably be influenced by Candler and other Republican power brokers. Was his vote to table an indication of how he would vote on ratification itself?

The motion to table having been defeated, the motion to ratify was next. Tabling was defeated by a tie; ratification had to be won by a majority. To say that all breaths were held would not be the half of it. However, this time, presumably seeing that his vote was needed to pass the bill and that he could no longer hide his indecision, Harry Burn voted aye. Ratification passed 49 to 47. Tennessee history records that Burn's vote for ratification was the result of a letter from his mother, asking him to "help Mrs. Thomas [sic] Catt with her rats."[104] Anita Pollitzer's descendants, among whom was her niece's husband, folk singer Pete Seeger, long carried the story that it was she who had convinced Burn to vote for suffrage.

Still the opposition was not done. "The enemies," as the *History of Woman Suffrage* observed, "died hard."[105] Legislative rules gave Seth Walker until midday on Saturday to make a motion to reconsider, and that was three more days to twist arms, offer emoluments, and defeat ratification. Young Harry Burn stayed his course, despite intense pressure to change his vote. He defended himself against charges that he had been bribed. "I believe in full suffrage as a right . . ." he later told reporters. "I appreciated the fact that an opportunity such as seldom comes to mortal man — to free 17,000,000 [*sic*] women from political slavery — was mine."[106]

Even as Walker did his best, the pro-ratification majority slowly inched up. Then, fearful that the pro-suffrage forces themselves would move to reconsider because they knew they had the votes to defeat it, thirty-eight opposition legislators left the state, but that was not enough to prevent a quorum, and the trick failed. On Saturday, the Tennessee House reconsidered and repassed ratification. Now it was up to the governor to send the official certificate of ratification to the U.S. secretary of state. Three more days went by as he hesitated in the face of an injunction filed by anti-suffragist lawyers to stop him, but on Tuesday, August 25, he signed the document and sent it to Washington, D.C., by train.

Tennessee's certification of ratification was delivered in the wee hours of August 26 to the home of U.S. Secretary of State Bainbridge Colby. A State Department employee was assigned to meet the train and rush the document to Colby. Then and there Colby signed the official Proclamation of Ratification with no suffragists or photographers present. A few hours later, Catt, Maud Wood Park, and Harriet Taylor Upton were invited to Colby's office for congratulations. The NWP delegation was scheduled to be received by Colby next, but a diplomatic emergency took him away before they could meet.

Later in the afternoon, Catt met with President and Mrs. Wilson. "Mrs. Catt was deeply affected by the alteration in the President's appearance since the last time she saw him . . ." her official biographer wrote. "She divined the bitterness in the unyielding man's soul at his physical incapacity to finish his own fight victoriously as she had finished hers."[107] Paul of course was persona non grata in the White House. For once, she regretted her determination to make the NWP a force for outside pressure. She let reporters know her resentment at being denied any presidential credit for the victory.

When on August 26, 1920, the secretary of state certified that ratification was completed, the Nineteenth Amendment became part of the Constitution. Tennessee anti-suffragists continued to try to obstruct. Anti-suffrage lawyers filed legal action after legal action. However, after their frustrating

Alice Paul, toasting ratification.

delay earlier in the year, the legislatures of Connecticut and Vermont ratified in September, providing state ratifications to spare should Tennessee lawyers succeed in undoing the legislature's action. Legal actions dragged on until 1922. August 26, 1920, remained the official date of ratification, the date at which women's right to vote became the law of the land.

Newspapers around the country put the news on their front pages, often with background stories recalling the long history of the woman suffrage movement, all the way back to Susan B. Anthony. Photographs of Catt and Paul were widely circulated, the former standing tall with a victory bouquet, the latter raising a nonalcoholic toast to the thirty-six stars sewn on the NWP ratification banner.

Both leaders gave comments to the public. Catt advised women to go into the party of their choice, though with a clear eye to the work that would be necessary to reach the higher circles of influence. By contrast, Alice Paul believed that women should not join the established parties. Neither Republicans nor Democrats had done anything substantial to help women win their votes, she insisted. It was the women of America, especially those who had been awakened to the need for militant action, who were responsible for the victory. She was going to keep the NWP alive as an independent political entity, dedicated to work against anti-woman discrimination, so that it could continue to pressure the established parties from the outside.

And what was Ida B. Wells-Barnett's reaction to suffrage ratification? She was no longer a force on the national stage. The National Association for the Advancement of Colored People (NAACP) and its leader W. E. B. Du Bois had taken over her anti-lynching work; and Mary B. Talbert, president of the National Association for Colored Women (NACW), had become the recognized spokeswoman, a less militant one, for the race. Wells-Barnett continued to work in close connection with the Republican Party. On the eve of the 1920 election, a reporter found her speaking to the Monroe County Republican Council in Rochester, New York. She "characterized the vote for women 'as a benefit to the race as a whole.'" She then went on to pay homage to those two great Rochester icons Frederick Douglass and Susan B. Anthony, who, Wells-Barnett wished, "could have been here to see the day when a woman's ballot will count equally with man's."[108]

Approximately thirty million women now had full rights to vote. How would it be possible to register the many newly enfranchised women as voters in time for the November 1920 presidential election, only nine weeks away? The NLWV set up classes to teach women how to get their names on the voter registries and then how to vote. Both major parties, hoping to reap this attractive new electoral resource, also mobi-

lized. As the default choice of most prominent suffragists, the Republican Party had
greater momentum going into the election.
Democrats, especially in the South, were
not able to keep up. In Tennessee, Governor
Roberts, who had presided over the final
state ratification, was defeated by a Republican candidate. Harry Burn, on the other
hand, was reelected, though party bosses,
angry at his heroic vote for the amendment,
refused to support him.

African American women benefited especially from these Republican initiatives, even
in the Democratic-dominated South, where
the Republicans hoped that these new voters might be able to bring the party back to
life. The *Baltimore Sun* reported that Republicans' high enrollments in Maryland were
"largely due to their success in getting the
negro women on the books."[109] "White
Women Lag At Polls. Negroes Rush to
Register" headlined a concerned *Louisville
Courier Journal.*[110] Historically affiliated
with the Republicans, black women had
great hopes that the Republican presidential
candidate, Warren G. Harding, would reverse the neo-segregationism of the Wilson
administration. Mary Church Terrell, appointed by the Republican Party to organize
the votes of African American women in

the eastern states, believed that "every colored woman in this section will vote for [Harding]."[111]

Their great enthusiasm notwithstanding, black women faced great obstacles in realizing their new voting rights. In Norfolk, Virginia, literacy test requirements developed against black men were aggressively applied to black women to deny them voting rights. In Georgia, requirements that voter registration be completed six months before the election were applied with discriminatory vigor to black women. Even in the face of these obstacles, the phenomenon of black women as eager, well-prepared, determined voters, made the news and headlined many accounts of the rush of women to register to vote.

Contemporary commentators settled on the estimate that between one-third and one-half of women who could vote did (as compared with two-thirds of men). This number stood as authoritative despite the fact that tabulating women's votes, both their overall numbers and their party choice, was impossible to do with any precision. Their political actions could not be determined by comparing precincts, because unlike poor people or black people, women are not geographically concentrated. Nor

Mary Church Terrell.

was there yet any scientific exit polling. Nonetheless, when Harding won the election by a landslide, women were credited (or blamed) for the result. Perhaps they would show their power, voting as a unified bloc, even more in future elections.

The era of woman suffrage was over. The era of women working their way up and through the political process had begun. It was, as Maud Younger had predicted, "the dawn of woman's political power in America."[112]

NINE:
THE AFTERSTORY

What difference did woman suffrage make? This is the question that looms over the history of this long struggle. Democracy doesn't end with the right to vote, but it certainly begins there. Carrie Chapman Catt called the Nineteenth Amendment "the first lap of this struggle for women's emancipation." Socialist feminist Crystal Eastman said that the ratification of the suffrage amendment "is a day to begin with, not a day to end with."[1]

The Nineteenth Amendment signaled the largest single enfranchisement in American history. It ended the official relegation of half the nation to the state of second-class citizens. Winning constitutional enfranchisement happened in the context of nonviolent protest, in contrast to the British movement. It was a glorious achievement and a major step in pursuit of the Declaration of Independence's dedication to pursue a "more perfect union." "In the last half century, more than any other group of people in this land," Carrie Chapman Catt declared, it was suffragists who "have kept the flying flag of the principles of the Declaration of Independence, the principles of the constitution, and have . . . educated the public in those principles."[2]

As for the impact on American women, full citizenship for women laid the basis for equality between men and women in the public arena. Securing the right to vote signaled the nation's recognition of each woman's independent existence, regardless of marital status. Winning the right to vote did not mean that women enjoyed equality in all spheres, not even equality and empowerment in electoral politics. But without the vote, all women's other aspirations would have been even more hobbled and halted than they were. "I did not expect any revolution when women got the ballot . . ." Rose Schneiderman, socialist and trade unionist, wrote in her autobiography, "but women needed the vote because they needed protection through the laws. Not having the vote, the lawmakers could ignore us."[3]

The woman suffrage movement was neither the beginning nor the conclusion of the pursuit of women's rights, of what became known by the early twentieth century as "feminism." In the wake of its victory, a new front in the battle for women's freedom, the birth control movement, emerged. It took the argument for selfhood, autonomy, and independence that Cady Stanton had invoked in the name of suffrage and extended it in a more personal and intimate way. Mary Ware Dennett was an officer in NAWSA before she founded the National Birth Control League, which sought to end the legal regime that had criminalized women's sexual choices since the days of Victoria Woodhull. Even Margaret Sanger, whose priority was always reproductive freedom, worked for suffrage through the Socialist Party in New York City in 1911.

And yet, the question of what difference suffrage made remained — and remains — unsettled. Almost immediately after enfranchisement, newspapers and periodicals were flooded with debates over whether woman suffrage had been a failure. The length of the battle, the final fury of the opposition, the militancy and determination that it had taken to secure this most basic of rights all inflated expectations and enlarged disappointments beyond what realistically might

Women voting, Lower East Side of New York City, 1922.

have been expected in the immediate post-suffrage years. The standard for the impact of the new female voting population was unachievably high. Women were expected to vote immediately in numbers equal to men but with radically different intentions and effects, as a bloc to cleanse politics. Voting hadn't solved all of men's political problems, but it was expected to do that for women.

Even before the 1924 presidential election, political commentators were already declaring that women's enfranchisement had been a failure, a judgment that was repeated by historians and political scientists for decades. Taking the most expansive suffragist claims as their guide — that all women would vote, that they would vote as a unified bloc, and that they would collectively purge corruption from politics — pundits had a field day saying that nothing of the sort had happened. "Nothing has changed," wrote socialist muckraker Charles Edward Russell in a much republished article, "except that the number of docile ballot-droppers has approximately doubled."[4] Although Russell "thinks he has conquered his cave man's complex," responded Carrie Chapman Catt, "he rises up and whacks women voters because they have not achieved a super-majority over men."[5]

What is undoubtedly true is that women did not vote, as political leaders initially expected (or feared), as a uniform bloc. They were half the population, half of every class, every race, every religion, every region. The majority of women had not fought for their voting rights and were politically inexperienced. They had to learn how to vote and to be socialized into electoral and partisan cultures. Even so, the first election brought out approximately one-third of eligible women voters, about half the rate of men.

Even the thousands who had participated

in the suffrage movement, who had been united so magnificently in its final years, were no longer linked by their common disfranchisement. They were divided, much like men, in their party allegiances, in their socioeconomic interests, between liberals and conservatives. "The effect of the ratification of the Nineteenth Amendment has been likened not inaptly to the demobilization of the defense forces after a war," observed social scientist Sophonisba Breckinridge. "Such demobilization is followed, naturally, by a great letting-down of moral energy and force, and second by the development of a diversification of aims and interest among and between those who had been united in the attack upon a common enemy."[6]

Granting women the right to vote did not automatically and of itself upend society and radically alter gender roles, the fearsome specter the opponents had raised. Enfranchisement gave women a crucial tool for change, of which only some women made immediate use. It was not simply being awarded the vote that had changed American women, altered American history, and affected political possibilities. The change came from the long struggle to win the vote, and from the heritage that left the women's rights movement, whenever it would fully revive again. It would take a long time after 1920 — almost as long as it took to win the constitutional amendment — for women to make the vote into a weapon to be wielded collectively on behalf of their sex. Ultimately it would require the incubation of another feminist movement before the greater promise of woman suffrage could be realized.

In the half decade after suffrage was won, while the possibility of a powerful, organized women's voting bloc still loomed, women political activists were able to make some important legislative gains. Maud Wood Park built a powerful congressional lobby around NAWSA's successor organization, the National League of Women Voters (NLWV), of which she was president. In 1922 this coalition secured the passage of one of its major goals, a law to reinstate American nationality to American women who had been forced by a 1907 law to forfeit it because they had married non-American men. The new law had its limits. Under nativist pressure, the 1922 Married Women's Independent Nationality Act excluded American women who had married Asian-born men. In 1931, in response to an international movement to protect married women's independent nationality, Congress passed and President Hoover signed legislation to remedy this exclusion.

The other great post-suffrage legislative achievement was won by the National Consumers League (NCL), which Florence Kelley headed. Under Kelley's leadership, in 1922 Congress passed the Sheppard-Towner Act, named after its congressional sponsors. This legislation designated federal money for maternal and child health care. Sheppard-Towner was the first major federal social welfare bill since Reconstruction. It was especially directed at remedying the nation's shockingly high infant and maternal mortality rates. The funding was modest — a million and a half dollars for each of seven years — and carefully constructed to funnel money through the states to avoid charges of federal usurpation of states' rights. "Of all the activities which I have shared during more than forty years of striving," Kelley declared, "none is . . . of such fundamental importance."[7]

Motherhood claims had always been among the most uncontroversial aspects of women's political activism, but now that women's formal political power had arrived, even these generated opposition. Senator

James Reed of Missouri called Sheppard-Towner "a Bill to authorize a board of spinsters to control maternity and teach the mothers of the United States how to rear babies."[8] The Daughters of the American Revolution, once part of the pro-suffrage coalition, turned dramatically to the right and attacked the bill as "a pernicious piece of legislation being an entering wedge of communism."[9] The American Medical Association also opposed the bill vigorously, fearing this as the first step in a public takeover of medical care. The law nonetheless passed and the program was refunded several times. However, by 1929, once it had become clear that women were not voting collectively to advance this and other reform goals, and as opponents no longer feared that women would join to punish them at the polls, the Republican-controlled Congress refused to reauthorize Sheppard-Towner. President Hoover looked the other way.

Florence Kelley also led efforts to tackle the bane of child labor. One would think this would be a supremely uncontroversial reform, but it was not. In 1916, the Supreme Court had ruled unconstitutional a federal law banning the employment of children under the age of fourteen, leaving a consti-

Women's Joint Congressional Committee advocates of Sheppard-Towner Act. Front row center: Maud Wood Park, with Jeannette Rankin and Florence Kelley to her left.

tutional amendment the only route. Kelley guided the amendment through both houses of Congress relatively easily in 1924, but political enthusiasm for constitutional amendments focused on social reform had evaporated. By the end of the decade, only six states ratified, effectively killing the anti-child-labor amendment. It was never resurrected. Congressional legislation in the 1930s eventually resolved the issue.

In any evaluation of this and other defeats in the post-suffrage decade, the opposition of conservative Republican administrations and especially the growth of a powerful right-wing reaction has to be taken into account. Indeed, women's entry into the electorate, after years of championing progressive political change, did a great deal to fuel this atmosphere of reaction. In 1923, the American Legion, Henry Ford, and others began to circulate a report prepared by the U.S. War Department, which depicted an insidious network of women's "Socialist-pacifist" organizations allegedly threatening American national security and values.[10] The wartime patriotism of suffragists could do nothing to shield them from these charges. This was a kind of voter suppression directed against the most determined and radical of the new women voters.

Right-wing attacks no doubt contributed to suffrage veterans' defensive moderation in the 1920s. Carrie Chapman Catt, once again a campaigner for world peace, reorganized her forces to pull them away from association with more left-wing groups. A major target of this right-wing insurgency was Jane Addams, one of America's most revered women. She was mercilessly maligned for her antiwar work, attacked as un-American, and portrayed as an unwitting and naive ally of the Communist conspiracy. Addams bore the attacks with her characteristic grace, and in 1931, four years before she died, she became the first American woman to win the Nobel Peace Prize, a matchless vindication of her work.

The other important post-suffrage congressional initiative, the Equal Rights Amendment, was first submitted to Congress in 1923, by the NWP. Alice Paul had kept the NWP out of larger women's political coalitions. Despite efforts by other NWP activists to devote the organization to issues such as peace, labor rights, and birth control, Paul was determined to concentrate the organization's energies exclusively on the elimination of all remaining legal discriminations against women. She proposed an Equal Rights Amendment to write into the federal constitution the principle that "men and women shall have equal rights throughout the United States and every place subject to its jurisdiction."[11] The amendment's deceptively simple formulation obscured a great deal of complexity and confusion about how equality was to be defined and which women would most benefit (or to put it another way, to which men would which women be compared in their claims for equality). Unlike the Child Labor Amendment, the Equal

Rights Amendment could not even get through Congress. Even the majority of suffrage veterans refused to support it, fearing that it would invalidate many state labor laws that exclusively protected women, such as those specifying maximum working hours but only for women. As a result, the factional split of the last suffrage years only deepened, dividing and weakening the remnants of the suffrage-era feminist spirit for decades to come.

Over the next forty years, the Equal Rights Amendment was introduced repeatedly in Congress, but it rarely made it out of committee. In 1940, the Republican Party endorsed the amendment in its platform, and four years later the Democrats did so as well, but it had no real chance of passing Congress. Still the NWP continued to make the ERA its national priority, and Alice Paul soldiered on. In 1972, a revived feminist movement carried the ERA through Congress. Five years later, Alice Paul died, age ninety-three. By this time, feminists were united behind the ERA and the major parties had reversed their positions, and the Republicans had become the home for a new generation of determined antifeminist opponents. When Congress passed the amendment in 1972, it did so with a seven-

First African American women voters, Ettrick, Virginia, 1920.

year limit (later extended by four years) for ratification. A well-organized, woman-led anti-ERA movement defeated the ratification drive, which remains, to this day, unfinished business.

At the beginning of the post-suffrage age, despite accelerating migration north, most black women were still living in the South, where they found themselves up against the same obstacles used to disfranchise African American men. Even so, their determination to vote took white political leaders by surprise. In the aftermath of ratification, black women in the South pressed for their right to vote from Atlanta to New Orleans to Jacksonville. In Daytona, Florida, forty-five-year-old educator Mary McLeod Bethune, a decade later to become the most politically powerful black woman in the country, stood up to the local Ku Klux Klan and succeeded in protecting almost four hundred black women in their voting rights.

As had been the case with respect to black male disfranchisement thirty years before, North Carolina was the epicenter of the battle between southern black women and their white opponents over voting rights. In late September 1920, newspapers across the state began charging a secret electoral plot among African American leaders for "capturing the state" by getting masses of black women to the polls while convincing white women to stay at home.[12] This was a distorted report of an actual plan devised by African American educator and clubwoman Charlotte Hawkins Brown to elude the state's notorious hostility to black voters by advising African American women to wait until the end of the registration period so as to take registrars by surprise. Her plan worked until, at the last minute, local Democratic leaders learned of the plans and were able to bring the black women's electoral insurgency to a halt.

Black women kept fighting to exercise their right to vote. Working with the NAACP, they sought a federal investigation into illegal acts by states of disfranchisement. In 1921, a deputation led by Addie Hunton came before the NWP Executive Committee to try to win support for congressional action against states that were suppressing their votes. Their appeal had the backing of NWP notables, including Florence Kelley, Harriot Stanton Blatch, and even John Milholland, who insisted that the struggle for black women's rights was dear to the heart of his martyred daughter Inez. But Alice Paul, single-minded as ever and still uninterested in a racially inclusive women's enfranchisement, insisted that the disfranchisement of black women was a race, not a sex, matter and of no interest to the NWP. "The colored women were disgusted," recalled Mary Church Terrell, spokeswoman for the delegation. Paul's response was "the most painful lack of tact I had ever seen."[13] Paul's action reignited an atmosphere of conflict between African American and white suffragists.

Through the rest of the decade, black women continued to focus their electoral efforts on the Republican Party. After campaigning for Harding in 1920, their leaders created a nationwide organization of Republican clubs to support Calvin Coolidge in 1924. The practice of lynching had come back into public focus with the return of African American soldiers from the Great War, and brought with it the rebirth of the Ku Klux Klan, which was gaining power over the Democratic Party. Working with the NAACP, black women organized a campaign against lynching, the same issue that had given birth to the black women's club movement a quarter century before. This time they highlighted African American female as well as male victims. They tried to get congressional Republicans to pass a federal law criminalizing lynching, but the party was moving further and further away from its Lincolnian legacy. Black voters, women as well as men, began to turn toward the Democratic Party.

In the aftermath of ratification, women were eager to move into elected office. The NLWV magazine, the *Woman Citizen*, listed 250 women who had run for office in the November 1922 elections, and estimated that there were perhaps at least an additional hundred. Most were running for state legislatures, though women sought seats in the U.S. House of Representatives in Indiana, Iowa, Pennsylvania, North Carolina, New Mexico, and West Virginia, and in the U.S. Senate in Minnesota, New York, Pennsylvania, and Wisconsin. Many ran as minor party candidates — Socialist, Prohibition — but there were also women seeking office as Republicans and Democrats.[14]

The problem, however, was that the major parties opened the doors to office for women only with the greatest care, and the higher circles of party leadership and decision-making remained closed to women. Emily Newell Blair, former Missouri suffragist, was one of the rare women with any major party standing. Serving as National Democratic Party vice chairwoman for most of the 1920s, she grew increasingly cynical. "Now at the end of ten years of suffrage, I find politics still a male monopoly," she wrote. "Women still have little part in framing political policies and determining party tactics."[15]

Most of the few women who had party backing and were able to win office were chosen precisely because they were reliably deferential to male party leaders, and were modest to the point of personal invisibility in their political ambitions. As a result, suffrage veterans, women with stamina forged of long battles for the vote, women who had their own political priorities, were not welcomed into political office. Anne Martin, a founding member of the NWP, ran in Nevada for the U.S. Senate as an independent in 1918 and 1920, losing both times. She and others were learning that winning the vote had broken down only one barrier to women's equality, leaving many others to be surmounted. Wives were still economically dependent, women workers were woefully underpaid, and in half the states, women could not even sit on juries. "The fundamental injustice is that our legal system is a masculine institution . . ." she wrote in 1922. "Very, very few women see that the next step toward equality must be winning woman's share, woman's *half* in man-controlled government."[16]

Seven women secured seats in the U.S. Congress between 1920 and 1928, none of them veterans of the suffrage struggle. Indeed, one, Alice Robertson, was an avowed anti-suffragist. "If people think I am going to do something sensational," she declared, "they are mistaken. I am conservative."[17] Then in 1928, Ruth Hanna McCormick announced her candidacy. If there was any suffrage veteran who was prepared to make her way into high political office, it was McCormick. Her suffrage bona fides were strong and her Republican Party credentials even more robust. Few women were better positioned to build bridges between the suffrage movement and the circles of political power. In 1916 her husband, Medill McCormick, was elected to Congress and two years later to the U.S. Senate. After he lost the 1924 Republican senatorial primary, he gave into the alcoholism and depression that had long haunted him, and he committed suicide. Ruth McCormick, now a widow with three children, had her own political ambitions, and resources that few other women could match. "We have carried water for the elephants long enough," she said. "Now we want to get in on the real show."[18]

After Jeannette Rankin, all but one of the seven women who had served in Congress had gained entry by inheriting their dead husbands' seats. Alice Longworth, Theodore Roosevelt's witty and acerbic daughter, quipped that they had "used their husbands' coffins as springboards."[19] Ruth McCormick was far more than a political widow. She had great wealth, political connections, and was a powerful political figure in her own right. Above all, she had her own constituency. She believed that she could

Ruth Bryan Owen and Ruth McCormick, 1929.

count on the backing of the expansive network of Republican Women's Clubs that she had been organizing even before ratification. She had, remarked one political observer, "an organization of 200,000 women," and she intended to use it.[20]

In 1928, McCormick ran an energetic, well-organized campaign for Congress. *Time* magazine put her on its cover. She made it through the Republican primary handily and won the general election by an unprecedented majority, thanking "the women who gave me my chance."[21] When she took her seat in 1929, it was a high point for women in Congress. There were eight other women in the House of Representatives that year.

One of them, Ruth Bryan Owen, was also a political daughter. As fate would have it, her father, William Jennings Bryan, had lost the presidency to William McKinley, promoted by Mark Hanna (McCormick's father), in the historic presidential election of 1896. Thus, there was much feminist symbolism when the two "Ruths," one Democrat and one Republican, walked into Congress arm in arm.[22]

Almost immediately after winning her seat in Congress, McCormick began to pursue her next goal, the U.S. Senate. The only previous woman senator was Georgia Democrat Rebecca Felton, an advocate for white women's rights. After the previous senator died, Felton was seated, but only for a day until a man replaced her. McCormick won the Illinois Republican Senate primary by a substantial 200,000 votes. "All women of America feel your victory as a step forward for womanhood," two of her sister Congresswomen predicted, "the biggest thing for women since the passage of the suffrage amendment."[23]

African American women worked closely with McCormick in her campaign. Ever since the days of Ida B. Wells-Barnett, the black women of Illinois had been well organized and knowledgeable in the ways of

569

electoral politics, working strategically with white women. In the two decades since 1910, the Chicago black community had grown 500 percent and now represented one-fifth of Chicago's Republican voters. Especially in a party primary, they could provide the crucial edge for victory. Recognizing this political reality, Ruth McCormick had marched alongside African American women in Chicago's 1914 suffrage parade and her husband had spoken forcefully in favor of antilynching legislation before Congress. In 1929 McCormick hired dozens of black women to campaign for her, headed by Mary Church Terrell. The burgeoning Chicago African American Republican political machine backed her candidacy.

Becoming one of the 432 members of the House of Representatives was one thing; winning one of the ninety-six seats in the U.S. Senate was quite another. McCormick soon discovered that, despite her moderate politics, her money, and her family connections, she could not even count on the support of the men of her own party. Senator Hiram Johnson, former leader of the California Progressives and Theodore Roosevelt's running mate in 1912, believed that "some of us consider" McCormick's election would be "a punch in the eye of the Senate. . . . Its thorough breakdown and demoralization will come with the admission of the other sex."[24] Illinois Republican leaders who were "disturbed about the possibility of extending petticoat rule" turned against her.[25] She might have made it through had it not been for the stock market crash and the Democratic wave it unleashed. In November 1930, at the general election, she was defeated by three quarters of a million votes.

The same year that Ruth McCormick ran for and failed to win a U.S. Senate seat, Ida B. Wells-Barnett ran for the Illinois Senate. Her path forward was much steeper. She had no significant backing, money, or reliable political support. African Americans were beginning to make their way up the Illinois political ladder, and she was running against two of them, both men. McCormick's run had inspired but also angered her. Shouldn't black women be their own leaders, she asked, and not just (as McCormick had said of women helping men) be water carriers for ambitious white women? Wells-Barnett finished third, winning less than .1 percent of the vote. She died a year later, age sixty-nine.

Statistics about how many, and how, women voted have been of considerable interest since the ratification of the Nineteenth Amendment. Answers had been very difficult to determine until the post–World War II years, when scientific electoral polling began. Recently, more elaborate quantitative measures developed by political scientists have provided new and more precise information.[26] A few basic facts are now clearer.

As previously stated, already in the early 1920s it was observed that women voted overall in smaller numbers than men. Now, however, it is possible to see that the turnout gap between men and women voters varied depending on region and state. The degree of women's lower turnout rates differed, depending not just on race but on the radically different voting policies of state political leaders. In southern states where legal constraints on voting were particularly severe, the female vote, of black women but also of white, was considerably suppressed. In Virginia, only 6 percent of eligible women voted in 1920. Female turnout was greatest in states where elections were competitive.

The percentage of eligible women who voted slowly but steadily increased over time. Sixteen years and five elections after ratification, in 1936, women's turnout rate was especially robust, its increase even greater than that of men. In Missouri, Illinois, and perhaps other states, women's voting rates rose to 80 percent of those of men.[27]

Second, through the 1920s and depending on the political culture in the state in which they participated, women voters were marginally more Republican than men. Republican strength was greatest in midwestern states. However, women were not, as many contemporaries insisted, responsible for the Republican landslide in 1920. In that election (in which voter turnout overall was very low) women voted overwhelmingly for Harding versus Cox, but so did men. Conversely, women were not, as many suffragists liked to believe, uniquely independent of parties. Through the 1920s, they were as loyal to their parties as men.

Third, the character of the electorate and so of the women who were part of it began to change dramatically during the election of 1928. In that election, even though the anti-Prohibition Democratic candidate, Al Smith, lost, the intensity of the election drew many Smith supporters among first- and second-generation immigrants, male and female both, into the electorate. First- and second-generation immigrant women followed the traditions of white working-class men and went into the Democratic Party. For the time being, Republicans maintained their edge with women voters, but that was beginning to slip.

Twelve years after the Nineteenth Amendment was ratified, the American political system changed dramatically. By the 1932 presidential election, worldwide economic depression had upended the American electorate, decisively ending many decades of Republican dominance over national politics, producing a historic Democratic victory, and beginning a new era of federal-government-supported reforms, known as the New Deal.

Few observers paid attention to how women voters participated and what they contributed. Nonetheless, though most explanations of the electoral realignment of 1932 focused on class, women voters played an important role. Male electoral involvement was already high, but because many women were not yet mobilized as voters, they were available to join the New Deal

Democratic Party as first-time voters in significant numbers. By Franklin Roosevelt's second term, the numbers of Democratic women voters had doubled. While the Republican Party continued to address women voters as wives and mothers, the Democratic Party began to speak to them as workers. "Women were a large and increasingly important source of electoral support for the emerging Democratic majority," according to a recent study.[28]

In 1932, riding the Democratic wave that elected Roosevelt, Hattie Wyatt Caraway of Arkansas finally broke the glass ceiling over the Senate to win election on her own (after a few months as her dead husband's surrogate). The Arkansas Democratic Party did not support her, but populist governor Huey Long of neighboring Louisiana did. Caraway had no historic connection to the suffrage movement, but she defended her seat and her Senate position by refuting charges from male opponents that a woman could not do the job of U.S. senator. Somewhat reluctantly, she cosponsored the Equal Rights Amendment in 1944, the year that her party put it on its platform. After two terms, she lost her seat to a young, charismatic Arkansas Democrat, J. William Fulbright.

Caraway was not the only woman benefiting from the new Democratic insurgency. Under the patronage of First Lady Eleanor Roosevelt, a remarkable group of politically experienced women gained considerable national political influence in the Roosevelt administration, taking positions in the Labor Department, the Social Security Administration, and the Foreign Service. Many of the legislative goals that suffrage veterans had failed to achieve during the Republican administrations of the 1920s were realized during the New Deal and can be attributed in large part to these women political activists. Child welfare funding, terminated by Republicans in 1929, was reinstated under Democratic sponsorship, as was, at last, anti–child labor legislation, in the Fair Labor Standards Act, which set sixteen as the minimum age for workers in most industries except agriculture. This time, the Supreme Court accepted the law's constitutionality.

While Herbert Hoover had failed to fulfill his promise to place a woman in a cabinet level office, Franklin Roosevelt did so with alacrity. Frances Perkins, who was a suffragist in college and then a labor reformer in the aftermath of the Triangle Fire of 1911, became secretary of labor, much to the astonishment of the male trade union leadership, which controlled that position.

The shift of African Americans from the Republican to the Democratic Party accelerated. Despite the Democratic Party's residual anti-black bias, African American voters were responding to its class politics and its attention to the needs of workers and of the poor. President Roosevelt, his party still answerable to a powerful southern wing, was no champion of racial equality, but his wife was. She pressed her husband repeatedly to support federal antilynching legislation, but his fear of alienating his southern base trumped her influence and he refused.

Eleanor Roosevelt brought African American activist Mary McLeod Bethune into the administration. Bethune was now president of the NACW, a position she took by defeating Ida B. Wells-Barnett in 1924. Her parents and the older of her sixteen siblings had been enslaved, and she too had first worked in the southern cotton fields. From there, she pursued an education and rose to be the founding president of a school for black girls, later to become Bethune-Cookman College, now a university.

From a less elite background than the previous generation of black women leaders, Bethune brought the African American women's movement down from the heights, away from the culture of racial uplift, and closer to the masses of black people. She was determined to prepare African American women "to take an active part in the political world."[29] Being brought into the Roosevelt administration made that possible. Bethune was appointed head of the Office of Minority Affairs of the National Youth Administration, and organized the Federal Council of Negro Affairs, commonly known as Roosevelt's "black cabinet." In 1935, she started a new black women's organization, the National Council of Negro Women, which rapidly eclipsed the NACW in influence.

After the Second World War, the difference in voting rates between men and women continued to narrow. According to newly established national polling, in 1952, 55 percent of eligible women voted, as compared with 63 percent of men. Women's rates of participation were rising while men's were declining.[30] College-educated and younger women were the most likely to vote, rural and southern women the least. When it came to office holding, however, the much vaunted contribution of women workers to the war effort did not translate into greater prominence or presence in electoral politics. In November 1946, only eight women were elected to the 80th Congress, all in the House of Representatives and none in the Senate.

In 1948, the nation's most popular magazine, the *Saturday Evening Post,* published an article entitled "We Women Throw Our Votes Away." The author was Susan B. Anthony II, named after her great-aunt. Born in 1916, she never knew her ancestor. "Women have a vote, thanks to Susan B. Anthony and her loyal co-workers," she wrote, "but they don't use it to benefit themselves." Women were voting, they just were not voting in unison, and they certainly were not voting to remedy continuing discrimination or add to their rights. "The most incredible blunder of organized women to my mind," she concluded, "is their failure to use the vote to get ahead in politics. . . . American women, after grasping the weapon of political action, the ballot, let it rust in their hands."[31] The article was published exactly a century after the Seneca Falls Convention, which other than local attention and the issuing of a three-cent commemorative stamp went largely unnoticed.

Susan B. Anthony II was active in peace, civil rights, and other progressive causes, and had helped found the left-wing Congress of American Women (CAW). In these years of domestic quietude, left-wing women helped to carry forward the feminist tradition, energized by knowledge of the history of suffrage triumphs.

Among the CAW's members was historian Eleanor Flexner, who did a great deal to enrich the women's rights historical record by emphasizing the roles of black and white working-class women. Eleanor Flexner was the daughter of accomplished parents, her father a highly influential social scientist and her mother a successful Broadway playwright. When Eleanor was eight, her parents had marched together in the New York suffrage parade of 1915. Flexner graduated from Swarthmore College, wrote about playwriting, and then, with no academic credentials or position, spent a decade researching the history of women's rights in the archives of Smith College. In 1959, when the history of the woman suffrage struggle had almost entirely disappeared from national memory, she published *Century of Struggle: The Women's Rights Movement in the United States,* the first truly definitive history of the woman suffrage movement.

The CAW and its progressive feminist membership became a target of a new anti-Communist crusade emanating from Congress. In an eerie echo of the right-wing attacks on the suffrage veterans and the campaign of voter suppression against women in the early 1920s, the House of Representatives Committee on Un-American Activities in 1949 issued an "elaborately illustrated" pamphlet condemning the CAW for fostering a "Red" infiltration into women's organizations. Anthony II's participation particularly caught the headlines, which charged her for "shamelessly capitalizing on the name of her great-aunt." Nora Stanton Barney, Elizabeth Cady Stanton's granddaughter and Harriot Stanton Blatch's daughter, was also active in the CAW and was similarly targeted.[32]

The Republican Party was beginning to experience a deep divide between traditional moderates and a newly aggressive right wing. A member of the former, Maine Republican Margaret Chase Smith, became the second woman to win a seat in the Senate in 1950. Just months after her election, Smith made headlines by becoming the first senator to criticize her fellow Republican, rabid anti-Communist Joseph McCarthy. "Those of us who shout the loudest about Americanism in making character assassinations are all too frequently those who, by their own words and acts, ignore some of the basic principles of Americanism," she declared.[33]

Smith made history again when, twelve years later, she was the first woman to make a serious major party bid for the presidency. The nomination went instead to Arizona conservative Barry Goldwater, the darling of the party's emerging right wing. As Smith's stature faded, another Republican woman was rising. Phyllis Schlafly did a great deal to advance Goldwater's candidacy. She would go on to create the most effective antifeminist women's movement since the anti-suffragists of the 1910s. Touting the danger of the gender revolution that loomed, she built a women's conservative Republican movement, the Eagle Forum. It kept the Equal Rights Amendment from being ratified when it finally emerged from Congress in 1972.

Through the 1950s and early 1960s, the boldest force for progressive social and political change was the civil rights movement. Although its most prominent leaders were men, African American women were its bedrock. From Topeka to Little Rock, women were in the lead in desegregating American public schools. Rosa Parks, the seamstress and NAACP leader, took the bold action that unleashed the 1956 Montgomery bus boycott.

At the forefront of these civil rights campaigns was the voting rights struggle in the Deep South. Fannie Lou Hamer, a Mississippi sharecropper, was its face, its heart, and its stirring voice. After she was kept from registering to vote, she dedicated herself to organizing a movement of black southerners to fight against their disfranchisement. For this, she was shot at, imprisoned, sexually assaulted, and nearly fatally beaten. In 1964, Hamer stood up to the National Democratic Party for refusing to oppose the all-white Mississippi state delegation. She went on to cofound the National Women's Political Caucus (NWPC). She died at age fifty-nine, weakened by the assaults she had suffered.

In 1968, after representing her Brooklyn district in the New York state legislature, Shirley Chisholm, daughter of Caribbean immigrants, became the first black woman elected to the U.S. Congress. She was a civil rights leader and also a feminist. In her political career, she claimed, she had "met more discrimination as a woman than for being black."[34] Four years later, Chisholm became the first black person to make a serious run for a major party presidential nomination. She ran in fourteen Democratic primaries but failed to win the nomination. She remained in Congress until 1980.

As of 1960, the prospects for a feminist revival were not promising. In newspapers, classified advertisements were separated by gender and most news having to do with women was segregated on the so-called society pages. The *New York Times,* the nation's newspaper of record, required information on a woman's marital status so that her name in its pages could be preceded correctly by "Miss" or "Mrs." Margaret Chase Smith was still the lone woman in the U.S. Senate. All the justices of the U.S. Supreme Court were still white men, as they had been for more than two and a half centuries. Popular images of women ran the small range from happy housewives to sexy starlets. Pop Freudians dismissed those who dared to come forward as feminists as women suffering from penis envy.

Major historic changes are not always easy to anticipate. Feminism was about to revive in dramatic fashion, and to reshape American politics, society, and economics in a massive way. In 1963, Congress passed and President John F. Kennedy signed the first piece of women's rights legislation since the 1920s. The Equal Pay Act of 1963 finally recognized that economic discrimination could be a matter of gender as well as race. Until then, the lower wages that women received were considered the natural, if unfortunate, consequence of women's primary family responsibilities and of men's obligations to support wife and children. The average wage at the time for women who were employed full-time was two-thirds that of men. Many women were employed only part-time or seasonally and earned much less.

That same year, Betty Friedan, left-wing journalist and trade unionist, published a blockbuster feminist manifesto, *The Feminine Mystique*. Discrimination against women was "the problem that had no name" — the word "sexism" had not yet been coined — but her book meant to change that. "It has been popular in recent years to laugh at feminism as one of history's dirty jokes," she began her chapter on "The Passionate Journey" that had been the women's rights movement. "Whenever, wherever in the world there has been an upsurge of human freedom, women have won a share of it for themselves."[35] Three years later, along with one man and more than a dozen black, white, and Hispanic women, trade unionists, academics, and state legislators, Friedan formed the National Organization for Women (NOW), often characterized as the feminist NAACP.

At virtually the same historical moment, another manifestation of the feminist revival was emerging among younger women, self-styled "radicals," the female wing of the so-called New Left. Like men of their ilk, they initially showed little interest in electoral politics. The Republican Party was a lost cause, but for them the Democratic Party was also fatally tainted by its conduct of the Vietnam War. Their concerns were more intimate than those that had predominated in the women's rights tradition. Taking for granted equality in the public arena, they focused on greater personal rights, on reproductive freedom, and on exposing the hidden history of violence against women. They were, in other words, redefining and expanding feminist politics. "The personal is political," they declared. Over the next decades, the issues that they brought to light would emerge as among the most powerful and divisive issues of American politics.

These younger women also turned back to the history of women's rights. In her 1970 manifesto, *The Dialectic of Sex,* twenty-five-year-old Shulamith Firestone was one of the first to speak of the feminist upsurge of which she was a part as a "second wave" following on the suffragist "first wave." With youthful bravado, she insisted that winning the right to vote had narrowed and compromised feminism's once revolutionary promise. Nonetheless, she was moved by the fortitude of the suffragists. Even though the vote was "not worth much to women as later events bore out," she had to admire the suffragists. "Even to read about the struggle for suffrage is exhausting, let alone to have lived through it and fought for it."[36]

With feminism's new energies rising quickly, NOW determined to stage a major celebration of suffragists' historic achievement. On August 26, 1970, the fiftieth anniversary of the ratification of the Nineteenth Amendment, NOW called for a Women's Strike for Equality. Women were encouraged to refuse to work, including their unpaid household labor, for one day. Previous anniversaries had passed with little public notice, but this time, more than fifty thousand women went out into the streets of their cities and towns. The celebration of women's enfranchisement was tied to a protest against the gender inequality that still persisted — wage discrimination, the hidden scourge of rape, women's unmet demand for control over their reproduction. Marchers saw themselves as part of a larger social justice movement. They not only called for the decriminalization of abortion and the passage of the Equal Rights Amendment, but also for an end to the Vietnam War and to institutionalized racism.

A new era had begun. In 1970, the number of women in state and federal legislatures finally began to take a visible upturn. In 1974, a majority of women voted as Democrats, a switch that continues to the present, and for which a new term, "gender gap," was coined. Women's votes were on the way to determining national elections.

A decade later, the male monopoly over Supreme Court appointments finally gave way with the appointment of Sandra Day O'Connor. Other benchmarks followed: the first woman speaker of the house, the first woman secretary of state, and the near election, defeated in a vicious and highly contested election, of a woman president.

American politics were being dramatically remade by women's involvement, by women politicians, by attitudes toward gender equality, and by the political salience of issues having to do with women's rights, women's welfare, women's concerns. American politics in the twenty-first century are unimaginable without the power of the female vote and the passions circulating around the "women's issues" of abortion and sexual violence. Efforts to undo women's rights gains had been met by a new determination to undo lingering practices of disregard and contempt for women.

The consequences of the woman suffrage movement continue to unfold in the rising of women's electoral mobilization, their growing political empowerment, and a reinvigorated commitment to undo male dominance wherever it exists. Like all great and powerful historical phenomena, its implications would evolve and its ultimate significance would shift. Our understanding of what the woman suffrage movement really means for American history continues to provoke and challenge us.

APPENDIX A

Declaration of Sentiments, 1848

When, in the course of human events, it becomes necessary for one portion of the family of man to assume among the people of the earth a position different from that which they have hitherto occupied, but one to which the laws of nature and of nature's God entitle them, a decent respect to the opinions of mankind requires that they should declare the causes that impel them to such a course.

We hold these truths to be self-evident: that all men and women are created equal; that they are endowed by their Creator with certain inalienable rights; that among these are life, liberty, and the pursuit of happiness; that to secure these rights governments are instituted, deriving their just powers from the consent of the governed. Whenever any form of government becomes destructive of these ends, it is the right of those who suffer from it to refuse allegiance to it, and to insist upon the institution of a new government, laying its foundation on such principles, and organizing its powers in such form, as to them shall seem most likely to effect their safety and happiness. Prudence indeed, will dictate that governments long established should not be changed for light and transient causes; and, accordingly, all experience hath shown that mankind are more disposed to suffer, while evils are sufferable, than to right themselves by abolishing the forms to which they were accustomed. But when a long train of abuses and usurpations, pursuing invariably the same object, evinces a design to reduce them under absolute despotism, it is their duty to throw off such government, and to provide new guards for their future security. Such has been the patient sufferance of the women under this government, and such is now the necessity which constrains them to demand the equal station to which they are entitled.

The history of mankind is a history of repeated injuries and usurpations on the part of man toward woman, having in direct object the establishment of an absolute tyranny over her. To prove this, let facts be submitted to a candid world.

He has never permitted her to exercise her inalienable right to the elective franchise.

He has compelled her to submit to laws, in the formation of which she had no voice.

He has withheld from her rights which are given to the most ignorant and degraded men — both natives and foreigners.

Having deprived her of this first right as a citizen, the elective franchise, thereby leaving her without representation in the halls of legislation, he has oppressed her on all sides.

He has made her, if married, in the eye of the law, civilly dead.

He has taken from her all right in property, even to the wages she earns.

He has made her, morally, an irresponsible being, as she can commit many crimes with impunity, provided they be done in the presence of her husband. In the covenant of marriage, she is compelled to promise obedience to her husband, he becoming, to all intents and purposes, her master — the law giving him power to deprive her of her liberty, and to administer chastisement.

He has so framed the laws of divorce, as to what shall be the proper causes of divorce, in case of separation, to whom the guardianship of the children shall be given;

as to be wholly regardless of the happiness of women — the law, in all cases, going upon a false supposition of the supremacy of man, and giving all power into his hands.

After depriving her of all rights as a married woman, if single and the owner of property, he has taxed her to support a government which recognizes her only when her property can be made profitable to it.

He has monopolized nearly all the profitable employments, and from those she is permitted to follow, she receives but a scanty remuneration. He closes against her all the avenues to wealth and distinction which he considers most honorable to himself. As a teacher of theology, medicine, or law, she is not known. He has denied her the facilities for obtaining a thorough education, all colleges being closed against her.

He allows her in Church, as well as State, but a subordinate position, claiming Apostolic authority for her exclusion from the ministry, and, with some exceptions, from any public participation in the affairs of the Church.

He has created a false public sentiment by giving to the world a different code of morals for men and women, by which moral delinquencies which exclude women from society, are not only tolerated, but deemed of little account in man.

He has usurped the prerogative of Jehovah himself, claiming it as his right to assign for her a sphere of action, when that belongs to her conscience and to her God.

He has endeavored, in every way that he could, to destroy her confidence in her own powers, to lessen her self-respect, and to make her willing to lead a dependent and abject life.

Now, in view of this entire disfranchisement of one-half the people of this country, their social and religious degradation — in view of the unjust laws above mentioned, and because women do feel themselves aggrieved, oppressed, and fraudulently deprived of their most sacred rights, we insist that they have immediate admission to all the rights and privileges which belong to them as citizens of the United States.

In entering upon the great work before us, we anticipate no small amount of misconception, misrepresentation, and ridicule; but we shall use every instrumentality within our power to effect our object. We shall employ agents, circulate tracts, petition the State and National legislatures, and endeavor to enlist the pulpit and the press in our behalf. We hope this Convention will be followed by a series of Conventions, embracing every part of the country.

The following resolutions were discussed by Lucretia Mott, Thomas and Mary Ann McClintock, Amy Post, Catherine A. F. Stebbins, and others, and were adopted:

WHEREAS, The great precept of nature is conceded to be, that "man shall pursue his own true and substantial happiness." Blackstone in his Commentaries remarks, that this law of Nature being coeval with mankind, and dictated by God himself, is of course superior in obligation to any other. It is binding over all the globe, in all countries and at all times; no human laws are of any validity if contrary to this, and such of them as are valid, derive all their force, and all their validity, and all their authority, mediately and immediately, from this original; therefore,

Resolved, That such laws as conflict, in any way, with the true and substantial happiness of woman, are contrary to the great precept of Nature and of no validity, for this is "superior in obligation to any other."

Resolved, That all laws which prevent woman from occupying such a station in society as her conscience shall dictate, or which place her in a position inferior to that of man, are contrary to the great precept of

Nature, and therefore of no force or authority.

Resolved, That woman is man's equal — was intended to be so by the Creator, and the highest good of the race demands that she should be recognized as such.

Resolved, That the women of this country ought to be enlightened in regard to the laws under which they live, that they may no longer publish their degradation by declaring themselves satisfied with their present position, nor their ignorance, by asserting that they have all the rights they want.

Resolved, That inasmuch as man, while claiming for himself intellectual superiority, does accord to woman moral superiority, it is pre-eminently his duty to encourage her to speak and teach as she has opportunity, in all religious assemblies.

Resolved, That the same amount of virtue, delicacy, and refinement of behavior that is required of woman in the social state, should also be required of man, and the same transgressions should be visited with equal severity on both man and woman.

Resolved, That the objection of indelicacy and impropriety, which is so often brought against woman when she addresses a public audience, come with a very ill-grace from those who encourage, by their attendance, her appearance on the stage, in the concert, or in feats of the circus.

Resolved, That woman has too long rested satisfied in the circumscribed limits which corrupt customs and a perverted application of the Scriptures have marked out for her, and that it is time she should move in the enlarged sphere which her great Creator has assigned her.

Resolved, That it is the duty of the women of this country to secure to themselves their sacred right to the elective franchise.

Resolved, That the equality of human rights results necessarily from the fact of the identity of the race in capabilities and responsibilities.

Resolved, therefore, That, being invested by the Creator with the same capabilities, and the same consciousness of responsibility for their exercise, it is demonstrably the right and duty of woman, equally with man, to promote every righteous cause by every righteous means; and especially in regard to the great subjects of morals and religion, it is self-evidently her right to participate with her brother in teaching them, both in private and in public, by writing and by speaking, by any instrumentalities proper to be used, and in any assemblies proper to be held; and this being a self-evident truth growing out of the divinely implanted principles of human nature, any custom or authority adverse to it, whether modern or wearing the hoary sanction of antiquity, is to be regarded as self-evident falsehood, and at war with mankind.

At the last session Lucretia Mott offered and spoke to the following resolution:

Resolved, That the speedy success of our cause depends upon the zealous and untiring efforts of both men and women, for the overthrow of the monopoly of the pulpit, and for the securing to woman an equal participation with men in the various trades, professions, and commerce.

APPENDIX B

*Declaration of Rights of the Women of the
United States, July 4, 1876*

While the Nation is buoyant with patriotism, and all hearts are attuned to praise, it is with sorrow we come to strike the one discordant note, on this hundredth anniversary of our country's birth. When subjects of Kings, Emperors, and Czars, from the Old World, join in our National Jubilee, shall the women of the Republic refuse to lay their hands with benedictions on the nation's head? Surveying America's Exposition, surpassing in magnificence those of London, Paris, and Vienna, shall we not rejoice at the success of the youngest rival among the nations of the earth? May not our hearts, in unison with all, swell with pride at our great achievements as a people; our free speech, free press, free schools, free church, and the rapid progress we have made in material wealth, trade, commerce and the inventive arts? And we do rejoice in the success thus far, of our experiment of self-government. Our faith is firm and unwavering in the broad principles of human rights, proclaimed in 1776, not only as abstract truths, but as the corner stones of a republic. Yet we cannot forget, even in this glad hour, that while all men of every race, and clime, and condition, have been invested with the full rights of citizenship, under our hospitable flag, all women still suffer the degradation of disfranchisement.

The history of our country the past hundred years, has been a series of assumptions and usurpations of power over woman, in direct opposition to the principles of just government, acknowledged by the United States at its foundation, which are:

First. The natural rights of each individual.

Second. The exact equality of these rights.

Third. That these rights when not delegated by the individual, are retained by the individual.

Fourth. That no person can exercise the rights of others without delegated authority.

Fifth. That the non-use of rights does not destroy them.

602

And for the violation of these fundamental principles of our Government, we arraign our rulers on this 4th day of July, 1876, — and these are our articles of impeachment:

Bills of Attainder have been passed by the introduction of the word "male" into all the State constitutions, denying to women the right of suffrage, and thereby making sex a crime — an exercise of power clearly forbidden in Article 1st, Sections 9th and 10th, of the United States Constitution.

The Writ of Habeas Corpus, the only protection against *lettres de cachet,* and all forms of unjust imprisonment, which the Constitution declares "shall not be suspended, except when in cases of rebellion or invasion, the public safety demands it," is held inoperative in every State of the Union, in case of a married woman against her husband, — the marital rights of the husband being in all cases primary, and the rights of the wife secondary.

The Right of Trial by a Jury of One's Peers was so jealously guarded that States refused to ratify the original Constitution, until it was guaranteed by the 6th Amendment. And yet the women of this nation have never been allowed a jury of their peers — being tried in all cases by men, native and foreign, educated and ignorant, virtuous and vicious. Young girls have been arraigned in our courts for the crime of infanticide; tried, convicted, hung — victims, perchance, of judge, jurors, advocates — while no woman's voice could be heard in their defence. And not only are women denied a jury of their peers, but in some cases, jury trial altogether. During the war, a woman was tried and hanged by military law, in defiance of the 5th Amendment, which specifically declares: "no person shall be held to answer for a capital or otherwise infamous crime, unless on a presentment or indictment of a grand jury, except in cases . . . of persons in actual service in time of war." During the last Presidential campaign, a woman, arrested for voting, was denied the protection of a jury, tried, convicted and sentenced to a fine and costs of prosecution, by the absolute power of a judge of the Supreme Court of the United States.

Taxation Without Representation, the immediate cause of the rebellion of the Colonies against Great Britain, is one of the grievous wrongs the women of this country have suffered during the century. Deploring war, with all the demoralization that follows in its train, we have been taxed to support standing armies, with their waste of life and wealth. Believing in temperance, we have been taxed to support the vice, crime, and pauperism of the Liquor Traffic. While we suffer its wrongs and abuses infinitely more than man, we have no power to protect our sons against this giant evil. During the Temperance Crusade, mothers were arrested, fined, imprisoned, for even praying and singing in the streets, while men blockade the sidewalks with impunity, even on Sunday, with their military parades and political processions. Believing in honesty, we are taxed to support a dangerous army of civilians, buying and selling the offices of government and sacrificing the best interests of the people. And, moreover, we are taxed to support the very legislators, and judges, who make laws, and render decisions adverse to woman. And for refusing to pay such unjust taxation, the houses, lands, bonds, and stock of women, have been seized and sold within the present year, thus proving Lord Coke's assertion, that "the very act of taxing a man's property without his consent, is, in effect, disfranchising him of every civil right."

Unequal Codes for Men and Women. Held by law a perpetual minor, deemed incapable of self-protection, even in the industries of the world, woman is denied equality of rights. The fact of sex, not the quantity or quality of work, in most cases, decides the pay and position; and because of this injustice thousands of fatherless girls are compelled to choose between a life of shame and starvation.

Laws catering to man's vices have created two codes of morals in which penalties are graded according to the political status of the offender. Under such laws, women are fined and imprisoned if found alone in the streets, or in public places of resort, at certain hours. Under the pretense of regulating public morals, police officers seizing the occupants of disreputable houses, march the women in platoons to prison, while the men, partners in their guilt, go free. While making a show of virtue in forbidding the importation of Chinese women on the Pacific coast for immoral purposes, our rulers, in many States, and even under the shadow of the national capitol, are now proposing to legalize the sale of American womanhood for the same vile purposes.

Special Legislation for Woman has placed us in a most anomalous position. Women invested with the rights of citizens in one section — voters, jurors, office-holders — crossing an imaginary line, are subjects in the next. In some states, a married woman may hold property and transact business in her own name; in others, her earnings belong to her husband. In some states, a woman may testify against her husband, sue and be sued in the courts; in others, she has no redress in case of damage to person, property, or character. In case of divorce, on account of adultery in the husband, the innocent wife is held to possess no right to children, or property, unless by special decree of the court. But in no state of the Union has the wife the right to her own person, or to any part of the joint earnings of the co-partnership, during the life of her husband. In some States women may enter the law schools and practice in the courts; in others they are forbidden. In some universities, girls enjoy equal educational advantages with boys, while many of the proudest institutions in the land deny them admittance, though the sons of China, Japan and Africa are welcomed there.

But the privileges already granted in the several states are by no means secure. The right of suffrage once exercised by women in certain States and Territories, has been denied by subsequent legislation. A bill is now pending in congress to disfranchise the women of Utah, thus interfering to deprive United States citizens of the same rights which the Supreme Court has declared the National Government powerless to protect anywhere. Laws passed after years of untiring effort, guaranteeing married women certain rights of property, and mothers the custody of their children, have been repealed in States where we supposed all was safe. Thus have our most sacred rights been made the football of legislative caprice, proving that a power which grants, as a privilege, what by nature is a right, may withhold the same as a penalty, when deeming it necessary for its own perpetuation.

Representation for Woman has had no place in the nation's thought. Since the incorporation of the thirteen original States, twenty-four have been admitted to the Union, not one of which has recognized woman's right of self-government. On this birthday of our national liberties, July 4th, 1876, Colorado, like all her elder sisters, comes into the Union, with the invidious word "male" in her Constitution.

Universal Manhood Suffrage, by establishing an aristocracy of sex, imposes upon the women of this nation a more absolute and cruel despotism than monarchy; in that, woman finds a political master in her father, husband, brother, son. The aristocracies of the old world are based upon birth, wealth, refinement, education, nobility, brave deeds of chivalry; in this nation, on sex alone; exalting brute force above moral power, vice above virtue, ignorance above education, and the son above the mother who bore him.

The Judiciary of the Nation has proved itself but the echo of the party in power, by upholding and enforcing laws that are opposed to the spirit and letter of the Constitution. When the slave power was dominant, the Supreme Court decided that a black man was not a citizen, because he had not the right to vote; and when the Constitution was so amended as to make all persons citizens, the same high tribunal decided that a woman, though a citizen, had not the right to vote. Such vacillating interpretations of constitutional law unsettle our faith in judicial authority, and undermine the liberties of the whole people.

These Articles of Impeachment Against Our Rulers we now submit to the impartial judgment of the people.

To all these wrongs and oppressions woman has not submitted in silence and resignation. From the beginning of the century, when Abigail Adams, the wife of one President and the mother of another, said, "we will not hold ourselves bound to obey laws in which we have no voice or representation," until now, woman's discontent has been steadily increasing, culminating nearly thirty years ago in a simultaneous movement among the women of the nation, demanding the right of suffrage. In making our just demands, a higher motive than the pride of sex inspires us; we feel that national safety and stability depend on the complete recognition of the broad principles of our government. Woman's degraded, helpless position is the weak point in our institutions to-day; a disturbing force everywhere, severing family ties, filling our asylums with the deaf, the dumb, the blind, our prisons with criminals, our cities with drunkenness and prostitution, our homes with disease and death.

It was the boast of the founders of the republic, that the rights for which they contended were the rights of human nature. If these rights are ignored in the case of one half the people, the nation is surely preparing for its downfall. Governments try themselves. The recognition of a governing and a governed class is incompatible with the first principles of freedom. Woman has not been a heedless spectator of the events of this century, nor a dull listener to the grand arguments for the equal rights of humanity.

From the earliest history of our country, woman has shown equal devotion with man to the cause of freedom, and has stood firmly by his side in its defence. Together, they have made this country what it is. Woman's wealth, thought and labor have cemented the stones of every monument man has reared to liberty.

And now, at the close of a hundred years, as the hour-hand of the great clock that marks the centuries points to 1876, we declare our faith in the principles of self-government; our full equality with man in natural rights; that woman was made first for her own happiness, with the absolute right to herself — to all the opportunities and advantages life affords, for her complete development; and we deny that dogma of the centuries, incorporated in the codes of all nations — that woman was made for man — her best interests, in all cases, to be sacrificed to his will.

We ask of our rulers, at this hour, no special favors, no special privileges, no special legislation. We ask justice, we ask equality, we ask that all the civil and political rights that belong to citizens of the United States, be guaranteed to us and our daughters forever.

APPENDIX C

*Nineteenth Amendment to the U.S.
  Constitution*

The right of citizens of the United States to vote shall not be denied or abridged by the United States or by any State on account of sex.

Congress shall have power to enforce this article by appropriate legislation.

ACKNOWLEDGMENTS

Since this book is the culmination of work that I began as a graduate student a half century ago, so my thanks are like the sands in the sea.

I begin by naming my teachers and mentors who have passed: Robert Wiebe, George Fredrickson, Anne Firor Scott, Gerda Lerner, and my beloved colleague Joyce Appleby.

I was first set on this path at Wellesley College by Dan and Helen Horowitz, who remain great friends and supporters.

While I was working on my first suffrage book, I was able to meet Alma Lutz, who received me warmly and shared her great archives. A few years later, Eleanor Flexner, forceful as any reading of *Century of Struggle* would indicate, agreed to meet with me. As I said goodbye, she finished with "Don't forget the Seventeenth Amendment!" Rhoda Barney Jenkins brought me close to her grandmother, Harriot Stanton Blatch. She, Coline Jenkins, and the rest of Elizabeth Cady Stanton's descendants have always been tremendously generous with their legacy and memories.

I have had a career's worth of wonderful students, graduate and undergraduate. Those whose researches have especially enriched this book include: Karin Blair, Chana Kai Lee, Rebecca Mead, Allison Sneider, Rumi Yasutake, Lisa Materson, Natalie Joy, Susan Englander, Carol Cini, Linda Frank, Mir Yarfitz, Sarah Pripas Kapit, Michelle Moravec, Kacey Calahane, and Trisha Franzen.

I cannot possibly name the many, many colleagues and friends of long standing who have accompanied me on the way, but I particularly wish to thank Eric Foner, Alice Wexler, Alice Echols, Robert Rosenstone, Nancy Cott, Liz Kennedy, Lynn Dumenil, Vivian Rothstein, Vicki Ruiz, William Graebner, and Dianne Bennett. The expansive visions and great prose of Vivian Gornick and Chris Stansell have continually instructed and inspired me.

Over the years, numerous archivists have helped me. I particularly want to mention the staffs of the Huntington Library, the Arthur and Elizabeth Schlesinger Library, and the Sophia Smith Collection of Smith College.

Thanks to Louise Caplan who helped me through the last stage of preparation.

I am grateful to the UCLA Faculty Senate for selecting me to give the 2018 Faculty Research Lecture, an extremely satisfying experience which sharpened my ideas and my skills at public presentation. The many, many colleagues at UCLA have been a great gift these last three decades, to name just a few: Joan Waugh, Lynn Hunt, Mary Yeager, Margaret Jacob, and Valerie Matsumoto. Brenda Stevenson, my supporter and champion (it is mutual), helped me so much along the way. Chairs and deans have supported my work: Ron Mellor, Teo Ruiz, Brenda Stevenson, David Myers, Steve Aron, Carla Pestana, and Scott Waugh.

Along my own long road to this book, I have enjoyed the company and benefited greatly from the work of other suffrage historians, among them: Susan Ware, Martha S. Jones, Marjorie Spruill, Paula Giddings, Mineke Bosch, Robert Cooney, Judith Wellman, and Jean Baker. While I was completing this book, the great dean of African American woman suffrage studies, Rosalyn Terborg-Penn, passed away. She is already sorely missed. Ellen Fitzpatrick, Ellen Chesler, Jeremi Suri, and Linda Lumsden kindly answered some recent queries.

I must particularly thank Kitty Sklar and Tom Dublin, whose magnificent work in establishing the *Women and Social Movements in the United States* website has made the rich heritage of the suffrage movement available, as my footnotes amply record. And last but not least, Ann D. Gordon, chief editor of the *Selected Papers of Elizabeth Cady Stanton and Susan B. Anthony,* has been a friend, editor, interlocutor, font of knowledge, and sister suffrage warrior from graduate school days to this moment.

My agent, Sandy Dijkstra, and I have been searching for a project on which we could collaborate for many years, and finally we found one. Sandy, Elise Capron, and Andrea Cavallaro showed me the pleasure and privileges of having a whole team working with me, not the least, of course, in getting me to Simon & Schuster as my publisher and Bob Bender as my editor. Bob's faith in this project and his guidance to gain the audience he believes the subject deserves have been a great blessing. I have done my best to return his confidence.

In the two years that I worked on this book, my life has changed dramatically: my mother passed away; I retired after three decades at UCLA; and I married for the first time. I dedicate this book to my mother and to my partner and husband, Arnold Schwartz, who has accompanied and supported me along these most recent steps to the ballot box.

NOTES

Introduction

1. Elizabeth Cady Stanton, Susan B. Anthony, and Matilda Joslyn Gage, eds., *History of Woman Suffrage* (hereafter *HWS*), v. 1 (Fowler & Wells, Publishers, 1881), 221.

2. Christine Stansell, *The Feminist Promise, 1792 to the Present* (Random House, 2010), 164.

3. Eastman, "Now We Can Begin," 1920, in Dawn Keetley and John Pettegrew, eds., *Public Women, Public Words: A Documentary History of American Feminism: 1900 to 1960* (Rowman & Littlefield, 2002), v. 2, 238.

4. Mary Gray Peck, *Carrie Chapman Catt: A Biography* (H. W. Wilson, 1944), 342–43.

One: The Sacred Right to the Elective Franchise, 1848–1861

1. Elizabeth Cady Stanton, *Eighty Years and More: Reminiscences, 1815–1897* (Simon & Schuster, 2020), 147.
2. Ibid., 148.
3. Ann D. Gordon, ed., *The Selected Papers of Elizabeth Cady Stanton and Susan B. Anthony* (Rutgers University Press, 1997), v. 1, 67.
4. Elizabeth Cady Stanton, Susan B. Anthony, and Matilda Joslyn Gage, eds., *History of Woman Suffrage* (hereafter *HWS*), v. 1 (Fowler & Wells, Publishers, 1881), 70–73. For full text see Appendix A.
5. "Address on Woman's Rights," September 1848, *Selected Papers,* Gordon, ed., v. 1, 99.
6. Rheta Childe Dorr, "The Eternal Question," *Colliers' National Weekly,* October 30, 1920.
7. Chris Densmore et al., *Lucretia Mott: The Essential Speeches and Sermons of Lucretia Mott* (University of Illinois Press, 2017), 44.
8. Judith Wellman, *The Road to Seneca Falls: Elizabeth Cady Stanton and the First Women's Rights Convention* (University of Illinois Press, 2004), 203.

9. Eleanor Flexner and Ellen Fitzpatrick, *Century of Struggle: The Women's Rights Movement in the United States (enlarged ed.)* (Belknap Press of Harvard University, 1973), 76.

10. Wellman, *The Road to Seneca Falls,* 203.

11. Douglass to the International Council of Women, 1888, https://1888-frederick-douglass-woman-suffrage/.

12. Stanton, Anthony, and Gage, eds., *HWS,* v. 1, 73.

13. Stanton, Address, September 1848, *Selected Papers,* Gordon, ed., v. 1, 105.

14. Stanton, Anthony, and Gage, eds., *HWS,* v. 1, 804.

15. "To the Editors of the *Seneca County Courier,*" after July 23, 1848, *Selected Papers,* Gordon, ed., v. 1, 88.

16. Stanton, Anthony, and Gage, eds., *HWS,* v. 1, 815.

17. Ibid., 91.

18. Ibid., 422.

19. Stanton, *Eighty Years and More,* 20.

20. Ibid., 443.

21. Ibid., 52.

22. Ibid., 53.

23. Ibid., 62–63.

24. Linda Frank, *An Uncommon Union: Henry B. Stanton and the Emancipation of*

Elizabeth Cady (Upstate New York History, 2017), 21.

25. Stanton, *Eighty Years and More,* 74.
26. Ibid., 59.
27. *Selected Papers,* Gordon, ed., v. 1, 4.
28. Stanton, *Eighty Years and More,* 71.
29. Frank, *An Uncommon Union,* 117.
30. Stanton, Anthony, and Gage, eds., *HWS,* v. 1, 350.
31. Ibid., 81.
32. Angelina Grimké, *Letters to Catharine Beecher, in Reply to an Essay on Slavery and Abolitionism* (Isaac Knapp, 1838), 118.
33. "American Anti-Slavery Society," November 1839, *Oberlin Evangelist.*
34. Ellen Carol DuBois, ed., *The Elizabeth Cady Stanton–Susan B. Anthony Reader* (Northeastern University Press, 1993), 11.
35. Stanton to Gerrit Smith, August 3, 1840, *Selected Papers,* Gordon, ed., v. 1, 16.
36. Stanton, *Eighty Years and More,* 80.
37. The full painting can be found at https://en.wikipedia.org/wiki/World_Anti-Slavery_Convention#Victuallers.
38. Stanton, *Eighty Years and More,* 83.
39. Stanton to Edward M. David, December 5, 1880, *Selected Papers,* Gordon, ed., v. 4, 27.
40. "Memorial Service for Lucretia Mott,"

January 18, 1881, *Selected Papers,* Gordon, ed., v. 4, 37.

41. *Our Famous Women: An Authorized and Complete Record of the Lives and Deeds of the Eminent Women of Our Times,* "Lucretia Mott" (A.D. Worthington & Co., Publishers, 1884), 490.

42. Stanton to Neall, January 25, 1841, *Selected Papers,* Gordon, ed., v. 1, 19.

43. Stanton to Neall, February 3, 1843, *Selected Papers,* Gordon, ed., v. 1, 41.

44. Stanton, Anthony, and Gage, eds., *HWS,* v. 1, 25.

45. Larry Reynolds and Susan Belasco Smith, eds., *"These Sad but Glorious Days": Dispatches from Europe* (Yale University Press, 1996), 222.

46. Ibid., 230.

47. Stanton, Anthony, and Gage, eds., *HWS,* v. 1, 221.

48. "Address on Woman's Rights," September 1848, *Selected Papers,* Gordon, ed., v. 1, 106.

49. Stanton, Anthony, and Gage, eds., *HWS,* v. 1, 805.

50. Stanton to Elizabeth Pease, February 12, 1842, *Selected Papers,* Gordon, ed., v. 1, 29–30.

51. "To the Legislature of New York," February 14, 1854, *Selected Papers,* Gor-

don, ed., v. 1, 246.

52. Stanton, Anthony, and Gage, eds., *HWS,* v. 1, 298.

53. Wellman, *The Road to Seneca Falls,* 154.

54. Stanton, Anthony, and Gage, eds., *HWS,* v. 1, 71.

55. Ibid., 102.

56. Ibid., 88–92.

57. *Proceedings of the Woman's Rights Convention, held at Worcester, October 23 and 24, 1850* (Prentiss and Sawyer, 1851), 3.

58. Paulina Wright Davis, et al. *A History of the National Woman's Rights Movement, for Twenty Years: with the Proceedings of the Decade Meeting, held at Apollo Hall, October 20, 1870, from 1850 to 1870* (Co-operative Association, 1871), 5.

59. Sally G. McMillen, *Lucy Stone: An Unapologetic Life* (Oxford University Press, 2015), 90.

60. Stanton, Anthony, and Gage, eds., *HWS,* v. 1, 821.

61. "Grand Demonstration of Pettycoatdom at Worcester," *Boston Daily Mail,* October 25, 1850, Women and Social Movements in the United States, 1600–2000 (hereafter WASMUS).

62. Truth's 1851 speech, delivered extemporaneously (as she was illiterate), appeared

multiple times, including by Harriet Beecher Stowe, in the decades afterward. Scholars now rely on the first account, from 1851, which quotes her as saying "Arn't I A Woman." They argue that "Ain't I A Woman," introduced in an 1863 version by Frances Gage, was altered to render Truth more folksy. Nell Irwin Painter, *Sojourner Truth: A Life, A Symbol* (W. W. Norton, 1996), 174–78.

63. Taylor, "Enfranchisement of Women," *Westminster and Foreign Quarterly Review,* July 1851, WASMUS.

64. Stanton to Anthony, April 2, 1852, *Stanton–Anthony Reader,* DuBois, ed., 55.

65. Grimké Weld to Stanton, c. April 1, 1851, *Selected Papers,* Gordon, ed., v. 1, 181.

66. Stanton, *Eighty Years and More,* 204.

67. "Women's Rights Convention at Worcester, Mass.," *New York Daily Tribune,* October 26, 1850, WASMUS.

68. McMillen, *Lucy Stone,* 119.

69. Stanton, Anthony, and Gage, eds., *HWS,* v. 1, 260–61.

70. Alice Stone Blackwell, *Lucy Stone: Pioneer of Women's Rights* (University of Virginia Press, 1930), 171–72.

71. Ida H. Harper, *The Life and Work of Susan B. Anthony* (Hollenbeck Press,

1908), v. 1, 52.

72. Ibid., 60.

73. Stanton, "A Brief Biography of Susan B. Anthony," *Our Famous Women,* 63.

74. Stanton, Anthony, and Gage, eds., *HWS,* v. 1, 458–60.

75. Harper, *Susan B. Anthony,* v. 1, 61.

76. Stanton, Anthony, and Gage, eds., *HWS,* v. 1, 457.

77. Harper, *Susan B. Anthony,* v. 1, 114.

78. "Bloomerism at the Crystal Palace," *The Freeman's Journal* (Dublin), September 19, 1851.

79. "The Bloomers in Florida," *Times-Picayune,* August 24, 1851, https://newspapers.com/newspage/25558664/.

80. Stanton, *Eighty Years and More,* 203.

81. Harper, *Susan B. Anthony,* v. 1, 115.

82. Ibid.

83. Stanton, "Temperance — Woman's Rights," July 1, 1852, *Selected Papers,* Gordon, ed., v. 1, 203.

84. Gordon, ed., *Selected Papers,* v. 1, 232.

85. Stanton to Anthony, January 16, 1854, *Selected Papers,* Gordon, ed., v. 1, 238.

86. Stanton, *Eighty Years and More,* 189.

87. Stanton, Anthony, and Gage, eds., *HWS,* v. 1, 595–605.

88. "Woman's Rights in the Legislature," *Albany Register,* March 7, 1854, Stanton,

Anthony, and Gage, eds., *HWS,* v. 1, 608–609.

89. Report of the Select Committee, March 27, 1854, Stanton, Anthony, and Gage, eds., *HWS,* v. 1, 616–18.

90. Anthony, Diary, January 5–12, 1855, *Selected Papers,* Gordon, ed., v. 1, 292–95.

91. Stanton, Anthony, and Gage, eds., *HWS,* v. 1, 630.

92. Anthony to Stanton, June 5, 1856, *Selected Papers,* Gordon, ed., v. 1, 322.

93. Anthony to Stanton, September 29, 1857, DuBois, ed., *Stanton–Anthony Reader,* 64.

94. Stanton, Anthony, and Gage, eds., *HWS,* v. 1, 462.

95. Anthony, Diary, March 29, 1854, DuBois, ed., *Stanton–Anthony Reader,* 72.

96. Stanton to Anthony, December 23, 1859, DuBois, ed., *Stanton–Anthony Reader,* 69.

97. Stone to Anthony, June 22, 1856, *Selected Papers,* Gordon, ed., v. 1, 327.

98. Harper, *Susan B. Anthony,* v. 1, 148.

99. Anthony to Stanton, November 4–5, 1855, DuBois, ed., *Stanton–Anthony Reader,* 59.

100. Stanton, *Eighty Years and More,* 210–11.

101. Henry Stanton to Elizabeth Stanton, January 12, 1861, *Selected Papers,* Gordon, ed., v. 1, 454–55.

Two: Now Let Us Try Universal Suffrage, 1861–1869

1. Ida H. Harper, *The Life and Work of Susan B. Anthony* (Hollenbrook Press, 1908), v. 1, 218.

2. Wright to Anthony, March 31, 1862, *Selected Papers of Elizabeth Cady Stanton and Susan B. Anthony,* Ann D. Gordon, ed. (Rutgers University Press, 1997), v. 1, 474.

3. Harriot Stanton Blatch and Alma Lutz, *Challenging Years: The Memoirs of Harriot Stanton Blatch* (G. P. Putnam Sons, 1940), 13.

4. Harper, *Susan B. Anthony,* v. 1, 226.

5. Ibid.

6. Deanne Blanton and Lauren M. Cook, *They Fought Like Demons: Women Soldiers in the Civil War* (Louisiana State University Press, 2002).

7. Elizabeth Cady Stanton, Susan B. Anthony, and Matilda Joslyn Gage, eds., *History of Woman Suffrage* (hereafter *HWS*),

v. 2 (Susan B. Anthony Publisher, 1886), 886.

8. http://alplm-cdi.com/chroniclingillinois/index.php/items/show/6642.

9. *Proceedings of the Meeting of the Loyal Women of the Republic, held in New York City, May 4, 1863* (Phair & Co. Printers, 1863), 67–68.

10. Harper, *Susan B. Anthony,* v. 1, 228.

11. Stanton, Anthony, and Gage, eds., *HWS,* v. 2, 61.

12. Harper, *Susan B. Anthony,* v. 1, 229.

13. "A Wisconsin Lady at the Loyal Women's Convention in New York City," *Semi Weekly Wisconsin,* May 19, 1863, 2.

14. Stanton to Mrs. Gerrit Smith, July 20, 1863, *Elizabeth Cady Stanton as Revealed in Her Letters, Diaries and Reminiscences,* Theodore Stanton and Harriot Stanton Blatch, eds. (Harper & Brothers, 1922), 94.

15. Ibid.

16. *Proceedings of the Meeting of the Loyal Women of the Republic,* 80.

17. "Speech by Anthony to the American Anti-Slavery Society," December 4, 1863, *Selected Papers,* Gordon, ed., v. 1, 506.

18. *Liberator,* Stanton to the Editor, December 13, 1863, *Selected Papers,* Gordon,

ed., v. 1, 507–508.

19. Anthony to Stanton, February 14, 1865, *Selected Papers,* Gordon, ed., v. 1, 535.

20. Anthony, Diary, May 9, 1865, *Selected Papers,* Gordon, ed., v. 1, 548.

21. Anthony, Diary, April 15, 1865, *Selected Papers,* Gordon, ed., v. 1, 542.

22. Anthony to Stanton, April 19, 1865, *Selected Papers,* Gordon, ed., v. 1, 543.

23. Remarks at Memorial Service for Abraham Lincoln, April 23, 1865, *Selected Papers,* Gordon, ed., v. 1, 546.

24. *Rochester Union and Advertiser,* August 31, 1865, *Selected Papers,* Gordon, ed., v. 1, 556.

25. "Universal Suffrage," July 29, 1865, *Selected Papers,* Gordon, ed., v. 1, 551.

26. Faye E. Dudden, *Fighting Chance: The Struggle over Woman and Black Suffrage in Reconstruction America* (Oxford University Press, 2011), 63.

27. Stanton to Wendell Phillips, May 25, 1865, *Elizabeth Cady Stanton,* Stanton and Blatch, eds., 104–105.

28. Harper, *Susan B. Anthony,* v. 1, 250.

29. Author's emphasis. There were other stipulations besides sex: being at least twenty-one, not being an Indian, not being found guilty of a crime. None of these

exclusions faced political opposition.

30. Stanton to Gerrit Smith, January 1, 1866, *Selected Papers,* Gordon, ed., v. 1, 569.

31. Stanton to Anthony, August 11, 1865, *Elizabeth Cady Stanton,* Stanton and Blatch, eds., 105.

32. Stanton, Anthony, and Gage, eds., *HWS,* v. 2, 91.

33. Ibid., 97.

34. Anthony to Sidney Clarke, January 21, 1866, *Selected Papers,* Gordon, ed., v. 1, 573.

35. Alma Lutz, *Created Equal: A Biography of Elizabeth Cady Stanton, 1815–1902* (John Day Company, 1940), 123.

36. Stanton to the American Anti-Slavery Society, May 9, 1866, *Selected Papers,* Gordon, ed., v. 1, 583.

37. Stanton, Anthony, and Gage, eds., *HWS,* v. 2, 153.

38. Ibid., v. 1, 694.

39. Eleventh National Woman's Rights Convention, May 10, 1866, *Selected Papers,* Gordon, ed., v. 1, 588.

40. Margaret Hope Bacon, "One Great Bundle of Humanity: Frances Ellen Watkins Harper, 1825–1911," *Pennsylvania Magazine of History* (1987), 21.

41. Eleventh National Woman's Rights

Convention, May 10, 1866, *Selected Papers,* Gordon, ed., v. 1, 587.

42. Elizabeth Cady Stanton for Congress, October 10, 1866, *Selected Papers,* Gordon, ed., v. 1, 593.

43. Stanton, Anthony, and Gage, eds., *HWS,* v. 1, 285.

44. Ibid., v. 2, 306. In the end, the full constitutional convention not only voted against a woman suffrage provision and refused to abolish black male suffrage property qualifications, but also postponed the submission of a revised constitution for two years, and even then voters rejected it.

45. Stanton to Theodore Tilton, September 15, 1867, *The Selected Papers of Elizabeth Cady Stanton and Susan B. Anthony,* Ann D. Gordon, ed. (Rutgers University Press, 2000), v. 2, 89.

46. Anthony speech in St. Louis, Missouri, November 25, 1867, *Selected Papers,* Gordon, ed., v. 2, 105.

47. Andrea Moore Kerr, *Lucy Stone: Speaking Out for Equality* (Rutgers University Press, 1995), 124.

48. Stone to Stanton, April 10, 1867, *Selected Papers,* Gordon, ed., v. 2, 49.

49. Meeting of the American Equal Rights

Association in New York, May 9, 1867, *Selected Papers,* Gordon, ed., v. 2, 69.

50. Stone to Stanton, April 20, and Stone to Anthony, April 20 and May 1, 1867, Stanton, Anthony, and Gage, eds., *HWS,* v. 2, 235, 237.

51. Stanton, Anthony, and Gage, eds., *HWS,* v. 2, 236.

52. Ibid., 239.

53. Stone to Anthony, May 9, 1867, *Selected Papers,* Gordon, ed., v. 2, 58.

54. Stanton, Anthony, and Gage, eds., *HWS,* v. 2, 234.

55. Stanton, Anthony, and Gage, eds., *HWS,* v. 2, 241.

56. Dudden, *Fighting Chance,* 112. He was the grandfather of the poet Langston Hughes.

57. Stanton, Anthony, and Gage, eds., *HWS,* v. 2, 183.

58. Ibid., 208.

59. Ibid., 225.

60. *Proceedings of the First Anniversary of the American Equal Rights Association in New York, held at the Church of the Puritans, New York, May 9 and 10, 1867* (R. J. Johnson, 1867), 20, 67.

61. Meeting of the American Equal Rights Association in New York, May 9, 1867, *Selected Papers,* Gordon, ed., v. 2, 63–65.

62. Elizabeth Stanton to Henry Stanton, October 9, 1867, *Selected Papers,* Gordon, ed., v. 2, 96.

63. Elizabeth Cady Stanton, *Eighty Years and More, Reminiscences, 1815–1897* (Simon & Schuster, 2020), 252.

64. Olympia Brown, *Acquaintances, Old and New, Among Reformers* (S. E. Tate Printing Co., 1911), 69.

65. Dudden, *Fighting Chance,* 118.

66. Anthony to Anna Dickinson, September 23, 1867, *Selected Papers,* Gordon, ed., v. 2, 93.

67. *Selected Papers,* Gordon, ed., v. 2, 95.

68. George Francis Train, *The Great Epigram Campaign of Kansas* (Prescott & Hume, Daily Commercial Office, 1867), 8.

69. Ibid., 31.

70. Anthony to Train, January 1, 1870, *Selected Papers,* Gordon, ed., v. 2, 288.

71. Anthony, Speech in St. Louis, Missouri, November 25, 1867, *Selected Papers,* Gordon, ed., v. 2, 108.

72. Stanton, Anthony, and Gage, eds., *HWS,* v. 2, 267.

73. Stanton, *Eighty Years and More,* 254.

74. Garrison to Anthony, January 4, 1868, *Selected Papers,* Gordon, ed., v. 2, 124.

75. Stanton, Anthony, and Gage, eds., *HWS,*

v. 2, 268.

76. Harper, *Susan B. Anthony,* v. 2, 290.

77. Wright to Stanton, February 20, 1868, *Selected Papers,* Gordon, ed., v. 2, 131.

78. Lutz, *Created Equal,* 160–61.

79. Stanton, "Roscoe Conkling," February 19, 1868, *Selected Papers,* Gordon, ed., v. 2, 130.

80. Anthony to Olympia Brown, January 1, 1868, *Selected Papers,* Gordon, ed., v. 2, 122.

81. Lutz, *Created Equal,* 191.

82. Stanton to Hooker, February 3, 1871, *Selected Papers,* Gordon, ed., v. 2, 413.

83. Stanton, "Manhood Suffrage," December 24, 1868, *Selected Papers,* Gordon, ed., v. 2, 196.

84. Stanton, "Address to the Anniversary of the American Equal Rights Association," May 12, 1869, *Elizabeth Cady Stanton, Feminist as Thinker: A Reader in Documents and Essays,* Ellen Carol DuBois and Richard Candida Smith, eds. (New York University Press, 2007), 198.

85. Stanton, "Editorial Correspondence," January 22, 1869, *Selected Papers,* Gordon, ed., v. 2, 204–5.

86. Stanton, Anthony, and Gage, eds., *HWS,* v. 2, 333.

87. Ibid., 373.

88. Stanton to Mott, after March 20, 1869, *Selected Papers,* Gordon, ed., v. 2, 231.
89. "May Anniversaries," *The Round Table: A Saturday Review of Finance, Literature, Society and Art,* May 22, 1869.
90. Stanton, Anthony, and Gage, eds. *HWS,* v. 2, 351.
91. Ibid., 382.
92. Gordon, ed., *Selected Papers,* v. 2, 238.
93. Harper, *Susan B. Anthony,* v. 1, 324.
94. Stanton, Anthony, and Gage, eds. *HWS,* v. 2, 383.
95. Ibid., 391.
96. Gordon, ed., *Selected Papers,* v. 2, 242.

Three: Are Women Persons? 1869–1875

1. Ellen Carol DuBois, *Woman Suffrage and Women's Rights* (New York University Press, 1998), 94.
2. Ann D. Gordon, ed., *Selected Papers of Elizabeth Cady Stanton and Susan B. Anthony* (Rutgers University Press, 2000), v. 2, 242.
3. "Meeting of the National Woman Suffrage Association," *New York Times,* May 18, 1869.
4. *Woman's Advocate,* May 29, 1869.
5. Remarks by Anthony to the American Woman Suffrage Association in Cleveland,

November 25, 1869, *Selected Papers,* Gordon, ed., v. 2, 284.

6. Sally G. McMillen, *Lucy Stone: An Unapologetic Life* (Oxford University Press, 2008), 203.

7. Andrea Moore Kerr, *Lucy Stone: Speaking Out for Equality* (Rutgers University Press, 1995), 146.

8. Elizabeth Cady Stanton, Susan B. Anthony, and Matilda Joslyn Gage, eds., *History of Woman Suffrage* (hereafter *HWS*), (Susan B. Anthony Publisher, 1881), v. 2, 428.

9. Anthony, Diary, October 9, 1870, *Selected Papers,* Gordon, ed., v. 2, 365.

10. Ida H. Harper, *The Life and Work of Susan B. Anthony* (Hollenbrook Press, 1908), v. 1, 376.

11. "Miss Anthony Evidently," *Pittsburgh Daily Commercial,* May 4, 1870, *Failure Is Impossible: Susan B. Anthony in Her Own Words,* Lynn Sherr, ed. (Crown, 2010), 132.

12. Harper, *Susan B. Anthony,* v. 1, 371.

13. Barbara Goldsmith, *Other Powers: The Age of Suffrage, Spiritualism, and the Scandalous Victoria Woodhull* (Knopf, 1998), 256.

14. Lois Beachy Underhill, *The Woman Who*

Ran for President: The Many Lives of Victoria Woodhull (Bridge Works Publishing, 1995), 68.

15. Stanton, Anthony, and Gage, eds., *HWS,* v. 2, 407–10, 444–45.

16. Appendix C: Women Who Went to the Polls, *Selected Papers,* Gordon, ed., v. 2, 645–54.

17. "Woman Suffrage in Vineland, New Jersey," *San Francisco Chronicle,* November 29, 1868.

18. Harper, *Susan B. Anthony,* v. 1, 376.

19. Anthony, Diary, January 14, 1871, *Selected Papers,* Gordon, ed., v. 2, 406.

20. Anthony to Woodhull, February 4, 1871, *Selected Papers,* Gordon, ed., v. 2, 415.

21. Stanton, Speech to Women in New York, May 17, 1870 and Stanton to Josephine Griffing, December 1, 1870, *Selected Papers,* Gordon, ed., v. 2, 343 and 382.

22. Stanton, Speech to Women in New York, *Selected Papers,* Gordon, ed., v. 2, 337.

23. Woodhull, "A Speech on the Principles of Social Freedom," November 20, 1871, *The Victoria Woodhull Reader,* Madeleine B. Stern, ed. (M&S Press, 1974), 23.

24. Goldsmith, *Other Powers,* 314.

25. Kerr, *Lucy Stone,* 168.

26. Stanton to Woodhull, December 29,

1871, *Selected Papers,* Gordon, ed., v. 2, 463.

27. Stanton to Mott, April 1, 1871, *Selected Papers,* Gordon, ed., v. 2, 428.

28. Harper, *Susan B. Anthony,* v. 1, 375.

29. Ibid., 388.

30. Stanton to Smith, September 18, 1871, *Selected Papers,* Gordon, ed., v. 2, 451.

31. Anthony to Stanton, September 10, 1871, *Selected Papers,* Gordon, ed., v. 2, 448.

32. Anthony, Diary, January 6, 1872, *Selected Papers,* Gordon, ed., v. 2, 468.

33. Anthony to Stanton and Hooker, March 13, 1872, *Selected Papers,* Gordon, ed., v. 2, 485.

34. Stanton, Anthony, and Gage, eds., *HWS,* v. 2, 516.

35. Anthony to Stanton and Hooker, March 13, 1872, *Selected Papers,* Gordon, ed., v. 2, 485.

36. *New York Herald,* May 10, 1872.

37. Alma Lutz, *Created Equal: A Biography of Elizabeth Cady Stanton* (John Day Company, 1940), 219–20.

38. *New York Times,* May 10, 1872, 8.

39. Harper, *Susan B. Anthony,* v. 1, 415.

40. *New Northwest,* May 31, 1872, 2.

41. Anthony, Diary, May 10, 11, and 12,

1872, *Selected Papers,* Gordon, ed., v. 2, 494.

42. Goldsmith, *Other Powers,* 400.

43. Stanton to Alonzo J. Grover, August 24, 1874, *The Selected Papers of Elizabeth Cady Stanton and Susan B. Anthony,* Ann D. Gordon, ed. (Rutgers University Press, 2003), v. 3, 103.

44. Goldsmith, *Other Powers,* 427.

45. *Philadelphia Inquirer,* June 5, 1872, 2.

46. Leslie Wheeler, ed., *Loving Warriors: Selected Letters of Lucy Stone and Henry B. Blackwell, 1853 to 1893* (Dial Press, 1981), 244.

47. Harper, *Susan B. Anthony,* v. 1, 417.

48. Stanton to Hooker, June 14, 1872, *Selected Papers,* Gordon, ed., v. 2, 511.

49. Stanton to Stone and Blackwell, July 13, 1872, *Selected Papers,* Gordon, ed., v. 2, 517.

50. Ibid.

51. Harper, *Susan B. Anthony,* v. 1, 419.

52. Ibid., 418.

53. *Rochester Democrat and Chronicle,* November 30, 1872, 4.

54. Anthony to Stanton, November 5, 1872, *Selected Papers,* Gordon, ed., v. 2, 524–25.

55. *Wyoming Democrat, Tunkhannock, Penn-*

sylvania, November 13, 1872.

56. Gordon, ed., *Selected Papers,* v. 2., 532.

57. Anthony to Wright, January 1, 1873, *Selected Papers,* Gordon, ed., v. 2, 548.

58. Woodhull to Anthony, January 2, 1873, *Selected Papers,* Gordon, ed., v. 2, 549.

59. Anthony, Diary, May 22, 1873, *Selected Papers,* Gordon, ed., v. 2, 609.

60. Anthony to Benjamin Butler, April 27, 1873, *Selected Papers,* Gordon, ed., v. 2, 602.

61. Anthony, "Is It a Crime for a U.S. Citizen to Vote?" January 16, 1873, *Selected Papers,* Gordon, ed., v. 2, 554–76. Anthony's italics.

62. *Rochester Democrat and Chronicle,* n.d., *Selected Papers,* Gordon, ed., v. 2, 609.

63. Anthony, "Is It a Crime," *Selected Papers,* Gordon, ed., v. 2, 562.

64. *Selected Papers,* Gordon, ed., v. 2, 611.

65. Anthony, Diary, June 18, 1873, *Selected Papers,* Gordon, ed., v. 2, 611.

66. Gordon, ed., *Selected Papers,* v. 2, 612–15.

67. Anthony, Remarks in the Circuit Court of the United States for the Northern District of New York, June 19, 1873, *Selected Papers,* Gordon, ed., v. 2, 613.

68. Anthony, Diary, June 18, 1873, *Selected*

Papers, Gordon, ed., v. 2, 616.

69. *Trial of Susan B. Anthony* (Prometheus Books, 2003), 127.
70. Women Who Went to the Polls, after June, New York, Gordon, ed., *Selected Papers,* v. 2, 654.
71. Anthony, Speech to the Centennial of the Boston Tea Party in New York City, December 16, 1873, *Selected Papers,* Gordon, ed., v. 3, 22.
72. Anthony, "Is It a Crime," January 16, 1873, *Selected Papers,* Gordon, ed., v. 2, 569.

Four: The Great Primitive Right from Which All Freedom Originates, 1876–1893

1. Mary Ashton Livermore, *The Story of My Life* (A. D. Worthington & Co., 1897), 578.
2. Stanton to Sister G, March 16, 1874, Ann D. Gordon, ed., *The Selected Papers of Elizabeth Cady Stanton and Susan B. Anthony* (Rutgers University Press, 2003), v. 3, 68.
3. Anthony to Daniel Anthony, May 5, 1874, *Selected Papers,* Gordon, ed., 73.
4. Anna Gordon, *The Beautiful Life of Frances Willard: A Memorial Volume* (Woman's Temperance Publishing Company, 1898), 1, 15.

5. Frances E. Willard, *Glimpses of Fifty Years: The Autobiography of an American Woman* (Woman's Temperance Publishing Company, 1889), 351.

6. Ibid., 470.

7. Ibid., 352.

8. Frances E. Willard, *Woman and Temperance: Or, The Work and Workers of the Woman's Christian Temperance Union* (James Betts & Co., 1883), 452–59.

9. Willard, *Glimpses of Fifty Years,* 352.

10. Anthony to Frances Willard, September 18, 1876, *Selected Papers,* Gordon, ed., v. 3, 261.

11. Willard, *Glimpses of Fifty Years,* 474.

12. Anthony to Rachel G. Foster, October 26, 1881, *The Selected Papers of Elizabeth Cady Stanton and Susan B. Anthony,* Ann D. Gordon, ed. (Rutgers University Press, 2006), v. 4, 116.

13. Willard, *Glimpses of Fifty Years,* 380.

14. Rosalyn Terborg-Penn, *African American Women in the Struggle for the Vote, 1850–1920* (Indiana University Press, 1998), 85.

15. Frances E. Willard, "The Southern People," *National Liberator,* August 28, 1881, Women and Social Movements in the United States, 1600–2000 (hereafter WASMUS).

16. Frances Smith Foster, *A Brighter Coming Day: A Frances Ellen Watkins Harper Reader* (Feminist Press, 1993), 281.

17. Watkins Harper, "Work Among Colored People," "Minutes of the National Woman's Christian Temperance Union, at the Eleventh Annual Meeting in St. Louis, Missouri, October 22nd to 25th, 1884," WASMUS.

18. Sarah J. W. Early, "A Word of Exhortation from Tennessee," *Union Signal,* 16 February 1888, WASMUS.

19. Sarah J. W. Early, "Work Among the Colored People of the Southern States," "National WCTU Annual Meeting Minutes of 1888," WASMUS.

20. Early, "A Word of Exhortation from Tennessee."

21. Willard, *Glimpses of Fifty Years,* 464.

22. Elizabeth Cady Stanton, Susan B. Anthony, and Matilda Joslyn Gage, eds., *History of Woman Suffrage* (hereafter *HWS*) (Susan B. Anthony Publisher, 1887), v. 3, 28.

23. "The Woman's Suffrage Movement," *Leavenworth Weekly Times,* July 20, 1876.

24. Anthony to Isabella Beecher Hooker, January 20, 1875, *Selected Papers,* Gordon, ed., v. 3, 145.

25. Stanton, Anthony, and Gage, eds., *HWS,*

v. 3, 29.

26. Ibid., 41.

27. Circular, "National Woman Suffrage Parlors," *Ballot Box,* June 1876.

28. Matilda Joslyn Gage and Sally Wagner, *The Declaration of Rights of Women* (Aberdeen Area NOW Chapter, 1975), 36.

29. "Centennial," *Ballot Box,* October 1876.

30. "Citizen Suffrage," *Philadelphia Inquirer,* July 20, 1876.

31. "Centennial," *Ballot Box.*

32. Anthony to Mathilde Anneke, September 27, 1875, *Selected Papers,* Gordon, ed., v. 3, 202.

33. "Declaration of the Rights of the Women of the United States," *Selected Papers,* Gordon, ed., v. 3, 234–39. For full text see Appendix B.

34. Stanton to Amelia Bloomer, December 13, 1880, *Selected Papers,* Gordon, ed., v. 4, 31.

35. Stone to Cady Stanton, August 3, 1876, *Selected Papers,* Gordon, ed., v. 3, 249.

36. Anthony to Hooker, October 12, 1875, *Selected Papers,* Gordon, ed., v. 3, 204.

37. Stanton, Anthony, and Gage, eds., *HWS,* v. 3, 717–19.

38. "Annual Meeting, American Woman Suffrage Association: Colorado Report," *Woman's Journal,* October 7, 1876, 327,

328, WASMUS.

39. "Gone Up," *Pueblo Chieftain* (October 19, 1877), reprinted in "Colorado Opponents of Woman Suffrage," *Woman's Journal,* 8 (November 3, 1877), 352, WASMUS.

40. Mamma to Alice, September 21, 1877, Leslie Wheeler, ed., *Loving Warriors: Selected Letters of Lucy Stone and Henry B. Blackwell, 1853 to 1893* (Dial Press, 1981), 274–75.

41. Anthony, "To the Editor of the Ballot Box," September 21, 1877, *Selected Papers,* Gordon, ed., v. 3, 321.

42. Susan M. Marilley, *Woman Suffrage and the Origins of Liberal Feminism in the United States, 1820–1920* (Harvard University Press, 1996), 96.

43. Marilley, *Woman Suffrage,* 96–97; Henry Blackwell, "Victory Deferred in Colorado," *Woman's Journal,* October 13, 1877, 324.

44. Stanton, Anthony, and Gage, eds., *HWS,* v. 4, 542–43.

45. Stanton, Anthony, and Gage, eds., *HWS,* v. 3, 691.

46. Blackwell to Alicekin, September 24, 1883, *Loving Warriors,* Wheeler, ed. 293.

47. Stanton, Anthony, and Gage, eds., *HWS,*

v. 3, 779.

48. Anthony to Butler, December 30, 1877, *Selected Papers,* Gordon, ed., v. 3, 343.

49. Carrie Chapman Catt and Nettie Rogers Shuler, *Woman Suffrage and Politics: The Inner Story of the Suffrage Movement* (University of Seattle Press, 1969), 113.

50. Carol Cornwall Madsen, "Emmeline B. Wells in Washington: The Search for Mormon Legitimacy," *Journal of Mormon History,* Fall 2000, 159.

51. Susan B. Anthony and Ida H. Harper, eds., *History of Woman Suffrage* (hereafter *HWS*) (Susan B. Anthony Publisher, 1902), v. 4, 44; "Resolutions of the NWSA," January 27, 1887, *Selected Papers,* Gordon, ed., v. 4, 549.

52. Harper, *Susan B. Anthony,* v. 2, 606.

53. Anthony and Harper, eds., *HWS,* v. 4, 90–91, 103.

54. Ibid., 94–95.

55. Cady Stanton to Anthony, January 8, 1887, *Selected Papers,* Gordon, ed., v. 4, 539.

56. "Susan B. on the Warpath," *Chicago Daily Tribune,* January 28, 1887.

57. "Interview with Anthony," January 26, 1887, *Selected Papers,* Gordon, ed., v. 4, 546.

58. "Executive Sessions of the National Woman Suffrage Association," April 3, 1888, *The Selected Papers of Elizabeth Cady Stanton and Susan B. Anthony,* Ann D. Gordon, ed. (Rutgers University Press, 2009), v. 5, 115.

59. Ibid.

60. "The Solitude of Self," *Selected Papers,* Gordon, ed., January 18, 1892, v. 5, 424–34.

61. Anthony to Elizabeth Smith Miller, February 15, 1892, *Selected Papers,* Gordon, ed., v. 5, 446.

Five: New Women, 1893–1906

1. Ida H. Harper, *The Life and Work of Susan B. Anthony* (Hollenbrook Press, 1908), v. 2, 743.

2. Jeanne Madeline Weimann, *The Fair Women: The Story of the Women's Building at the Columbian Exposition, Chicago, 1893* (Academy Chicago, 1981), 323.

3. Ibid., 527.

4. May Wright Sewall, ed., *The World's Congress of Representative Women,* 2 vols. (Rand, McNally & Co., 1894), 482.

5. "Women Have Their Theme," *Chicago Tribune,* May 19, 1893.

6. Joseph G. Brown, *The History of Equal*

Suffrage in Colorado, 1868–1898 (New Publishing Printing Co., 1898), 22.

7. Brown, *Equal Suffrage,* 19.

8. Meredith, "How Colorado Was Carried," *Woman's Journal,* November 18, 1893, 361.

9. Susan B. Anthony and Ida H. Harper, eds., *History of Woman Suffrage* (hereafter *HWS*) (Susan B. Anthony Publisher, 1902), v. 4, 513.

10. Meredith to Anthony, June 14, 1893, Ann D. Gordon, ed., *The Selected Papers of Elizabeth Cady Stanton and Susan B. Anthony* (Rutgers University Press, 2009), v. 5, 524.

11. Anthony to Olympia Brown, September 3, 1890, *Selected Papers,* Gordon, ed., v. 5, 321.

12. Harper, *Susan B. Anthony,* v. 2, 694.

13. Colorado Equal Suffrage Association, "To the Women of Colorado," 1893, Women and Social Movements in the United States, 1600–2000 (hereafter WAS-MUS).

14. Meredith, "How Colorado Was Carried," *Woman's Journal,* November 18, 1893.

15. "Why They Did It," *The Weekly Gazette,* December 14, 1893.

16. Anthony to Meredith, November 23,

1893, *Selected Papers,* Gordon, ed., v. 5, 548.

17. Elizabeth Ensley, "Election Day," 1894, WASMUS.

18. Ida H. Harper, ed., *History of Woman Suffrage* (hereafter *HWS*), v. 5 (National American Woman Suffrage Association, 1922), 101.

19. Anthony to Lillie Devereux Blake, April 22, 1894, *Selected Papers,* Gordon, ed., v. 5, 593.

20. Anthony, interview, June 22, 1894, *Selected Papers,* Gordon, ed., v. 5, 633.

21. Mary Gray Peck, *Carrie Chapman Catt, a Biography* (H. W. Wilson Company, 1944), 80.

22. Lecture to AME Zion Church, San Francisco, May 3, 1896, *Selected Papers,* Gordon, ed., Anthony, v. 6, 69.

23. Anthony to Mary Anthony, September 30, 1896, Ann D. Gordon, ed., *The Selected Papers of Elizabeth Cady Stanton and Susan B. Anthony,* v. 6 (Rutgers University Press, 2013), 106.

24. Anna Howard Shaw, *The Story of a Pioneer* (Harper & Brothers Publishers, 1915), 196.

25. "Will Ratify Their Planks," June 20, 1896, *San Francisco Call.*

26. Harper, *Susan B. Anthony,* v. 2, 880.

27. Ibid., 883.

28. Rebecca J. Mead, *How the Vote Was Won: Woman Suffrage in the Western United States, 1868–1914* (New York University Press, 2004), 92.

29. Harper, *Susan B. Anthony,* v. 2, 891.

30. "Mrs. Sarah Cooper," *Woman's Column,* December 26, 1896.

31. Ida B. Wells and Frederick Douglass, *The Reason Why the Colored American Is Not in the Columbian Exposition* (privately published, 1893), 4, 11.

32. Ibid., 6–7.

33. Ibid., 26.

34. Alfreda M. Duster, ed., *Crusade for Justice: The Autobiography of Ida B. Wells* (University Press, 1970), 151.

35. Ibid., 209.

36. Paula Giddings, *When and Where I Enter: The Impact of Black Women on Race and Sex in America* (William Morrow, 1984), 13.

37. "The Progress of Colored Women," 1898, Maureen Moynagh with Nancy Forestall, eds., *Documenting First Wave Feminisms, Volume 1: Transnational Collaborations and Currents* (University of Toronto Press, 2012), 191.

38. Duster, *Crusade for Justice,* 255.

39. Ibid., 265.

40. Ibid., 310.

41. Ibid., 319.

42. Wells-Barnett, "How Enfranchisement Stops Lynching," 1910, Mia Bay, ed., *Ida B. Wells, The Light of Truth: Writings of an Anti-Lynching Crusader* (Penguin Books, 2014), 422–24.

43. Faye E. Dudden, *Fighting Chance: The Struggle over Woman Suffrage and Black Suffrage in Reconstruction America* (Oxford University Press, 2011), 93.

44. Stanton, "Educated Suffrage Justified," November 3, 1894, *Selected Papers,* Gordon, ed., v. 5, 656.

45. Ellen Carol DuBois, *Harriot Stanton Blatch and the Winning of Woman Suffrage* (Yale University Press, 1997), 73.

46. Anthony to Clay, January 30, 1893, *Selected Papers,* Gordon, ed., v. 5, 506.

47. Anthony, Diary, February 4, 1895, *Selected Papers,* Gordon, ed., v. 5, 674.

48. "The Atlanta Convention," *Woman's Journal,* February 16, 1895.

49. National Woman Suffrage Association, *Report of the International Council of Women: Assembled by the National Woman Suffrage Association, Washington, D.C.,*

U.S. of America, March 25 to April 1, 1888, vol. 1 (R. H. Darby, 1888), 330.

50. Duster, *Crusade for Justice,* 230.

51. Marjorie S. Wheeler, *New Women of the New South: The Leaders of the Woman Suffrage Movement in the Southern States* (Oxford University Press, 1993), 118.

52. Logan, "Adella Hunt Logan," in *Votes for Women! The Woman Suffrage Movement in Tennessee, the South, and the Nation,* Marjorie Spruill Wheeler, ed. (University of Tennessee Press, 1995), 102.

53. Shaw, *Story of a Pioneer,* 312.

54. Harper, ed., *HWS,* v. 5, 59.

55. Sewall, *World's Congress of Representative Women,* 871.

56. Kathryn Kish Sklar, ed., *The Autobiography of Florence Kelley: Notes of Sixty Years* (Charles H. Kerr Publishing Company, 1986), 79.

57. Kelley to Anthony, January 21, 1884, *The Selected Letters of Florence Kelley, 1869–1931,* Kathryn Kish Sklar and Beverly Wilson Palmer, eds. (University of Illinois Press, 2009), 19.

58. Sklar, ed., *Autobiography,* 64.

59. Jane Addams, *Twenty Years at Hull-House: with Autobiographical Notes* (Signet Classics, 2010), 59.

60. Ibid., 140–41.

61. Mary Kenney O'Sullivan, unpublished autobiographical manuscript, n.d., Schlesinger Library, Harvard University.

62. "How They Live on $3 a Week," *Chicago Tribune,* April 16, 1893.

63. Sklar, ed., *Autobiography,* 85.

64. Ibid., 87.

65. Addams, *Hull-House,* 142.

66. Kelley, *Some Ethical Gains Through Legislation* (Macmillan Company, 1905), 199.

67. Kelley to Nicholas, February 18, 1906, *Selected Letters,* Sklar and Palmer, eds., 137.

68. Anthony and Harper, eds., *HWS,* v. 4, 311.

69. Harper, ed., *HWS,* v. 5, 143.

70. Kelley to Nicholas, February 7, 1906, *Selected Letters,* Sklar and Palmer, eds., 136.

71. Steven M. Buechler, *The Transformation of the Woman Suffrage Movement: The Case of Illinois, 1850–1920* (Rutgers University Press, 1986), 162.

72. Anthony to Harper, October 28, 1902, *Selected Papers,* Gordon, ed., v. 6, 455.

73. Harper, ed., *HWS,* v. 5, 173.

74. Ibid., 165.

75. "What the Woman Suffragists Will Do

Today," *Baltimore Sun,* February 12, 1906, 14.

76. Harper, ed., *HWS,* v. 5, 165.

77. Ibid., 189–90.

78. *Washington Evening Star,* February 15, 1906, *Selected Papers,* Gordon, ed., v. 6, 577.

79. Rheta Childe Dorr, *A Woman of Fifty* (Funk & Wagnalls Company, 1924), 340.

80. Lucy Anthony to Elizabeth Smith Miller, March 2, 1906, *Selected Papers,* Gordon, ed., v. 6, 580.

81. Shaw, *Story of a Pioneer,* 233.

82. Mabel Nichols to Maude Nichols, March 13, 1906, *Selected Papers,* Gordon, ed., v. 6, 581.

Six: A Political Cause to Be Carried Politically, 1907–1915

1. Martin Pugh, *The Pankhursts: The History of One Radical Family* (Vintage Books, 2008), 137.

2. "A New Word," January 26, 1906, *Morrisville Vermont Messenger.*

3. "American 'Uncrowned Queens' Lead Pageant in London of Women Comprising Classes from the Nobility to Scullery Drudges in Favor of Suffrage," *Oakland Tribune,* June 24, 1908, 8.

4. Clara Colby, "A-Foot with My Vision," *Woman's Tribune,* August 8, 1908, 39.

5. "Votes for Women: Do You Want It?" *Seattle Star,* May 5, 1910.

6. Mary Kenney O'Sullivan, "Women and the Vote," *Labor Journal, Everett, Washington,* January 10, 1909, 3. This brief opinion piece was later republished as a pamphlet entitled "Women and the Vote" and widely circulated by NAWSA.

7. College Equal Suffrage League of Northern California, *Winning Equal Suffrage in California* (College Equal Suffrage League of Northern California, 1911), 19.

8. Susan Englander, *Class Conflict and Coalition in the California Woman Suffrage Movement, 1907–1912* (Edwin Mellen Press, 1992), 112.

9. "Wage Earning Line Divides Suffragettes," *San Francisco Call,* October 4, 1908.

10. "Labor Unions Indorse Plea to Give Vote," *San Francisco Call,* August 18, 1911.

11. Herbert Ruffin, *Uninvited Neighbors: African Americans in Silicon Valley, 1769–1990* (University of Oklahoma Press, 2014), 45.

12. Rebecca J. Mead, *How the Vote Was*

Won: Woman Suffrage in the Western United States, 1868–1914 (New York University Press, 2004), 138; Eileen Wallis, *Earning Power, Women and Work in Los Angeles, 1880–1930* (University of Nevada Press, 2010), 94.

13. Louise Herrick Wall, "Moving to Amend," *Sunset Magazine,* September 11, 1911, 378.

14. College Equal Suffrage League, *Winning Equal Suffrage in California,* 46.

15. Ibid., 11.

16. "Suffrage Poster to Go on Display," *Oakland Tribune,* August 19, 1911.

17. College Equal Suffrage League, *Winning Equal Suffrage in California,* 113–114.

18. Wall, "Moving to Amend," 378.

19. College Equal Suffrage League, *Winning Equal Suffrage in California,* 106.

20. Ibid., 107.

21. Ibid., 111.

22. Mead, *How the Vote Was Won,* 147.

23. "California's Victory," *Woman's Standard,* November 1911.

24. Antoinette Brown Blackwell to Caroline Severance, July 21, 1913, Severance Papers, Huntington Library; thanks to Glenna Matthews for this citation.

25. Mead, *How the Vote Was Won,* 1.

26. Annelise Orleck, *Common Sense and a Little Fire: Women and Working Class Politics in the United States, 1900–1965* (University of North Carolina Press, 1995), 60.

27. David von Drehle, *Triangle: The Fire That Changed America* (Grove Press, 2003), 57.

28. Harriot Stanton Blatch and Alma Lutz, *Challenging Years: The Memoirs of Harriot Stanton Blatch* (G. P. Putnam's Sons, 1940), 114.

29. "Federation Women Fight Over By-Laws," *New York Times,* December 3, 1909.

30. Nancy Schrom Dye, *As Equals and as Sisters: Feminism, the Labor Movement, and the Women's Trade Union League of New York* (University of Missouri Press, 1980), 132.

31. Blatch and Lutz, *Challenging Years,* 93–94.

32. Ibid., 236.

33. Ibid., 110.

34. Ibid., 120.

35. Ibid., 111.

36. Ibid., 127.

37. Ibid., 97.

38. Ellen Carol DuBois, *Harriot Stanton*

Blatch and the Winning of Woman Suffrage (Yale University Press, 1997), 33.

39. "Protection from Fire," *Brooklyn Eagle,* April 3, 1911.

40. Orleck, *Common Sense and a Little Fire,* 103.

41. Blatch and Lutz, *Challenging Years,* 164–65.

42. DuBois, *Harriot Stanton Blatch,* 140.

43. Johanna Neuman, *Gilded Suffragists: The New York Socialites Who Fought for Women's Right to Vote* (New York University Press, 2017), 92.

44. "Suffering Suffragettes," *The Crisis,* June 1912.

45. W. E. B. Du Bois, "Editorial," *The Crisis,* October 1911.

46. "Votes for Women," *The Crisis,* September 1912.

47. Terrell, "The Justice of Woman Suffrage," *The Crisis,* September 1912.

48. Logan, "Colored Women as Voters," *The Crisis,* September 1912.

49. Ann D. Gordon, ed., *Selected Papers of Elizabeth Cady Stanton and Susan B. Anthony* (Rutgers University Press, 2006), v. 4, 209.

50. Grace Wilbur Trout, "Sidelights on Illinois Suffrage History," *Journal of the Il-*

linois State Historical Library, July 1920, 96.

51. Ida H. Harper, ed., *History of Woman Suffrage* (hereafter *HWS*), v. 6 (National American Woman Suffrage Association, 1922), 155–56.

52. "The Suffrage Conquest of Illinois," *The Literary Digest,* June 28, 1913, whole no. 1410.

53. "Banners Greet Suffrage Parade," *Chicago Tribune,* July 2, 1913.

54. *Chicago Defender,* July 5, 1913.

55. Susan B. Anthony and Ida H. Harper, eds., *History of Woman Suffrage* (hereafter *HWS*), (Susan B. Anthony Publisher, 1902), v. 4, 445.

56. Inez Haynes Gillmore, *The Story of the Woman's Party* (Harcourt, Brace and Company, 1921), 19–21.

57. This aspect of the parade remains highly contested in the historical literature. The accounts which I have relied on are: Jill Zahniser and Amelia Fry, *Alice Paul Claiming Power* (Oxford University Press, 2014); Adele Logan Alexander, "Adella Hunt Logan: The Tuskegee Woman's Club, and African Americans in the Suffrage Movement," in *Votes for Women! The Woman Suffrage Movement in Tennessee,*

the South and the Nation, ed. Marjorie Spruill Wheeler (University of Tennessee Press, 1995); Katherine H. Adams and Michael L. Keener, *Alice Paul and the American Suffrage Campaign* (University of Illinois Press, 2008); and Rosalyn Terborg-Penn, *African American Women in the Struggle for the Vote, 1850–1920* (Indiana University Press, 2008).

58. Wanda Hendricks, *Gender, Race and Politics in the Midwest* (Indiana University Press, 1998), 91–93.

59. "Women's Beauty, Grace and Art Bewilder the Capital," *Washington Post,* March 4, 1913.

60. "Illinois Women Feature Parade," *Chicago Tribune,* March 4, 1913.

61. "Marches in Parade Despite Protest," *Chicago Defender,* March 8, 1913.

62. *The Crisis,* May 1913.

63. Mary Walton, *A Woman's Crusade: Alice Paul and the Battle for the Ballot* (Palgrave Macmillan, 2010), 67.

64. "Now to Fix Guilt," *Washington Post,* March 7, 1913.

65. Walton, *A Woman's Crusade,* 75.

66. Blatch and Lutz, *Challenging Years,* 197.

67. United States Congress, U.S. Senate, Committee on the District of Columbia,

Women's Suffrage and the Police; Three Senate Documents (Arno Press and the *New York Times,* 1971), xv.

68. Harper, ed., *HWS,* v. 5, 366.

69. "Suffragists Fear Split on Report," *Washington Times,* December 5, 1913.

70. Blatch and Lutz, *Challenging Years,* 247.

71. Gillmore, *Story of the Woman's Party,* 50–51.

72. Blatch and Lutz, *Challenging Years,* 210.

73. Walton, *A Woman's Crusade,* 101.

74. Gillmore, *Story of the Woman's Party,* 76.

75. Ibid., 80–83.

76. Ibid., 97.

77. "Crowd in House Hears Debate on Suffrage Bill," *St. Louis Post-Dispatch,* January 12, 1915.

78. "House Defeats Suffrage Bill," *Hartford Courant,* January 13, 1915.

79. "Suffragists Lose Fight in House of Representatives," *Burlington Free Press,* January 13, 1915.

80. Robert Fowler, *Carrie Catt, Feminist Politician* (Northeastern University Press, 1984), 126.

81. Mary Gray Peck, *Carrie Chapman Catt, a Biography* (H. W. Wilson Company, 1944), 243.

82. Ibid., 222.

83. Carrie Chapman Catt and Nettie Rogers Shuler, *Woman Suffrage and Politics: The Inner Story of the Suffrage Movement* (Charles Scribner's Sons, 1926), 287–88.

84. Harper, ed., *HWS,* v. 6, 461.

85. Peck, *Carrie Chapman Catt,* 231.

86. Harriet Hyman Alonso, *Peace as a Women's Issue: A History of the U.S. Movement for World Peace and Women's Rights* (Syracuse University Press, 1993), 61.

87. "Anti-Suffragists Exult in Victory," *Rochester Democrat and Chronicle,* November 15, 1915.

88. Peck, *Carrie Chapman Catt,* 233–34.

Seven: How Long Must Women Go On Fighting for Liberty? 1915–1917

1. Ida Husted Harper, ed., *History of Woman Suffrage* (hereafter *HWS*) (National American Woman Suffrage Association, 1922), v. 5, 8.

2. Mary Gray Peck, *Carrie Chapman Catt: A Biography* (H. W. Wilson Company, 1944), 236.

3. Ibid., 243.

4. Ibid., 238.

5. Harper, ed., *HWS,* v. 5, 460.

6. Ibid., 752.

7. "Mrs. Blatch Pours Out Wrath on Root,"

New York Times, November 4, 1915.

8. Harper, ed., *HWS,* v. 5, 453.

9. "Suffrage War to Continue," *Washington Herald,* December 18, 1915.

10. "Suffrage Envoys Arrive in Butte," *Anaconda Standard,* May 8, 1916.

11. Ellen Carol DuBois, *Harriot Stanton Blatch and the Winning of Woman Suffrage* (Yale University Press, 1997), 194.

12. Ibid., 191.

13. Inez Haynes Gillmore, *The Story of the Woman's Party* (Harcourt, Brace and Company, 1921), 159.

14. "Helen Keller Sees Dawn of Freedom," *Wausau Daily Herald,* June 7, 1916.

15. Genevieve McBride, *On Wisconsin Women: Working for Their Rights from Settlement to Suffrage* (University of Wisconsin Press, 1993), 266.

16. Carrie Chapman Catt and Nettie Shuler, *Woman Suffrage and Politics: The Inner Story of the Suffrage Movement* (Charles Scribner's Sons, 1926), 251–52.

17. Catt and Shuler, *Woman Suffrage and Politics,* 254.

18. Harper, ed., *HWS,* v. 6, 349.

19. Catt and Shuler, *Woman Suffrage and Politics,* 254.

20. Margot Ford McMillen, *The Golden*

Lane: How Missouri Women Gained the Vote and Changed History (Arcadia Publishing, 2011), 93.

21. Peck, *Carrie Chapman Catt,* 250.
22. Maud Wood Park, *Front Door Lobby* (Beacon Press, 1960), 170.
23. Peck, *Carrie Chapman Catt,* 251.
24. Harper, ed., *HWS,* v. 5, 489.
25. Ibid., 498.
26. Eleanor Flexner and Ellen Fitzpatrick, *Century of Struggle: The Women's Rights Movement in America* (Belknap Press of Harvard University, 1975), 289.
27. Park, *Front Door Lobby,* 15–16.
28. Jacqueline Van Voris, *Carrie Chapman Catt: A Public Life* (Feminist Press, 1987), 134.
29. DuBois, *Harriot Stanton Blatch,* 201.
30. "Last Appeal from Unenfranchised Women," *Suffragist,* October 14, 1916.
31. Linda J. Lumsden, *Inez: The Life and Times of Inez Milholland* (Indiana University Press, 2004), 174.
32. Ibid., 173.
33. Gillmore, *Story of the Woman's Party,* 195.
34. Lumsden, *Inez,* 173.
35. Doris Stevens, *Jailed for Freedom* (Boni & Liveright, 1920), 51.

36. Gillmore, *Story of the Woman's Party,* 203.

37. "Vassar Suffrage Sentinel Tells What It Is to Picket White House," *Washington Post,* January 29, 1917.

38. Doris Stevens, *Jailed for Freedom,* 79.

39. Van Voris, *Carrie Chapman Catt,* 144.

40. Inez Haynes Irwin, *Adventures of Yesterday* (Schlesinger Library, 1976), 209.

41. Maud Wood Park, "What I am and who I believe," 1903, Melanie Gustafson, ed., Women and Social Movements in the United States, 1600–2000 (hereafter WASMUS).

42. Park, *Front Door Lobby,* 17.

43. Ibid., 21–22.

44. Ibid., 130.

45. Adelaide Washburn, "Biography of Helen Hamilton Gardener," WASMUS.

46. Harper, ed., *HWS,* v. 5, 567.

47. Park, *Front Door Lobby,* 39.

48. Maud Wood Park, "The Federal Amendment," *Woman's Journal,* March 3, 1917.

49. Van Voris, *Carrie Chapman Catt,* 248.

50. Park, *Front Door Lobby,* 76.

51. "Suffragists Vote to Retain Pickets," *New York Sun,* May 30, 1917.

52. "Suffrage Hurt by Picketing," *San Francisco Examiner,* June 1, 1917.

53. "Suffragists Mobbed at White House Gates," *New York Evening World,* June 21, 1917.

54. http://academic.brooklyn.cuny.edu/history/johnson/espionageact.htm.

55. "Crowd Destroys Suffrage Banner at White House," *New York Times,* June 21, 1917; "Flaunt Fresh Banner," *Washington Post,* June 21, 1917.

56. Stevens, *Jailed for Freedom,* 101–102.

57. Ibid., 108.

58. Ibid., 155.

59. Doris Stevens, "Justice as Seen at Occoquan," *Suffragist,* August 11, 1917.

60. Stevens, *Jailed for Freedom,* 116.

61. Gillmore, *Story of the Woman's Party,* 228.

62. Stevens, *Jailed,* 123–24.

63. Ibid., 147–48. Stevens misspelled her name as Gvinter.

64. Mary Church Terrell, *A Colored Woman in a White World* (Ransdell Inc., 1940), 316.

65. Stevens, *Jailed,* 213.

66. "Nine More Suffragists Seized at White House," *Baltimore Sun,* June 27, 1917, 3.

67. Stevens, *Jailed,* 225.

68. Gillmore, *Story of the Woman's Party,* 292.

69. Stevens, *Jailed,* 221.

70. Ibid., 177–78.

71. Ibid., 198.

72. Ibid., 201.

73. Linda Ford, "Alice Paul and the Politics of Nonviolent Protest," in *Votes for Women,* Jean Baker, ed. (Oxford University Press, 2002), 183.

74. Stevens, *Jailed,* 208.

75. Peck, *Carrie Chapman Catt,* 277.

76. "President Wilson Endorses National Suffrage," *Suffragist,* November 3, 1917.

77. Harper, ed., *HWS,* v. 6, 465.

78. Susan Goodier and Karen Pastorello, *Women Will Vote* (Cornell University Press, 2017), 172.

79. Mrs. Norman Whitehouse, "990,000 New York Women Want the Vote," *Woman Citizen,* September 8, 1917, 273.

80. Annelise Orleck, *Common Sense and a Little Fire: Women and Working Class Politics in the United States, 1900–1965* (University of North Carolina Press, 1995), 110.

81. "Female Suffrage Notes," *New York Age,* October 11, 1917.

82. "20,000 March as Living Plea for Suffrage," *New York Sun,* October 28, 1917.

83. Peck, *Carrie Chapman Catt,* 278–79.

84. "New Suffrage Parade Idea," *New York*

Times, October 21, 1917.

85. "President Lends Aid to New York Suffrage Party," *Washington Times,* August 30, 1917.

86. Goodier and Pastorello, *Women Will Vote,* 184.

Eight: Enemies Died Hard, 1918–1920

1. Maud Wood Park, *Front Door Lobby* (Beacon Press, 1960), 120–21.
2. Emily Newell Blair, *Women's Committee, United States Council of National Defense: An Interpretive Report* (U.S. Government Printing Office, 1920), 23.
3. Harriot Stanton Blatch and Alma Lutz, *Challenging Years: The Memoirs of Harriot Stanton Blatch* (G. P. Putnam's Sons, 1940), 284.
4. Harriot Stanton Blatch, *Mobilizing Woman Power* (Woman's Press, 1918), 88–90.
5. Elaine Weiss, *The Woman's Hour: The Great Fight to Win the Vote* (Viking, 2018), vii.
6. Rheta Childe Dorr, *A Woman of Fifty* (Funk & Wagnalls, 1920), 405.
7. Ibid., 385.
8. Addie W. Hunton and Kathryn M. Robinson, *Two Colored Women with the American Expeditionary Forces* (Brooklyn Eagle

Press, 1920), 11–12.

9. Ibid., 22.

10. Ibid., 157.

11. Susan Chandler, "Addie Hunton and the Construction of an African American Peace Perspective," *Affilia,* August 1, 2005, 271.

12. Ida Husted Harper, ed., *History of Woman Suffrage* (hereafter *HWS*) (National American Woman Suffrage Association, 1922), v. 5, 579.

13. *Extending the Right of Suffrage to Women: Hearing Before the Committee on Suffrage, House of Representatives, Sixty-Fifth Congress, Second Session, January 3–7, 1918* (U.S. Government Printing Office, 1918), 44.

14. Ibid., 176.

15. Katherine H. Adams and Michael L. Keene, *Alice Paul and the American Suffrage Campaign* (University of Illinois Press, 2008), 216.

16. Inez Haynes Gillmore, *The Story of the Woman's Party* (Harcourt, 1921), 346.

17. Park, *Front Door Lobby,* 143.

18. Ibid., 137–38.

19. "House Passes Suffrage Amendment to Exact Vote Required by Law," *Arizona Republic,* January 11, 1918, 1.

20. Gillmore, *Story of the Woman's Party,* 347.

21. Ibid.

22. Ibid.

23. Ibid., 328.

24. Amelia Fry, *Rebecca Hourwich Reyher: Search and Struggle for Sex Equality and Independence,* Suffragists Oral History Project, Women and Social Movements in the United States, 1600–2000 (hereafter WASMUS), 75.

25. Park, *Front Door Lobby,* 163.

26. Ibid., 183.

27. Ibid., 185–86.

28. Helen Gardener to Woodrow Wilson, August 18, 1918, Gardener Papers, Schlesinger Library, Harvard University.

29. Mary Gray Peck, *Carrie Chapman Catt: A Biography* (H. W. Wilson Company, 1944), 297.

30. Gillmore, *Story of the Woman's Party,* 377–78.

31. Park, *Front Door Lobby,* 210.

32. Doris Stevens, *Jailed for Freedom* (Boni & Liveright, 1920), 294.

33. Peck, *Carrie Chapman Catt,* 297.

34. Gillmore, *Story of the Woman's Party,* 380.

35. Park, *Front Door Lobby,* 212.

36. "Woman Suffrage Up Again," *Topeka*

Daily Journal, November 30, 1918.

37. "How to Defeat a Senator," Woman's Journal, November 16, 1918.

38. Peck, Carrie Chapman Catt, 299.

39. "How to Defeat a Senator."

40. "Miss Rankin Retires with 'Swan Song' of Praise for Solons," Muncie Indiana Star Press, March 10, 1919.

41. Park, Front Door Lobby, 220.

42. Ibid., 223.

43. Marjorie Spruill Wheeler, New Women of the New South: The Leaders of the Woman Suffrage Movement in the Southern States (Oxford University Press, 1993), 165.

44. Ibid., 169.

45. Stevens, Jailed for Freedom, 313.

46. Rebecca Hourwich Reyher, Search and Struggle for Equality and Independence (Regents of the University of California, 1977), 88.

47. Ibid., 329.

48. Wheeler, New Women of the New South, 31.

49. Gillmore, Story of the Woman's Party, 429.

50. Park, Front Door Lobby, 267–68.

51. Carrie Chapman Catt, "Woman Suffrage Will Be Ratified," Wisconsin State

Journal, June 5, 1919.

52. Ada James to Theodora Youmans, 1917, in Megan Schade, *Ada James: From Conservative to Radical Woman in Life and Politics.* Undergraduate thesis, University of Wisconsin Eau Claire, 2006.

53. Pollitzer to O'Keeffe, August 17, 1919, *Lovingly, Georgia: The Complete Correspondence of Georgia O'Keeffe & Anita Pollitzer,* ed. Clive Giboire (Simon & Schuster, 1990), 267.

54. Pollitzer, "Working for Suffrage for the Special Session in Virginia on August 13," *Suffragist,* August 16, 1919.

55. "Advocates of Equal Suffrage Advance Arguments for Votes," *Times Dispatch Richmond,* September 8, 1919.

56. "Susan B. Anthony Amendment Causes Hot Fight," *Natchez Democrat,* September 4, 1919, in *HWS,* ed., Ida Harper, v. 6, 671.

57. Betty Gram and Anita Pollitzer, "Virginia and the Susan B. Anthony Amendment," *Suffragist,* September 20, 1919.

58. M. W. Pidgeon, "From the Virginia Battle Front," *Woman's Journal,* February 2, 1919.

59. Peck, *Carrie Chapman Catt,* 319.

60. Carrie Chapman Catt and Nettie Shuler, *Woman Suffrage and Politics: The*

Inner Story of the Suffrage Movement (Charles Scribner's Sons, 1926), 358.

61. Peck, *Carrie Chapman Catt,* 317.

62. "Legislature to Be Convened by Governor Says Capital Report," *Caspar Wyoming Star Tribune,* December 11, 1919.

63. "Suffrage Index of Good and Bad Governors," reprinted from *New York Times* in *Suffragist,* September 20, 1919.

64. "Women Are Urged to Go into Parties," *Atlanta Constitution,* February 15, 1920.

65. Catt and Shuler, *Woman Suffrage and Politics,* 382.

66. Gillmore, *Story of the Woman's Party,* 453–54.

67. Catt and Shuler, *Woman Suffrage and Politics,* 384.

68. "The Triumphant Thirty-Fifth," *Woman Citizen,* April 10, 1920.

69. Harper, ed., *HWS,* v. 6, 638.

70. Catt and Shuler, *Woman Suffrage and Politics,* 404.

71. Ibid., 400.

72. Carol E. Hoffecker, "Delaware's Woman Suffrage Campaign," *Delaware History,* 1983, 158.

73. "Suffragettes Hold Meeting," *Baltimore Afro-American,* March 28, 1914.

74. Alice Dunbar-Nelson, "Urges Free Bal-

lot for Colored Women," *Wilmington Sunday Star,* August 22, 1920, WASMUS.

75. "Forward Delaware," *Woman's Citizen,* May 1, 1920.

76. "Antis Return Their Thanks," *Wilmington Evening Journal,* June 3, 1920.

77. "Suffragists to Continue Fight," *Wilmington Evening Journal,* June 3, 1920.

78. Catt and Shuler, *Woman Suffrage and Politics,* 400.

79. "Suffrage Beaten in Delaware Finally: Republicans Blamed," *Raleigh News and Observer,* June 3, 1920.

80. Elaine Weiss, *The Woman's Hour: The Great Fight to Win the Vote* (Penguin, 2018), 103.

81. Harper, ed., *HWS,* v. 5, 717.

82. Catt and Shuler, *Woman Suffrage and Politics,* 427.

83. Ibid., 428.

84. Carol Lynn Yellin and Janann Sherman, *The Perfect 36: Tennessee Delivers Woman Suffrage* (Vote Press, 2016), 99.

85. Harper, ed., *HWS,* v. 5, 580.

86. Anita Shafer Goodstein, "A Rare Alliance: African American and White Women in the Tennessee Elections of 1919 and 1920," *Southern Historical Quarterly,* May 1998, 239.

87. Weiss, *The Woman's Hour*, 34.

88. "Force Bills and Race Prejudice," *Woman Patriot,* July 10, 1920.

89. Weiss, *The Woman's Hour*, 191.

90. Ibid., 277.

91. Yellin and Sherman, *The Perfect 36*, 87.

92. Jacqueline Van Voris, *Carrie Chapman Catt: A Public Life* (Feminist Press, 1987), 160.

93. Weiss, *The Woman's Hour*, 220.

94. Catt and Shuler, *Woman Suffrage and Politics*, 443.

95. Yellin and Sherman, *The Perfect 36*, 100.

96. Weiss, *The Woman's Hour*, 272.

97. Catt and Shuler, *Woman Suffrage and Politics*, 442.

98. Weiss, *The Woman's Hour*, 86, 274–86.

99. Van Voris, *Carrie Chapman Catt*, 160.

100. Yellin and Sherman, *The Perfect 36*, 103.

101. Catt and Shuler, *Woman Suffrage and Politics*, 448.

102. Weiss, *The Woman's Hour*, 304.

103. Gillmore, *Story of the Woman's Party*, 460.

104. Phoebe Burn to Harry Burn, August 17, 1920, http://cmdc.knoxlib.org/cdm/compoundobject/collection/p265301coll8/id/699/rec/2.

105. Harper, ed., *HWS,* v. 5, 642.

106. Harper, ed., *HWS,* v. 6, 624. The correct number was more like 27 million women.

107. Peck, *Carrie Chapman Catt,* 339.

108. "Says Woman's Task Is to See Man Uses Vote," *Rochester Democrat and Chronicle,* October 8, 1920.

109. *Baltimore Sun,* October 13, 1920.

110. *Louisville Courier Journal,* October 7, 1920.

111. Anna L. Harvey, *The Legacy of Disfranchisement: Women in Electoral Politics, 1917–1932* (PhD diss., Princeton University, 1995), 143.

112. Gillmore, *The Story of the Woman's Party,* 429.

Nine: The Afterstory

1. Crystal Eastman, "Now We Can Begin," 1920, *Public Women, Public Words: A Documentary History of American Feminism: 1900 to 1960,* Dawn Keetley and John Pettegrew, eds., v. 2 (Rowman & Littlefield, 2002), 238.

2. Carrie Chapman Catt, "The Victory Convention," 1920, Keetley and Pettegrew, eds., v. 2, 237.

3. Annelise Orleck, *Common Sense and a Little Fire: Women and Working Class Politics in the United States, 1900–1965* (University of North Carolina Press, 1995), 100.

4. Charles Edward Russell, "Is Woman Suffrage a Failure?" *The Century* (March 1924), 724–30.

5. Carrie Chapman Catt, "The Cave Man Complex Versus Woman Suffrage," *Woman Citizen,* April 5, 1924.

6. Sophonisba Breckinridge, *Women in the Twentieth Century: A Study of Their Political, Social and Economic Activities* (McGraw-Hill Professional Publishing Company, 1933), 255.

7. J. Stanley Lemons, *The Woman Citizen: Social Feminism in the 1920s* (University of Illinois Press, 1973), 155.

8. Ibid., 160.

9. Jacqueline Van Voris, *Carrie Chapman Catt: A Public Life* (Feminist Press, 1987), 193.

10. Lucia Maxwell, "The Spider Web Chart: The Socialist-Pacifist Movement in America Is An Absolutely Fundamental and Integral Part of International Socialism," *Dearborn Independent,* March 22, 1924, Women and Social Movements in the

United States, 1600–2000 (hereafter WAS-MUS).

11. By the time the amendment finally passed through Congress in 1972 the wording had changed significantly, now posed in the negative: "Equality of rights under the law shall not be denied or abridged by the United States or by any State on account of sex."

12. "Colored Women's Rights Association Gives Advice to Negro Voters," *Lincoln County News,* September 30, 1920.

13. Dorothy Sterling, *Black Foremothers: Three Lives* (Feminist Press, 1988), 147.

14. "Women Entries in Election Races," *Woman Citizen,* November 4, 1922.

15. "Emily Newell Blair Tells Why I Am Discouraged about Women in Politics," *Woman's Journal,* January 1931.

16. Anne Martin, "Women's Vote and Woman's Chains," 1922, *Public Women,* Keetley and Pettegrew, eds., v. 2, 260.

17. *Women in Congress, 1917–2006* (U.S. Government Printing Office, 2006), 26.

18. Kristie Miller, *Ruth Hanna McCormick: A Life in Politics, 1880–1944* (University of New Mexico Press, 1944), 143.

19. Ibid., 159.

20. Ibid., 160.

21. Ibid., 196.

22. Jo Freeman, *We Will Be Heard: Women's Struggle for Political Power in the United States* (Rowman & Littlefield, 2008), 107.

23. Miller, *Ruth Hanna McCormick,* 222.

24. Ibid., 223.

25. Ibid., 232.

26. Kevin Corder and Christina Wolbrecht, *Counting Women's Ballots: Female Voters from Suffrage Through the New Deal* (Cambridge University Press, 2016). The authors selected ten states to develop their argument. The only region they were not able to investigate, for complex statistical reasons, was the Far West.

27. Ibid., 137, 227.

28. Ibid., 250.

29. Joyce A. Hanson, *Mary McLeod Bethune: Black Women's Political Activism* (University of Missouri Press, 2003), 112.

30. Barbara C. Burrell, *Women and Political Participation: A Reference Handbook* (ABC Clio, 2004), 92.

31. Susan B. Anthony II, "We Women Throw Our Votes Away," July 17, 1948, *Public Women,* Keetley and Pettegrew, eds., v. 2, 279–82.

32. "Probers List 'Pro-Red' U.S. Women," *New York Daily News,* October 23, 1949.

33. Ellen Fitzpatrick, *The Highest Glass Ceil-*

ing: *Women's Quest for the American Presidency* (Harvard University Press, 2016), 108.

34. "Shirley Chisholm, 'Unbossed' Pioneer in Congress, Is Dead at 80," *New York Times,* January 3, 2005.

35. Betty Friedan, *The Feminine Mystique* (W. W. Norton & Co., 1963), 137, 143.

36. Shulamith Firestone, *Dialectic of Sex: The Case for Feminist Revolution* (Bantam Books, 1971), 22.

Anderson, Kristi. *Women in Partisan and Electoral Politics Before the New Deal.* University of Chicago Press, 1996.

Aptheker, Bettina. *Woman's Legacy: Essays on Race, Sex, and Class in American History.* University of Massachusetts Press, 1982.

Baker, Jean H. *Sisters: The Lives of America's Suffragists.* Hill and Wang, 2005.

Baker, Noelle A., ed. *Stanton in Her Own Time: A Biographical Chronicle of Her Life, Drawn from Recollections, Interviews, and Memoirs by Family, Friends, and Associates.* University of Iowa Press, 2016.

Bay, Mia. *To Tell the Truth Freely: The Life of Ida B. Wells.* Hill and Wang, 2010.

Beeton, Beverly. *Women Vote in the West: The Woman Suffrage Movement, 1869–1896.* Garland Publishing, Inc., 1986.

Behn, Beth. *Woodrow Wilson's Conversion*

Experience: The President and the Federal Woman Suffrage Amendment. Ph.D. diss., University of Massachusetts, 2012.

Benjamin, Anne M. *A History of the Anti-Suffrage Movement in the United States from 1895 to 1920.* Edwin Mellen Press, 1991.

Bordin, Ruth. *Women and Temperance: The Quest for Power and Liberty, 1873–1900.* Rutgers University Press, 1990.

Bredbenner, Candice. *A Nationality of Her Own: Women, Marriage and the Law of Citizenship.* University of California Press, 1998.

Brown, Dorothy. *American Women in the 1920s: Setting a Course.* Twayne Publishers, 1987.

Buhle, Mari Jo. *Women and American Socialism, 1870–1920.* University of Illinois Press, 1981.

Burrell, Barbara C. *Women and Political Participation: A Reference Handbook.* ABC Clio, 2004.

Clarke, Ida C., ed. *Women of 1924 International.* Women's News Service, Inc., 1924.

Cooney, Robert. *Winning the Vote: The Triumph of the American Woman Suffrage Movement.* American Graphic Press, 2005. Comprehensive image history of the movement.

Cooper, Anna Julia. *A Voice from the South: Published by a Black Woman of the South.* Aldine Printing House, 1892.

Cott, Nancy F. *The Grounding of Modern Feminism.* Yale University Press, 1987.

Cott, Nancy F., ed. *A Woman Making History: Mary Ritter Beard Through Her Letters.* Yale University Press, 1991.

Decosta-Willis, Miriam, ed. *The Memphis Diary of Ida B. Wells.* Beacon Press, 1995.

Denton, Sally. *The Pink Lady: The Many Lives of Helen Gahagan Douglas.* Bloomsbury Press, 2009.

Dillon, Mary Earhart. *Frances Willard, from Prayer to Politics.* University of Chicago Press, 1944.

Dumenil, Lynn. *The Second Line of Defense: American Women and World War I.* University of North Carolina Press, 2017.

Duniway, Abigail Scott. *Path Breaking: An Autobiographical History of the Equal Suffrage Movement in Pacific Coast States* (originally published 1914). Schocken Books, 1971.

Dye, Nancy Schrom. *As Equals and as Sisters: Feminism, the Labor Movement, and the Women's Trade Union League of*

New York. University of Missouri Press, 1980.

Edwards, Rebecca. *Angels in the Machinery: Gender in American Party Politics from the Civil War to the Progressive Era.* Oxford University Press, 1997.

Finnegan, Margaret. *Selling Suffrage: Consuming Culture and Votes for Women.* Columbia University Press, 1999.

Flanagan, Maureen A. *Seeing with Their Hearts: Chicago Women and the Vision of the Good City, 1871–1933.* Princeton University Press, 2002.

Foner, Philip S., ed. *Frederick Douglass on Women's Rights.* Da Capo Press, 1992.

Franzen, Trisha. *Anna Howard Shaw: The Work of Woman Suffrage.* University of Illinois Press, 2014.

Free, Laura E. *Suffrage Reconstructed: Gender, Race and Voting Rights in the Civil War Era.* Cornell University Press, 2015.

Freeman, Jo. *We Will Be Heard: Women's Struggle for Political Power in the United States.* Rowman & Littlefield, 2008.

Fuller, Paul E. *Laura Clay and the Woman's Rights Movement.* University Press of Kentucky, 1975.

Gardener, Helen Hamilton. "Sex in Brain." In *Facts and Fictions: Third Edition.* Arena

Publishing Company, 1893.

Garvey, Ellen Gruber. "Alice Moore Dunbar-Nelson's Suffrage Work: The View from Her Scrapbook." *Legacy: A Journal of African American Women Writers,* 2016.

Gilley, B. H. "Kate Gordon and Louisiana Woman Suffrage." *Louisiana History: The Journal of the Louisiana Historical Society* 24 (Summer 1983).

Ginzburg, Lori. *Elizabeth Cady Stanton: An American Life.* Hill and Wang, 2009.

———. *Untidy Origins: A Story of Women's Rights in Antebellum New York.* University of North Carolina Press, 2005.

Gluck, Sherna, ed. *From Parlor to Prison: Five American Suffragists Talk About Their Lives. An Oral History.* Vintage Books, 1976.

Goldberg, Michael Lewis. *An Army of Women: Gender and Politics in Gilded Age Kansas.* Johns Hopkins University Press, 1997.

Gordon, Ann D., Bettye Collier-Thomas, and John Bracey, eds. *African American Women and the Vote, 1837–1965.* University of Massachusetts Press, 1997.

Gordon, Sarah Barringer. *The Mormon Question: Polygamy and Constitutional Conflict in Nineteenth Century America.*

University of North Carolina Press, 2002.

Gornick, Vivian. *Solitude of Self: Thinking About Elizabeth Cady Stanton.* Farrar, Straus and Giroux, 1996.

Green, Elna C. *Southern Strategies and the Woman Suffrage Question.* University of North Carolina Press, 1997.

Griffith, Elisabeth. *In Her Own Right: The Life of Elizabeth Cady Stanton.* Oxford University Press, 1985.

Gullett, Gayle. *Becoming Citizens: The Emergence and Development of the California Women's Movement, 1880–1911.* University of Illinois Press, 2000.

Gustafson, Melanie, Kristie Miller, and Elisabeth Israels Perry, eds. *We Have Come to Stay: American Women and Political Parties, 1880–1960.* University of New Mexico Press, 1999.

Gustafson, Melanie. "Women in Politics Since 1920." In *The Oxford Encyclopedia of American Political and Legal History.* Donald Critchlow and Philip Vandermeer, eds. Oxford University Press, 2012.

Guy-Sheftall, Beverly, ed. *Words of Fire: An Anthology of African-American Feminist Thought.* The New Press, 1995.

Hamilton, Tulia Brown. *The National Association of Colored Women, 1896–1920.*

Ph.D. diss., Emory University, 1978.

Harley, Sharon and Rosalyn Terborg-Penn, eds. *The Afro-American Woman: Struggles and Images.* Kennikat Press, 1978.

Harvey, Anna L. *Votes Without Leverage: Women in American Electoral Politics, 1920–1970.* Cambridge University Press, 1998.

Hendricks, Wanda A. *Fannie Barrier Williams: Crossing the Borders of Region and Race.* University of Illinois Press, 2014.

Higginbotham, Evelyn. *Righteous Discontent: The Women's Movement in the Black Baptist Church, 1880–1920.* Harvard University Press, 1994.

Hine, Darlene Clark. *Black Women in America,* 2 volumes. Oxford University Press, 2005.

Hoffert, Sylvia D. *Alva Vanderbilt Belmont: Unlikely Champion of Women's Rights.* Indiana University Press, 2012.

Howard, Anne Bail. *The Long Campaign: A Biography of Anne Martin.* University of Nevada Press, 1985.

Huehls, Betty Sparks. *Sue Sheldon White: Lady Warrior.* Ph.D. diss., University of Memphis, 2002.

Jensen, Joan M. "All Pink Sisters: The War Department and the Feminist Movement in the 1920s." In *Decades of Discontent: The Women's Movement 1920–1940*. Lois Scharf and Joan M. Jensen, eds. Northeastern University Press, 1987.

Jensen, Kimberly. *Mobilizing Minerva: American Women in the First World War*. University of Illinois Press, 2008.

Johnson, Joan Marie. *Funding Feminism: Monied Women, Philanthropy, and the Women's Movement, 1870–1967*. University of North Carolina Press, 2017.

Jones, Martha S. *All Bound Up Together: The Woman Question in African American Public Culture, 1830–1900*. University of North Carolina Press, 2007.

Kaptur, Representative Marcy. *Women of Congress: A Twentieth Century Odyssey*. Congressional Quarterly, Inc., 1996.

Kraditor, Aileen S. *The Ideas of the Woman Suffrage Movement 1890–1920*. Columbia University Press, 1965.

Kroger, Brooke. *Suffragents: How Women Used Men to Get the Vote*. State University of New York Press, 2017.

Larson, Erik. *The Devil in the White City: Murder, Magic and Madness at the Fair that Changed America*. Crown Publishers, 2003.

Lemert, Charles, and Esme Bhan, eds. *The

Voice of Anna Julia Cooper. Rowman & Littlefield, 1998.

Lerner, Gerda. *The Grimké Sisters of South Carolina: Pioneers for Women's Rights.* University of North Carolina Press, 1967.

Lerner, Gerda, ed. *The Feminist Thought of Sarah M. Grimké.* Oxford University Press, 1998.

Lunardini, Christine A. *From Equal Suffrage to Equal Rights: Alice Paul and the National Woman's Party 1910–1928.* New York University Press, 1986.

Maillard, Mary, ed. *Whispers of Cruel Wrongs: The Correspondence of Louisa Jacobs and Her Circle, 1879–1911.* University of Wisconsin Press, 2017.

Matterson, Lisa G. *For the Freedom of Her Race: Black Women and Electoral Politics in Illinois, 1877–1932.* University of North Carolina Press, 2009.

McMillen, Sally G. *Seneca Falls and the Origins of the Women's Rights Movement.* Oxford University Press, 2008.

Mitchell, Michele. *Righteous Propagation: African Americans and the Politics of Racial Destiny After Reconstruction.* University of North Carolina Press, 2004.

Morgan, David. *Suffragists and Democrats: The Politics of Woman Suffrage in America.*

Michigan State University Press, 1974.

Noun, Louise R. *Strong-Minded Women: The Emergence of the Woman-Suffrage Movement in Iowa.* Iowa State University Press, 1969.

Nutter, Kathleen Banks. *The Necessity of Organizing: Mary Kenney O'Sullivan and Trade Unionism for Women, 1892–1912.* Garland Publishing, 2000.

Palmer, Beverly, ed. *Selected Letters of Lucretia Coffin Mott.* University of Illinois Press, 2002.

Poplett, Carolyn O., with Mary Ann Poucznik. *The Woman Who Never Fails: Grace Wilbour Trout and Illinois Suffrage.* Historical Society of Oak Park and River Forest, 2000.

Sander, Kathleen Walters. *Mary Elizabeth Garrett: Society and Philanthropy in the Gilded Age.* Johns Hopkins University Press, 2008.

Schechter, Patricia A. *Ida B. Wells-Barnett and American Reform, 1880–1930.* University of North Carolina Press, 2001.

Schuyler, Lorraine Gates. *The Weight of Their Votes: Southern Women and Political Leverage in the 1920s.* University of North Carolina Press, 2006.

Showalter, Elaine, ed. *These Modern*

Women: Autobiographical Essays from the Twenties. Feminist Press, 1978.

Sklar, Kathryn Kish. *Florence Kelley and the Nation's Work: The Rise of Women's Political Culture, 1830–1900.* Yale University Press, 1995.

Smith, Norma. *Jeannette Rankin: America's Conscience.* Montana Historical Society Press, 2002.

Sneider, Allison L. *Suffragists in an Imperial Age: U.S. Expansion and the Woman Question 1870–1929.* Oxford University Press, 2008.

Solomons, Selina. *How We Won the Vote in California: A True Story of the Campaign of 1911.* New Woman Publishing Company, 1912.

Stansell, Christine. *The Feminist Promise: 1792 to the Present.* Modern Library, 2010.

Stefano, Carolyn. "Networking on the Frontier: The Colorado Women's Suffrage Movement, 1876–1893." In *The Women's West,* Susan Armitage and Elizabeth Jameson, eds. University of Oklahoma Press, 1987.

Steinson, Barbara J. *American Women's Activism in World War I.* Garland Publishing, 1982.

Sterling, Dorothy. *We Are Your Sisters: Black Women in the Nineteenth Century.* W. W. Norton, 1984.

Stern, Madeline. *Purple Passage: The Life of Mrs. Frank Leslie.* University of Oklahoma Press, 1970.

Suhl, Yuri. *Ernestine Rose and the Battle for Human Rights.* Reynal & Company, 1950. The first biography of Rose, authorized by the Jewish women's rights organization, the Emma Lazarus Federation.

Sumner, Helen L. *Equal Suffrage.* Harper & Brothers Publishers, 1909.

Swerdlow, Amy. *Women Strike for Peace: Traditional Motherhood and Radical Politics.* University of Chicago Press, 1993.

Terborg-Penn, Rosalyn. "Discontented Black Feminists: Prelude and Postscript to the Passage of the Nineteenth Amendment." In *Decades of Discontent: The Women's Movement, 1920–1940,* Lois Scharf and Joan M. Jensen, eds. Northeastern University Press, 1987.

"The Anti-Lynching Crusaders: The Lynching of Women." 1922. Women and Social Movements in the United States, 1600–2000.

Thomas, Mary Martha. *The New Woman in Alabama: Social Reforms and Suffrage,*

1890–1920. University of Alabama Press, 1992.

Trigg, Mary K. *Feminism as Life's Work: Four Modern American Women Through Two World Wars.* Johns Hopkins University Press, 2014.

Tsenes-Hills, Temple. *I Am the Utterance of My Name: Black Feminist Victorian Discourse and Intellectual Enterprise at the Columbian Exposition, 1893.* iUniverse, 2006.

Van Burkleo, Sandra F. *Gender Remade: Citizenship, Suffrage, and Public Power in the Northwest, 1879–1912.* Cambridge University Press, 2015.

Van Wagenen, Lola. *Sister Wives and Suffragists: Polygamy and the Politics of Woman Suffrage, 1879–1896.* PhD. diss., New York University, 1994.

Von Drehl, David. *Triangle: The Fire That Changed America.* Grove Press, 2003.

Ware, Susan. *Beyond Suffrage: Women in the New Deal.* Harvard University Press, 1981.

Washington, Margaret. *Sojourner Truth's America.* University of Illinois Press, 2009.

Weigand, Kate. *Red Feminism: American Communism and the Making of Women's Liberation.* Johns Hopkins University Press, 2002.

Weimann, Jeanne Madeline. *The Fair Women: The Story of the Women's Building, World's Columbian Exposition, 1893.* Academy Chicago, 1981.

Wheeler, Marjorie Spruill, ed. *One Woman, One Vote: Rediscovering the Woman Suffrage Movement.* New Sage Press, 1995.

White, Deborah. *Too Heavy a Load: Black Women in Defense of Themselves, 1894–1994.* W. W. Norton, 1998.

Willard, Frances E. *Women & Temperance, or The Work and Workers of the Woman's Christian Temperance Union.* Park Publishing Co., 1883.

Williams, Lillian S. "And Still I Rise: Black Women and Reform, Buffalo, New York, 1900–1940." *Afro-Americans in New York Life and History,* 14, July 1990.

Yellin, Jean Fagan, ed. *The Harriet Jacobs Family Papers, Volume One.* University of North Carolina Press, 2008.

Youmans, Theodora. "How Wisconsin Women Won the Ballot," *The Wisconsin Magazine of History* (September 1921).

Young, Rose. *The Record of the Leslie Woman Suffrage Commission, Inc., 1917–1929.* The Leslie Woman Commission, 1929.

Zahniser, Jill D., and Amelia R. Fry. *Alice*

Paul: Claiming Power. Oxford University Press, 2014.

ILLUSTRATION CREDITS

Page number

Canada

ABOUT THE AUTHOR

Ellen Carol DuBois is Distinguished Research Professor in the History Department of UCLA. She is the author of numerous books on the history of woman suffrage in the United States, among them: *Feminism and Suffrage: The Emergence of an Independent Women's Movement in America, 1848–1869; Harriot Stanton Blatch and the Winning of Woman Suffrage;* and *Suffrage: Women's Long Battle for the Vote.* She is the coauthor, with Lynn Dumenil, of the leading textbook in U.S. women's history, *Through Women's Eyes: An American History with Documents* and coeditor, with Vicki Ruiz, of *Unequal Sisters: In Inclusive Reader in U.S. Women's History.*

The employees of Thorndike Press hope you have enjoyed this Large Print book. All our Thorndike, Wheeler, and Kennebec Large Print titles are designed for easy reading, and all our books are made to last. Other Thorndike Press Large Print books are available at your library, through selected bookstores, or directly from us.

For information about titles, please call:
    (800) 223-1244

or visit our website at:
    gale.com/thorndike

To share your comments, please write:
    Publisher
    Thorndike Press
    10 Water St., Suite 310
    Waterville, ME 04901